IF WOMEN COUNTED

If Women Counted

A New Feminist Economics

Marilyn Waring

Introduction by
Gloria Steinem

HarperSanFrancisco
A Division of HarperCollins*Publishers*

The author and the publishers wish to gratefully acknowledge the following for permission to reproduce material:

Hazel Henderson for the conceptual figure, "The Economy as a Layered Cake," in *The Politics of the Solar Age: Alternatives to Economics.* First Edition by Doubleday, N.Y., 1981. New Edition, 1988 with new Introduction by the author from Knowledge Systems, Inc. of Indianapolis, Indiana.

W.W. Norton & Co. Inc., Worldwatch Institute, and Lester Brown for adaptation of the table "Nuclear Reactors as of December 31, 1984" in *State of the World 1986.* Copyright © by Worldwatch Institute.

Worldwatch Institute and Lester Brown for excerpts from "Worldwatch Paper 64: Investing in Children" by William N. Chandler.

W.W. Norton & Co. Inc., Worldwatch Institute, and Lester Brown for excerpts from *Sisterhood of Man* by Kathleen Newland. Copyright © by Worldwatch Institute.

Gena Corea, for quoting from personal correspondence.

Women's Center, Cambridge, MA, for the table "What is a Wife Worth?" in *Houseworker's Handbook,* published in 1973 by Leghorn & Warrior.

Acknowledgments continue on page 387.

FIRST HARPERCOLLINS PAPERBACK EDITION PUBLISHED IN 1990

Library of Congress Cataloging-in-Publication Data

Waring, Marilyn, 1952–
    If women counted.

    Bibliography: p.
    1. Sex discrimination in national income accounting.
2. Women—Economic conditions. I. Title.
HC79.I5W384   1988   339.3'0723   88-45160
ISBN 0-06-250933-0

ISBN 0–06–250940–3 (pbk.)

90 91 92 93 94 RRD(H) 10 9 8 7 6 5 4 3 2 1

This edition is printed on acid-free paper that meets the American National Standards Institute Z39.48 Standard.

For my grandmothers
Louie and Mary Olive
and my parents
William Allan and Audrey May
who tried to
teach me about the value
of things

Contents

Abbreviations   xi

Acknowledgments   xii

Introduction by Gloria Steinem   xvii

Prologue: Women as Nonproducers   1

  What Brought Me to Write This Book   1
  What This Book Is About   5

1. A WOMAN'S RECKONING: AN INTRODUCTION TO THE
   INTERNATIONAL ECONOMIC SYSTEM   14

    Tell Me a Riddle: Who Works and Who Doesn't   15
    Blind Man's Buff: How Economic Theory Constructs
      Reality   17
    Defining Economic Terms   20
      Value   21
      Work, Labor, and Economic Activity   25
      Production and Reproduction   27
    Counting Women Out of the Labor Force   29
    And What of Mother Earth?   31
    The Boundaries of the UNSNA   33
    Co-option to Unreality: How Economics Is Taught   36
    Beyond the Boundary: Scientific Method in Economics   39
    My Context   43

2. A CALLING TO ACCOUNT: WHO DEVELOPED THE UNSNA
   AND WHY   46

    This System's a Winner: The Power of the UNSNA   47
    Once Upon a Time: A Short History of the UNSNA   49

How to Pay for the War   54
Vital Statistics: The Demand   58
Vital Statistics: The Supply   69

3. THE BOUNDARY OF CONCEPTION: HOW THE UNSNA
MAKES WOMEN INVISIBLE   74

For the Sake of Convenience: Devising the UNSNA
    Rules   75
Invisible Women: Applying the UNSNA Rules   81
Feudalism Lives On: Defining "Household"   88
In Summary   90

4. NOTHING SEXIST HERE: STATISTICIANS IN ACTION   92

The Head Office   92
How Statisticians Think: Responding to a Feminist
    Politician   93
How Statisticians Think: Revising Reality   103
Nepal: A Case Study in Statistics Gathering   108
    Encountering the People   109
    Compiling the Statistics   111

5. THE STATISTICAL CONSPIRACY: SOURCES FOR THE
NATIONAL ACCOUNTS   115

The Census   117
    The Census of Population   118
    The Census of Agriculture   130
    Household Labor Force Surveys   136
A Strategy for Making Change   138
In Summary   143

6. VILLAINY AND INCOMPETENCE: PROBLEMS ECONOMISTS
SEE IN THEIR OWN SYSTEM   144

The Problem of Pricing   147
Three Problems Acknowledged by Economists   149
    The Hidden Economy   149

Environmental Pollution   154
Leisure Time   159

7. THE VALUE OF DEATH: HOW WAR, POVERTY, AND
   POISONS HELP THE ECONOMY   165

   War and the Economy: Death Visible as Production   166
   When War and Poverty Mix: Death Invisible as Debt   172
   Lip Service Is Generous   176
   Poverty and the Economy: The Unaccounted for Costs   178
   The Other Benefits of Growth: Poisons and Pills   181
   Looking for Alternatives   184

8. A VALUE ON YOUR TIME: WOMEN, CHILDREN, AND THE
   ECONOMICS OF REPRODUCTION   187

   The Technological Medical Market   189
   The Legal Market   193
   The Social and Cultural Market   199
   The Labor Market   203
   The Sexuality Market   204
   The Economics of Breast-feeding   206
   The Social Welfare Market   211
   The Propaganda Market   215
   Wheeling and Dealing: The Power Politics of
       Reproduction   217
   Naming the Market   222

9. THE EYE OF THE BEHOLDER: THE UNSNA AS APPLIED
   PATRIARCHY   224

   Urban Housework   225
   Rural Housework   228
   How Much Work Doesn't Count   230
   Making the Connections: Nutrition   235
   Making the Connections: Trade and Productivity   238
   Making the Connections: The Laws of Property and
       Ownership   240
   Making the Connections: Fertility   242
   And Many More Connections   246

10. "YOUR ECONOMIC THEORY MAKES NO SENSE":
    ECONOMICS AND THE EXPLOITATION OF THE PLANET   250

    If Counting Were the Answer   252
    What Counts on This Boundary of Production   254
    The Treatment of Water   256
    The Market for Trees and Crops   260
    What Am I Bid for a Giant Panda?   265
    Growth's Legacy—War's Waste Material   269

11. IF COUNTING WERE THE LIMIT OF INTELLIGENCE:
    MY SEARCH FOR AN ALTERNATIVE TO THE UNSNA   276

    Stage One: Imputing a Value for Women's Work   276
      Public Policy Implications   284
      Problems with Imputing Women's Work   286
      The Environment   287
    Stage Two: Economic Welfare   291
    Stage Three: Coming Full Circle   297

12. GLIMPSING THE WHOLE: A NEW MODEL FOR GLOBAL
    ECONOMICS   299

    Pietilä's Alternative   300
    Reasons for Inaction: Patriarchy's Perspective 304
    In Summary   312

Epilogue: A Call to Action   316

Appendixes   327

Notes   335

Bibliography   349

Index   365

Abbreviations

DOD	(U.S.) Department of Defense
DOE	(U.S.) Department of Energy
EEC	European Economic Community
EPA	(U.S.) Environmental Protection Agency
FAO	(UN) Food and Agriculture Organization
GDP	Gross Domestic Product
GNP	Gross National Product
ILO	(UN) International Labor Organization
IMF	(UN) International Monetary Fund
INSTRAW	International Research and Training Institute for the Advancement of Women
LSMS	Living Standards Measurements Survey
MEW	Measure of Economic Welfare
MPS	Material Product System
NASA	(U.S.) National Aeronautics and Space Administration
NBER	(U.S.) National Bureau of Economic Research
OECD	Organization for Economic Cooperation and Development
OSHA	(U.S.) Occupational Safety and Health Agency
UNECA	UN Economic Commission of Africa
UNESCO	UN Educational, Scientific, and Cultural Organization
UNICEF	UN International Children's Emergency Fund
UNSNA	UN System of National Accounts
USAID	U.S. Agency for International Development
USDA	U.S. Department of Agriculture
WFUD	Wildlife Fish User Days
WHO	(UN) World Health Organization

Acknowledgments

The gestation of this book has now spanned more than a decade, beginning with newspaper clippings and diary entries and continuing through the research and writing.

I owe my greatest debt to thousands of women. There are those whose names I never knew, whom I watched for hours or days, taking notes and photographs in more than three dozen countries around the world. There are those who trusted me as a politician, who confided in me and became my teachers. The rural women of my former political constituencies in New Zealand inspired and encouraged me always in this work. To Elizabeth Reid, Nalini Singh, and Antoinette Clark I owe the impetus, given in 1980, for the original conception for this book. Robin Morgan's trust in me was an inspiration, and to her I owe the existence of this book. I owe particular thanks to Isel Rivero at the United Nations, whose commitment to making UN documents available to me was selfless and utterly reliable.

Several people have commented on the ideas or on drafts of the chapters. I owe particular thanks to Bella Abzug, Tony Andreas, Ruth Busch, Gena Corea, Elizabeth Darlison, Elizabeth Dawe, Dale Lethbridge, Marcella Martinez, Robin Morgan, Paula de Perna, Elizabeth Reid, Marcia Russell, Sue Sayer, Pat Schroeder, Gloria Steinem, Elizabeth Vaneveld, and Wendy Vivian. Sue Sayer was also tireless and endlessly patient in assisting with footnoting and the bibliography.

The following economists supported and commented on my work: John Kenneth Galbraith, Gar Alperovitz, Stuart Rabinowitz, Marianne Ferber, and Michele Naples (in the United States); Brian Easton, Len Bayliss, Alf Kirk, Tony Andreas, John Chetwin, and Conrad Blyth (in New Zealand). Other social scientists whose support was invaluable were Margaret Gilling,

Andrea Pamphilis, Kathleen Gomez, Ynestra King, Dove Bing, and Nita Crawford of the Institute for Defence and Disarmament Studies; Lester Brown and Edward Woolf at the Worldwatch Institute in Washington; statisticians Ron Fergie and Sharon Evans; Lindsay Nieman in the Canadian Ministry of External Affairs; and feminist theorists Berit Ås and Hilkka Pietilä. To Jan von Tongeren, head of the UN statistical office, and to UN demographer Joanne Vanek, I owe thanks for their time and their honesty under intense questioning.

I owe special thanks to the Institute of Politics at the Kennedy School at Harvard University, where I was a Fellow (sic) in 1981, and to the Institute for Research on Women and the Eagleton Institute of Politics at Rutgers University, where I did my final research work in 1985. I am especially grateful to librarians Lil Maman at Rutgers; to Catherine Bouvin, deputy librarian at the United Nations library in New York; to many staff at the General Assembly library in Wellington, New Zealand; and to Geraldine Hay, reference librarian at the University of Waikato.

My work at Rutgers would have been impossible without the generous financial support I received from the following benefactors: the Ploughshares Fund, the Unitarian Universalist Service Committee, the L. J. and Mary C. Skaggs Foundation, Marge Benton, Susanna Dakin, Genevieve Vaughan, the Ms. Foundation for Education and Communications, and Marie Wilson of the Ms. Foundation for Women.

I would not have been able to complete my work without the assistance of students Virginia Ahearn, Lynn Dolce, and Jennifer Klot, who were employed in endless rounds of indexing cards, photocopying, reading, and "fetching."

The manuscript has been typed and assembled in its various manifestations by Marg Comer, Donna Cressy, Annette Dibley, Mary McGuinness, Gaye Miller, Bid Molnar, and Jane Wilson, without whose help I would still be writing.

In the last two years of travel and homelessness, I have been nurtured, fed, comforted, and humored by many dear friends, to whom I am especially grateful. My special thanks to my parents, Audrey and Bill Waring, to my godparents Vivian and Noel Bunn, and to Katherine O'Regan, Rosemary Ronald, Wendy Vivian, Lindsay Quilter, Michele Naples, Robin Morgan, Maggie Eyre, Sandi Hall, Elizabeth Dawe, Maurice Knuckey, Sue Sayer, Ngahuia te Awekotuku, Lorae Parry, Bronwyn Gray, and Lesley Boyles.

Finally to Bridget Williams, my editor at Allen and Unwin/ Port Nicholson Press in New Zealand; to Edite Kroll, my literary agent; to Robin Morgan; and to Yvonne Keller of Harper & Row (San Francisco) go my sincere thanks for the guidance and suggestions for change that established the final product.

I do not claim that this is "all my own work," but I am quite content to take full responsibility for it.

Marilyn Waring
Wellsford, New Zealand
November 1987

We should be on our guard not to overestimate science and scientific methods when it is a question of human problems; and we should not assume that experts are the only ones who have a right to express themselves on questions affecting the organization of society.

—Albert Einstein

Introduction

If you have any question about the worth of reading this book, try an experiment.

Close one eye and look across the room you are in, or at a scene outside your window, or at any vista. Note what you see in front of you. Test your peripheral vision.

That was a view of the world *before* this book.

Now open both eyes and look at the same scene. Note the new depth in front of you, the rounded reality of two peripheries, and the feeling of wholeness that comes from perceiving in balance.

This is the world *after* this book.

Marilyn Waring changes our worldview. Some of the ways she does this are on a large scale: for instance, adding the existence, unique contributions, and experience of the female half of humanity to traditional, one-eyed, inaccurate economics. Others are simple and basic: for instance, she questions why a tree has a measurable value when chopped down and sold, but not while it is growing and giving us oxygen? Thanks to her, when we look at what is, and what could be, we permanently enlarge our vision.

But there are three other features of this book that, as an impatient activist and a noneconomist, I especially want to commend to you.

First, it not only synthesizes research on the invisibility of women's labor and on the lack of an imputed value for the environment, but it also tells us how these invisibilities have been institutionalized. We have had far-sighted environmentalists before. We have had brilliant feminist theorists. But this is the first time that someone who is *both* has also been the Chair of the Public Expenditure Select Committee in the Parliament of a major country and had the international experience to rethink megaeconomics. In other words, it's one thing to blow the whistle on industries that pollute, or to question why water carried through pipes has a value but water carried daily and a long distance by women does not. It's something else to name, challenge, and propose a substitute for the way that these injustices are enshrined and perpetuated by the economic record-keeping of most nations, and even by the United Nations System of National Accounts.

Second, Marilyn Waring demystifies both national and international economics. As the rare expert who is also witty, a populist, and an excellent explainer, she not only puts human beings and human values into economics, but also vice versa. Since many economists are so insecure that they deliberately obfuscate in order to demonstrate their indispensability or to hide possible errors, it is both a practical help and a pleasure to find a secure and happy economist.

Third, this book does not just tell us how bad the situation is. (And it is very bad.) Unlike many apocalyptic writers, Marilyn Waring does not seek the moral superiority of singing the blues and being a messenger of doom. On the contrary, she tells us exactly what we could do to reverse invisibility, inaccuracy, and damage. With practical ideas that can be found throughout the book, and in an unusual, activist chapter at its end, she makes pragmatic proposals for ways to change everything from definitions and boundaries that hide both the depletion of environmental capital and the real scope of production, to instituting census and other economic data-gathering that could document our real problems and assets. She also provides new schemata for understanding our national economies; suggests alternate ways of attributing value to women's unpaid work; and includes tables of indicators for computing environmental damage.

For women readers, especially—and for men who have been wondering whatever happened to the female half of the world—Waring makes reality visible. Homemakers in industrial countries and women who do most of the agricultural work in the Third World will be equally grateful to this book for putting an end to their shared semantic slavery: no reader should refer to such workers as "women who don't work" ever again. The status of female human beings in general could be transformed by Waring's insistence on making human reproduction finally visible as the most basic form of production. And the double standard that calls what happens to men "politics," but what happens to women "culture," is permanently broken.

Indeed, this book reveals that women are a Third World wherever we are: low on capital, low on technology, labor intensive, and a source of raw materials, maintenance, and underpaid or unpaid production for the more powerful.

Nonetheless, men have just as much stake in this thesis and its call to action as women do. It offers large rewards, from economic models that actually work, to the possibility of survival itself. It should motivate overdeveloped countries, which are in as much environmental danger as underdeveloped ones. And the thoughtful, rich diversity of Waring's examples from different cultures and countries makes this message one of the most globally inviting and universal ever included in a book.

Indeed, the story of the ozone layer alone, the mistakes that led to its unnoticed damage, and the implications of that damage for this Spaceship Earth, could bring together the most time-honored of enemies.

I have only one remaining worry in the invisibility department: the author herself. Though her value is evident throughout this book, her impact may not be. Here is just one example. As a member of Parliament in New Zealand, on a crucial day in 1984, she withdrew from the conservative government caucus and voted to transform New Zealand into a nuclear-free zone. She thus became the deciding factor that brought down the government in power, forced a snap election, and made her country the first to refuse to harbor or fuel a superpower's nuclear ships. She had also been the major architect of the parliamentary political strategy that brought the antinuclear movement to that crossroads. Ironically, Prime Minister David

Lange, who became enthusiastic about a nuclear-free zone only after its political victory, was nominated for a Nobel Prize as a result of this successful effort, while Waring was passed over; clearly a case of female invisibility in itself.

Since a 1984 Nobel Prize was awarded to British economist Sir Richard Stone for his pivotal role in creating the United Nations System of National Accounts—the international system that supports and formalizes the national invisibility of women's labor, environmental values, and the like—the Nobel Prize Committee has more than invisibility to answer for. It has not just overlooked virtue, but rewarded error itself.

Perhaps current Nobel Prize Committee members will read this book and see the magnitude of its past blindness and consider making its importance more visible with a Nobel Prize.

Finally, I hope that readers will take a personal step inspired by the activist last chapter: adapting this book's philosophy and its new systems for imputing value to their individual and family economics. Reproduction and human care-taking, natural assets and environmental damage, can be writ small in the reality of our own lives even while we analyze them writ large.

After all, political philosophers always have told us that the family is a microcosm of the state. Unfortunately, they didn't take the next logical step: only democratic families can produce and sustain a real democracy.

—Gloria Steinem

IF WOMEN COUNTED

Prologue

Women as Nonproducers

A synopsis, some chapter headings, a draft first chapter, and now a book contract, lie on the table in front of me. This goat farmer sits here surrounded by ten years of paper clippings, political papers, notes, and diary entries from visits to every political bloc and continent.

What Brought Me To Write This Book

This inquiry began when I was appointed to and then chaired the Public Expenditure (Public Accounts and Budget) Select Committee during my terms as a Member of the New Zealand Parliament from 1975 to 1984. At one point in my tenure as Chair, New Zealand revised its System of National Accounts in accordance with changes suggested by the United Nations. It was then that I underwent a rude awakening as to the importance of the United Nations System of National Accounts (UNSNA). I learned that in the UNSNA, the things that I valued about life in my country—its pollution-free environment; its mountain streams with safe drinking water; the accessibility of national parks, walkways, beaches, lakes, kauri and beech forests; the absence of nuclear power and nuclear energy—all counted for nothing. They were not accounted for in private consumption expenditure, general government expenditure, or gross domestic capital formation. Yet these accounting systems were used to determine all public policy. Since the environment effectively counted for nothing, there could be no "value" on policy measures that would ensure its preservation.

Hand in hand with the dismissal of the environment, came evidence of the severe invisibility of women and women's work. For example, as a politician, I found it virtually impossible to prove—given the production framework with which we were faced—that child care facilities were needed. "Nonproducers" (housewives, mothers) who are "inactive" and "unoccupied" cannot, apparently, be in need. They are not even in the economic cycle in the first place. They can certainly have no expectation that they will be visible in the distribution of benefits that flow from production.

These injustices result from the System of National Accounts, an international system of economic measurement. Any annual report of the World Bank, the International Monetary Fund (IMF), United Nations (UN) agencies, or national governments, is based on national account statistics. The UN uses national accounts to assess annual contributions, and to appraise the success of regional development programs. Aid donors use the UNSNA to identify deserving cases, need being determined by per capita gross domestic product. The World Bank uses these figures to identify nations that most urgently need economic assistance. Multinational corporations use the same figures to locate new areas for overseas investments. Companies project the markets for their goods on the basis of the national accounts projections and plan their investment, personnel, and other internal policies.

And that's only part of the story. For individual countries the uses made of national accounts and their supporting statistics are manifold and have far-reaching effects. They are used for creating frameworks or models for the integration of economic statistics generally. They are used to analyze past and current developments in the national economy and are the basis of projections of the possible effects of changes in policy or other economic changes. They are used to quantify all areas of what is considered the national economy so that resource allocation decisions can be made accordingly. Governments project public service investment and revenue requirements for the nation—and plan new construction, training, and other programs necessary to meet those needs—all by using their national accounts. They are used to forecast short- and medium-term future trends. They are also used internationally to compare one nation's economic performance with another's.

The national accounts by themselves do not indicate what economic policies a government should implement. They are simply a mechanism—but one which operates for specific ends. The appropriate size of the budget deficit or correct amount of any taxation cuts, for example, cannot be inferred directly by the national accounts. Policy measures are based on a *selective* understanding of economic stimulus. The national accounts just record a pattern of economic activity. But from the outset, the figures are rigged.

Early national income accounts were evolved, as we shall see, in order to justify paying for wars. Since the institutionalization of national income accounting by the United Nations, however, the motive has expanded. A major reason that only cash generating activities are taken into account is to ensure that countries can determine balance of payments and loan requirements—not as a comparative exercise, but as a controlling exercise. Those to whom money is owed (First World governments, multinational banks, and multilateral agencies) now impose this system on those who owe them money. They are interested only in seeing the *cash generating* capacity of the debtor countries, not their *productive* capacity. But whatever the change of motive, two things are constant. Those who are making the decisions are men, and those values which are excluded from this determination are those of our environment, and of women and children.

The current state of the world is the result of a system that attributes little or no "value" to peace. It pays no heed to the preservation of natural resources or to the labor of the majority of its inhabitants or to the unpaid work of the reproduction of human life itself—not to mention its maintenance and care. *The system cannot respond to values it refuses to recognize.*

In 1980 I had another experience that forced me to examine more closely the patriarchal nature of economics. I was a member of the New Zealand delegation to the UN Mid-Decade Conference on Women, in Copenhagen. When we fought there for the recognition of women's unpaid productive and reproductive work, the counterattacks were fivefold. An extraordinary alignment of the male delegation heads from India, the USSR, and the Holy See (yes, the Vatican has a permanent seat in the UN), told us:

- An interest in women in any role other than mother is culturally imperialistic, imposing a Western feminist ideology on other quite different cultures.
- Support for women's nonmothering roles must necessarily lead toward destruction of the family.
- Development problems must be solved first, and then we can deal with equal opportunities, rights, and benefits for women.
- Attempts to employ women will necessarily exacerbate employment problems.
- If one takes care of development, women's roles and status will automatically be improved.

Nevertheless, an alignment of women delegates from all political blocs saw for the first time a mention in a UN document of women's roles as producers *and* reproducers. Using the insights of this conference, I prepared a theoretical paper on the UN System of National Accounts for the Women and Food Conference in Sydney, Australia, in February 1982. At that time, as a member of Parliament, I discussed the draft paper with officials in the New Zealand Treasury, the External Aid Division of the Ministry of Foreign Affairs, and the Department of Statistics. The Australian deputy-chief statistician, Ron Fergie, was on an exchange visit to Wellington at the time, and I have in front of me my first draft, with his comments and editing throughout. His memo of reply to me—a classic of sexist economic assumption—was one of the major incentives to write this book.

What This Book Is About

If Women Counted is not preoccupied with debating economics with men. If my desire was to establish my own credibility within the male world, then I would make those ritual bows. But while women may not be visible to the governing ideology of the world, I do not see why we need to mimic its standards or methods to make ourselves understood or heard.

Perhaps there is a need for that sort of book, but someone else should take it on. I do confess that the temptations are phenomenal. For example, what feminist wouldn't enjoy responding to Frederick Engels's discussion of Dühring's "Force" theory and his discussion of slavery.[1] He suggests, "in the case of Robinson Crusoe and Friday, *so in all cases of domination and subjection up to the present day . . . subjugation has always been . . . a means through which food can be secured.*"[2] (my emphasis)

So who "secures food"? I ask myself. Then Engels quotes Karl Marx as writing,

In order to make use of a slave, a man must possess two kinds of things: First, the instruments and material for his slaves' labour [a household?] and secondly, the *minimum* means of subsistence for him. . . . Before slave labour could become the dominant mode of production in a whole social group an even far higher increase in production, trade and accumulation of wealth was essential. . . .[3]

Property turns out to be the right, on the part of the capitalist, *to appropriate the unpaid labour of others* or its product, and, on the part of the labourer, the impossibility of appropriating his [*sic*] own product. *Separation of property from labour has become the necessary consequence* of a law that apparently originated in their identity.[4] (my emphasis)

So it has separated, has it? Then what is marriage?

As an undergraduate student of political philosophy, I was afraid to write this—i.e., my own perspective—afraid of the ridicule of the males who would 'mark' my work, afraid of writing in the first person. Yet now I delight in exposing these tyrannous ideologies. For example, following a period of despotism, communities see, according to Engels,

their first economic advance consisting in the increase and development of production by means of *slave labour*. . . . This was an advance even for the slaves; the prisoners of war, from whom the mass of the slaves was recruited, now at least kept their lives, instead of being killed as they had been before, or even roasted, as at a still earlier period. . . .

So long as the really working population was so much occupied in their necessary labour that they had no time left for looking after the common affairs of society—the direction of labour, affairs of the state, legal matters, art, science, etc.—so long was it always necessary that there should exist *a special class, freed from actual labour, to manage these affairs*; and *this special class never failed to impose a greater and greater burden* of labour, for its own advantage, *on the working masses*. Only the immense increase of the productive forces attained through large scale industry *made it possible* [note tense] to distribute labour among all members of society without exception, and thereby to limit the labour time of each individual member [for which read: men] to such an extent that all have enough free time left to take part in the general—both theoretical and practical—affairs of society.[5] (my emphasis)

You see what a feminist can do with this. It is a description of women's universal enslavement. Women are still roasted if they are not recruited into slavery. If, for example, their dowries are insufficient then they are killed, often by "accidental" fire. When their 'useful' lives are over (that is, their husbands die), they are expected to commit 'sati' by burning themselves on the funeral pyre. And in a "still earlier period" they were burned at the stake. As for the assumption that workers have leisure, well, of course they do. Since "workers" are defined as males, since male workers are now capitalists, and since the property imbued in them is womankind, then what Engels describes is a very apt portrayal of the current position of *women*. One could, for the sake of socialist feminists, say a great deal more about this, but again, it is not the point.

Neither does this book nor this argument have to do with wages for housework, though both share Maria della Costa's original intention of providing a tool for raising consciousness and for mobilizing women everywhere.[6] I am not arguing that a woman should be paid an assessment lower than the average wage to reproduce herself as a beneficiary in the system. I am talking about attributing a monetary valuation to unpaid work, productive and reproductive. This process, called imputation, would make this work visible, influencing policies and concepts, and questioning values.

This is also not a book about the invisibility of women's work. In various ways, Barbara Rogers, Ester Boserup, Lourdes Beneria, Kathleen Newland, and others have written that book.[7] I often used to wonder why they had not dealt in some detail with the UN System of National Accounts. I am beginning to understand why. The rhetoric of these accounts is so removed from us, and requires so much in the translation, that it is difficult to breathe any life onto the page when trying to demystify them. Yet demystify them we must, because the UNSNA is an essential tool of the male economic system. So I will have to trust my sisters to stay with the text, and trust that as I show how this system treats our lives, my analysis will become clear.

The context is introduced in chapter 1. I introduce the players, so to speak, the language of economics, and a brief history of how the national accounts came into being. This already involves a critique of how the economic system touches each of our lives, and the life of the biosphere itself. Indeed, there seems no way to avoid this book being about everything on the planet. To acknowledge that may seem arrogant, yet true arrogance would be to silence or edit myself.

In chapter 2, I explain the derivation of this system; how recent it is, who the men responsible for it were and are; and the political exigencies of the time that brought about this particular "solution." I explain in chapter 3, step by step, the United Nation's rules for national accounts, what they are, and how they are used. Then, in chapter 4, I use several diverse countries to illustrate the difference between the conception and the practice involved in the accounts. In chapter 5, I explain the tools for collecting information and developing indices in these accounts—and the part that women do or do not play in that. (As much as the practitioners will protest that the national accounts are not welfare indicators, the fact remains that in the absence of any other indicator this is how they are used.) U.S. Senator Daniel Moynihan has written:

> If American society recognized home-making and child rearing as productive work to be included in the national economic accounts the receipt of welfare might not imply dependency. But we don't. It may be hoped the women's movement of the present time will change this. But as of the time I write, it had not.[8]

From personal experience I know that the policymakers, to whom figures such as per capital Gross National Product (GNP) are fed, are not educated in the uses and abuses of these statistics. Most with whom I worked over the years would not have known that the accounts exclude the services of housewives or that conservation and environmental issues are quite beyond the sphere of any so-called balanced economic analysis. Women's household production is not the only work that is excluded. Census data are often not collected for smaller enterprises or for the self-employed in the informal sector or for the informal sector trading that we see in markets everywhere. Then there is the voluntary work that women everywhere perform in the majority. Chapter 6 examines acknowledged "measurement difficulties" in the national accounts, and the motives for continued use of the accounts even in the face of that. How unsubtle it is, for example, that the underground economy, where a large number of men are involved in crime, corruption, drug abuse, and pornography, is a source of much concern and guesstimation for *inclusion* in the accounts.

Which brings us to chapter 7: an exploration of the "value" of human life—or, rather, given the current economic system, the "value" of death. This question has always been spoken of in the realms of philosophy and religion. By adding economics to the mix, we can address some interesting perspectives. It seems to me that our planet's stockpile of murderous bombs should give us a clue about the realm of economics. For example, when Western policymakers sit around their cabinet and executive tables trying to decide whether or not to build more bombs, shouldn't one of the questions (in terms of their own "cost benefit analyses") be, "Well, how much are we prepared to spend to wipe out each Russian citizen? What is a Soviet child standing in Red Square worth?" It is not an irrelevant question. It is, in fact, what they are deciding.

The weapons systems that have been accumulated have the capacity to annihilate our world's population twelve times over. The amount spent on these weapons should give us an indication of the economic value of human life.*

The U.S. military budget, for example, is larger than the GNPs of all but eight countries in the world. (The budget of the U.S. Department of Defense is the largest centrally planned economy outside the Soviet Union.) In 1986, the Pentagon was spending nearly $1 billion a day, $41 million an hour, $700,000 a minute. This statistic does not include expenditure for the manufacture of nuclear fuel and all things nuclear, which in the United States is paid for by the Department of Energy. A

---

*What I would most like to have done, of course, was to have fed into a computer the world's annual population since 1945, a rough estimate of the megatonnage of nuclear weaponry produced per year, and a rough estimate of spending on such weapons and their delivery systems for each year, so that we might have had a comprehensive forty-years' documentation of what the decision makers thought our lives were worth. I thought someone must have asked this question before, or if not, then some software mixture in some major disarmament study could produce the cross-tabulations. I spent four months looking for that in the major research institutes in the United States in 1986, and checking with all the possible references they could give me. The Senior Research Assistant in Joseph Nye's Harvard Study Group told me that the "accuracy of missiles in targeting was such that it was not a relevant question." In the light of the then recent failures of Cruise missile launches, a global failure of satellite launches, a failed Titan launch, the failed Challenger launch, and the Chernobyl disaster, I was not convinced.

feminist analysis must ask: does economics factor a "value for human life" into its cost-benefit analyses of such "growth" and "development"? Does economics address, for instance, the issue of "reproduction"?

Chapter 8 focuses on the reproduction of the species. Do the national accounts take into account women's time and effort in birthing and raising a child? Is that all there is to "reproduction"? And how is reproduction in its fullest sense different from women's unpaid, unacknowledged "productive" work? And what about such issues as in vitro fertilization, "test tube babies," bride price, custody battles, "ownership" of children, reproductive freedom, and sexual preference?

One of the difficulties of being a woman is that we have to try to do everything. It is the same, as I discovered in chapter 9, in feminist writing. Mary O'Brien draws attention to this in the introduction to her book *The Politics of Reproduction*:

Feminist scholarship cannot engage in the disciplinary fragmentation which currently pervades social science, nor can it afford the ahistorical indulgences of here and now empiricism. A feminist social science, responding to the cultural pervasiveness of male supremacy, must be a unified social science, a unification which also transcends the partiality of political economy.[9]

"The partiality of political economy." How well we all know it, even if we haven't named it. It is arbitrary. It is linear. It is fragmented. And it is found everywhere. But a feminist analysis, as O'Brien describes, makes the connections. The descriptions of women's lives in chapter 9 raise the question: is the economics discipline a functionary and tool of patriarchy—or is patriarchy a functionary and tool of economics? Does it matter? This chapter provides data for you to draw your own conclusion.

Albert Einstein wrote:

The discovery of general laws in economics is made difficult by the circumstance that observed economic phenomena are often affected by many factors which are very hard to evaluate separately. In addition, the experience which has accumulated since the beginning of the so-called civilised period of human history has—as is well-known—been largely influenced and limited by causes which are by no means exclusively economic in nature.[10]

Indeed, nature itself is not considered "economic." Which is the subject of chapter 10. It is no accident that our much-loved and much-pillaged and raped planet is often called Mother Earth. The analogies of ravage and exploitation between women and our environment have been the focus of writers such as Rachel Carson, Susan Griffin, Ngahuia te Awekotuku, and the women writers of Greenham Common.[11] The economic point of view discussed in chapter 10 continues those analogies. I examine the links between economics and such factors as the alarming shrinkage of the earth's forests, the dependency of women on wood for fuel, the pressure created on such a limited resource by a rapid population increase, and the consequent soil erosion and desertification. For example, rough estimates of the cost of providing safe water and sanitation for human and animal species alike are $20 billion (less than a fortnight's world expenditure on armaments), yet half our planet's population lacks such facilities. Unsafe water and inadequate sanitation account for 75 percent of illnesses in poor countries. What value, if any, does the world's economic system attribute to the interdependencies of the world's ecosystem?

In chapter 11, I deal with the question of whether imputing the value of women's work into the national accounts would make any difference. If survey data were collected on a microcosmic level (e.g., individual as opposed to "household"), significant information would emerge about the production-related time spent by women and children. A survey in Kenya showed that 80 percent of household cereal production is done by women;[12] yet we can spy out the policy interest because agricultural training institutions are directed almost wholly towards men. Women know these things because we keep our eyes open, but it appears multilateral agencies have to have empirical evidence before they are able to move to redirect their investments. And if unpaid productive and reproductive labor remain invisible, then women remain invisible. There seems no doubt that if housewives were included in the labor force and the value of their unpaid work was added to the total cost of services (which, with the costs of goods, constitutes GNP), the repercussions would be felt in various fields of social policy: Certain forms of social security would be extended to them, as would access to adult vocational training programs presently restricted to the "working" population, and greater investment would be made in social facilities such as child care centers. To what level would this method be effective, and at what point would patriarchy reassert its power?

In aid programs the definition of women as "non-producers" is particularly obvious. Either women are denied access to aid on the grounds that they are "less productive" or "too traditional," or they are not recognized as a development problem— because it is assumed that they would be cared for by male heads of households and that their marginalization from economic activities is both inevitable and appropriate. Foreign assistance programs may be directed toward women but only as mothers (nutrition and maternal and child health programs) or potential mothers (population programs). Women are seen (narrowly) as reproducers not producers, welfare cases not workers. This perception on the part of policy planners is not confined to developing countries. It reflects the national policy practice of aid donors. In addition, the impact of technological change on rural women is class-specific. Whereas women in the middle and landlord class can benefit from time saved, technological change in the processing of food and crops can eliminate supplementary sources of employment on which poor women have to depend. In our own Western, industrialized countries, major changes in taxation structure affect women in a similarly class-specific way.

There is another way, as chapter 12 explains, a different economic conception and new way to act. For example, what changes might occur in global economic policy and practice if the *worth* of the planet itself, as well as that of the majority of its human population, were *valued*? I want so much for our lives to be different, for my sisters to find some joy and a real freedom. I want to *do* something about it all. So I conclude with a call for action, for us and our sisters, both powerful and powerless, and a plan of action of things to do. I suggest a strategy, something each of us can do as we refuse to be cogs in the machinery of perpetuating this barren and murderous economic system.

I love my country and deeply feel the privilege of calling this environment of Aotearoa* "home." It was my sister New Zealander Katherine Mansfield who wrote in her journal, "Risk—risk anything. Care no more for the opinion of others, for those voices. Do the thing hardest on earth for you to do. Act for yourself. Face the Truth."[13] So I've written it down. As I see it. I would like it to be of some "use value."

Aotearoa is the name given by the indigenous Maori people to New Zealand.

1. A Woman's Reckoning

An Introduction to the International Economic System

I am awake in a glistening morning ready to write. From the window, the lush green grass, thick with autumn dew, leads to the empty beach. The sea and sky beyond—both blue and unpolluted—are washed clear and clean by the sun. The only sounds are the early dawn chorus and the roaring of the waves. I sit, as writers and artists have sat for centuries, laboring unpaid. Yet I am sure this is work. I am sure it is productive, and I hope it will be of value. But as far as the International Labor Organization (ILO) is concerned, on this late summer day in 1986, it is none of the above.

I consider the hills rising directly from the sea. They were once covered in thick native bush, which must have been nonproductive, for it was burned or cleared off. Now thousands of pine trees inch their way to a harvest at twenty years. That will make them "productive." If the mineral prospecting licenses on the hills reveal minerals in quantity, the hills, too, will be productive. As they are—untouched, unscathed—they have no value. That's what the international economic system says.

My tenancy of this house is unproductive. While its owner will have a market rental value of the house imputed for the sake of the national accounts, I contribute nothing, as I am a guest here. I consume a little water and electricity. Now that has value! If modern plumbing conveniences were not providing water and I walked with my bucket to the foothills four hundred meters away to collect it from the streams there, it would be worthless. That's what the international economic system says.

If I were to take commercially prepared, prepackaged food from the refrigerator, I would be economically consumptive. But I choose to eat the feijoas, tamarillos, and apples from the domestic garden, items of no value. All in all, I seem to be having a very worthless sort of day—like the beach, the birds, and the clear and unpolluted skies.

Tell Me a Riddle: Who Works and Who Doesn't

Consider Tendai, a young girl in the Lowveld, in Zimbabwe. Her day starts at 4 A.M., when, to fetch water, she carries a thirty-litre tin to a borehole about eleven kilometers from her home. She walks barefoot and is home by 9 A.M. She eats a little and proceeds to fetch firewood until midday. She cleans the utensils from the family's morning meal and sits preparing a lunch of sadza for the family. After lunch and the cleaning of the dishes, she wanders in the hot sun until early evening, fetching wild vegetables for supper before making the evening trip for water. Her day ends at 9 P.M., after she has prepared supper and put her younger brothers and sisters to sleep. Tendai is considered unproductive, unoccupied, and economically inactive. According to the international economic system, Tendai does not work and is not part of the labor force.

Cathy, a young, middle-class North American housewife, spends her days preparing food, setting the table, serving meals, clearing food and dishes from the table, washing dishes, dressing and diapering her children, disciplining children, taking the children to day-care or to school, disposing of garbage, dusting, gathering clothes for washing, doing the laundry, going to the gas station and the supermarket, repairing household items, ironing, keeping an eye on or playing with the children, making beds, paying bills, caring for pets and plants, putting away toys, books, and clothes, sewing or mending or knitting, talking with door-to-door salespeople, answering the telephone, vacuuming, sweeping, and washing floors, cutting the grass, weeding, and shoveling snow, cleaning the bathroom and the kitchen, and putting her children to bed. Cathy has to face the fact that she fills her time in a *totally* unproductive manner. She, too, is economically inactive, and economists record her as unoccupied.

Ben is a highly trained member of the U.S. military. His regular duty is to descend to an underground facility where he waits with a colleague, for hours at a time, for an order to fire a nuclear missile. So skilled and effective is Ben that if his colleague were to attempt to subvert an order to fire, Ben would, if all else failed, be expected to kill him to ensure a successful missile launch. Ben is in paid work; he is economically active. His work has value and contributes, as part of the nuclear machine, to his nation's growth, wealth, and productivity. That's what the international economic system says.

Mario is a pimp and a heroin addict in Rome. He regularly pays graft. While Mario's services and his consumption and production are illegal, they are, nonetheless, marketed. Money changes hands. Mario's activities are part of Italy's hidden economy. But in a nation's bookkeeping, not all transactions are accounted for. A government treasury or a reserve bank measures the money supply and sees that more money is in circulation than has been reported in legitimate business activities. Thus some nations, including Italy, regularly impute a minimal value for the hidden economy in their national accounts. So part of Mario's illegal services and production and consumption activities will be recognized and recorded. That's what the international economic system says.

Ben and Mario work. Cathy and Tendai do not. Those are the rules. I believe that women all over the world, with lives as diverse as those of Cathy and Tendai, are economically productive. You, too, may believe that these women work full days. But according to the theory, science, profession, practice, and institutionalization of economics, we are wrong.

Blind Man's Buff: How Economic Theory Constructs Reality

The major twentieth century British economist, John Maynard Keynes, called economics "a method rather than a doctrine, an apparatus of the mind, a technique of thinking which helps its possessor to draw correct conclusions."[1] My "technique of thinking" has me conclude that Cathy and Tendai work, that they are productive, and that their economic activity is of value. My technique of thinking leads me to conclude that Ben and Mario work, that they are destructive, and that their economic activity is a major cost and threat to the planet. But that is not how the established economic theory views their activities.

Theory is used, first of all, in order to decide what facts are relevant to an analysis. As the lives of Tendai, Cathy, Ben, and Mario illustrate, only some everyday experiences are stated, recognized, and recorded by economic theory. Overwhelmingly, those experiences that are economically visible can be summarized as *what men do*.

Most propositions in economics are explained and illustrated by using words and mathematics. These are seen to be alternative languages that are translatable into each other. Mathematical formulas assist the illusion that economics is a value-free science: propaganda is less easily discerned from figures than it is from words. The process of theorizing takes place when economists reason about simplified models of an actual economy or some part of an economy. From this model, "factual predictions" are made. Clearly, if you do not perceive parts of the community as economically active, they will not be in your model, and your "correct conclusions" based on the model will not include them.

The belief that value results only when (predominantly) men

interact with the marketplace means that few attempts are made to disguise this myopic approach.

For example, Baron Lionel Robbins, an economist who was a member of the British House of Lords, wrote:

The propositions of economic theory . . . are all *assumptions* involving in some ways *simple* and *indisputable* facts of *experience*. . . . We do not need controlled experiments to establish their *validity*: they are so much *the stuff of our everyday experience* that they have only to be stated to be recognized as *obvious* (my emphasis).[2]

Whatever else Baron Robbins's "everyday experience" might involve, it will not account for the everyday experience of Cathy and Tendai. We are taught to read through or over such rhetoric, never to question it. It is the language of economic texts, and their assumptions that the male experience encompasses female experience have enslaved women in the male economic system.

Feminist theorist Sheila Rowbotham reminds us:

Language conveys a certain power. It is one of the instruments of domination. . . . The language of theory—censored language—only expresses a reality experienced by the oppressors. It speaks only for their world, for their point of view.[3]

And something else happens to language in its colonizing by male theorists.

Xenophon coined the word *oikonomikos* to describe the management or rule of a house or household. In general usage, the word *economy* still retains some links with its Greek origins. *Roget's Thesaurus* lists as synonyms management, order, careful administration, frugality, austerity, prudence, thrift, providence, care, and retrenchment.[4] These synonyms are unlikely candidates for what is called the "science" of economics. The meanings of words, our words, change inside a "discipline."

When I look at the index of any major journal of economics, it is difficult to think of subjects that have remained unscathed in terms of invasion by this discipline. Nobel Prize winner Paul

Samuelson, Professor of Economics at Massachusetts Institute of Technology, writes:

In recent years, economists have begun to infiltrate the field of demography. This is part of the imperialist movement in which we economists try to apply our methodologies to everything—to the law, to the sociology of the family, courtship, marriage, divorce, and cohabitation.[5]

But women are generally presumed to know little about economics, or the world's or a nation's economy. Yet a "simple and indisputable fact of everyday experience" is that most women know how to be economical, to use things sparingly, to cut down on expenses. For some this knowledge and skill sustains the lives of themselves and their children from one hour or one day to the next. But what "everyday experience" would British Baron Lionel Robbins call on to give the "obvious" answers to some simple questions?

- Case studies in Gambia show that women's working time in agriculture rose from nineteen to twenty hours when improved methods were introduced, but men's working time fell from eleven to nine hours.[6] How does that happen?
- Why do nutritional deficiencies result, when family food availability declines as subsistence (nonmonetary) farmland is taken for cash crops and men get paid an income?
- Why, when men take over responsibility for women's tasks as soon as they are mechanized, or when they are transformed from subsistence into market production, are the tasks suddenly "productive"?
- Housework is implicitly taxed by not being valued. Shouldn't it then be recognized in the distribution of benefits?
- A chemical spillage creates increased value in the labor and expenditure required to clean it up; it contributes to a nation's growth. Why is that so?
- As I write, NASA has announced a "successful" Star Wars experiment. Two missiles were launched and chased each other about the sky before one deliberately blew up the other

and then self-destructed. This success follows a failed Challenger shuttle mission, failed Titan and Cruise missile tests, and failed satellite launches. But for the purpose of recording production, both the success and the failures contributed billions of dollars in growth to the U.S. economy.

This is not a sane state of affairs. What is the origin of such madness?

According to Baron Robbins the authoritative definition of economics is "the study of human behaviour in disposing of scarce means which have alternative uses to satisfy ends of varying importance."[7] Then shouldn't the basic questions of economics involve those who are seen to be "economically inactive"? What particular mix of goods and services best meets the needs and wants of a community—how they are to be produced, from whom they are to be provided, and how they are to be distributed—are questions that should include the community and the environments in which we live. But the system says that forests, rainfall, water resources, fossil fuels, seafood, soil, grasslands, and the quality of the air that we breathe are worthless when preserved for future generations. It is their use, exploitation, and payment for them in the market that, in Robbins's terms, "establishes their validity." It is in their destruction that they become "simple and indisputable facts of experience."

Defining Economic Terms

Disciples of economics are likely to see it as a science that treats things from the standpoint of price. Words that we think we all understand (such as *value, work, labor, production, reproduction,* and *economic activity*) have been hijacked into the service of this science. As a result, such words come to have two very different definitions: an economic definition and a noneconomic one.

Value

Value is the most important word to understand in its economic and noneconomic contexts. The word is derived from the Latin *valere*, meaning "to be strong or worthy." The *Oxford English Dictionary* now lists its principle meaning in purely economic terms: "that amount of some commodity, medium of exchange, etc., which is considered to be an equivalent for something else; a fair or adequate equivalent or return." But I know what I think is "strong or worthy" in my life. I know about the value of friendship, fresh air, daily exercise. I frequently weigh the value of my time: how will I spend it, in which activity? For me, value is a sense, a feeling—not a tangible measure, despite the *Oxford English Dictionary*.

The notion of value has had a varied literary history. It's found in the Bible, of course, in St. Matthew's Gospel: "Are not two sparrows sold for a farthing? And one of them shall not fall on the ground without your Father. The very hairs of your head are all numbered. Fear ye not therefore, ye are of more value than many sparrows."[8] And in "Much Ado About Nothing," William Shakespeare wrote:

> For it so falls out
> That what we have we prize not to be worth
> While we enjoy it, but being lacked and lost,
> Why then we rack the value.

In the sixteenth century, Montaigne wrote in his *Essays*, "The value of life lies not in the length of days but in the use you make of them."

Addison and Steele, seventeenth century English essayists, had their versions. "It was very prettily said, that we may learn the little value of fortune by the persons on whom heaven is pleased to bestow it,"[9] and "I value my garden more for being full of blackbirds than of cherries, and very frankly give them fruit for their songs."[10]

In the eighteenth century, William Hazlitt put it more austerely: "Those who make their dress a principal part of themselves, will, in general, become of no more value than their dress."[11] Ralph Waldo Emerson, nineteenth century U.S. poet, wrote, "The one thing of value in the world is the active soul."

From the fourteenth to the seventeenth century, sources of value were seen, in literature and in politics, to be scarcity, utility, and desirability.

Language is power, but literary concepts of value find few friends in economics. Like much of our language, this strong, worthy word has been taken from us and led along a very narrow path.

In the sixteenth and seventeenth centuries, English writers Thomas More and Thomas Hobbes argued in political and moral terms about what was of "value" in society. Their visions were very different, but the conflicts that they observed—between freedom and authority, community and private property, cooperation and competition—are ever with us and no closer to resolution.

The economist Adam Smith, writing in the eighteenth century, was perhaps the first to use the concept of value in relation to the market. He distinguished "market" from "moral" value and identified the market as the place where values are expressed. That this distinction was in itself not objective but a specific moral and political viewpoint does not attract much debate. Writing at the time of the emergence of a new manufacturing class, Smith wanted to know what was responsible for the growth of national wealth. He established the logical foundation for his work by identifying what he thought was essential human nature. He developed an image of humans as materialistic, egoistic, selfish, and primarily motivated by pursuit of their own self-interest. This is also not a "scientific opinion," it seems to me, but a created, and moral, judgment. He writes:

Man [sic] has almost constant occasion for the help of his brethren and it is in vain for him to expect it from their benevolence only. He will be more likely to prevail if he can interest their self love in his favour, and show them that it is for their own advantage to do for him what he requires of them. . . . It is not from the benevolence of the butcher, the brewer, or the baker that we expect our dinner, but from their regard to their own interest.[12]

In this description, the male gender is subject. Smith did not acknowledge women's (or men's) altruism and benevolence. In ignoring women he characteristically presumed their idiosyncracies to be those of his "brethren." If Adam Smith was fed daily by Mrs. Smith, he omitted to notice or to mention it. He did not, of course, pay her. What *her* interest was in feeding him we can only guess, for Adam Smith saw no "value" in what she did.

A much more accurate view of the concept of value in economics comes from a woman, the economist Joan Robinson. Economics textbooks are generally alienating, turgid, bludgeoning. But the works of Joan Robinson did not affect me in that way. A pupil of Alfred Marshall, and a colleague of John Maynard Keynes, Robinson was, until her death, a professor of economics at Cambridge University. On the question of value she wrote:

One of the great metaphysical ideas in economics is expressed by the word "value." . . . It does not mean market prices, which vary from time to time under the influence of casual accidents; nor is it just an historical average of actual prices. Indeed, it is not simply a price; it is something which will explain how prices come to be what they are. What is it? Where shall we find it? Like all metaphysical concepts, when you try to pin it down it turns out to be just a word.[13]

And:

A metaphysical belief, as in the law of value, cannot be wrong, and this is the sign that there is nothing to be learned from it.[14]

And further:

The awkwardness of reckoning in terms of *value* . . . accounts for much of the obscurity in Marx's exposition, and none of the important ideas which he expresses in terms of the concept of value cannot be better expressed without it.[15]

Robinson was wary of importing a specious scientific quality into her discussions. She recognized that *value* should be examined in terms of the motives of the writer and *evaluation* in terms of the ultimate ends that it was designed to serve. If value is "a quality of an object or experience which arouses and/or satisfies our interest, appreciation, or desire,"[16] then it is most certainly in the eye of the beholder.

Despite Robinson's warnings, economists from Adam Smith onward have maintained that their moral judgment—that the market was the source of value—was a judgment devoid of self-interest. The concept of value used in articles in modern economic journals is far from metaphysical. The value of much is measured or guessed at. For example, an article entitled "The Value of Safety" shows economic value at its "objective" and absurd best:

[I]f decisions are to be taken in a systematic and consistent manner and scarce resources are to be allocated efficiently and to the greatest advantage, it would seem necessary to have a method of associating explicit values with anticipated improvements in safety—and costs with deteriorations—in order that these effects can be weighed in relation to other desirable and undesirable consequences of the decision.[17]

Thus, the value of safety is not a moral value of averting injury, saving life, ensuring healthy working conditions. Such considerations play no part. The value of safety is its costs and benefits relative to lost or gained production, possible legal suits, different groups of workers, and the allocation of scarce resources.

Another commentator, John Broome, suggests that one motivation for *valuing life* at the moment is by means of people's *willingness to pay* for safety. He "believes at the moment we have no sound basis for valuing life," and points out that people argue that it is: "manifestly inefficient not to have a uniform value (of life) established for all of Government's decision making. If two branches of Government use different values, then the resources used on life saving would save more lives if they were redistributed between the branches."[18] Broome argues that establishing a uniform value for life would not be the best thing to do because "we" do not know what the right objective is. *We* do: *life* is the right objective.

I turn back to the mountains. If minerals were found there, the hills would still be worthless until a mining operation commenced. And then as cliffs were gouged, as roads were cut, and smoke rose, the hills would be of value—their value would be the price the minerals would fetch on the world market. No price would be put on the violation of the earth, or the loss of beauty, or the depletion of mineral resources. This is what value means, according to economic theory.

Work, Labor, and Economic Activity

When I was a child, one of my grandmothers would bring her work into the sitting room. She would sit sewing buttons and darning socks while we sat reading at leisure, listening to the radio in front of the fire. My grandmother never stopped. When I got up in the morning she would already be in the kitchen working the dough for the day's baking. My other grandmother was a member of the church and a number of charity organizations. She did what our village called good works. Arriving home from school, I might see the clothesline flagged with washing or piles of weeds in the pathways or bottles full of freshly preserved fruit on the kitchen bench, and I would know my mother had been working hard. I, in turn, would have to do my schoolwork.

Every time I see a mother with an infant, I know I am seeing a woman at work. I know that work is not leisure and it is not sleep and it may well be enjoyable. I know that money payment is not necessary for work to be done. But, again, I seem to be at odds with economics as a discipline, because when work becomes a concept in institutionalized economics, payment enters the picture. *Work* and *labor* and *economic activity* are used interchangeably (though different schools of economics will argue that this is not the case). So my grandmother did not work, and those mothers I see with their infants are not working. No housewives, according to this economic definition, are workers.

The criterion for "productive" work proposed over fifty years ago by home economist Margaret Reid was that any activity culminating in a service or product, which one can buy or hire someone else to do, is an "economic activity" even if pay is not involved.[19] Yet in major texts used in college economics courses in North America, it is not unusual to find sentences such as "Most of us prefer no work to work with no pay."[20] Who is "us," I wonder. Adam Smith defined work as an activity requiring the worker to give up "his [sic] tranquility, his freedom and his happiness."[21] Charlotte Perkins Gilman, a leading intellectual of the women's movement in the United States in the early twentieth century, called this a particularly masculine view:

Following that pitiful conception of labour as a curse, comes the very old and androcentric (i.e., male-centered) habit of despising it as belonging to women and then to slaves . . . for long ages men performed no productive industry at all, being merely hunters and fighters.

Our current teachings in the infant science of political economy are naively masculine. They assume as unquestionable that "the economic man" will never do anything unless he has to; will only do it to escape pain or attain pleasure; and will, inevitably, take all he can get and do all he can to outwit, overcome, and if necessary destroy his antagonist.[22]

But the view of the world that Gilman despised has been institutionalized, so that work, according to Katherine Newland, "is still the primary means by which people establish a claim to a share of production. To be without work is to place that claim in jeopardy."[23] Housewives clearly do not "work." Mothers taking care of children are not working. No money changes hands.

Those who are in the grey area of informal work—between the recognized labor market and the housewife—may not claim to be workers either, in this economic sense. Invisible, informal work includes bartering, the trading of goods in informal settings (for example, in flea markets), and "off the books" or "under the table" employment. Workers who do not report work or pay income taxes on earnings and workers who are paid in cash at below minimum wages fall into this category. In addition, volunteer work can be considered informal work.[24] (And note that volunteer *work* is generally done by women while *financial contributions* to voluntary organizations—which take place in the market, are tax-deductible, and have special rules within the economic system—are generally made by men.)

"Home-based work activities"—including housekeeping, home repair and maintenance, do-it-yourself building, and child care—are informal work. So are "deviant work activities"—which include anything from organized crime to petty fraud. The social exchange of services, which is the giving and receiving of services within social networks of relatives, friends, neighbors, and acquaintances, is also regarded as economically unimportant and remains unacknowledged.

The *labor force*, then, is defined in economics as all members of the working age population who are either employed formally or are seeking or awaiting formal employment. The labor force consists of the employed and unemployed but not the underemployed, the marginally employed, the would-be employed, and certainly not those who work in the informal sector or who work as housewives.

Production and Reproduction

The skewed definitions of work and labor that are used by economists result in an equally skewed concept of *production*. As we have seen, economists usually use *labor* to mean only those activities that produce surplus value (that is, profit in the marketplace). Consequently, labor (work) that does not produce profits is not considered production.

So, for example, the labor of childbirth may be work for a

paid surrogate mother or for the paid midwife, nurse, doctor, and anaesthetist. Despite the *Oxford English Dictionary's* description of labor as "the pains and effort of childbirth: travail," the woman in labor—the reproducer, sustainer, and nurturer of human life—does not "produce" anything. Similarly, all the other reproductive work that women do is widely viewed as unproductive. Growing and processing food, nurturing, educating, and running a household—all part of the complex process of *reproduction*—are unacknowledged as part of the production system. A woman who supplies such labor is not seen by economists as performing work of value. Yet the satisfaction of basic needs to sustain human society is fundamental to any economic system. By this failure to acknowledge the primacy of reproduction, the male face of economics is fatally flawed.

We frequently hear from politicians, theologians, and military leaders that the wealth of a nation is its children. But, apparently, the creators of that wealth deserve no economic visibility for their work.

But what value is a unit of production which cannot guarantee its own continuous and regular reproduction? As a means of reproduction, woman is irreplaceable wealth. Reproducing the system depends on her. Gold, cloth, ivory, and cattle may be desirable, but they are only able to produce and reproduce wealth in the hands of progeny. Control derives ultimately not from the possession of wealth, but the control of reproduction. In terms of value, reproduction of the human species is either the whore, debased, of no worth, or the virgin on the pedestal, valued beyond wealth.

In support of this point of view, Gerda Lerner, Professor of History at the University of Wisconsin, argues that women's reproductive power was the first private property amassed by men, and that domination over women provided the model for men's enslavement of other men.[25]

The basic definitions and concepts in the male analyses of production and reproduction also reflect an unquestioned acceptance of biological determinism. Women's household and child care work are seen as an extension of their physiology. All the labor that goes into the production of life, including the labor of giving birth to a child, is seen as an activity *of* nature, rather than as interaction of a woman *with* nature. "Nature" apparently produces plants, animals, and Homo sapiens unconsciously, and women play no active or conscious part in the process.

Pivotal to this analysis is the fixation on paid labor alone as productive. Even Frederick Engels's brief insight on reproduction is now forgotten. Engels was the long-time friend of Karl Marx and Marx's collaborator on *The Origin of the Family, Private Property and the State*. In it, Engels wrote:

According to the materialist concept . . . the determining factor of history is, in the final instance, the production and reproduction of the immediate essentials of life. This, again, is of a two-fold character. On the one side, the production of the means of existence of articles of food and clothing, dwellings and of the tools necessary for that production; on the other side, the production of human beings themselves, the propagation of the species.[26]

Yet today the liberal-conservative spectrum of economists speak of reproduction (in some of its forms) as privatized and domestic (and thus only of its microeconomic significance). The Marxist economists speak of it (in some of its forms) as having only "use value." Reproduction in all its forms is not fully addressed within any discipline. While recent feminist writers are an exception (see, for example, Gena Corea's *The Mother Machine* or Mary O'Brien's *The Politics of Reproduction*), reproduction is generally seen as part of nature and, thus, not within the scope of analysis or change.

Counting Women Out of the Labor Force

In the rain forest of southern Cameroon, the Beti people practice a form of agriculture that involves clearing two new half-acre fields each year and cultivating them for two or three years. Thus, the food farmer, always a woman, has four to six fields under cultivation at any one time. The major crops are groundnuts, cassava, cocoyams, plantain, and a variety of vegetables. Men's agricultural labor consists primarily of the cultivation of cocoa, one of Cameroon's major exports.

Beti men labor for a total of seven and a half hours a day. They spend less than an hour a day on food-related tasks, about two hours a day on their cocoa plots, and four hours on work such as beer or palm-wine production, house building and repair, production of baskets, production of housing materials or other simple commodities intended for the market, and part-time wage work.

Beti women, on the other hand, labor for eleven hours a day. They spend about five hours a day on food production—four hours to provide for family needs and one hour to produce surplus for the urban market. In addition, they spend three to four hours a day for food processing and cooking and two or more hours for water and firewood collection, washing, child care, and care of the sick.[27]

The International Labor Organization (ILO), a UN agency, counts the Beti man as an "active laborer." But since none of the Beti woman's working day is spent "helping the head of the family in his [sic] occupation"[28]—and since housework done by members of a family in their own homes is also specifically excluded—the ILO concludes that she is not an active laborer.*

Thus the international economic system constructs reality in a way that excludes the great bulk of women's work—reproduction (in all its forms), raising children, domestic work, and subsistence production. Cooking, according to economists, is "active labor" when cooked food is sold and "economically in-

---

*The I.L.O. will also exclude Tendai and Cathy, and much of the world's invisible child labor force. International guidelines set the age of eligibility for the economically active population at 15 years, although countries may set lower limits. In 25 of 40 countries for which comparisons are possible by age, females form a significantly higher proportion of child labor than of adult labor. In 14 countries the sex ratios are similar for both age groups, and in only one is the child labour force disproportionately male.

active labor" when it is not. Housework is "productive" when performed by a paid domestic servant and "nonproductive" when no payment is involved. Those who care for children in an orphanage are "occupied"; mothers who care for their children at home are "unoccupied."

The American contributor to the *International Encyclopedia of Social Science,* A. J. Jaffe, further demonstrates the peculiar reasoning inherent in the international economic system. In the section "The Labour Force—Definitions and Measurement," he writes that "housewives are excluded from what is measured as the working force because such work is outside the characteristic system of work organization or production. Moreover their inclusion in the working force would not help policy makers to solve the significant economic problems of American society."[29]

I would have thought that domestic work was about the oldest "system of work organization or production." And as for "significant economic problems of American society," what about the problems of the more than 30 million Americans—77.7 percent of them women and children—who lived below the poverty line in 1980? What about the fact that 36 percent of all female-headed households in America and 56.2 percent of black female-headed households were at or below the poverty level in 1982? And how about the 20 percent of all American children and 50 percent of all American black children who lived in poverty in 1983?[30] Doesn't such poverty represent a significant enough problem for policymakers to address? Evidently not, since most women and children do not count in the reckoning of the international economic system.

And What of Mother Earth?

Women and children have not been the only losers in this system. Many of the environmental resources we value are excluded from measure in the economy. They cannot be sold in private markets, so it is said to be difficult to determine what they are worth. Yet their destruction, and the costs of cleaning up after the destruction, are labeled "growth" and "production."

Lester Thurow, professor of economics and management at Massachusetts Institute of Technology and a highly-regarded writer on economics, sees cause for four major concerns: the pollution of air, land, and water; the exhaustion of nonrenewable natural resources; wilderness and species preservation; and the health and safety factors in industrial production.

He sums up the problem nicely:

Pollution controls are often opposed on the grounds that they will lower economic growth and will reduce our real standard of living. This simply isn't true. Using our present measures of economic output, while costs of cleaning it up do appear, the benefits of a clean environment do not appear. This is a problem produced by inadequate statistics and not a basic characteristic of pollution control.[31]

He suggests that the system invites us to see pollution control only as a cost, without counting the benefits generated as output. One of the difficulties for the system to cope with, of course, is that the characteristics of our environment that are being destroyed have been thought of as the free gift of nature. So a cool breeze is of no value, but cool air produced through an air conditioner is. Since we have no property rights to air, we cannot pursue a claim even when our air is damaged. The nuclear accidents at Chernobyl and Three Mile Island would suggest that air property rights may have to become collective property rights. There's not much point worrying about our growth rate and our standard of living if we are all dying of radiation poisoning.

But on the world political stage there is a great deal more concern about growth rates than about a planet becoming more poisoned each day. Summit conferences of political leaders of all political blocs, the UN General Assembly, the International Monetary Fund (IMF) and the World Bank, multinational corporations, and the world's leading banking and lending institutions have no time for nuclear fallout, acid rain, ozone layer depletion, or dioxin in water supplies. They are obsessed with growth. What then is growth, and how is it measured?

The Boundaries of the UNSNA

As we have learned, the method for measuring production and growth throughout most of the world is called the United Nations System of National Accounts (UNSNA). [An alternative system, the "Material Product System" (see Appendix I) is in use in the Soviet Union and countries of Eastern Europe.] This system measures the value of all goods and services that actually enter the market. It also measures the value of other production that does not enter the market, such as government and nonprofit services provided free or at a nominal charge and accommodation provided by owner-occupied dwellings.

The UNSNA has also decided that certain areas of human activity lie outside what it calls the *production boundary*. These areas are excluded from measurement in the national accounts. Generally, the UNSNA excludes household activities, the products which are "observed" as seldom or never marketed. In other words, the service of housewives and other family members, household maintenance and production, and illegal transactions are all outside the UNSNA's production boundary.

Yet among the Turu people of East Africa, the most valuable of the services exchanged in the market is female productive labor, obtained through marriage, for which bridewealth is exchanged. When a husband dies, his wife is inherited by his brother. To be a successful "producer," a man must own three essentials: land, livestock, and laborers—that is, wives, whom we may also call slaves. Behind all marriages is the expectation that production will increase. All domestic labor and the bulk of agricultural labor is carried out by women. Food is always served first to the male head of the household and to other males present, including boys.[32]

The key products marketed among the Turu are the services

of housewives and their work in household maintenance and in subsistence production. Yet the UNSNA treats the labor of Turu women the same way it treats Cathy's labor in North America—both are excluded from its measurements of production and growth.

This treatment, and the attitudes that condone it, also pervades the Material Product System (MPS) used to measure production and growth in the Soviet Union and in East European countries (see appendix 1). In 1975, the deputy editor of *Izvestia* wrote to *Soviet Women*, "However tired a woman may be when she comes home from work, however exhausted physically and mentally, the first thing she does after coming through the door is to put on an apron and prepare dinner. Why? Because 'women' and 'homemaker' are inseparable concepts."[33] Likewise the East European sociologist, Zsuzsa Ferge, has written, "the results of housework do not serve economic justification in a satisfactory manner because they are accepted as natural and are only noticed when they are absent."[34]

Vladimir Illich Lenin, leader of the Bolshevik revolution in the USSR, blamed women's subordinate position in society on their work within the confines of the household. The solution he advocated was to involve women in social production outside the household and to socialize housework. I'm not sure who he thought would perform housework once it became social production if it wasn't the newly freed woman. It is clear that by housework he had in mind that work labeled unpaid household activities. But the conception of housework adopted by the international economic system includes the reproduction and nurturance of human life, subsistence food production, and community work. There is no consistency from country to country in the activities that are or are not "economic." But there is one unwritten rule: If women do it in an unpaid capacity in their homes, in their garden plots, or in the community, it is housework. Women need no convincing about the necessity of this work. Some of us enjoy parts of it. Some of our sisters, for whom it has been a totally debilitating experience, have been sent to psychiatric hospitals for refusing to do it.

It is not as if the work involves lack of competence. To grow plants for food, for example, requires information and experience. Gwen Wesson has developed a tentative analysis of skills and knowledge involved in the production and preparation of plant foods.[35] She points out that to prepare seeds one needs to know about germination requirements, seed preparation, and soil choice. Seed preparation requires visual discrimination, fine motor coordination, and sensitivity to humidity levels and weather predictors. To sow and strike seeds one needs to know about seasons, climate, plant requirements, weather conditions, microclimatic factors, soil enrichment, and moon phases. Sowing seeds requires physical dexterity and strength, and a tolerance of harsh weather and difficult conditions. To care for plants properly, one needs information about the nature of the plant, diseases, pruning, staking, water supplies, companion planting, predators, sequences, growing seasons, and soil maintenance. Plant propagation also requires persistence and patience, physical strength, and attention to plant needs. Harvesting a crop requires judgments in relation to weather, ripeness, labor, grading and packing, and knowledge about preserving, immediate use, and propagation. Proper harvesting requires sensitivity to plants' performances, judgment about weather predictors, and physical staying power.

The majority of the world's women have acquired these skills and this information without the benefits of literacy, education courses, or development projects. They probably learned them from "economically inactive," "unoccupied" women. The contributions that all these women make to their families and their communities are not measured by either the UNSNA or the MPS as production or growth.

Co-option to Unreality: How Economics Is Taught

Harvard economist and liberal U.S. writer John Kenneth Galbraith writes:

That many women are coming to sense that they are instruments of the economic system is not in doubt. But their feeling finds no support in economic writing and teaching. On the contrary, it is concealed, and on the whole with great success, by modern neo-classical economics—the everyday economics of the textbook and classroom. This concealment is neither conspiratory nor deliberate. It reflects the natural and very strong instincts of economics for what is convenient to influence economic interest—for what I have called the conventional social virtue. It is sufficiently successful that it allows many hundreds of thousands of women to study economics each year without their developing any serious suspicion as to how they will be used.[36]

One of the prime neo-economists taught to our prospective student is John Maynard Keynes. An industrialized, monetarized society based on private property—Britain in the 1920s and 1930s—formed the background for his work. Keynes's logic led him to the conclusion that free markets left to their own devices produced short-term depression and long-term stagnation.

Joan Robinson, who worked with John Maynard Keynes at Cambridge, says that his work is characterized by uncertainty, incompatible decisions, and unrealizable expectations. Robinson insists that Keynes's General Theory is set in a strictly short period where "a state of expectations, controlling a given level of effective demand, is given only momentarily and is always in the course of bringing itself to an end."[37] But Keynes is seldom taught in this context, and decades of decision-makers believing otherwise become, as Keynes himself described at the end of The General Theory, "the slaves of some defunct economist."

Our student will be taught that the 1971 Nobel Prize winner for economics, Simon Küznets, argued for institutional changes (i.e., state intervention) in the economy to promote economic growth. The 1976 Nobel Prize winner, Milton Friedman, attributing inflation to government expenditure, argued that the government should get out of the market, both as a regulator and participant.

Wherever one of these students of economics looks, she will find women's experience excluded or numbed by language. The complicated, heart-wrenching, ambivalent, rich, joyous, rewarding (and enslaving) experience of motherhood and mothering becomes, in the Marxist school, "reproducing the future commodity labor power," while in Western economic theory it is reduced to a matter for "welfare." The writings of feminist economists Olive Schreiner and Charlotte Perkins Gilman will not be part of the curriculum. Ritual bows may be made in the direction of equal pay or discrimination against women in the labor force or comparable worth (equal pay for work of equal value). Yet even these are more likely found in "women's studies" publications than in mainstream economic journals.

Then our young woman student will be introduced to the Chicago School, or "new home economics." The patron of the Chicago School is Gary Becker, author of a major work called *A Treatise on the Family*.[38] Our student will soon understand that Becker is the new high priest of patriarchal economics. If Karl Marx is the patron saint for her Soviet sister, Becker must become hers, because a good grade and any hope of proceeding to a postgraduate degree necessitates the surrender of her intellect to the theory of the Chicago School. This "new home economics" should not be confused with what women have always understood by that phrase—the original Greek study of the management of a household. From a discipline that excludes the household from its system of valuation because it is not part of the market, Becker lifts the current market concepts and superimposes them on the family and household.

Becker's theory of marriage contains three main parts. The first tells who will be married and to whom, "all things being equal." It assumes that individuals maximize their income, defined broadly, by attempting to marry partners with whom they can jointly make the most money. Marriage is viewed as a game in which each player has a fixed known "shadow price." The shadow prices, which reflect productive capacities, define rankings of men and women from most to least desirable. (Becker continually refers to "superior" and "inferior" persons.) Becker assumes away conflicts concerning values and the distribution of income and power. Equality of opportunity is subsumed in the argument that anatomy is destiny—that a women's physiological specialization in infant care tips the balance towards female specialization in home production and male specialization in market work. He conceives that the value of a child is its expected worth as an adult.

Women academic economists Marianne Ferber and Bonnie Birnbaum comment that the complex reality of the world is ignored time and again by the simple, elegant models the Chicago School constructs. The basic assumption of all Becker's work is that men (he calls them "people") always behave rationally. This leads to the baffling implication generally found in this work "that all outcomes are in some sense optimal," that is, the best compromise for all the "people," given all the available options. Ferber and Birnbaum comment that this approach amounts to a tacit endorsement for the status quo of male domination.[39]

In his recent writings on families and households, Chicago School economist Robert Pollack illustrates further characteristics of modern economists. One is the use of jargon from other disciplines, such as political science and psychology. Another is the way in which the qualities of the power functions of the male world are attributed to the family and household management. Pollack writes:

The transaction cost approach uses marriage as a "governance structure," emphasises the role of "bargaining" within families, and draws attention to the advantages and disadvantages of family organisation in terms of incentives and monitoring, and to the special roles of "altruism" and "family loyalty." It also recognises the disadvantages of family governments: conflict spillover, the toleration of inefficient personnel, inappropriate ability match, and inability to realise economics of scale. If activities are assigned to institutions in an efficient or cost-minimising fashion, the balance of these advantages and disadvantages plays a major role in determining which activities are carried out within families and which are performed by firms, non-profit institutions, or the state.[40]

A neoclassical economist would not see this description of the family as empty rhetoric. Economists take these sorts of pronunciations terribly seriously. Women do not analyze the family in this extraordinary language, not because we are not that clever, but because we are not that stupid. But this is an example of what Galbraith meant about the use of women students. Women who must listen to, read, discuss, use, and write about this sort of thinking daily for four or more years—knowing that their degree and job security are dependent on perpetuating this ideology—are likely to lose sight of themselves. The discipline offers no relief, holds up no mirrors to women's experience.

Beyond the Boundary: Scientific Method in Economics

Donald N. McCloskey superbly points out the outmoded value that economics still puts in the authority and objectivity of science. He starts out with a list of "tenets of scientific method":

1. Prediction (and control) is the goal of science.
2. Only the observable implications (or prediction) of a theory matter to its truth.
3. Observability entails objective, reproducible experiments.
4. If (and only if) an experimental implication of a theory proves false is the theory proved false.
5. Objectivity is to be treasured; subjective observation (introspection) is not scientific knowledge.

6. Kelvin's dictum: "When you cannot express it in numbers, your knowledge is of a meagre and unsatisfactory kind."

7. Introspection, metaphysical belief, aesthetics, and the like may well figure in the discovery of a hypothesis but cannot figure in its justification.

8. It is the business of methodology to demarcate scientific reasoning from nonscientific reasoning, positive from normative.

9. A scientific explanation of an event brings the event under a covering law.

10. Scientists (for instance, economic scientists) have nothing to say as scientists about values, whether of morality or art.

11. The rule known as Hume's Fork: "When we run over libraries, persuaded of these principles, what havoc must we make. If we take in our hand any volume—of divinity or school metaphysics, for instance—let us ask, does it contain any abstract reasoning concerning quantity or number? No. Does it contain any experimental reasoning concerning matter or fact or existence? No. Commit it then to the flames, for it can contain nothing but sophistry and delusion."

McCloskey comments, "Few in philosophy now believe as many as half of these propositions. A substantial, a respectable and growing miniority believes none of them. But a large majority in economics believes them all."[41]

The obsession with numbers and the institutionalization of concepts based on scientific method has been a colonizer. Since the preservation of natural resources cannot be easily expressed in numbers, the environment has been colonized. In the traditional sense of the developing world, other cultures and values have been colonized. And on the pretense that male observation is unbiased, this system has colonized women and children.

The question of what entails "economic activity" revolves around the question of value. It is said that obvious exclusions from such activity are goods and services on which no one could put a market price because their values are spiritual, psychological, social, or political. It is then argued that women's role as socializers, as articulators of class and gender ideology, and as (too often the easy) collaborators in reproducing the conditions of their own subordination, has no value. Yet nonprofit organizations such as churches and clubs are included as productive services in the national accounts; so are therapists and voluntary agencies where the cost of production is met by members and benefactors. Agents of social reproduction— teachers, crime prevention officers, health workers—are included, as are political campaigners, and government administrative services on the grounds that the services have an economic price in terms of the cost of labor, capital, and materials to produce them. An infant born through the new "test-tube" technology or womb implant, or a child raised in an institution, is considered "products." Those who bring the fetus to term in the laboratory, or who care for the child in the orphanage or juvenile facility are seen as workers. They are economically active. But a mother, daily engaged unpaid in these activities, is "just a housewife."

I am not the first to raise some of these questions. Chinese writer, novelist, and commentator Han Suyin has written,

Woman as creator of wealth has been totally ignored. Yet the development of civilization from spinning and weaving by hand to the industrial manufactures of today require women's labour. Woman the consumer is also a factor in the economics of any country. Throughout the ages, the role of woman as wealth accumulator has been slighted. Her role as traditional teacher of arts and language and skills, in dance and music and singing and many other fields, is taken for granted and not properly valued.[42]

While the UN International Decade for Women (1975–85) produced many documents and many gallant statements about women and development, Ester Boserup's classic book,

Women's Role in Economic Development, demonstrated as long ago as 1970 that women's invisibility as workers retarded any real process of growth.[43] Collating previously unpublished data from official censuses, official statistics, and special surveys, Boserup's study provided a substantial body of literature that reinforced her conclusions. Many others have produced profound and substantial reasons for change. Their target tended to be policies, not the UN System of National Accounts. Token gestures were made. Rhetoric changed—but little else.

Other feminist writers have concentrated on exposing the bias against women that pervades economic theory. Among them, French theorist Christine Delphy was concerned to avoid the tempting trap that the answer for women lay with socialism. Using the language of the Marxist school, she discusses their analyses of labor.

A woman's agricultural labour, for instance, is not paid if it is performed within the family; she cannot exchange her family production on the market. Therefore, she does not make use of her own labour power. Her husband makes use of it, since he alone can exchange his wife's production on the market. In the same way a woman does not make use of her housework as long as it is performed within the family; she can only exchange it outside the family. Thus women's production always has an exchange value—can be exchanged by them—except within the framework of the family. With industrialization, family production is limited to housework; or more precisely, we call housework that to which the unpaid labour of the housewife has been limited.[44]

Microeconomic studies bear out this analysis. When women enter the paid work force, their work is valued. They pay for laundry, processed foods, and so on, and it is generally assumed that their housework burden is lighter. But as former Norwegian parliamentarian Berit Ås reports:

Women researchers are concerned about the fact that growth in many sectors of the economy takes place by adding more work to the existing unpaid work performed by women. For instance, all over the Western world, supermarkets replace small retailers. This requires housewives to increase the time needed for shopping. A Swedish study revealed that a majority of women customers had no car at their disposal. Either they had to shop every day and walk longer distances or they had to carry heavier burdens and use bus transportation when it was available. Reducing the number of sales personnel in the supermarkets and hiring of unqualified people make it necessary for housewives to inform themselves more thoroughly by reading labels and comparing products. Good advice and consumer information can no longer be expected. American studies of consumerism have shown that the average shopping time per family amounts to about eight hours weekly compared to about two hours per week only a few decades ago.[45]

While many women see reproduction, and the maintenance of human and ecological resources, as primary principles of economics, that is not the tradition of the discipline. And while feminist scholars and many others have pieced together part of the jigsaw, I could never see the full picture. I couldn't understand how or why such madness ruled our lives. I determined to satisfy my need to know.

My Context

As I write in 1986, more than twenty-five wars are in progress, and the global expenditure on armaments is at record levels. The number of illiterate people is still growing.

The UN Food and Agricultural Organization (FAO) estimates that from 1974 to 1976, 436 million people were undernourished in ninety developing countries, as measured by calorie intake levels below which an individual's ability to carry out minimum necessary activity is seriously impaired. If present trends continue, the number of seriously undernourished people will reach 590 million by the year 2000. Lack of safe drinking water and adequate sanitation are major causes of the death of millions of children every year in the developing countries. Nearly three-fifths of the population of developing countries (excluding China) still did not have access to safe drinking water in

1986, and only about one-quarter had any sort of sanitary facility.

While women are more than 50 percent of the world's enfranchised population, they hold no more than 10 percent of the seats in national legislatures. In one government in three, no women are in the highest decision-making body.

The sky is being poisoned with nuclear fallout. The world's ozone layer is diminishing, and the seas are polluted. No economic model provides the means for understanding how both economic growth and ecological sustainability might be possible.

Joan Robinson has written:

To learn from the economists regarded as scientists, it is necessary to separate what is valid in their description of the system from the propaganda that they make, overtly or unconsciously, each for his own ideology. The best way to separate out scientific ideas from ideology is to stand the ideology on its head and see how the ideas look the other way up. If they disintegrate with the ideology, they have no validity of their own. If they still make sense as a description of reality, then there is something to be learned from them, whether we like the ideology or not.[46]

The UNSNA and its rules and regulations govern the measurement of national income in all countries. It is my confirmed belief that this system acts to sustain, in the ideology of patriarchy, the universal enslavement of women and Mother Earth in their productive and reproductive activities.

If I am wrong, then the system, when turned on its head to include recognition of *all* economic activity, will be operative. If it is not possible for the UNSNA to function by way of such inclusion, then the role of propaganda in the system will be clear. For example, if women's work cannot be successfully incorporated in a system which purports to measure all economic activity, if the system at that point disintegrates, then it is invalid. The sole function of the system is to legitimize the propaganda.

Whose propaganda would we be examining?

Harvard biology professor Ruth Hubbard, in commenting on the medical profession, said, "The system . . . , by which I mean both the structure and content of the scientific and technical professions, has been constructed by one particular, limited social group, composed of the economically privileged, university-educated, white men, and it serves their need more than ours."[47] The economic system has been constructed in exactly the same way. The profession of economics is that of a limited social group—economically privileged, university-educated, white men. It serves neither the majority of humankind nor our fragile planet. Its structure and content have a design and a beguiling propaganda.

2. A Calling to Account

Who Developed the UNSNA and Why

The successful transmission of propaganda relies heavily on cliché or rhetoric. It also relies on inducing fear (of, for example, the unknown or uncontrollable) in a submissive public who will not ask too many enlightened questions. It is not surprising then, that many people, and women in particular, have "economics anxiety." Mathematical, mechanical, and medical anxieties, and other mystifications may represent a deliberate obfuscation: an effort to remove the discipline and its information from the powerless. Such political exclusivity is also useful to disguise vulnerability and to keep from telling the truth. It is reinforced by a lack of direct access to the discipline through sex-role stereotyping or tracking.

The anxiety is also evidence of a quite sane alienation from the subject matter. This occurs when I tell any housewife that she is unoccupied, economically inactive, and doesn't work. If a system treats you like that, you won't spend much time examining it.

Alternatively, such an alienation, without explanation, can lead people to think that they are intellectually inferior, that they can't understand the economic system. They have heard terms like *national income*, *balance of payments*, *Gross National Product* (GNP), and *Gross Domestic Product* (GDP) used with seeming alacrity by businessmen, politicians, and newspaper editors. After having served for ten years in public political office, it is my distinct impression that, with the exception of those trained in economics, most of these people don't know what they're talking about. They bluff it, reliant on human nature, intimidation, and embarrassment to silence those who might be curious to ask just what the national income is.

To overcome such anxiety, information is a key—to demystify, to empower, and frequently to enrage. This chapter begins that task. Some his/story is called for to begin to unravel the answer to the questions how and why the system works as it does. The United Nations System of National Accounts (UNSNA) is the internationally recognized system for measuring and recording the values that economic theorists have observed. Its development springs from the classical Western economic theory of such men as Adam Smith, Alfred Marshall, and John Maynard Keynes. The evolution of the system was politically motivated, and the rules made about what would and would not be recorded as production were also political choices.

Most of us are familiar with political concern about whether our Gross Domestic Product (GDP) is rising or falling. But do you suppose that the Japanese people feel better when their GDP rises? Not all of them do: Japan, with one of the highest GDPs in the world, has the world's highest suicide rate among older women. I doubt that the still surviving victims of Hiroshima and Nagasaki think about it. The all too frequent presumption that the well-being of a community or nation improves because of a rise in their GDP is based on a statistic derived from the UNSNA. And while most people have heard the terms GDP or GNP, few have heard of these national accounts. Yet every country has them.

This System's a Winner: The Power of the UNSNA

Most economists today would hail the development of the national accounts as one of the greatest achievements of modern economists. With admitted problems, the national accounts are thought of as the best description and analysis of the operation of the global economic system. Politicians, economists, bureaucrats—the power brokers—believe that economics can only be an effective tool for a government's economic planning and management if it is supported by an adequate system of national accounts.

The Nobel Prize in Economics in 1984 was won by Sir Richard Stone, British representative on the United Nations committee that formalized the UNSNA. The Nobel Selection Committee described Sir Richard as the person mainly responsible for creating an accounting system for nations that has been indispensable in monitoring their financial position, in tracking trends in national development, and in comparing one nation's economic workings with another's. An indication of the esteem given this system by the economists of the world is the fact that Sir Richard had been among the final ten candidates considered for the prize every year since an award in the category of economics was first given in 1969.

In announcing the prize, Rajnar Bentzel, secretary of the Award Committee, said young people who follow economics might be surprised by this selection. "The system has become accepted as so self-evident that it is hard to realize that someone had to invent it." That is very true. It *is* hard to realize that a system so philosophically and practically omnipresent for centuries has only recently been institutionalized globally and with the blessing of governments everywhere. This happened quite simply.

The Statistical Office of the United Nations published *A System of National Accounts and Supporting Tables* in 1953.[1] The report was prepared by a "group of experts" appointed by the secretary general. The five men were Loreto M. Dominguez of the Pan American Union, Kurt Hansen of Denmark, George Jaszi of the United States, Moni Mohan Muckherjee of India, and Sir Richard Stone, who acted as chairperson.

The report sought to give a "coherent picture of economic structure" from economic statistics. "The main impetus for this development was the practical need for information about the working of *the economic system as a whole* and the way in which its various parts are related to each other (my emphasis)."[2] So the aim was a system that would offer economic explanations of the way the world worked. "As a whole" implies for me (though clearly not for the designers) all human beings as well as all natural resources, and even so-called "Acts of God." The report explained, "While national accounting information is useful in all fields of economic decision making because of the factual background which it provides, *its outstanding use has been in connection with public policy* [my emphasis]."[3] This, as we shall see, was a key, both in terms of the motivation of the system's authors and in terms of the system's fallacies. For if national accounting provides factual information (and that is debatable), then the facts are highly selected. And they are highly selected in a way that predetermines public policy. The information is not collected for what it might teach us but to further the ends for which the methodology was devised.

With minor structural changes, the UNSNA has remained conceptually intact since 1953. When international reports and writers refer to women as statistically or economically invisible, it is the UNSNA that has made them so. When it dawns on you that militarism and the destruction of the environment are recorded as growth, it is the UNSNA that has made it so. When you are seeking out the most vicious tools of colonization, those that can obliterate a culture and a nation, a tribe or a people's value system, then rank the UNSNA among those tools. When you yearn for a breath of nature's fresh air or a glass of radio-active-free water, remember that the UNSNA says that both are worthless.

Once Upon a Time: A Short History of the UNSNA

Economic historians trace the origins of the system to Sir William Petty, who prepared guesstimates of the income of the English nation (as distinct from the income of the government) in 1665.[4] In a double-entry account, he defined the "Income of the People" as the annual value of their labor and the annual stock or wealth (in terms of rent, interest, and profit). The "Annual Expense of the People" included consumption and any surpluses remaining thereafter.

In a manuscript published in 1698, Gregory King made rudimentary efforts to quantify the prosperity of a country by examining all its sources of income.[5] He adopted Petty's framework and estimated for more than two dozen socioeconomic groups in England the number of families and the average income, expense, and saving per family.

After the French Revolution, in the late eighteenth century, Frenchman François Quesnay led a movement that identified national income with agricultural product. He argued that only agriculture produced a net product over and above costs. Other sectors were thought of as nonproductive. Services, such as those provided by household servants, lawyers, and the clergy, were excluded.

For over a century, there was much debate as to whether or not "services" were productive labor. Adam Smith's influence was strong. In his book *The Wealth of Nations* (1776),[6] he argued that *all* commodity production and distribution could be productive but defined productive labor as follows:

There is one sort of labour which adds to the value of the subject upon which it is bestowed: There is another which has no such effect. The former, as it produces a value, may be called productive; the latter, unproductive labour. Thus the labour of a manufacturer adds, generally to the materials which he works upon, that of his own maintenance, and of his master's profit. The labour of a menial servant, on the contrary, adds to the value of nothing.[7]

Services were excluded, according to him. Adam Smith specifically excluded the "sovereign" from the productive realm, but it is not clear which category he deemed appropriate for soldiers.

This restrictive concept has never been totally abandoned. It was accepted by nineteenth century philosophers David Ricardo and John Stuart Mill. It was adopted by Karl Marx in *Das*

Kapital.[8] Marx, writing in 1860 and 1870, did not include services in his concept of the "material product." (This became the foundation of the Material Product System (MPS) used in Eastern European countries today as an alternative to the UNSNA. A brief description of the key difference between the two systems is found in appendix 1.)

Cambridge economist Alfred Marshall dominated the accepted British and American teaching from the 1880s to the 1920s. When he wrote that the annual "net aggregation of commodities, material and immaterial, including services of all kinds, is the true net annual income, or revenue of a country,"[9] services became accepted as part of the national income; they could be measured in the market. In his mind, national income itself was a market concept. Marshall once said that economics is merely the study of mankind (*sic*) in the ordinary business (*sic*) of life. He was, and has been, interpreted literally.

By the late nineteenth century, economists had estimated national income figures for England and France. S. N. Prokopovitch, a Marxian reformer, prepared estimates for Russia in 1906 using the MPS. These were updated in 1917 under the Kerensky government as a basis for wartime planning. By the end of World War I, estimates had also been prepared in the United States, Austria, Australia, Norway, Germany, Japan, Switzerland, the Netherlands, Italy, and Bulgaria. Beginning with Canada and the Soviet Union in 1925 and Germany in 1929, central governments took over national income estimation. Thereafter, people, events, and decisions in the United States and in Great Britain dominated the history, and it is important to trace these in some detail.

In the United States, the report "Income in the United States: Its Amount and Distribution 1909–1919" was published by the National Bureau of Economic Research (NBER). The definition of income used in this report corresponds in most major ways to that used today. It included essentially the market economy (where money must change hands), with the addition of home-produced food and fuel, and an estimate of the rental value of owner-occupied homes. The inclusion of the food, fuel, and rental value involves *imputation*, which, as we'll see later, is one of the problems of national income accounting.

British economist Arthur C. Pigou set out criteria in 1928 that the national product or income should include the values of the production of goods and services that "can be brought directly or indirectly into relation with the measuring rod of money." This he interpreted narrowly in 1932 as covering "everything that people buy with money income, together with the *services* that a *man* obtains from a house owned and inhabited by *himself*" (my emphasis).[10] In this it is presumed he meant that a value for having a home would be imputed as a service for the national accounts. But in the context of other "services" that a man receives from a household "owned" by himself, it is open to a quite different interpretation. Hundreds of millions of men believe that they "own" their wives and daughters and their services.

The gentlemen estimators thus either discounted services entirely or conceived of them as contributors only when directly measurable by money. There was no progress in this thinking when estimates were taken over by central governments and recorded and published on a regular basis.

Generally, governments did not give a high priority to national income accounting until the Depression of the late 1920s. There were few trained or professional statisticians or economists employed in any arm of any administration. But after the Depression began in the United States, the overwhelming problem facing the government was how to achieve economic recovery. The staff of the NBER was soon expanded. This was the political background and impetus for the need to establish national accounts.

In June 1932, the U.S. Senate resolved that reports of national income for the years 1929, 1930, and 1931 should be prepared. The most experienced person to head this effort was Lilian Epstein, who had been an assistant on the earlier NBER reports and who was available for the task. But a man, Simon Küznets, was appointed over her, in that sleight of hand familiar to employed women elsewhere. Küznets was a former student of the director of research at the NBER, Wesley C. Mitchell. In recording the story of responding to the Senate resolution, statistical historians Joseph W. Duncan and William C. Shelton list the names of all the professional young men hired to work on the task. They add, "five clerks, all women with substantial experience and know-how, assisted importantly in the work."[11] The invisibility of these nameless experts mirrors precisely the invisibility of women in the reports on which they worked.

For the next twenty years Küznets was at the forefront of development and debate on the national accounts. In 1941 he published a two-volume work entitled *National Income and Its Composition 1919–1938*,[12] based on his nineteen-page article in 1933 on national income for the *International Encyclopedia of Social Sciences*. His work was notable for its accuracy and volume of detail. He revised definitions and excluded capital gains from the accounts.*

Küznets was later a Nobel prize winner in economics, but not for his work on national income accounting. For many years of his academic life, Küznets was denied a university chair in economics, being termed a "statistician." He eventually became one of the few knowledgeable critics of the evolving system. By 1947, Simon Küznets wrote:

The refusal to extend discussion in (social welfare) directions to a fuller coverage of consumption levels, of levels of living, and of experimentally established functional equivalents—is not due to the possibly low yield of such explorations. On the contrary, they promise results of great value. They might explain more satisfactorily . . . the basic differences between industrial and pre-industrial economies, and the conditions on which the latter can be industrialized. . . . [T]hey might provide a more effective basis for comparison and help overcome the difficulties imposed by differences in the goods composition of na-

---

*Capital gains are the positive difference between the purchase price of an asset and the price obtained for it when it is resold. Houses, land, stocks, antiques, jewelry, and artworks often show significant capital gains when resold.

tional product. Studies of nutrition indicate unmistakably that pre-industrial societies manage to obtain the basic vitamin supply at much lower economic costs, and hence at much lower prices, than a price comparison of identical commodities would indicate.

That we have paid so little attention to these aspects of the comparison is due largely to a feeling that the study has not advanced sufficiently to permit abandonment of the more traditional approach.[13]

Küznets is referring here to the consequences of the refusal to extend coverage in the system of national accounts to include such things as subsistence production. If we are concerned solely with market measurement, we are unable to establish the true living conditions (as opposed to an average standard of living) of a population. His example of nutrition is one that is particularly relevant to women's lives, both for domestic policy planning and for international comparison. Diet, as opposed to household income, may well be a far better indicator of the "well-being" of the community.

While Küznets was a major influence on national income accounting in the United States, his view, expressed in 1947, did not prevail. Developments in Britain took a different path.

How to Pay for the War

In 1939, John Maynard Keynes returned from a period of illness to work in the British treasury. E. A. G. Robinson, a friend and colleague of Keynes at this time, recalls that "within a few weeks of the outbreak of war he had developed ideas of the scale of the British war potential and of the methods of war finance which were later to form the basis of the whole operation of the British war economy."[14]

Keynes asked (later, Sir) Richard Stone to join him, and the two coauthored a paper entitled "The National Income and Expenditure of the United Kingdom, and How to Pay for the War." The title is appalling in its blatancy and clear in its intention. This document formed the foundation of Stone's further work, during peacetime, to develop the uniform accounting system subsequently adopted by the United Nations.

Keynes offered the general theory that the total amount of income (or economic activity) in a country is heavily determined by a combination of three factors: consumption, investment, and government spending. Stone took matters further, defining how each of these three elements could be measured and specifying interactions between them. The uniform accounting system, not unlike that which corporations at the time used, was then developed to measure the national income *of a country at war*.

Robinson records that by 1942

the broader problems of internal war finance had . . . in the main been reduced to order. In the British system the economic planning of the war was by then conducted almost exclusively in terms of *the real resources*, in manpower allocations, in raw materials allocations, in shipping allocations, in building allocations, and the like; *the needs of civilian consumption were taken into account at that stage*, and the problems of war finance increasingly became, as Keynes had argued that they should, those of seeing that taxation and savings mopped up so much as possible of the redundant purchasing power, and that inflation was thus kept within as narrow bounds as possible. (my emphasis)[15]

The war was the priority. The well-being of the population was a secondary consideration.

The United States, while still neutral, was mobilizing, and U.S. industry was heavily involved in the supply of raw materials and armaments to Germany, Japan, and to Britain and its allies. Milton Gilbert, a student of Simon Küznets, became chief of the National Income Division of the Department of Commerce in the U.S. government in 1941. He was totally persuaded by the Keynes and Stone publication, "How to Pay for the War."

Gilbert presented a paper in December 1941 entitled "Measuring National Income as Affected by the War." Statistical historians Duncan and Shelton claim that this paper is the first clear, published statement of Gross National Product (GNP).[16]

That is, GNP equals consumer expenditures plus gross investment outlays plus government expenditures on goods and services. (A full description of these terms is found later in this
chapter.)

Gilbert's paper "did not insist that GNP was the one, the
good, and the true concept." On the contrary it stated, "There
is no one correct measure of income or output that can be used
indiscriminately in every type of economic problem." This
might have given hope for flexibility, a creative and more inclusive approach. But Gilbert's purpose and economic problem
was "how to pay for the war." He strongly supported the use
of GNP as the *proper measure in analyzing the economic relationship
between defence expenditures and total output.* The point of view
of the article is *measurement* rather than programming or *feasibility.* Gilbert's conception of GNP was constructed for specific
political purposes.

National income figures didn't support President Roosevelt's
budget expenditures of (U.S.) $56 billion for the year ending
June 1943. But another way of dressing them up, in the framework of the GNP, could justify it. Gilbert wrote a paper entitled
"War Expenditures in National Production" and argued that the
defense program was entirely possible. He pointed out that the increase in output would come (1) from the new defense plants
and equipment that were already built, under construction, or
being converted; (2) from a decline in unemployment and an
increase in labor force hours per week; and (3) from shifting
production from civilian goods to raw materials, where the pay
rates for the factors of production would be much higher. This
meant, for example, that the same amount of silk used in parachutes, instead of in the manufacture of stockings, would reg-
ister a larger contribution for the national income.

The impressive successes in the use of the national income
and product statistics for war purposes made their use in post-
war planning apparently logical and certainly inevitable. Yet
one feature was set in concrete: national income estimates

everywhere continue, to this day, to be an assessment of *how best to pay for the war.*

Gilbert established a new form of accounts in 1947, based on his war successes. As mentioned earlier, Küznets did not accept the new emphasis, which excluded a measure of welfare.* He also cautioned against reliance on GNP because it ignored working conditions and certain nonmarket activities.

Gilbert's reply to Küznets listed five advantages to his accounting framework:

1. It reveals the *structure* of the economy.
2. It aids in the solution of conceptual problems by *forcing consistency.*
3. It is useful *pedagogically.*
4. It provides a *framework* from which emerges a statistical shopping list *to improve the estimates.*
5. It makes it clear that there are two ways to *measure* nearly every item (from buyer or seller) and permits a few items to be measured by subtraction (my emphases).

Gilbert's approach leaves no room for alternative perception, for change, for flexibility, for the human response to life. It admits to a fascistic forced consistency.

Küznets became increasingly concerned with the *end use* of the statistics and gave great emphasis to welfare and long-run considerations. He was very aware of the deficiencies of GNP as a measure of economic well-being. Gilbert defended himself in 1945: "I can only repeat that we are not trying to measure welfare but the value of production from a business point of view."

Yet Küznets was not alone in his concern. Other economists were aware that both aggregate and per unit increases in national income were inadequate as indicators of economic growth because they said nothing about changes in the abso-

---

*"Welfare" in this context means "well-being," not the narrower usage as "government assistance."

lute extent of poverty. A system developed to win a war had no interest in measuring a nation's poverty. It might well measure changes in market wealth, but it did not measure the distribution of that wealth.

British economist J. Viner wrote in 1953, "The numbers of those living at the margin of subsistence may have grown steadily consistent with a rise in the average income of the population as a whole."[17] This would, of course, invalidate the "growth"—either real or imagined. Viner recognized, however, that if he made the reduction of mass poverty the crucial test of economic growth—which simple logic tells us it should be— then he would be separating himself from the whole body of literature on the subject. Market measures, he argued, also assume that growth of output implies or accompanies a rise in *qualitative* satisfaction—which may not necessarily be the case, or in any event is the case only with those affected by that growth. The suicide rate among elderly Japanese women tells such a story. According to research on the conditions of aged people done by the ministry of welfare in Japan, 84 percent of aged men and 56 percent of aged women have some income. Almost half of the elderly women in a nation with one of the world's highest rates of growth have no income.[18] Thus national income statistics disclose nothing about the distribution of wealth.

But the seeds of criticism sown by Küznets and Viner bore no fruit. The UNSNA has become even more entrenched in the intervening decades.

Vital Statistics: The Demand

National income is recorded arithmetically according to basic accounting rules. The great amount of the data recorded in national income accounts is recorded primarily for accounting purposes, then wedged into the framework of the national accounts. Sales and purchases, payments and receipts, assets and liabilities, visible and recorded in the market, are the key sources for figures. Table 1 illustrates how these are presented finally. For those of you who feel anxious at this point, I want to explain each line entry on this table, what it records, and how it is recorded.

Consumption is seen as the amount spent by households on currently produced goods and services. Consumption refers to spending, not to eating or wearing clothes out or using newly purchased products. When I buy an old house or a used car, economists do not call this consumption but the exchange of one asset (money) for another asset. Similarly, if I want to buy treasury bonds or some stock market shares, this is not seen as spending but as the exchange of one asset for another. But the fee that I pay the land agent or stockbroker is consumption—of a service.

Durable goods include cooking utensils, cleaning appliances, and gardening tools. *Nondurable goods* include food, clothing, and fuel. *Services* include health care, footwear repairs, and laundries. Owning your own home is also recorded as a service consumption, as Pigou described.

When you build your home, the new construction is considered investment, not a personal consumption expenditure. This is because, according to the logic of the system, residential dwellings are often occupied on a rental basis. Housing produces the service of providing a shelter year after year. So each year a value for the potential rental an owner-occupied house might get on the market is imputed as a consumption of a service for the expenditure side of the accounts. The same rule applies to every dwelling, whether it is a mansion or a mud hut.

The contributor to the *Encyclopaedia of Economics* suggests that there are two reasons why economic theory defines consumption in this way.[19] First, the reasons (motives) that households spend and save are different from the profit motive and opportunities that dominate investment decisions. Household spending and saving intentions do not correspond with business investment and intentions or with the government's aims

Table 1.
National Income Accounts for 1981 (Billions of Dollars)

Aggregate Demand [Expenditure]			Cost of Production [Income]	
Consumption		$1858	Wages	$1637
Durable goods	232		Unincorporated business	135
Nondurable goods	743		Rent	34
Services	883		Dividends from profits	61
Investment (gross)		451	Interest	309
Nonresidential fixed	329		Net transfer payments	229
Residential fixed	106		Depreciation	322
Inventory change	16		Indirect business taxes and transfers	
Government purchases		591	and statistical discrepancy	198
Federal	230			
State and local	361			
Net Exports		26		
Exports	367			
Imports	341		Equals	
Equals			Gross National Product	$2925
Gross National Product		$2925		

Source: U.S. Department of Commerce, *Survey of Current Business.*

in public policy (!). Second, the contributor suggests that it is spending on currently produced goods and services that determines how much is produced, how many are employed, and whether or not inflation occurs.

The first reason assumes that men (and, let's be clear about it, this is a description of the male economic world) behave differently and with different motives inside the household, as opposed to in government or in business or in the labor force. This is one of the unquestioned "observations of fact" that is a commencement step in the development of economic theory. Quite clearly, women were not consulted on this score. As for the second reason, how can the true motives of households be observed when the vast proportion of their consumption, throughout the world, is of production and services that never enter the market?

The UN System of National Accounts lists the following main items of consumption expenditure. If the goods have been purchased in the market or if the goods are being consumed by a person whose primary production in the labor force is of that commodity, the consumption is visible. If the goods have been produced and are being consumed by Tendai or Cathy, by my grandmothers, my mother, or myself, or any of the millions of so-called unoccupied women, neither the production nor the consumption is visible.

The list includes:

1. All food, including purchases in restaurants or boarding houses, consumption of own products by producers, and food provided to employees, including members of the armed forces.
2. Beverages, including soft drinks and all alcoholic beverages.
3. Tobacco.
4. Clothing and other personal effects, including footwear, leatherwear, jewelry, and watches.

5. Rent, rates, and water charges, including all gross rent paid by tenants, imputed gross rent on owner-occupied dwellings, and indoor repairs and upkeep paid for tenants.

6. Fuel and light, including the purchases of coal, gas, electricity, firewood, etc.

7. Furniture, furnishings, and household equipment, including purchases of durable household goods such as furniture, household textiles, electrical appliances, wireless sets, televisions, etc.

8. Household operation, including wages paid to domestic servants; purchases of nondurable household goods; and all repair, insurance, and similar services incidental to durable household goods and clothing.

9. Personal care and health expenses, including purchases of toilet articles and medicines, payments to doctors and hospitals.

10. Transportation and communication, including purchases and operating cost of transporting equipment, purchases of transportation and communication services.

11. Recreation, including expenditures on entertainment, hotels, restaurants, hobbies, and purchases of books and other printed matter.

12. Miscellaneous services, including actual and imputed bank charges; operating expenses of life insurance companies; administrative charges of private pension schemes, household finance companies, and other financial institutions rendering services to households; education and research; and various personal services.

13. Expenditure abroad of residents, including all expenditure on foreign travel, except that part which is charged to business expense.[20]

The second factor on the expenditure side of the accounts in table 1 is *investment*. We might think we've done some investing in our lives, but investment in economics is not buying antiques or artworks or stock market shares. That is financial investment. Investment, as economists use the term, means physical capital. And just to complicate this process further, capital is not money but new buildings, equipment, structures, and machinery used in the further production of goods and services for sale. Investment in previously produced goods is not counted, because it makes no demands on the productive capacity. Investment in property is not in itself investment for the national accounts, as it does not contribute to the aggregate demand for goods and services. Governments purchase capital goods to be used in producing other goods and services, and often sell the product. The reasons to buy these goods and the processes of political decisions are, according to the UNSNA authors, different from the profit motive of businesses. So government purchases of capital goods are classified as government expenditure.[21] By definition, in national income theory and national income accounting, only businesses invest.*

In my recent experience of buying a small farm I was concerned to secure a home, a small farming business, and an investment. I did not distinguish between my motives for a home and my motives for a business. In making my investment, some primary considerations were the topography, the soil type, the climate, a water supply, a small stand of native bush, and the prevailing winds. But what I apparently "invested" in were the capital goods: fencing, drainage, tree removal, farm buildings, and artificial fertilizers. This is because the classifications for capital investment for residential and nonresidential categories are defined as follows:

1. Land, including legal and other transfer fees but excluding buildings on site.
2. Dwellings representing all expenditure on new construction and major alterations to residential buildings but ex-

---

*National income should not be confused with the total wealth of a country. The total wealth would include the value of all the capital, land, and natural resources and every other material thing of value.

cluding the value of land before improvement. (The expenditure covers the cost of all permanent fixtures such as furnaces, fixed stoves, central heating and water supply installations, and all equipment currently installed before renting.)

3. Nonresidential buildings, including industrial buildings, warehouses, office buildings, stores, restaurants, hotels, farm buildings, and buildings for religious, educational, and similar purposes.

4. Other construction and works, comprising such projects as permanent ways of railroads, subways, and tunnels; harbor facilities; car parking facilities; airports; athletic fields; roads; streets; sewers; electricity lines; gas mains and pipes; telephone and telegraph lines.

5. Transport equipment, including ships; motorcars, trucks, and commercial vehicles; aircraft; tractors for road haulage; and vehicles used in public transport systems, railways, tramway rolling stock, carts, and wagons.

6. Machinery and other equipment, covering all capital expenditure not included in the above groups, including power generating machinery; agricultural machinery; office machinery, equipment, and furniture; metal working, mining, construction, and other forms of industrial machinery.[22]

The final category of investment recorded in the national accounts (see table 1) is *inventory changes* that are added or subtracted from investments. Inventories are records of raw materials or partly processed (intermediate) goods that firms buy to use in production. They include such things as coal stocks, nuts and bolts, and bulk linen for manufacturing. Goods are counted in inventories in the year they are produced. Inventories also include finished goods held in stock for future customers. In the rules governing inventories, we find a clue to the how and why questions concerning the exploitation of our planet's ecosystem. The rules state:

Changes in farm stock, such as grain and livestock, are included in this flow while increases in natural resources due to growth, as in the case of forests and standing crops, and new discoveries, as in the case of mineral deposits, are excluded from capital formation. Changes in stocks in the hands of marketing authorities are included here.[23]

The UN System of National Accounts and supporting tables thus recommends that expenditure on *forest clearance*, land reclamation and improvement, and on the development of plantations, orchards, vineyards, and forests should be included but that increases in natural resources due to *growth* (as with forests and standing crops) be *excluded*. Practice with regard to the natural increase in livestock varies, but it is also obvious that wildlife in whatever numbers (increasing or depleting) is of no account at all. This neatly ensures that consequences to the world's food chain, which flow from public policy decisions based on national income statistics, count for nothing.

After consumption and investment, the third major flow on expenditure in table 1 represents the current expenditure on goods and services undertaken by *general government*. In a close examination of these flows it is important to notice the different treatment accorded the military and to remember that a key use and derivation of this system was to "win the war."

Transfers between general government and the rest of the world, whether in cash or in kind, are excluded from the consumption expenditure of the government making the grant, and are treated as international transfers, except that military equipment, purchased for use by another government, is included in the consumption expenditure of the government making the purchase.[24]

You will notice that the consumption side of the national accounts is also labeled the "demand" side of the accounts. Public policy and the international rules operate so that we apparently "demand" to "consume" military equipment.

Government final consumption expenditure is recorded by *purpose* or by *function*, as table 2 demonstrates. Different countries adopt different procedures for recording within the same basic framework. This is particularly the case in respect to the first three categories: general public services, defense, and public order and safety.

Given the concentration of the system of the market and that the market price of most general government activity is nil, "government" is not sold on the market. There are exceptions, such as the fees of hospitals, schools, and other charges of government. If the market price valuation were used for general government activity in the same way as for business activity, the product (that is, the value added in the general government sector) would be a substantial negative amount. The government's purchases of intermediate goods and services from other sectors would exceed its sales to other sectors. The measure of the services that government provides is thus taken to be the cost of producing them. Despite the lack of a market price, a value of production attaches. The measure of the same services provided within a household apparently costs nothing to produce and is valued at nothing or assumed to be household consumption, if any expenditure is involved.

Government consumption expenditure is split into a number of *types* of expenditure. Keynes, Stone, and Gilbert's wartime categories remain. One item, wages and salaries, comprises the remuneration of general government employees *except* members of the armed forces, whose pay and allowances are included in another item. Wages and salaries for government servants include social security contributions and contributions to pension funds of government employees.

Another item, pay and allowances of members of the armed forces, includes *all* remuneration regardless of the type and duration of the service. Such payments include the value (at cost) of food and standard clothing, including uniforms provided free.

Purchases from enterprises and purchases abroad for military purposes are separated out again. This includes expenditure on arms, munitions, aircraft, road vehicles, ships, the costs of new buildings for military use, and of such military works as

Table 2.

Government Final Consumption Expenditure by Function in Current Prices, 1982

	Ecuador[a]	India[b]	Korea, Republic of[c]	Sweden[d]
General public services	7543	35.57		23727
Defence	6982	56.73	} 4017.4	
Public order and safety	2936	—		} 19089
Education	17394	21.61	117.9	37718
Health	3544	10.22	18.2	46811
Social security and welfare	3460	4.46	33.1	31396
Housing and community amenities	1855	3.24	8.4	3109
Recreational, cultural, and religious affairs	159	1.36	19.3	10017
Economic services	6882	24.33	155.6	9309
Fuel and energy	1421	2.38		
Agriculture, forestry, fishing, and hunting	2024	9.29		
Mining, manufacturing, and construction, except fuel and energy	580	2.22		
Transport and communication	2293	6.50		
Other economic affairs	564	3.94		
Other functions	11174	1.30	0.2	1535
Total government final consumption expenditure	61929	158.82	4370.1	182711

Source: *National Accounts Statistics, Government Accounts and Tables 1983* (New York: United Nations, 1986).

[a] Million Ecuadoran sucres
[b] Thousand million Indian rupees
[c] Thousand million Korean won
[d] Million Swedish kroner

the construction of military airfields, training grounds, etc. An item for civilian purposes comprises all purchases other than compensation of general government employees and includes the costs of operating schools, hospitals, social service, police forces, roads, and other transport installations.

The fourth flow of expenditure in table 1 records the *exports and imports* of goods and nonfactor services (e.g. insurance, transportation), sold to the rest of the world. The flow includes the value of gifts in kind and other exports that are financed by means of international transfers, but it excludes the value of military equipment transferred between governments. The "war" is again afforded a different treatment.

Certainly there are many rules for special treatments in the expenditure approach. For example, if a UN agency is providing free medicine to the poorer members of the community, the cost of the free medicine is regarded as a purchase by the general government sector and is entered as general government consumption expenditure, not as private consumption expenditure. But if a village woman, who is recognized as an expert midwife, poultice maker, or herbalist, is involved in a similar dispensation of medicine, the consumption is recorded nowhere.

In another special treatment, private *nonprofit* institutions are grouped with the household sector because they are not established primarily with the aim of earning a profit, nor are they principally concerned with providing services to enterprises.*

The value of private nonprofit institutions' services would be much greater if they were included in the costs of an imputation for the services provided by people working in a vol-

---

Profit organizations serving households include such diverse organizations as private schools, religious orders, trade unions, charitable bodies, clubs and nonprofessional sporting organizations, and other cultural and recreational groups. Some of these bodies do receive income from selling goods and services for members, but most of their income is from fees and dues from members, subscriptions, investments, and grants from enterprises and from the government.

untary capacity. An unnamed New Zealand treasury official wrote recently, "It has not been possible (nor necessarily desirable) to value these unpaid services."

The statement is incorrect and blatantly a value judgment. It *is* possible to value these unpaid services. In the United States in 1980, 52.7 million women participated in voluntary work that was valued at $18 billion. It was not calculated in the nation's accounts.[25]

Vital Statistics: The Supply

Figure 1 is a simple model of the arithmetical information presented in table 1 and serves as a guide to analyze the income or cost of production side of the national accounts. The largest single contributor on the income side of the U.S. national accounts is the item *wages and salaries*. This category includes the monetary values of such things as fringe benefits, tips, bonuses, and paid vacations.

Proprietors' incomes are those received by owner-operated businesses, such as corner stores or gas stations. Incomes received from partnerships (for example, in law or accountancy) or from professional associations and from unincorporated farms are included in this category. This is the category where "primary production," produced and consumed on the farm, is counted. In the United States, where there are fewer and fewer small farms and businesses, proprietors' income has been a declining percentage of the national income.

Corporate profits are used to pay income taxes and, according to the company's policy, to pay dividends. Most corporations retain some profits to finance expansion or to use for immediate running costs and commitments.

Rental income is usually associated with leasing property, such as land, houses, and offices, but in theory includes anything obtained from renting any asset. In high-rise development it is not uncommon to find air space being rented. *Interest*

Figure 1.
Expenditure and Income Approach to GNP

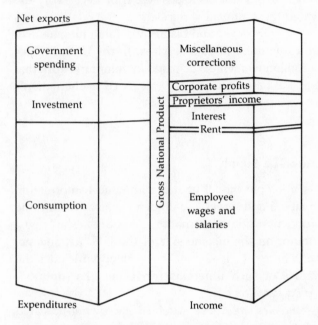

Source: Howard J. Sherman and Gary R. Evans, *Macroeconomics* (New York: Harper and Row, 1984), 37.

is the payment made for the use of borrowed money, usually to banks or to the holders of bonds.

Miscellaneous corrections includes the *statistical discrepancy* (see table 1). In the collection of data for national income accounts some mistakes are unavoidably made. The right column will not exactly match up with the left column. The difference is unashamedly called the statistical discrepancy. As can be seen in table 1 and figure 1, in the national income accounts, the right column equals the left because both add up to GNP, including the statistical discrepancy. This does not imply that the economy is in equilibrium. A disequilibrium in which the value of production exceeds demand will appear as a large growth in inventory change. This is how the production of nuclear weapons is treated—the value of production exceeds the demand for their use—thus far. Even if the economy is truly in disequilibrium, these accounts will not show that. The wartime methodology of development of the income accounts ensured this as one of their purposes. The statistical discrepancy of $198 billion in the 1981 U.S. national income accounts in table 1 exceeds the annual total income of many of the world's nations.

Gross National Product (GNP) and *Gross Domestic Product* (GDP) are derived from the national accounts. Each can be estimated by using either the expenditure or income approach (see table 1 and table 2). The concept of GNP has now been dropped from the United Nations statistical office vocabulary in favor of GDP, although the United States in particular continues to use GNP in its domestic publications and policy statements.

This is because GNP supposedly measures the production that generates income for a country's residents. GDP supposedly measures production that generates income in a nation's economy, *whether the resources are owned by that country's residents or not*. Thus interests, profit, and other forms of transfer from income generated in a country's economy—but accruing to nonresidents—is part of GDP but not part of GNP.

This subtle transition occurred without a murmur on the world stage during the U.N. development decade. After five years of the decade, little or no growth had occurred in "developing" countries when GNP was used as the indicator. But GDP produced different figures, and political leaders in the developing world, who have generally sought to encourage overseas investment, were content to be party to figures that recorded "growth" (and, in turn, attracted more investment) rather than those figures that more readily indicated the well-being of their own populations.

In many cases, especially in developing countries, there will be a significant difference between the figures of per capita GNP and per capita GDP. This has major consequences in terms of the assessment of growth rates (and the opportunities for multinational investment) and in terms of the assessment of basic human needs and well-being of the population (and the provision of aid). The shift to GDP gives priority to economic growth and investment and obscures the needs of a people.

This distinction is crucial—even within a misguided system—in terms of the end use of the figures. In this context we should recall that the 1953 UN group of experts stated that the system "yields information on certain structural properties of the economy which is a useful if not *essential background for public policy* formulation [my emphasis]."[26]

Like the GNP, the GDP is used to monitor rates and patterns of growth, to set priorities in policy making, to measure the success of policies, and to measure "economic welfare." Activities that lie outside the production boundary—that is, in every nation, the great bulk of labor performed by women in an unpaid capacity—are left out of the GDP, as they are left out of the GNP. It is not a large step from that point to leaving them out of policy considerations altogether. This is part of the reason why cuts of $636 million can be proposed in the largest U.S. government cash benefit program, Aid to Families with Dependent Children, while the Pentagon, for $614 million apiece, can order more SSN 688 nuclear attack submarines.

The GNP of the United States, as reported by the U.S. Department of Commerce, includes only "final products." This means that the value of a product is counted only once, even when that product is found at intermediate stages in the production process within a short time span. Wheat is a good example: produced first by the farmer, it is then transported, processed, and milled into flour. The flour producer then sells the product to the baker, who processes it to a final product for sale for consumption. The correct procedure is to count the wheat at point of first sale, then to include only the "value added" by labor at each point in the further production process.

If a woman does all this herself it is neither production nor consumption. It is economic inactivity. It lies outside the production boundary.

In reality, economic production covers the whole range of human activities devoted to the creation, with limited resources, of goods and services capable of satisfying human wants. Because of their limited supply, these activities have definite economic value in terms of an actual or imputed value in market exchange. The national accountants choose which transactions—of all the exchanges that take place—are to be deemed production. Like a photographer with a zoom lens, they can choose to show us selected details of a scene or the whole scene. The choice to date has been, in all cases, to assume the scene from selected details.

This brings us back to the question of observation that the example of Baron Lionel Robbins raised so clearly. His is the unquestioned approach, adapted from such earlier writing as *The Scope and Method of Political Economy* by John Neville Keynes (father of John Maynard Keynes). Keynes senior saw three stages in the economic discipline. First, the economist *observes* the *facts* (my emphasis) of the actual world to gain an insight into economic relations. Second, from clearly stated premises drawn from prior observation, he (*sic*) deduces the general laws of political economy. Third, these laws are tested by inductive verification.

If Keynes senior is correct, then much of the economic discipline is a matter of perception, and what does or does not constitute production could depend on the way you see the world. And it does.

3. The Boundary of Conception

How the UNSNA Makes Women Invisible

Chapter 2 examined the categories that form the basis of the national accounts. These categories give an indication of the "facts of the actual world" as observed by economists. But having established these categories, what general "laws" of political economy did the economists enshrine? The answer lies in a closer examination of the UNSNA, and its rules. To decide what did or did not constitute production, a production boundary was decided upon. All things of no "value" were excluded from the production boundary. Of particular importance for the operation of the system was the definition of a household—which lay outside the boundary.

In this chapter I show the system in operation and its effects on the lives of women and children. This examination shows whose public policy interests are served by the system.

The 1974 Bangladesh census redefined the categories related to women's work from "productive economic activity" in the 1961 census to "housewife." Women engaged in nonwage labor or in in-kind exchange relations have been defined as inactive. All those designated as housewives are also considered to be nonproductive and are classified in the economically inactive category. This grossly underestimates the nature and extent of productive labor in which rural women are involved as well as the actual number of women employed.[1]

The underreporting of female agricultural labor, particularly for the category of family workers, affects Palestinian refugees in the Arab world. With respect to the large number of Palestinians in the country, the government of Jordan reported the following in 1968:

The traditional social attitude of the people considers the wife who is helping her husband in his agricultural work as being economically non-active and leads, therefore, to her exclusion from the members of the labour force in agriculture. The same attitude applies to all female family members helping men in agricultural work.[2]

Elise Boulding, prominent U.S. social commentator, says that the only information about women that governments now require concerns the production and fertility rates, the size of the economically inactive female reserve labor force, and the educational level of the current and future female labor force. Yet even when governments seek to acquire such minimal figures, the census guidelines are such that they are continually underestimated or simply not counted. In most Latin American countries, only 20 percent or even fewer of the women and girls over ten years of age are classified as economically active. For women, work opportunities exist in agriculture, handicrafts, and personal services generally carried out within the home by unpaid family workers, independent workers, or paid domestics. But from 1950 on, these women were not counted as workers.[3]

For the Sake of Convenience: Devising the UNSNA Rules

On the question of production, the UNSNA states that it is "convenient to draw a production boundary."[4]

A definition of producer is needed. As a first approximation it may be supposed that the transactors, that is the producing and consuming entities in the economy, can be exhaustively and exclusively classified as either enterprises or households and that producers can be identified with the former category.[5]

So, from the start, production wasn't to be found in households. With a few exceptions:

The distinction between enterprises and households is not in all cases sufficient to draw a satisfactory production boundary. In the simplest case, households may buy direct services, such as domestic services, from other households and it seems reasonable to regard these services as part of production. *This can be done by recognizing a limited amount of production within households.* The household that buys the direct services rendered by other households is thought of as buying at cost, in its capacity as a consumer, the direct services from a production account to which is debited the cost of the services. This production account, like any other, lies within the production boundary and what flows out of it is part of the final product.[6] (my emphasis)

This is the paragraph that gives rise to the much-commented upon result that when a man marries his housekeeper the GNP goes down. So we start with a sexist definition, just because a definition is needed. Yet if the original definition is challenged, the only correction needed is to make an exception, i.e., "recognize a limited amount of production" within the still officially excluded territory.

Households in rural areas were also to be treated differently. The UNSNA rules stated,

Farm households are not only households from a consuming point of view, but also enterprises which engage in agricultural production. These two aspects of their activity must be separated and this may be done by setting up a production account to which purchases and sales *in respect of their productive activity* are debited and credited and a consumption account to which is credited their income and to which is debited their consumption expenditure.[7] (my emphasis)

Since these households usually produce agricultural goods for their own consumption as well as for the market, the UNSNA suggests that one impute a sale to account for their own consumption. Sometimes a transaction is invented (or imputed) when there is an economic process that is considered to need recording, but no actual commercial transaction accrues. The imputation in this case is the price that the stock or produce would have found in the local market. If the "head of the household" classifies *himself* as a cattle farmer and kills a beast for his family, it is counted as if it went to market. If all the rest of the food that accompanies the meat is grown in a garden plot by the wife of the "head of the household," no valuation is imputed. The vegetable garden is not the primary agricultural enterprise, not *the* productive activity.

Economically inactive Cathy, our North American friend in chapter 1, presents few problems for these rules. She is simply not productive, despite the long list of chores I cited earlier.

In industrialised economies in which monetary exchange and the division of labour have *progressed* [my emphasis] far, the separation of households from enterprises and the inclusion in total product of production for home consumption do not constitute important practical problems in national accounting because by far the greater part of production takes place for sale in the market by enterprises which in most cases are clearly defined. In underdeveloped countries, however, the reverse is the case and so it is important to set up clearly defined rules for drawing the production boundary.[8]

Such rules might have allowed Tendai, in the Lowveld, to be recorded as economically productive. Water, fuel, food, household services are all, if exchanged in the market, items for consumption expenditure. But the 1953 UNSNA report draws the distinction, for "convenience," between primary and other producers. A housewife by definition cannot be a primary producer. In fact, she cannot be a producer. The woman may be agriculturally productive, but her primary role is still defined as housework, and so any recognized production will be seen as secondary production. In this catch-22, she will be excluded from the definition of primary producer.

In the limited vision of the authors of the 1953 UNSNA, the definitions of primary producer and the production boundary were narrow. In addition, the report clearly imposed the values of industrialized countries on agrarian and subsistence (non-

monetary) societies, in an illustration of neocolonialism that is
further described at later points in this book.

In the case of primary producers, that is those engaged in agriculture,
forestry, hunting, fishing, mining and quarrying, all primary production whether exchanged or not and all other goods and services produced and exchanged are included in the total of production. In the
case of other producers, that is those engaged in all other industries
listed in the international standard industrial classification [housewife
is not included in this list] the total of their primary production is
included as for primary producers.[9]

The description of primary producers includes all the stereo-
typical male roles. Women *might* be covered by agriculture, apparently. But the paragraph that followed rules out that possibility.

These rules are in close agreement with the imputation procedures
used for *industrialised economies*. The farming imputation made for such
economies accords with the rules given for primary producers and the
rental imputation accords with the rules given for other producers if
account is taken of the fact that home ownership is regarded as a
trade. In practice no other imputations of this kind are made *since
primary production and the consumption of their own produce by non-primary
producers is of little or no importance.*[10] (my emphasis)

In other words, women's work is of little or no importance!
Over the years I have read and reread the last sentence of the
above quote. It still makes me gasp for breath. It embodies
every aspect of the blindness of patriarchy, its arrogance, its
lack of perception—and it enshrines the invisibility and enslavement of women in the economic process as "of little or no
importance."

That sentence has caused a relatively small amount of debate
in the international arena, but it is important to examine the
parameters of that debate.

In 1953, while there was considerable argument about the
definition of production boundaries and coverage rules, there
was general unspoken agreement about the exclusion of house-

wives. A working party of African statisticians recommended in 1960 that in addition to all nonmonetary activities, such as agriculture, forestry, and fishing, estimates might also be useful for a group of activities that they termed rural household services.

These consisted of the following:

1. Building construction and landworks by households.
2. Processing, storage, transportation, and distribution of own primary output.
3. Processing of primary products, including the manufacture of clothing, footwear, household equipment, furniture and furnishings, and the carriage of water.[11]

On first reading it appears that women's productive work was recommended as included under items 2 and 3. The working party took the view that it was most important to give proper coverage in the national accounts to subsistence food production and own account capital formation in rural areas. In other words, if dams or homes were built or pottery or chairs made by members of a family or household for themselves, a value should be imputed for these activities into the national accounts. While the statisticians suggested the inclusion of the carriage of water (primarily women's work), *housework, weeding* of primary productive land crops, and the *processing, storage, transportation, and distribution of food* from subsistence farming was still excluded. And while women may well process primary products, they do not manufacture them. They just do housework.

Another UN committee of experts appointed by the Statistical Commission, and again chaired by Richard Stone, revised the UNSNA in 1968 and accepted many of these recommendations. The system now allows for coverage of further nonmonetary activities. The notable exclusions are still the carriage of water, weeding, the collection of firewood, subsistence crop production, and housework. The production boundary now includes:

1. Production of primary products, that is, the characteristic products of agriculture, fishing, forestry, mining, and quarrying.
2. Imputed rental incomes of owner-occupiers.
3. Building and construction.
4. Processing of primary commodities by the producers of these items in order to make such goods as butter, cheese, flour, wine, oil, cloth, or furniture for their own use, whether or not any of these manufactures are offered for sale.
5. Production of other commodities that producers consume in their households and that they also produce for the market. [12]

The rules for market valuation of such production are as follows:

In the case of non-monetary transactions, that is, barter and production for own use, the prices to be applied are those at which the producer sells, or if he [sic] does not sell, those at which producers of similar products sell in the same or neighbouring localities. [13]

There is no obligation to cover all these activities in the UNSNA. Individually, governments, policy makers, politicians, economists, and statisticians decide where the demarcation line governing production will be drawn. In practice, there is a cabal that ensures that the production of any of these goods by a housewife still counts for nothing.

Reasons given by men for their failure to account for women's work are (1) conceptual problems and (2) the practical difficulties of collecting data. It does not seem to occur to them that if you have a conceptual problem about the activity of half the human species, you then have a conceptual problem about the whole. As a result, the categories of work for which information is collected are ill-defined and biased towards market activity. They include activities in agriculture, trade, industry (usually defined by sectors such as weaving, sewing, iron works), or services (teaching, domestic service). *Unpaid domestic work is specifically excluded from the definition of work in UN census manuals—but nowhere is domestic work defined.* As a result, it becomes a residual category that includes, besides cooking, child care, and domestic services, all food processing, kitchen gardening, animal tending, food and water collection, fishing, hunting, gathering, and manufacturing for home use—activities generally performed on a large scale within the household in the subsistence sector. Let's look at some examples of how all this works.

Invisible Women: Applying the UNSNA Rules

Kathleen Newland describes the situation precisely:

Among the nomad people of Iran's Zagros mountains, the men look after the animals. The women do almost everything else. They do the nearly universal women's work of preparing meals and looking after the children. They haul water into the camp on their backs; they milk and shear the animals, mostly sheep and goats. They collect such edible plants as the surroundings afford—primarily berries, roots, and fungi.
They churn butter, make cheese and yogurt, and refine the leftover whey into the daily beverage. They spin the wool and goat hair into threads and press it into felt and make clothes, tent cloth, and carpets for their family's use. From each tent household of an extended family, a woman goes daily to collect wood from the bush. On the average, she spends half a day at the task, plus another hour at the camp breaking the torn-off branches of thorn bush into pieces small enough for the cooking fire.[14]

For these women only their work, crops, livestock, and their handicraft are visible, even as non-monetary production. In other parts of the Arab world, in Jordan and Saudi Arabia, they would count food-processing as well. Crop storage would count in Malawi and the Sudan, and also in Bangladesh—

which doesn't count food-processing. Water carrying is the least counted of all unpaid productive activities.

The UN has noted in numerous publications "the ambiguity of the labour force concept in rural areas of developing countries, where women undertake various productive but unpaid activities which may or may not be counted in theory or in practice, as economic production."[15]

While the subject is debated with relish—by the UN Statistical Commission, by the authors of the World Bank Living Standards Measurement Series, by researchers at the Organization for Economic Cooperation and Development (OECD) in major recent studies of the UN agency INSTRAW, by conferences of the International Labor Organization—in the end, most commentators embrace the UN definition of the boundary of production. Harold Copeman, a former undersecretary in the British treasury, wrote in 1981

The national income statistician has to decide how far the imputation process should go. *Should one impute an income to the partner in a marriage who does the housework or gardening, and a purchase of services by the other partner? A trend towards the production of home vegetables, and home decorating and repairs would* then affect not only sector accounts, *but the level and rate of growth of national income and GNP. This could be significant* as social habits, working hours, retirement ages, and unemployment change. The United Kingdom and international practice is to confine production mainly to goods and services which are in fact exchanged for money, and to impute transactions which are closely similar to those where money passes.[16] (my emphasis)

"This could be significant" reveals the extent to which the statistics could change. Presumably the policies that flow from them would change, too—and in a way that would not suit the currently dominant power cabals. It is not, as is often claimed, that it cannot be done. An unnamed New Zealand Treasury official writes

The scope of production is in fact an elastic boundary which can be expanded or contracted depending on the values of national accountants concerned. . . . Although international comparability is improved by the inclusion of some non-marketed activity, it is generally accepted that such imputations be restricted to only a few significant instances. In recent times it has been proposed that production should include negative elements such as the *costs of environmental destruction or pollution* and intangible elements embracing educational investments or returns to technical know-how. *To this end the national accounting system is adaptable* and these possibilities could be included as additions to the existing system. It is not recommended that they be incorporated within the accounts themselves. The inclusion of too much non-marketed activity, based on questionable imputations, *greatly reduces the usefulness* of national accounts as a tool for economic analysis.[17] (my emphasis)

As a tool for whom? Note the objective tone, the lack of clarity as to who will use the accounts. The tool is certainly not meant to be used for women, the environment, or the poor.

In the most substantial commentary on the coverage of non-monetary activities I have seen, OECD statistician Derek Blades writes

For virtually all planning applications the national accounts must give a realistic picture of the *growth* of output income and expenditure. To do this the non-monetary production boundary should be drawn fairly widely, since output or income increase only when more is produced, not simply because a larger proportion of a fixed total is exchanged for cash. . . . The production boundary should encompass non-monetary activities which are likely to be replaced by monetary activities as an economy becomes more specialised. The prime candidates here include subsistence agriculture, food processing, handicrafts and building. In some cases forestry activities, water collecting and crop storage will need to be included too. Because of the practical difficulties of measurement, the case for including housewives' general services is considerably weaker.[18]

But again he misses the point. As long as "housewives' general services" are excluded, so is the collection of water and wood and the storage of crops. For in nonmonetary economies these tasks are overwhelmingly performed by women classed as housewives.

Blades makes a second point that the kind of people who generate most nonmonetary output—the poor in general and peasant farmers in particular—are to an increasing extent the central concern of economic policymakers. But Blades fails to identify the poor—the overwhelming majority everywhere are women. In his study, the activities covered least in the accounts are handicrafts, water collection, crop storage, and housewives' services. Of fifteen developing countries in the Caribbean and South America, only Jamaica covered food processing in their national accounts; only Argentina, Haiti, Jamaica, and Mexico included handicrafts. Table 3 shows the results of Blades's survey carried out in 1973. This is not a survey of who does what work, but of what work is visible.

Yet another example of female invisibility: In Africa, women and men share labor and planning and caring for domestic animals. Women do 60 percent of the marketing of excess crops and harvesting, 70 percent of the hoeing and weeding, 80 percent of transport of crops from farm to home, 80 percent of crop storage, 90 percent of carrying water and fuel and processing food crops, and 95 percent of feeding and caring for children, men, and the aged. In accordance with standard economic practices, *only the petty marketing labor of these women is likely to be visible* in Blades's study. And yet, on these figures are based development planning, socioeconomic policy formation, and the establishment of national priorities. The women simply do not show up when policymakers plan.

This invisibility is also the destiny of Pakistan women in small peasant households who work fifteen hours a day, even in nonpeak periods. It is a fate shared by the wife of a small farmer or farm laborer in Central America who starts her day at 3 or 4 A.M. It is also the fate of 49 percent of all women on farms in New Zealand. It is unquestionably the case in Brazil, where census interviewers were instructed that any activity

Table 3.

Non-Monetary Activities Covered in the National Accounts of Seventy Developing Countries

Region and country	Crops	Livestock	Forestry	Hunting	Fishing	Food processing	Handicrafts	Dwellings	Other buildings	Construction[b]	Urban	Rural	Water carrying	Other activities[c]
AFRICA:														
Angola	X	X	X	X	X	X	—	X	X	—	X	X	X	X
Botswana[a]	X	X	X	X	X	X	X	X	—	—	X	X	—	—
Burundi	X	X	X	—	X	—	X	—	—	—	—	—	—	—
Cameroon	X	X	X	X	X	—	X	X	—	—	—	—	—	—
Congo-Brazzaville	X	X	—	X	X	X	—	X	—	—	X	X	—	—
Dahomey	X	X	X	X	X	X	X	X	—	X	X	X	—	—
Ethiopia	X	X	X	X	—	—	X	X	X	X	—	X	—	—
Gambia	X	X	X	—	X	—	—	—	—	X	X	—	—	—
Ghana	X	X	X	X	X	X	X	X	X	—	X	X	—	—
Ivory Coast	X	X	X	X	—	X	—	—	—	—	—	—	—	—
Kenya	X	X	X	—	X	—	—	X	X	X	—	X	X	—
Madagascar	X	X	X	—	—	—	—	X	X	—	X	X	—	—
Malawi	X	X	X	—	X	X	X	X	X	—	X	X	—	X
Mali	X	X	X	—	X	X	X	X	—	—	X	—	—	—
Mauritania	X	X	X	—	X	X	X	X	—	—	—	—	—	—
Mauritius	—	—	—	—	X	—	—	—	—	—	X	X	—	—
Morocco	X	X	X	X	X	X	X	X	—	—	X	—	—	—
Mozambique	X	X	X	X	X	X	—	X	X	—	X	X	X	X
Niger	X	X	X	—	X	—	X	X	—	—	X	X	—	—
Nigeria	X	X	X	—	X	X	X	X	—	—	X	X	—	—
Rhodesia (Zimbabwe)[a]	X	X	X	—	—	X	X	X	X	—	X	—	—	—
Rwanda	X	X	X	X	X	X	X	X	—	—	—	—	—	—
Senegal	X	X	X	—	X	—	—	—	—	—	X	X	—	—
Sierra-Leone	X	X	X	X	—	—	—	X	X	—	X	X	—	—
Sudan	X	X	X	X	X	X	X	X	—	—	X	X	X	X
Swaziland	X	X	X	—	—	—	X	X	—	—	X	—	—	—
Tanzania	X	X	X	X	X	—	—	X	X	—	X	X	—	—
Togo	X	X	X	X	X	X	X	—	X	—	X	X	—	—
Tunisia	X	X	—	—	—	—	—	X	—	—	X	X	—	—
Uganda	X	X	X	X	X	—	—	X	—	—	—	X	—	—
Upper Volta (Burkina Faso)	X	X	X	X	X	X	X	X	X	—	—	X	—	—
Zaire	X	X	—	—	X	—	—	—	—	—	X	X	—	—
Zambia	X	X	—	—	X	—	—	X	—	X	X	X	—	—
AMERICA:														
Argentine	X	X	—	X	—	—	X	—	X	—	X	—	—	—
Brazil	X	X	—	—	X	X	—	X	—	—	X	—	—	—
Chile	X	X	—	—	—	—	—	—	—	—	X	X	—	—
Colombia	X	X	X	—	X	X	—	X	X	—	X	X	—	—
Costa Rica	X	X	—	—	—	—	—	—	—	—	X	X	—	—
Dominican Republic	X	X	X	—	—	—	—	X	X	—	X	X	—	—

Table 3 continued

Region and country	Agriculture, etc.					Food processing	Handicrafts	Building & construction			Urban	Rural	Imputed rents	
	Crops	Livestock	Forestry	Hunting	Fishing			Dwellings	Other buildings	Construction[b]			Water carrying	Other activities[c]
Ecuador	X	X	—	—	X	X	—	—	—	—	X	X	—	—
Guyana	X	X	—	—	X	X	—	X	—	X	X	X	—	—
Haiti	X	X	X	—	X	X	X	X	—	X	X	X	—	—
Jamaica	X	X	X	X	X	X	X	X	X	—	X	X	—	—
Mexico	X	X	X	—	—	—	X	X	X	X	X	X	—	—
Nicaragua	X	X	X	—	X	X	—	—	—	—	X	X	—	—
Panama	X	X	—	—	X	X	—	—	—	—	X	X	—	—
Peru	X	X	—	—	X	X	—	—	—	—	X	X	—	—
Venezuela	X	X	—	—	—	—	—	—	X	X	X	X	—	—
ASIA:														
Bangladesh	X	X	X	—	X	—	X	X	X	—	X	X	—	X
Hong Kong	X	X	—	—	X	—	—	—	—	—	X	X	—	—
India	X	X	X	X	X	X	X	X	X	X	X	X	—	—
Indonesia	X	X	X	X	X	X	X	X	X	—	X	X	—	—
Iran	X	X	—	—	—	—	X	—	—	—	X	X	—	—
Iraq	X	X	—	—	X	—	X	X	—	—	X	X	—	—
Israel	X	X	—	—	X	—	—	—	—	X	X	X	—	X
Jordan	X	X	—	—	X	X	X	X	X	—	X	X	—	—
Khmer Republic	X	X	—	—	X	—	X	—	—	—	—	—	—	—
Korea (South)	X	X	—	—	X	X	—	X	X	X	X	X	—	—
Malaysia	X	X	—	—	X	X	X	—	—	—	X	X	—	—
Nepal	X	X	—	—	X	X	X	X	X	—	X	X	—	—
Philippines	X	X	—	—	X	X	X	X	X	X	X	X	—	—
Saudi Arabia	X	X	—	—	X	X	X	X	X	X	X	X	—	—
Singapore	X	X	—	—	X	—	—	—	—	—	X	X	—	—
Sri Lanka	X	X	—	—	—	—	X	X	—	—	X	X	—	—
Taiwan	X	X	—	—	X	X	—	X	X	X	X	X	X	—
Thailand	X	—	—	—	—	—	—	—	—	—	X	X	—	—
Vietnam (South)	X	—	—	—	—	X	—	—	—	—	X	X	—	—
EUROPE:														
Cyprus	X	X	X	X	X	—	—	—	—	—	X	X	—	—
Greece	X	X	X	X	X	—	X	X	—	—	X	X	—	—
Malta	X	X	—	—	—	—	—	—	—	—	X	X	—	—

Sources: For *Mauritania* and *Khmer Republic* the coverage of non-monetary activities was obtained from their most recent national accounts publications. For other countries the information was obtained from a mail survey. See Derek W. Blades, *Non-Monetary (Subsistence) Activities in the National Accounts of Developing Countries* (OECD, October 29, 1975), 14.

X indicates that the activity is covered in the country's present national accounts series.
[a]The coverage shown for Botswana and Rhodesia (Zimbabwe) refers to the "traditional" sector.
[b]Land clearance, boreholes, roads, and bridges.
[c]"Housewives' services" in *Angola* and *Mozambique*; "crop storage" in *Bangladesh*, *Malawi*, and *Sudan*; and "personal services" by Kibutzim members in *Israel*.

declared by a housewife that was not housework should not be taken into account, as this did not count as work.[19]

Housework is not work. But since housework is seen as a woman's primary activity, and is not defined, anything else that she does is not work either, because it is secondary to housework.

This invisibility is not simply the fate of rural women. In the 1971 census in India, when the registration was allowed both of lacemaking as a household industry and of lacemakers as workers, only 6,449 male and female workers were recorded in the whole Narsapur district as engaged in manufacturing. But in 1977–78, 8 million rupees worth of lace goods were exported from Narsapur to Australia, the Federal Republic of Germany, Italy, Denmark, Sweden, the United Kingdom, the United States, Ireland, and the Netherlands. Lace worth $1–2 million was sold in major Indian cities, mainly to tourists. And, according to an official statement, 95 percent of the foreign exchange earnings from the export of handicrafts from the state of Andhra Pradesh came from the lace industry of Narsapur. Yet the more than 200,000 women who work in what is called a household industry are nowhere to be found in the census statistics.[20]

So, you might ask, why does that matter? The reasons are extensive, but among the more important are the following. Only 6,500 people are credited with the production of thirty times that number. These figures will be the basis of any government or multinational investment aimed at boasting foreign exchange earnings in the state. The invisibility of the workers draws no attention to their per capita exchange earnings in the state. The invisibility of the workers draws no attention to their appalling work conditions and extraordinary exploitation as profits accrue only to the visible workers—owners, managers, entrepreneurs—the male face of the industry. Further, the visibility of *all* the other workers would begin to change the labor content component of the nation's GDP. Countries who rely on the production of statistics to demonstrate relative levels of poverty so that they might receive aid have an interest in understating such figures. As outlandish as it may sound, some countries have a vested interest in retaining their status as a "least-developed country" (ldc), and others in recording a negative growth rate, to qualify for some forms of assistance. From time to time statisticians who took their jobs too seriously have "disappeared," and international meetings of statisticians have voiced concern at such occurrences.[21]

In the UN and ILO international guidelines for censuses of business organizations in the mining, industrial, and service sectors, all but the "very small units" should be included. But as the Narsapur example demonstrates, the "very small units" are very numerous.

Just in case you are unwittingly beginning to think that these examples occur only in less-developed or overpopulated countries, let's look at the New Zealand system, where women don't count either. Here the national accounts give numerical expression to the main features of economic activity covering production, expenditure, and income distribution. The New Zealand national accounts contain information collected on the transactions of the 200,000 establishments that produce goods and services and on the 900,000 households that consume the bulk of this output. The most important transactor is called the *production unit* or *establishment*. It may be a farm, a factory, a shop, a government department, or an old people's home. It may not even have a location, because it is strictly an accounting unit that brings together factors of production (land and/ or labor and/or capital) and produces a good or service. It may sell its product, it may produce it for free distribution, or—as is the case with many government services—it may be produced only for the common good. But it may not be a household.

Feudalism Lives On: Defining "Household"

The *United Nations Multi-lingual Demographic Dictionary* defines a household as a socioeconomic unit consisting of individuals who live together. It defines *family* primarily in terms of relationships associated with the reproductive process that are regulated by law or custom. In deciding on household composition, there are three broad approaches: (1) a common source of the major part of income; (2) sleeping under one roof or within one compound; and (3) a common source of food.[22] We are now familiar with the belief that households lie outside the production boundary and have no output. For those of us who are unfamiliar with the economic dogma, this comes as a surprise. But there are more similar surprises in store when we look at the concept of the household.

According to the UNSNA,

- The household is not a family-operated enterprise because it does not produce income. Therefore, persons who work unpaid in households are not employed.
- Income brought into the household and saved is consumption. Income saved within the household (for example, because a woman bakes a cake instead of buying one) is invisible as either production or consumption.
- Despite the fact that the household is both the center of consumption and the supplier of all the factors of production, it is not a family-operated enterprise.

Households are similarly excluded from the scope of production activities in the Material Product System used by the countries of Eastern Europe (see appendix 1 for a discussion of this system). While the concepts of production may differ between the two systems, the concepts of labor are the same. Women are invisible as producers in their capacities as housewives. Women are just as likely to be invisible in that role in the distribution of government benefits under either system. Soviet social scientist Svetlana Turchaninova reflects the same ideas and biases as Western economists. In "Women's Employment in the USSR," an article in a 1976 ILO publication, she writes,

The 1970 national census showed 7.5% of all women of working age or 5.9 million in absolute figures to be employed in the domestic economy as against 25.4% in 1959. Women's employment in the domestic economy, above all as housewives, is seen in present day Soviet society as necessary not only for the individual mother, but also for the proper rearing of a new generation, and hence, at least for the time being, as an indispensable element of a rational employment system. But this confinement to the domestic economy of a certain number of women for a certain period of time does not in any way signify that they are forever withdrawn from productive employment. A typical Soviet woman today is not a housewife permanently chained to her kitchen sink, nursing a garden plot, but a full citizen active in *productive employment and interrupting it* only for a while to bear and look after her children [my emphasis].[23]

These attitudes are part of the "inductive verification" that Keynes spoke of in the testing of economic laws. This magnitude of the invisibility of women's work (even to other women) was a major lesson I learned from my parliamentary experience. For example, as a politician, it was virtually impossible for me to prove—given the production framework—a need for child care facilities. "Nonproducers" who are "inactive" and "unoccupied" cannot, apparently, be in need. They can certainly have no expectation that they will be visible in the distribution of benefits, such as child care, that might flow from production.

In Summary

In the planting season, a Zambian woman will wake at 5 A.M. She will walk for thirty minutes to the field with a baby on her back. She will spend nine and a half hours ploughing, planting, and hoeing until 3 P.M. For an hour she will collect firewood and carry it home. Then she will spend one and a half hours pounding or grinding grain or vegetables. It will take forty-five minutes to fetch water and an hour to light the fire and cook the meal for her family. After dishing out food, eating, and cleaning up, she will wash her children, herself, the family's clothing, and go to bed. If she is paid, her work in the fields may be considered productive. If the census is taken during this planting season, she may be classified as a worker. Whatever the situation, she is duly laboring as she nurtures and cares for a child at the same time. And whatever the situation, this last will be discounted. Zambia includes crops and livestock in its boundary of production. But food processing, handicrafts, water carrying, fuel collection, and, of course, housework are excluded.

The conceptual boundaries of the scientific method used by the UNSNA authors are limited to the male world. *Institutional* child care would be a service. The use of electricity, gas, kerosene, or coal as a fuel purchased in the marketplace would be consumptive. The processing or manufacture of foodstuffs in a factory is production. Water delivered through a tap has market value. A visit to a restaurant or laundry would be an economic activity.

But when a Zambian woman does it all herself—it is housework.

By now, evidence of this patent injustice raises the question, How can they get away with this? They do have a rationale. Remember, the two primary reasons economists and statisticians give for the global invisibility of women are (1) conceptual difficulties, and (2) the difficulties of collecting data.

4. Nothing Sexist Here

Statisticians in Action

The conceptual difficulties surrounding *work, production, economic activity*, or the *household* appear to be a problem of observation and the participant observer. But in my ten years of political experience and research on this book, my questions about the hows and whys of such observations consistently met with stock answers from the three groups involved: the policymakers, the economists, and the statisticians. The policymakers said that they could only work with, and from, the economists' models and the statisticians' figures. The economists said that they worked within policy guidelines that required particular statistics. And the statisticians said that they just produced the figures the policymakers and the economists' models required of them. No one, it seems, is responsible for the dismal state of economics. But is this possible? To examine more closely the issue of responsibility, let's look at the practices of just one of the groups involved—the statisticians.

The Head Office

The UNSNA is administered by the Statistical Office of the United Nations, located in New York. It provides information, and it summarizes and publishes the data on national accounts. The staff services the Statistical Commission of the United Nations, which is attended by diplomatic and statistical representatives of member countries, the overwhelming majority of whom are men.

Statistical data are based on submissions from individual governments and from the International Labor Organization (ILO), the Food and Agricultural Organization of the United Nations (FAO), the United Nations Educational, Scientific, and Cultural Organization (UNESCO), and the World Health Organization (WHO). Other agencies of the United Nations system that collaborate closely with the Statistical Office are the United Nations Family Planning Agencies (UNFPA), the International Civil Aviation Organization (ICAO), the World Bank, and the International Monetary Fund (IMF).

A substantial percentage of the staff expenditure of the Statistical Office for both headquarters staff and field experts is used to provide technical support for executing statistical projects in developing countries. However, within the UN system, as inside individual countries, statistics is not a priority for investment and expenditure.

While the Statistical Office of the United Nations has no comprehensive list of the users of the statistics it produces, the office sees the primary group as the UN system, including the Secretariat, the specialized agencies, the General Assembly, the Economic and Social Council, and their subsidiary bodies.[1] A second major group of users consists of the governments of member states of the United Nations, and intergovernmental organizations, e.g., the European Economic Community (EEC) and the Organization for Economic and Cultural Development (OECD). The third group of users is universities, research bodies, and nonprofit organizations, as well as nongovernmental organizations, private companies, and individuals.

In overwhelming numbers the decision makers and users employed in all these institutions are male.

How Statisticians Think: Responding to a Feminist Politician

To begin, let's examine the perceptions of a mainstream, typical male statistician when he is confronted with a feminist perspective.

Ron Fergie, then deputy statistician for the Australian government, was on a year's exchange to the Department of Statistics in Wellington, New Zealand, in 1981. Well known in the international statisticians community, Fergie had been responsible for the recent establishment of a system of national accounts in Papua New Guinea and later worked in Jamaica. I asked him to look at a draft of a presentation I had written for the Women and Food Conference in Sydney in February 1982. It was the first time I had committed to paper the ideas that were to become the framework for this book.

At the outset I declared, "This paper can be read as a global strategy proposal to overcome one area of women's oppression or as a total and absolute undermining and ridiculing of the national and international national income accounting measurements."

Fergie leaves the first part of the statement standing and corrects the second to read, "or as an argument for the development of *more valid* measures of income product and consumption in the *standard systems* by which we measure economic activity" (my emphasis). In the margin he comments, "Why set out to destroy something which would have to be rebuilt but with suitable additions? I suggest you state your objectives in positive terms."

In the following paragraph I wrote, "The broad theses are (1) if women's work as producers and reproducers is invisible as a contribution in the national accounts, women are invisible in the distribution of benefits."

Fergie omitted the word *if* and replaced it with "to the extent that." He crossed out "and reproducers" and commented, *"Isn't reproduction just a special case of production* [my emphasis]?"

My second thesis was "the assumption that women's unpaid work is household-confined reinforces the invisibility of all work that women do." Fergie altered it to read, "the fact that so much of women's unpaid work is household-confined and not visible leads to an understatement of their contribution to national product vis-à-vis that of men."

My third thesis was "the absence of the contribution of women's work from national accounts is a deliberate patriarchal ideological bias and nothing but this lies in the way of inclusion." Fergie corrected this to read, "the absence of the contribution of women's unpaid household services from national accounts is indicative of an ideological bias running through our whole value system, of which the national accounts are the tip of the iceberg." And in the margin he noted, "Your evidence is purely circumstantial and very thin. Where is the motivation?" With an arrow pointing toward the words *ideological bias*, he underlined the word *nothing* and wrote, "Nothing but massive conceptual and practical data collection problems!"

Then I wrote, "the invisibility of women globally in the national accounts is a common denominator of the caste struggle. It is an *oppression* common to all patriarchal governments irrespective of their professed ideology." He wrote, "It is a *feature of economic accounting* common to all patriarchal governments irrespective of their professed ideology."

I commented next on the obvious—that the universal, significant omissions from the system of national accounts are the unpaid services of housewives and other members of the household. At this point Fergie underlined "other members of the household" and commented, "i.e., there is no distinction on the basis of sex." Theoretically, this is true. But any woman anywhere knows that there is a major distinction on the basis of sex in terms of who spends the greatest amount of time in unpaid services both in and for the household. And those distinctions are not marginal or small in terms of the hours worked.

That was just the first page. Accompanying my helpfully and revealingly edited manuscript on its return was a substantial memo, which I also wish to highlight. I had commented in my paper on the political function of the statistician in ensuring women's invisible work. I had noted the reasons offered by the authors of the World Bank Living Standards Measurement Series for omissions from statistics, who wrote:

Participating in the debate on which data are most needed for policy purposes, *the statistician cannot avoid a responsibility* for the wise deployment of resources. . . . If the purpose . . . is to develop concepts, methods and manuals on procedure which will make it easier for countries to collect particular types of data, then the responsibility *for being selective* cannot be avoided.[2] (my emphasis)

Fergie commented as follows:

In offering constructive criticism of the draft paper I am assuming that your intentions are polemic rather than academic. So I have confined myself to an attempt to improve the credibility of the argument that the contribution of women to welfare is undervalued in the conventional *economic welfare aggregations* of the national accounts. (my emphasis)

My paper was to be delivered to a largely academic audience. So the assumption that my intentions were polemic, not academic, must have arisen because the paper was, unapologetically, informed by a feminist ideology in form and content. To Fergie, my observations of facts are not, apparently, academic, though views informed by a patriarchal ideology apparently are, and such views are also, of course, scientific. The statement about conventional welfare aggregations refers to a worldview (not confined to statisticians, and universally recognized as public policy) that goes very simply: When women *are* visible, women are problems. Women are welfare.

Fergie continued:

I think this is a fair and worthwhile target for comment, insofar as this is one of a number of areas in which one would like a much more comprehensive, elaborate and reliable accounting system if we had the capability to produce and use it properly. But I don't believe you can sustain an argument that this lack of coverage is a result of any sexist bias on the part of the accounting fraternity. I have therefore tried to draw attention to or modify some of the assertions that are most likely to be shot at (outside of an all feminist audience) and that would weaken the authority of your argument.

Interesting, isn't it, that he talks of there being no "sexist bias on the part of the accounting *fraternity*." He concedes that the invisibility of women is a problem area and that their inclusion (along with other unspecified things) would make the national accounts more comprehensive, elaborate, and reliable. The "capability to produce," in this context, means more money from governments. Nevertheless, funds *are* allocated, and statisticians (generally) decide what questions will be asked, for example, in the census of population. This apparently has nothing to do with patriarchy. And, apparently, feminist audiences being of a like-minded polemic persuasion will not have the capability of scientific criticism.

Then Fergie wrote:

Essentially I think you should be pointing the finger not at the national accountants but at our value system generally. When the time comes that *households* generally think it worthwhile to account for the unpaid efforts of their members (rather than just the acquisition and use of their family pay packet) the national accountants will have the material and incentive to build this into the national accounting system.

Feminists *are* pointing the finger at our value system generally and vigorously. But how can *households'* thoughts be known when they are assumed to be those of the "head" or "reference person"—overwhelmingly the man? The system operates to ensure a political invisibility (except as welfare problems) for those who are economically invisible.

Fergie continued:

In the early part of the paper particularly you seem to be asserting a deliberate bias against measuring the productive activity of women. But you really haven't substantiated this. The world standard (UNSNA) in essence urges countries to measure non-market production of the kind of output which is *generally sold on the market* (i.e., sold extensively enough for a value to be imputed to the non-market production).

The failure to cover this non-market production (whether by males or females) in many countries is not for want of urging by the designers of the UNSNA. The problem is that the national accountants of the least developed countries haven't the expertise or the data to make these estimates as they would like to. The larger the proportion of agricultural and other regular production activity outside the market, the more horrendous the conceptual and methodological problems that arise. Some developing countries have been more heroic in their attempts to cope with this than others.

You *can* substantiate an accusation that the national accounting conventions lead all countries to exclude the unpaid *domestic* services of women (as distinct from their *unpaid participation in the production of goods and services which in the general case are marketed*) [my emphasis]. But, to be fair, you would have to admit that the exclusion is due to the demonstrable difficulty of producing meaningful and reliable estimates of the market value of such activities where appropriate market prices do not exist. (It is *not* appropriate to value a Papua New Guinea housewife's time on domestic duties in a rural household at the hourly wage rate for women at the local plantation—the fact is that a very much lower wage rate than that would have to be accepted if all the housewives entered the very limited market for the kind of services they could offer.)

The reader will judge whether or not a case for deliberate bias against measuring the productive effort of women (and the destructive effort of men) is established. But, again, domestic services—their full possible range from prostitution to health care to maintenance worker to counsellor to domestic servant—are the production of goods and services that, in the general (i.e., male) case, are marketed. Childbearing and childrearing and children may not, in the general case, be marketed, but markets are most certainly established for them. In addition, I would hotly dispute the proposal that the goods and services (other than domestic) that the UNSNA says women produce are generally marketed. That assumption is not "an indisputable fact of experience" and in my observation is quite the reverse.

Then comes a *very* interesting paragraph from Fergie:

Certainly there is nothing sexist in this limitation of "economic" production to the kind of goods and services which are generally marketed and therefore capable of measurement in money value terms. The unpaid domestic activities of men are also considerable and equally defy measurement on a basis that would allow legitimate comparison over time or between different communities. Consider, for example, the role of men in a country like [Papua New Guinea] who provide such unpaid services as tribal government, law making, family discipline, security from attack, witchdoctoring, etc., which they might assert occupies all their spare time outside of their "economic production" and recreational and sleeping time. And how does one put a "true" value on the unpaid services of the warrior or on the underpaid services of the conscripted soldier?

Is he saying that the sexism in the limitation of economic production is simply coincidence? No, he says that men's unpaid activities don't count either. This would include household repairs and car maintenance. Measurement has been made of this, and the invisibility of this sort of unpaid work by men is a fraction of that of women. But then note the rural Papua New Guinea examples: tribal government, law making, family discipline, security from attack, "witchdoctoring." All of these have their urban, paid (and overwhelmingly male) equivalents. Men are paid to *reproduce social relationships* or to reproduce patriarchy. Women have their equivalent forms of unpaid reproductive work (and much more besides), but they are called community relations, problem solving, childrearing and family relations, protector, healer. They perform these functions, while men have recreation time. And as for the true value of a warrior or soldier—my contention would be, as I discuss later, that the cost is a negative, that war is not growth or development, that legitimized murder is destructive and a debit to our global accounts.

In the body of my paper I wrote, "The work on imputing a value to what women do has been largely conducted in academic institutions in developed countries with an urban bias. This has fallen into the trap of assuming that what women do is housework."

Fergie wrote in the margin, "What is your point here? This

is the main omission in developing countries (the other unpaid household activities like house and car maintenance and family chauffeur are omissions that relate mainly to men)."

Fergie's marginalia demonstrate that half the human species needs some assistance in seeing clearly. First, women do a great deal more than housework, which is quite clear in the description of Cathy and Tendai's work at the beginning of chapter 1. Second, if one in every three households on earth is headed by women, then the unpaid household activities that Fergie outlines as referring mainly to men do not occur in anything like the percentage that he would estimate. Third, his comments make it quite clear that he is speaking about middle to upper class populations in the developed world, and it is hardly a generalization that one would expect of a statistician who had worked for a significant period of time in Papua New Guinea and in Jamaica. Finally, it demonstrates that he does not understand the extent to which "housework" includes household maintenance—as if continual cleaning, tidying, laundry, and so on have nothing to do with maintenance.

At one stage of the draft paper, I discussed the research on definitions of housework and drew attention to those of Kathryn E. Walker and Margaret E. Woods of Cornell University.[3] They see housework as a sum of all useful activities performed in the home with a view to providing the goods and services that enable a family to function. The categories of activities that they use are (1) food preparation, (2) care of family members, (3) care of clothing, and (4) shopping, household management, and maintenance of accounts. According to my "participatory observation," the categories are, in fact, insufficient. For example, in respect to food preparation, I commented, "This apparently includes processing but not growing." Fergie crossed out the word *processing* and inserted, "cooking," and in the margin he wrote, "Is it being assumed that these are all female functions? Men are doing all of these things—do you want to have them measured separately by sex?" But if men are doing all of these things, it is extraordinary that Mr. Fergie hadn't noticed that in food preparation a great deal more than cooking goes on.

At one stage in my draft paper I drew attention to a paper by W. H. Garjer on the potential contribution to the GNP of valuing household work. Garjer had commented that "lack of recognition of housework penalizes women who work outside the home because it conceals the fact that these women have two occupations considering the unequal division of household duties within the home." The paper was prepared for the Family Economics–Home Management Section of the American Home Economics Association meeting in Atlantic City in June 1973. At this point on my paper, the Australian deputy statistician wrote, "How authoritative is this forum?"

In the developing world, the omission of women's unpaid work from the national accounts leads to the omission, not simply of cooking and washing, but of hauling water, collecting wood, animal raising activities, and subsistence agriculture. I commented, "In many developing countries the work input of rural women is higher than that of men when measured in terms of time limits." Fergie, displaying at this point his particular conceptual vision, questioned, "Have they considered the input of men in government, security, and other higher level unpaid activities?"

First of all, note the hierarchy operating. These are "higher level activities." Second, you and I both know that, in most time-unit studies, the time that men apparently spend in such occupations is counted as work and is quite differentiated from leisure. But not so for women when they take part in the same sorts of activities. But what, after all, is the distinction between the conversation (as an activity) of men sitting in the sun, chewing their beedlenut and drinking their imported beer while discussing matters of "government security and other higher level activities," and the conversations conducted by women over the wells, collecting water, working together collecting firewood, pounding maize or sorghum, or other "unproductive" household activities?

Statisticians argue that it is difficult to impute a value for any unpaid work in the developing world, whether done by men or women, and that the exclusion is not gender specific. But in my paper I gathered quite sufficient data to describe how, from country to country and from activity to activity, work done by women is, to an overwhelming degree, excluded from the production boundary. I think the evidence overwhelmingly demonstrates that women's invisibility, institutionalized in the so-called developed world, was exported to the rest of the world via the national accounts as another tool of colonization. At this point in my paper, Ron Fergie's excitement could scarcely be contained. He commented that this was not so, not from the perspective of "my thirty years of national accounting experience. What was *exported* was a money value account system that was less than adequate in largely subsistence economics—I don't think it was institutionalising anything other than a method (the only one offering) that enabled diverse activities to be aggregated via the common measuring rod of money value."

Fergie concluded his memo with the following comments:

My feeling about the paper is that you are somehow trying to hang the blame for the (fast disappearing) subservient economic role of women on to the national accountants. This is a bit like blaming the business accounting fraternity for the wrongdoings of corporate directors. Basically the national accountant provides the reporting system *his masters* [my emphasis] want and are prepared to pay for and there is a limit to how far he can go in accounting for activity which the actors do not themselves bother to record. You really should be asking why householders don't bother to account for their non-market activities in money value terms.

I wish you success with your talk. I hope I don't have to rise to the defence of the national accountants who really are innocent bystanders and don't deserve to have their life's work demolished without cause and without promise of anything in its place.

So "it is not my fault"—it is the "householders'" fault. "I do not want my life's work in the service of my masters demolished." Spoken like a good soldier—and good soldiers often display their ideology in the field.

It was at this point that I realized it mattered not at all who was most culpable—the policymakers, the economic theorists, or the statisticians. Each group understood the other, the other's needs, interest, and rules, and comprehended its own self-interest in that cabal.

How Statisticians Think: Revising Reality

As I mentioned, Ron Fergie was largely responsible for the establishment of the UNSNA in Papua New Guinea and in Jamaica. Papers he has written recording this experience enable me to set out some of the methods Fergie used when he assisted in the establishment of national accounts in Papua New Guinea in 1973.

Papua New Guinea needed national accounts in 1973 principally to establish its status for international aid and trade concessions. Fergie outlines the transition in the economy and in the policy priorities of the newly independent administration. Then he describes the problems he was faced with as a statistician and how he overcame these. He writes:

Expatriate economists, who were still in control of development planning in Papua New Guinea, were preoccupied with balance of payments figures. The coalition government did not just want to know about the level of national income, but also about how it was distributed between sectors, profits and wages and rural areas and towns. Perhaps the most notable characteristic of the economy which a system of national accounts needed to monitor was the quite extraordinary transition taking place from a near stone age subsistence economy condition for much of the population to a modern market economy heavily dependent on overseas markets.

Papua New Guinea is one country in which production outside the market is so large and the national price system so imperfect that *the existence of a national income in money value terms is open to challenge on conceptual grounds*. Certainly it could be argued that for a larger part of the population living in the rural villages, the attempt to represent their total market and non-market economic activity in money value terms was far more artificial than it would be for countries where subsistence production is a relatively minor element of total production. It would also have to be conceded that *there was a danger of misusing the accounts in pursuing theoretical problems* of resource allocation on the basis that Keynes's theory was as appropriate to a substantially subsistence economy as to a modern market economy.

In the event, *the statistician made the judgement* [which casts a different light on Fergie's claim that national accountants are "innocent bystanders"] that the influence of the market had become so pervasive and transition towards production mainly for the market was proceeding so rapidly that it was necessary to attempt to monitor the shift from pure subsistence production to mixed market, non-market production. It was necessary to measure both forms of production, consumption and income in common money value terms within the framework of a set of national accounts.

At the same time the decision was made to record non-market components separately from the market components throughout the accounts as well as in combination. This would enable broad generalisations to be made along the lines of (say) "subsistence production in this country is 20% of the gross domestic product today whereas ten years ago it was 50% whilst in that country it is still 45%."

A further advantage of elaborating the [UNSNA] presentation in this way is that it would be possible to distinguish between the reasonably sound elements of the national accounts and the part which is subject to considerable reservations on both conceptual and operational grounds. Thus the statistician warns that while attempts have been made to estimate the volume of non-market transactions and to place monetary value on them, such estimates should be used with reservation since they are somewhat conjectural in nature [my emphases].

Fergie's final caveat actually applies to the whole system, not simply nonmarket transactions. Everything recorded in the national accounts has a value assignment on it. The whole system should be "used with reservations." It is all "somewhat conjectural in nature."

Fergie's warning did not mean to suggest that the nonmonetary or subsistence productive work of women would be included in the accounts. The statistics collected of population and work force characteristics make that immediately apparent. The strong presumption seems to be that women don't work. Here is the list of population and work force characteristics used by Fergie for data collection:

1. Nonindigenous population
2. Indigenous male work force
3. Indigenous males aged ten years or more
4. Indigenous males aged ten years or more per indigenous male worker
5. Indigenous females aged ten years or more
6. Indigenous females aged ten years or more per indigenous male worker
7. Indigenous children under ten years
8. Indigenous children under ten years per indigenous male worker
9. Indigenous male work force
   a) wholly or mainly money-raising
   b) wholly or mainly subsistence

Notice there is no item called "indigenous female work force." Women, along with children, are invisible except as the vicarious liabilities of men (see items 4, 6, and 8).

Much of the value of unpaid work done by the rural male labor force was thought to be imputable—and is imputed. An example of one such transaction, recorded as the production of rural nonvillage producers, is the free or partly paid work of villagers who traditionally provide labor to various agencies (such as local government councils and religious missions). Conceptual problems abound here, but evidently these can be solved if they concern men.

Papua New Guinea is one of the few countries where, Fergie says, it has been "practicable and useful" to distinguish the category "producers of private non-profit services to households." But *only the missions* have been allocated to this cate-

gory.* He claims that data are not available for other bodies—
social clubs, trade unions, professional associations, and political parties. Fergie argues that "the economic activity of these
bodies is not thought significant" compared with the missions.
So it *is* possible, after all, to include nonmonetary work in the
national accounts. But the statisticians decide whose work will
be counted—and, once again, women's work is "not thought
significant."

Where free or partially paid labor is contributed to mission
work or to local government, estimates of the following items
are obtained for each district:

1. The adult population providing such labor.
2. The average number of days' labor provided per person
   per year for district works (e.g., construction and maintenance of major roads, airfields, etc.).
3. The average number of days' labor provided per person
   per year for local government works (e.g., construction
   and maintenance of minor roads).
4. The average number of days' labor provided per person
   per year for mission works (e.g., construction and maintenance of church, school, and hospital buildings and the
   grounds).
5. The average number of days' labor provided per person
   per year for village and tribal works (e.g., construction
   and maintenance of paths, river crossings, ceremonial
   buildings, and areas used for communal activities).
6. The value of payments made in cash or kind to villagers
   for providing labor for district or local government works.

The contribution of free and partly paid labor in the above
categories is imputed by using the ruling minimum-wage rate
in rural areas and then deducting the cash or kind payments
to estimate the value of uncompensated labor provided.

---

*Major contributors to neocolonization in the Pacific area have been conven-
tional and fundamentalist Christian churches.

Somehow one suspects that "construction" does not include the forms of work that women do: weaving for the inside of the mission buildings. One similarly fears that "maintenance" does not include the forms of work that women do: sweeping, for example.

One of the more difficult areas of measurement for imputation in the national accounts of Papua New Guinea is the estimate of production of food for own consumption. Estimates of the value of nonmarket food production (traditional foods consumed in rural villages) are nonetheless made by Fergie's system. An estimation of the total calorie intake from consumption of traditional foods by the indigenous population each year is converted to volume, or the equivalent physical quantity of each food item at harvest. These quantities are valued at the estimated prices current in main centers and rural areas each year. To give estimates of food produced for own consumption in rural villages, the total quantity of each traditional food item harvested or purchased by nonrural village households is subtracted from the total. So, when need be, statisticians *can* devise ways to account for nonmarket food production. But Fergie's work force categories, listed above, would suggest that the labor for all this production is attributed to the indigenous male work force—wholly or mainly subsistence— which is, of course, an outright lie.

Fergie also rises to the challenge in another area of traditional difficulty for imputation—firewood gathering. He estimates that the number of families in rural villages that gather firewood for their own use is 55 percent of the number of males (*sic*) in the wholly or mainly subsistence work force. This is multiplied by the average quantity of firewood used per family per year and by the average price of firewood in order to estimate the value of production of firewood for own consumption in rural villages. Again, a way is devised to account for a nonmarket activity—and, again, the system contains faulty presumptions. It presumes that men collect firewood—or that the collection of firewood is only valuable when men do it. In fact, with some exceptions, the women report that the men simply watch while the women do the work.

In the eyes of statisticians such as Ron Fergie, reality thus shrinks into a cramped picture that includes only hard-working men and nonproductive women. But I have met with rural women from the highlands of Papua New Guinea. I have listened to them speak at a regional conference of the International Council of Women. They spoke of days of enormous physical toil. Yet this toil did not appear on the statistician's ledger sheets. Bride prices, for example, were openly advertised in Port Moresby newspapers, but Fergie excluded "housewives' services"—whether a price was paid or not. When these rural women carried water up and down steep hills as they did for two to three hours a day, it was not productive, Fergie said, because it had no market value. When these rural women gathered firewood as they did several times daily, it was not productive, Fergie concluded, because there was no market price for that firewood in remote rural areas. If wood could be bought in the local town market, then the value could be imputed for the gathering of firewood. But the presumption would still be that it was gathered by the subsistence male work force. In Papua New Guinea, a rural woman is labeled a housewife, not a primary producer.

Fergie himself proved you can impute if you choose to. But the choice of what unpaid activities will be made visible depends entirely on the perception of the participant observer— that is, the statistician in the field.

Nepal: A Case Study in Statistics Gathering

The statistical office of the UN lists the following major difficulties in establishing good statistics in any country:

1. The problem of staff shortages and turnovers.

2. The lack of overall planning and coordination by governments for the collection of statistics.
3. The limit of capacities in a number of countries for the collection of statistics and the high cost of such data collection.
4. The deficiencies in the statistical programs and in the data collected.
5. Delays and bottlenecks in data processing.
6. Problems in statistical training.
7. A limited scope for the application of data collected and a limited amount of money available for analysis of such data.[4]

But even this list does not give one a feel for the magnitude of the practical difficulties of collecting data. Let me describe more of the situations that confront the statistician, first using my own experiences in the country of Nepal. These observations are those of a white, educated New Zealand woman and make her value judgment.

Encountering the People

The buildings below me, and the cattle wandering about the landing strip, signaled my arrival in Kathmandu in 1980. Nepal is, according to international statistics, one of the poorest and least developed countries in the world. More than 90 percent of the population lives in rural areas, dependent on polluted water that hastens the spread of disease. Less than 5 percent of the population has access to electricity. Life expectancy is 41.1 years for females and 43.4 years for males. The infant mortality rates of 137.9 for girls and 128.4 for boys are among the highest in the world. The literacy rate for women is 5 percent and for men 33 percent.[5]

I remember our raft stopping along the Trisuli River on the day of a total eclipse of the sun. On the banks, two women and three girls, aged 4 to 10, were gathering firewood in baskets. My companions asked them whether they knew not to look at the sun. Here, in this country of high illiteracy and, presumably, no transportation or communication systems, they knew that "the tiger was eating the sun" and that their eyes would be harmed if they gazed toward it.

The eyes of the women in the factory I visited in Kathmandu would not be so lucky. As I arrived, at the top of narrow stairs off a side street, I was led into a room that appeared to me at first sight to be totally dark. I had just distinguished figures behind pale candles when a light was switched on—to show the foreigner potential purchases. For the rest of the time, these young women, many of whom may have been sold as workers to the city, worked at their hand-sewing by candlelight. This was in stark contrast to the daylight booths of those with treadle sewing machines—men who operated their own small businesses.

On either side of the river valleys I traveled, the steep slopes were farmed. Though terraced, a vicious cycle of erosion was still evident. In some places the deforestation on the steepest slopes cleared for farming had been the cause. In other areas the need for wood fuel had led to the problem. Aid schemes had sought to preserve and regenerate forestry growth in national parks. The local people had been prohibited from collecting firewood. The only alternative fuel for them was cattle dung. If they burned dung, then they had no fertilizer for their crops, and the crop failures led to further erosion.

For those who lived in Kathmandu, fuel was also a problem. The effects of the international oil price rise, and the landlocked nature of Nepal with its dependency on India for routes to and from the rest of the world, made a fuel price rise inevitable. The price of kerosene, the fuel for the cooking stoves of the urban poor, rose 40 percent. The price of gasoline, consumed by the wealthy families, foreign aid officials, and diplomatic missions, rose 7 percent. Discontent was also on the rise. During my visit I viewed a demonstration march against the government, one of the first in living memory.

Naturally, fuel was consumed by the trucks that transported

anything and everything over the road to India and the road to China. On my trip on the China road, our truck stopped many times to wait its turn for one-way passage on hair-raising narrow mountain ledges. The axle frequently scraped the ground. Slips were often in evidence. Along the sides of the road, women and children squatted, sharp pointed stones in their hands. With these they pounded a larger stone that was placed on a substantial piece of rock. In this way, they made road gravel.

In Nepal, the transportation sector in large part consists of porters, not vehicles. Porters who carry supplies for tourist trekking parties are part of the transportation network (women who carry water for several hours a day are not). Ropeways stretched high above ravines are another frequent form of transportation. Families stand in a small, open, boxlike container, and one of them reaches forward on the rope and hauls the primitive gondola forward.

Compiling the Statistics

It occurs to me that, in 1953 when the UNSNA was first published, the greater part of humanity lived in conditions like those of Nepal, rather than those of wartime Britain or the United States. The arrogance of those who imposed the UNSNA on the rest of the world is, on its own, extraordinary. The conceptual and intellectual leap involved in the imposition itself would be hilarious, if it were not so criminal. Occasionally a person with some consciousness and sensitivity to such impositions can be found, as with Barkay in the case of Nepal.

Nepal is an agricultural country: about 90 percent of the labor force is employed in agriculture; agriculture is the main source of exports and of domestic products. The 1971 Nepal census reported an economic activity rate for population aged 10 years and above of approximately 83 percent for males and 35 percent for females. In contrast, the World Bank's Living Standards Measurement Survey of eight villages reported that adult females spend 4.62 hours daily on activities that fall within the conventional definition of employment, while men spend 5.81 hours on these activities.[6] Anthropological literature on Nepal describes Nepalese women as performing most of the farm work.

The orthodox statistician, working from census data, can be seen already to have understated women's employment. The distortion is even greater if *all work* is considered. Time-use data from the World Bank study show that adult men in Nepal work 7.5 hours a day and women 10.8 hours a day. Male children in the 10 to 14 age group work 4.8 hours a day and female children 7.3 hours. They work at even younger ages—but are seen in the study data only in economic or subsistence activities. A nine year old "playing" with her five-year-old brother is not, according to the World Bank, engaged in child care for the household sector.

Richard M. Barkay, a statistician of twenty-five years field experience, was responsible for the establishment of an estimating procedure for national accounts in the Kingdom of Nepal. Barkay's political mandate was to establish indicators that could assist primarily in domestic policy planning. This in itself distinguishes him from mainstream statisticians. On the question of comprehension and reliability of data, he wrote:

At every turn arbitrary decisions must be made; at the same time one must make the degree of one's lack of knowledge explicit. . . . Great precision of measurement is not always necessary because the important and interesting changes will be sufficiently marked to show up with even crude measurements. . . . It is surprising how much can be learned if the right questions are asked. . . .[7]

Nor was Barkay insensitive to the direct political connection of the statistician with the economist and policymaker.

The task of a dynamic national accounts estimator is to maintain a constant and forceful interest in every aspect of the changing economy. He does not make economic policy, but should provide a continuing stimulus, repeatedly challenging the policy-maker to consider all the issues and the choices.[8]

Barkay also comments on the logistical difficulties, described by the UN Statistical Commission as inhibiting good statistics, that were outlined at the beginning of this section.

The experience of Nepal shows that basic information for many significant sectors of the economy is not lacking; what is lacking is an efficient reporting system, able to supply an up-to-date flow of the required information. By expediting this flow even a meagre statistical staff can supply the planner with national accounts data suited to his purpose. The trouble is that the required information and concepts should be planning oriented, and at the same time should fit statistical categories and methods.

Even in a country with a very narrow data base and scarce statistical resources a modified system of national accounts can be established. The prevailing belief, that Nepal simply does not have the apparatus needed to gather the sort of statistics necessary for a real understanding of the economy, is not justified. The system of accounts, essential for development planning and analysis, can be produced within the planning agency timetable and can be sufficiently detailed and accurate for short-term planning, provided the data collection methodology is adapted to the sources of data.[9]

Barkay advocated adopting flexible observation and measurement procedures. He acknowledged the arbitrariness of both the boundary of production and the concept of value. For Barkay, economic activities includes food processing, fuel and water collection, and manufacturing for home use—i.e., all activities that result in increasing material resources within the household. He argues that in industrial countries, the major part of food processing, fuel and water collection, and home construction is performed outside the household and, hence, are considered income-generating activities. The fact that these same activities are often performed within the household in Nepal and other developing countries is not sufficient reason for excluding them from the definition of economic activities. Unfortunately, Barkay is one of a few statisticians whose work includes women. That work fails to influence the U.N. Statistical Commission.

But Barkay joins Fergie in distinguishing between developed and developing countries, as if the more difficult conceptual problems occur only in nonmarket economies. Together, their work implies that Tendai is a problem, but Cathy is not as difficult. My own suspicion is that the activities of women in developing countries are so dramatically different in nature (but not in effect) from the activities of women in the so-called developed world, that Western men *notice* it. Cathy does not appear a difficulty, for her chores fit in the class of taken-for-granted tasks of "housework." Cathy does not see things this way, as we shall see in chapter 5.

5. The Statistical Conspiracy

Sources for the National Accounts

In practice, the national accounts for any country are compiled from a wide range of statistics derived from a variety of sources. While some of these sources provide a direct measure of economic activity during a period, others are used as indicators of movements, such as consumer price indexes. To give an idea of the variety of sources involved, let me briefly summarize those used by economists in my own country, New Zealand. While New Zealand has a small population (3.3 million) and only about 200,000 "transactors," the methods of data collection are comparable with those of most developed countries.

The main sources for the New Zealand national accounts are economic and other censuses conducted by the Department of Statistics. The economic censuses collect statistical data within the national accounting framework; examples of these are the censuses of manufacturing, financial services, and local authorities. Other censuses, such as the annual agricultural census, collect a wider range of data. More frequent than censuses are sample surveys conducted by the Department of Statistics. These include the quarterly manufacturing and retail trade surveys and the annual household income and expenditure survey. Administration records of central and local government agencies include income tax returns, import and export documents, and building permits. Other government departments or other agencies also carry out surveys. The labor department's quarterly employment information survey, the mines department survey of mineral production, or producer board survey (e.g., Wool Board, Dairy Board, Meat Board) statistics are included.

Material is also collected from the central government public accounts and the financial accounts of other organizations funded or effectively controlled by central government. The published financial accounts of private enterprises such as listed public companies, producer boards, and nonprofit organizations are all consulted and used, as is price data from ad hoc surveys conducted by the Department of Statistics to support the construction of price indexes. The price indexes (such as the consumer price index, the producer price index, the capital expenditure price index, nominal weekly wage rate index, and the farm input price index) are used to deflate current price national accounts aggregates to produce the constant price accounts. This is the technique used to arrive at expressions of costs in "constant dollar" terms.

The current position in regard to key sources material and indices used in the establishment of the national accounts is well summarized by a recent letter I received from a friend, Janine Haines, deputy leader of the Australia Democratic party. I had written asking her for some more detail on the collection of data and questions of imputation in the Australian economy. A member of her staff contacted the Australian Bureau of Statistics and received the following reply:

There are at least three hundred different forms used in collecting data for the national accounts. None of the forms contains any information on the labour performed by women in the home. The principle behind collection of data for the national accounts is that no data is included of production where the producer is also the consumer.

Further, it is difficult to put a value on work performed in the home. One could look at how much a family with both partners working spent on people to come in and do the cleaning, mind the kids, etc. We could measure how many hours work a woman spends cleaning, cooking, child minding, etc., and attribute award wages for this labour. All the methods are arbitrary and imperfect, and the household surveys have never attempted to gather such data, nor, given the fact that our surveys are compulsory, is there likely to be much support for our asking questions like "how much time did you spend cleaning, cooking, etc."

If therefore the Senator wants to find out if women's domestic labour is measured in the household accounts the answer is no. Looking at three hundred forms won't tell her any more, but if she is crazy enough to still want a copy of all three hundred we will of course send them.[1]

There seems to be an extraordinary consistency of tone in the communications we politicians received from Australian statisticians. And since I cannot deal with three hundred forms, it seems practicable to look at the most universal, the census.

The Census

Every country is expected to conduct a census of population every ten years. The more "statistically developed" repeat the survey every five years. This census of population, supplemented by labor force surveys and censuses of business and agriculture, forms a major part of the data base for the compilation of national accounts and for that key derivative, per capita GDP.

The primary topics recommended by the UN for the 1980 global round of censuses included the following:

1. sex
2. age
3. relationship to head or other reference person
4. marital status
5. place of residence
6. educational attainment
7. economic activity status
8. occupation
9. industry
10. employment status

Time worked, income, and sector of employment were also included in some censuses.

But don't be too encouraged by that list. Neither Tendai nor Cathy, the women we met in chapter 1, have an occupation, industry, or employment status and neither worked for any time. The brotherhood of economics is intent on its conspiracy.

Large numbers of women remark at the anger they feel as respondents to their country's census, anger at the lack of interest in their lives, anger at their invisibility. But then the form disappears, and the anger abates—until next time, when they are again confronted by their institutionalized invisibility: a bitter mixture of the economists' theories, the policy planners' conceptual framework, and the statisticians' data-recording difficulties.

The population census, the census of agriculture, and the household labor force survey serve as examples of this bitter mixture. They will now be examined so that we might assess the degrees, in Joan Robinson's words, of "validity" and "propaganda" to be found in them. But however profoundly inadequate and universally sexist we might find the conceptual basis of these examples, their sexism is not the "problem" with which the economists and statisticians are preoccupied—as we shall see.

The Census of Population

Most of us have seen a census form. As a child I remember being very put out that I did not have a form of my own to fill in. I also remember that, while both my parents sat at the table with the interviewer, it was my father who responded to all the questions. That memory points to one of the major problems with the census: it focuses on households, not individuals, and in doing so it leaves out women and children.

Of the developed countries, Canada is generally recognized as having a highly sophisticated statistical arm of government. The last census of Canada was completed on June 3, 1986. In form and content, it is representative of census forms in the Western countries, so we will use it as our chief example.

If this questionnaire comes to the household of Cathy, our North American friend from chapter 1, she and her spouse will fill in the first seven questions independently (see table 4).* The first task will be for the household to nominate a *reference person*—the term now adopted in Canada (and elsewhere) in preference to head of the household.

The next six questions relate to the physical characteristics of the dwelling. The census defines a dwelling as "a separate set of living quarters with a private entrance from the outside or from a common hallway or stairway inside the building. This entrance should not be through someone else's living quarters." Then the census asks for the name of the person who is *primarily responsible* for paying the rent, mortgage, taxes, and electricity for the dwelling. Even if Cathy has asserted that she is the reference person, she now names her spouse. But aren't there myriad possibilities in the structures of households I've discussed and those you can think of? And is primary responsibility a category possible only for the earners of income—or might the savers and household budgeters, who technically pay for these items, lay claim to this role? Why is this question necessary?

The remaining questions in this section of the census query the number of persons who live in the dwelling, its age, its size, the main type of heating or fuel used, and the yearly payments for the same fuel. Tendai, our friend in Zimbabwe, collected wood for her household's fuel, and there were no payments for it. Similarly in my home, my heating is a fireplace, fuelled by firewood collected by me from fallen pine boughs. In both cases, in the Canadian census, fuel would be collected and used without any production or consumption taking place. If, to quote the census, "the main type of heating

---

*You may like to answer this according to your own circumstances and see if it makes you feel as enraged as I feel.

Table 4.

Census of Canada Questionnaire, Questions 2–7

---

2. Relationship to Person 1.

Husband or wife of Person 1
Common-law partner of Person 1
Son or daughter of Person 1
Father or mother of Person 1
Brother or sister of Person 1
Son-in-law or daughter-in-law of Person 1
Father-in-law or mother-in-law of Person 1
Brother-in-law or sister-in-law of Person 1

Grandchild of Person 1
Nephew or niece of Person 1
Other relative of Person 1 (print below)
Lodger
Lodger's husband or wife
Lodger's son or daughter
Roommate
Employee
Other nonrelative (print below)

3. Date of Birth

——— ——— ———
Day   Month   Year

4. Sex

☐ Male

☐ Female

5. Marital Status

Now married
(excluding separated)
Separated
Divorced
Widowed
Never married
(single)

6. What is the language you first learned in childhood and still understand?

English
French
Italian
German
Ukrainian

————————————
Other (specify)

7. Do you consider yourself an
   Aborignal person or a native
   Indian of North America, that
   is, Inuit, North Amercan Indian, or Metis?

   _____ No, I do not consider
   myself Inuit, North
   American Indian, or
   Metis
   _____ Yes, Inuit
   _____ Yes, status or regis-
   tered Indian
   _____ Yes, nonstatus Indian
   _____ Yes, Metis

Source: 1986 census of Canada.

equipment for the dwelling" is "other, e.g, fireplace" and if
"the fuel or energy used most for heating this dwelling" is
"wood" and if "for this dwelling the yearly payments" for wood
are "none," then that is the case. But in one season both Tendai
and I spend hours working to ensure a supply of that fuel.
Why isn't this of interest to the census-takers?

Renters and owners are then asked the monthly cash rent or
monthly mortgage payments and property taxes for the dwelling. Also included is the question "If you were to sell this
dwelling now, for how much would you expect to sell it?"
These figures are collected to impute the value of properties
for the purpose of national accounts.

Questions 14 to 24 in the 1986 Canadian census are included
in table 5 to demonstrate the range of questions deemed of
priority importance in the population census.* These vary from

---

*The 1980 census of the United States asked seven population questions of
every person and nine housing questions about every housing unit. Twenty
additional questions were asked of a sample (about 19 percent nationwide) of
households. "Children ever born" was one such sample question in 1980. Responses were used in the computation of fertility rates. After being asked sev-

time to time and country to country and tend to reflect some response to public pressure for policy change in areas such as racism, disability, or fertility.

In the Canadian census of 1986, it was questions 25–32 (see table 6) that ensured that Cathy disappeared from the economically productive population. She would have been expected to answer "None" to question 25(a); to check "No, personal and family responsibilities" in response to question 25(e); and on declaring, at question 26, that she had "last worked" before 1985, Cathy would be directed to "Go to question 32." At that point, since housework (undefined) has become the generic term for *all* unpaid work that women do, Cathy is not encouraged to record her unpaid economic activity. But if Cathy is one of those increasing number of women who protest enforced compliance in their own enslavement and invisibility, she will describe her work whether or not the census asks for it. Table 6 includes the responses, that every woman on the planet has the opportunity to make, in kind, in the 1990 global round of censuses.

But assuming that Cathy does not take that step, you can see that the policymakers will derive from the statistics a picture, small though it is, of Cathy's spouse. They will know little about Cathy. The system says that "the average number of economically active is an indicator of the economic base of the family." Cathy, you will remember, is "economically inactive." She apparently adds nothing to the economic base of her

---

eral times in previous censuses, this question was omitted in the 1986 New Zealand census. A discussion paper issued by the U.S. Bureau of the Census in 1986 ("Alternatives and Issues Concerning the 1990 Census Subject Content, Data Products, and Geographic Areas") suggests replacing this question with one that asks if a woman has had any children and/or whether she has had a birth in the last year. This would "permit the development of a current population profile of mothers with newborn children."

I wonder why that is wanted? I'm sure it's not to offer assistance to such mothers. The motive would seem to me to more likely be connected with the higher birth rates in the black and hispanic communities, particularly among teenage women.

Table 5.

Census of Canada Questionnaire, Questions 14–24

---

14. Where were you born?
15. Of what country are you a citizen?
16. In what year did you first immigrate to Canada?
17. To which ethnic or cultural group(s) do you or did your ancestors belong?
18. What language do you **yourself** speak at home now?
19. Can you speak English or French well enough to conduct a conversation?
20. (a) Are you limited in the kind or amount of activity that you can do because of a long-term physical condition, mental condition, or health problem?
    (b) Do you have any long-term disabilities or handicaps?
21. (a) What is the **highest** grade (or year) of **secondary** (high) or **elementary** school you ever attended?
    (b) How many years of education have you ever completed at **university**?
    (c) How many years of schooling have you ever completed at an institution **other than** a university, secondary (high), or elementary school? Include years of schooling at community colleges, institutes of technology, CEGEPs (general and professional), private trade schools or private business colleges, diploma schools of nursing, etc.
22. What degrees, certificates, or diplomas have you ever obtained?
23. What was the major field of study of your **highest** degree, certificate, or diploma (**excluding** secondary or high school graduation certificates)?
24. Where did you live five years ago, that is, on June 1, 1981?

Source: 1986 Census of Canada.

household. Cathy is subsumed in a vicarious relationship with her spouse and his income. She is not alone in this.

It seems to me that if we are to recognize the productive and consumptive work of Cathy and millions of women and children everywhere as economic activity, then the concepts of

Table 6.

Census of Canada Questionnaire, Questions 25–32 (including sample responses from Cathy, a woman who considers housework genuine work)

---

25. (a) Last week, how many hours did you work (not including housework, maintenance, or repairs for your own home)? Include as work:
- working without pay in a family farm or business (e.g., assisting in seeding, doing accounts);
- working in your own business, farm, or professional practice, alone or in partnership;
- working for wages, salary, tips, or commission.

   _[96]_ Number of hours (to the nearest hour). Go to Question 27

   OR,

   _____ None. Continue with Questions 25(b) to 32

   (b) Last week, were you on temporary lay-off or absent from your job or business?
   Mark one box only
   ☑ No
   ☐ Yes, on temporary lay-off from a job to which I expect to return
   ☐ Yes, on vacation, ill, on strike or locked out, or absent for other reasons

   (c) Last week, did you have definite arrangements to start a new job within the next four weeks?
   ☑ No
   ☐ Yes

   (d) Did you look for work during the past four weeks? For example, did you contact a Canada Employment Centre, check with employers, place or answer newspaper ads?
   Mark one box only
   ☑ No. Go to Question 26
   ☐ Yes, looked for full-time work
   ☐ Yes, looked for part-time work (less than 30 hours per week)

Table 6 continued

(e) Could you have started work last week had a job been
available?

Mark one box only

☐ Yes, could have started work

☑ No, already had a job

☐ No, temporary illness or disability

☐ No, personal or family responsibilities

☐ No, going to school

☐ No, other reasons

26. When did you last work, even for a few days (not including
housework, maintenance, or repairs for your own home)?

Mark one box only

☑ In 1986 ⎫
☐ In 1985 ⎬ Answer Questions 27 to 32
⎭

☐ Before 1985—Go to Question 32

27. **NOTE:** Questions 27 to 30 refer to your job or business last
week. If you held no job last week, answer for your job of
longest duration since January 1, 1985. If you held more than
one job last week, answer for the job at which you worked the
most hours.

(a) For whom did you work?

_____

  [My husband and family]
_____

Name of firm, government agency, etc.

_____

  [Household]   ╲
_____

Department, branch, division, section, or plant

(b) What kind of business, industry, or service was this?

_____

  [Production and reproduction of conditions of life]
_____

Give full description, for example, wheat farm, trapping, road
maintenance, retail shoe store, secondary school, temporary help
agency, municipal policy.

_____

  [see attached (prepared list, as per chapter 1)]
_____

Table 6 continued

28. At what address did you work? If no usual place of work, see Guide.

Mark one box only

(i) ☑ Worked at home (includes living and working on the same farm)

(ii) ☐ Worked outside Canada

(iii) ☐ Worked at the address below (please specify) _____

> If street address is not known, give the building name, shopping centre, or street intersection, etc.

[Cathy's household address]

Number   Street

> If you worked in a suburban municipality within a large urban area, specify that municipality, not the main city.

City, town, village, township, other municipality, or Indian reserve

---

County   Province or territory

29. (a) What kind of work were you doing?

[slave labor]

For example, accounting clerk, door-to-door salesperson, civil engineer, secondary school teacher, chief electrician, food processing laborer, fishing guide. (If in the Armed Forces, give rank.)

(b) In this work, what were your most important activities or duties?

[multiple]

For example, verifying invoices, selling cosmetics, managing the research department, teaching mathematics, supervising construction electricians, cleaning vegetables, guiding fishing parties.

Table 6 continued

30. (a) In this job were you mainly:

☐ working for wages, salary, tips, or commission?

☑ working without pay for your spouse or another relative in a family farm or business?

} Go to Question 31

☐ self-employed without paid help (alone in partnership)?

☐ self-employed with paid help (alone or in partnership)?

} Continue with Question 30 (b)

(b) If self-employed, was your farm or business incorporated?

☐ No

☐ Yes

31. (a) In how many weeks did you work during 1985 (not including housework, maintenance, or repairs for your own home)?
Include those weeks in which you:

• were on vacation or sick leave with pay;
• were self-employed or an unpaid worker in a family farm or business;
• worked full time or part time.

☐ None.   Go to question 32

OR

52 Number of weeks

(b) During most of those weeks, did you work full time or part time?
Mark one box only

☑ Full time

☐ Part time

Table 6 continued

32. During the year ending December 31, 1985, did you receive any income or suffer any loss from the sources listed below?

- If yes, please mark the "Yes" box and enter the amount; in case of a loss, also mark the "Loss" box.
- If no, please mark the "No" box and proceed to the next source.
- Do **not** include family allowances and child tax credits.
- Please consult the Guide for details.

AMOUNT

(a) Total wages and salaries including commissions, bonuses, tips, etc., before any deductions
☐ Yes _____ ☐ Loss
☐ No

(b) Net nonfarm self-employment income (gross receipts minus expenses) from unincorporated business, professional practice, etc., on own account or in partnership
☐ Yes _____ ☐ Loss
☐ No

(c) Net farm self-employment income (gross receipts minus expenses) from agricultural operations on own account or in partnership
☐ Yes _____ ☐ Loss
☐ No

(d) Old age security pension and guaranteed income supplement from federal government only (provincial income supplements should be reported in (g)
☐ Yes _____
☐ No

Table 6 continued

(e) Benefits from Canada or Quebec Pension Plan ☐ Yes _____

☐ No

(f) Benefits from Unemployment Insurance (total benefits before tax deductions) ☐ Yes _____

☐ No

(g) Other income from government sources including provincial income supplements and grants and social assistance, e.g., veterans' pensions, workers' compensation, welfare payments (do not include family allowances and child tax credits) (See Guide) ☐ Yes _____

☐ No

(h) Dividends and interest on bonds, deposits and savings certificates, and other investment income, e.g., net rents from real estate, interest from mortgages ☐ Yes _____ ☐ Loss

☐ No

(i) Retirement pensions, superannuation, and annuities ☐ Yes _____

☐ No

(j) Other money income, e.g., alimony, scholarships ☐ Yes _____

☐ No

(k) Total income from all of the above sources ☐ Yes _____ ☐ Loss

☐ No   [*nil*]

Source: 1986 Census of Canada.

head of household and reference person have to go. The census must be of individuals, not of households.

The Census of Agriculture

While censuses of agriculture were devised primarily for income and production accounts, the greater importance now of these statistics is to assist in dealing with issues of poverty, unemployment, malnutrition, and with policies for special groups such as landless agricultural laborers, women, children, and refugees. While the needs for and uses of the data might have changed, the conceptual base of collection has not. As we shall see, it continues to perpetuate the invisibility of the vast majority of the world's food producers—women.

In a census of agriculture we meet another conceptual difficulty—that of a *holding* and a *holder*. The UN Food and Agriculture Organization (FAO), which sets the international guidelines for such a census, defines a holding as a unit of agricultural production comprising all the land used completely or partly for agricultural purposes and all livestock operated under the management of an individual or group without regard to legal ownership.

The holder is the person who exercises control over the operations of the holding and is responsible for the utilization of available resources. FAO consultant statisticians Casley and Lury note:

Many apparent holders are not truly so. The holder must be taking the responsibility for the production of the crops and their disposal. A holder may not make day-to-day decisions about the operation of part or all of his holding because he is satisfied with the way his son or his wife is acting on his behalf. He would interfere if he became dissatisfied with the operations carried out. For example if the wife of the head of the household omits to weed the maize on a piece of land for which she appears to be taking operational responsibility the head may instruct her to do so. In such a case it is the head of the household who is the holder.[2]

For the purpose of collecting data on agriculture and in survey programs, identification of agricultural households is recommended as follows: "A household is considered to be an agricultural household when at least one member of the household is operating a holding (farming household) or when the household head, reference person, or main income earner is economically active mainly in agriculture."[3]

For millions of men, being "economically active mainly in agriculture" principally comprises overseeing and bossing their wives and children, who do the work on the men's land.

It is possible that a proportion of households connected with agriculture will not be covered. This includes those households that do not operate a holding or those where the head, reference person, or main income earner is not "economically active mainly in agriculture." In censuses of agriculture, the concept of holding has usually been limited to those above a certain size in area. Consequently, the most vulnerable section of the agricultural population has not been investigated at all.

Among the characteristics of holdings that the FAO suggests collecting, we find the following topics. The information collected will include the total time (in work days per year) worked on each of these agricultural operations.

1. preparation of the land
2. sowing or planting
3. crop husbandry (care of growing crop)
4. harvesting
5. animal husbandry
6. marketing the produce
7. administration and supervision
8. other

Perhaps weeding is supposed to be included under crop husbandry. Perhaps food processing and storage are collected under harvesting or marketing the produce. Perhaps the vast bulk of the labor hours that many women perform are all supposed to be included under "other." What may appear to be a subtle slip of gender blindness in categorizing activities, is symptomatic of a calculated disregard for what women do.

Citizens of Canada who "operated a farm, ranch, or other agricultural holding (feedlots, greenhouses, nurseries, institutional farms, mushroom houses, and fur farms) with sales of agricultural products during the past twelve months of $250 or more" were required to fill in the 1986 census of agriculture. Agricultural products included livestock and poultry, dairy products and eggs, field crops, fruits and vegetables, mushrooms, greenhouse and nursery products, sod, fur-bearing animals, honey and beeswax, and maple products.

The "operator," the person responsible for the day-to-day decisions made in the operation of the holding, was legally required to fill in the census. If the holding was operated as a partnership, the name and address of one of the partners was to be entered as the operator. Of all the agricultural produce that was home-processed or home-consumed, the operator was invited to include only "poultry production for use at home" on the census. Under "farm business expenses," cash wages paid for housework are specifically excluded. Under "hired agricultural labour," the operator was instructed not to include housework or custom work or other nonagricultural work.

The Canadian census of agriculture is used to "ascertain the importance and wellbeing of Canadian agriculture in relation to the total economy, and to evaluate the impact of agricultural policies and programmes. The data on hired labour are used by agricultural and manpower researchers and administrators for estimating and evaluating labour requirements and planning training programmes. Questions on off-farm work make it possible to identify the number of part-time and full-time farmers and to measure the impact on agricultural production." Or at least that is the theory.

In the Canadian census of agriculture, as in so many others, a woman whose hours of work on the farming venture would be the equivalent to a full-time paid worker, but who works in an unpaid capacity, is utterly invisible both as a producer and a consumer. She will also be invisible as a beneficiary in all the policies that flow to the agricultural sector of the Canadian economy.

The Ministry of Agriculture and Food in Ontario estimates that rural women are involved in those "economic inactivities" from 80 to 101 hours weekly. If Cathy had a sister who had married an Ontario farmer, her sister would typically accept more of the responsibility for childrearing than her partner. She would prepare the meals, clean the house, do the laundry for her family and, in some cases, for the hired farm labor as well. Except for some financial management advice and shopping, her husband would be unlikely to help with domestic chores. Along with 85 to 90 percent of the other rural women in Ontario, she would help in the operation of the total farm enterprise. About 50 percent of those women would help with physical work on the farm, 25 percent of them doing it the year round. Involved in a variety of crop, livestock, and dairy operations, she would help operate, maintain, and repair farm equipment. In addition, along with 80 to 90 percent of her sisters in the region, she would assist in the business aspects of the farm—keeping records and accounts, preparing tax returns, paying bills, ordering and collecting farm supplies, and checking market prices. She would make daily and seasonal decisions jointly with her husband and other business partners about cropping plans, livestock, and machinery, and about negotiating loans and mortgages.[4]

The rural Canadian woman's experience is mirrored in many ways in the United States. Carolyn Sachs, in her book *The Invisible Farmers*,[5] gives us a picture of the daily lives of rural American women (see table 7). Dr. Rachel Rosenfeld, a sociologist at the University of North Carolina, whose data was the basis of Carolyn Sachs's table, says that on their tax forms very few of these farm women identified themselves as farmers.* At

---

*Studies in Australia show more women than previously filing returns to the taxation office as "employer" or self-employed "primary producer." But of

the same time, over half of the women considered themselves to be operators of their farms or ranches. And over half the married women thought that they could continue farming if something happened to their husbands. Thus there seemed to be a relatively high sense among these women of their roles as current or potential farmers.[6] But do American agricultural economists share that sense? Let's take a look.

The United States census of agriculture, produced by the Department of Commerce, collects primary data on commodity production, prices, resource use, and the characteristics of farmers, farm households, and farm workers. From these primary data, government agencies then generate statistical information (including price indexes, costs of production, indicators of farm income and wealth, and sectoral value added), with productivity and other aggregate indicators, for the national accounts. The substantial addition to social and economic statistics on farm households in the 1964 U.S. census has never been repeated. In that year, a special survey on farm labor collected information on *all* workers, including unpaid family members. This supplies the best data base for agricultural policy planning. The failure to continue with this base has had serious consequences in the lack of government policy response to the major rural depression in the U.S.

Instead, the U.S. Department of Agriculture (USDA) index of labor-input weights all hours, regardless of the difference in education, age, sex, and occupation of workers. Furthermore, the USDA labor-input data are not determined from surveys of hours worked or workers committed to agricultural production. Rather the labor-input is calculated on a requirement basis using estimated quantities of labor required for various production activities.

---

these, most have stated "housewife" as their occupation for census purposes (see Kerry James, "Women on Australasian Farms: A Conceptual Scheme," *Australian and New Zealand Journal of Sociology* 18 [1982]: 305). Statements on taxation returns more likely reflect an accountant's advice to avoid taxes than the woman's concept of her role or the reality of her work.

Table 7.

Farm Women's Invovlement in Farm and Home Tasks

	Percentage responding		
	Regular Duty	Occa-sionally	Never
Plowing, disking, cultivating, or planting	11	25	63
Applying fertilizers, herbicides, or insecticides	5	12	83
Doing other field work without machinery	17	25	58
Harvesting crops or other products, including running machinery or trucks	22	29	49
Taking care of farm animals, including herding or milking dairy cattle	37	29	34
Running farm errands, such as picking up repair parts or supplies	47	38	15
Making major purchases of farm or ranch supplies and equipment	14	23	63
Marketing products—that is, dealing with wholesale buyers or selling directly to consumers	15	18	67
Bookkeeping, maintaining records, paying bills, or preparing tax forms for the operation	61	17	22
Doing household tasks like preparing meals, house cleaning, and so on	97	2	1
Supervising the farm work of other family members	24	26	50
Supervising the work of hired farm labor	11	25	64
Taking care of a vegetable garden or animals for family consumption	74	14	12
Looking after children	74	13	13
Working on a family or in-home business other than farm or ranch work	34	13	53

Source: Carolyn E. Sachs, *The Invisible Farmers: Women in Agricultural Production* (Totowa NJ: Rowan & Allanheld, 1983), 39.

Yet for years or even decades it has been assumed that a certain rate of productivity flows from a certain number of visible paid workers. Government policies are made on this basis. The assumptions of per capita production will be far in advance of the truth. If the per capita production of unpaid and invisible family workers were taken into account, government policies that attempt to hold the tide of recession in agriculture would be different in developed as well as developing countries.

Economists often argue that the magnitude of such work is of little or no importance. It is not an argument advanced by mothers or housewives. In 1977 the USDA's nationwide food consumption survey indicated that 18 percent of the total money value of vegetables used at home was home-produced. An average gardening household saved approximately $40 per year on vegetables. This was approximately 20 percent of the average amount spent on vegetables in 1977 by nongardening households. Quite apart from the fact that this is significant enough to measure in the consumer price index, it has obvious health and nutrition policy implications. The study showed that rural households were more likely than urban to engage in such production and that home owners were more likely than tenants to garden. Households with a nonearning homemaker gardened more; households with only a single adult or preschool children gardened less. Households with members aged fifty-five or more had a high probability of gardening.

This significant production is not recorded anywhere as work or as production. My suspicion is that the results of the 1977 survey were used more for the marketing implications for major national and multinational food producers than for determining well-being, health, nutrition, and income substitution priorities in the policy machine.

Household Labor Force Surveys

Household surveys are among the most flexible of all data-gathering mechanisms. In principle, any subject can be explored, and the concepts and level of detail can be adapted to the requirements of the investigation.[7]

Whatever their flexibility, such surveys are still designed to meet specific objectives in terms of national accounts. The statistics are used to construct consumer price indexes and to furnish data on levels and distribution of household income. They are used to show differences in consumption and expenditure between rural and urban groups. In turn, these figures provide the data for compiling household accounts in the system of national accounts, and they provide data for estimating the distributed effects of taxation and social benefits.

Despite the boasts of flexibility inherent in the household survey system, the well-being of a population will never be truly assessed while households remain the respondent unit. The vast majority of populations become invisible when subsumed by income earners. A good example of this approach is given by Casley and Lury in their description of international practice.

We prefer to call a household survey one in which the household is the final sample unit and also provides the unit of reference for the major focus of this survey. Questions may be asked of individual members of the household, but these are aimed at itemising individual components of household activities in order to obtain the household data by aggregation. Surveys of subjects such as *fertility, child nutrition, food intake* and *energy expenditure* are surveys of *individuals*, although the individuals are also household members and membership of the household will determine to some extent the individual's fertility, health and consumption habits.[8]

Since Casley and Lury also define a household as "comprising a person or group of persons, generally bound by ties of kinship, who live together under a single roof or within a single compound and who share a community of life in that they are answerable to the same head and share a common source of food," it should be obvious that the perceived head of household won't know the answers to these individual questions. It is difficult to escape the conclusion that the male world is concerned with the well-being of the community (that is, the community of men) and that the female world is concerned with individuals. But the (manifestly strained) demarcation established by Casley and Lury enables the establishment of an invisibility of the majority of the human species by way of statistical treatment.

The New Zealand government's labor force survey serves as an example of such household surveys. The New Zealand Department of Statistics boasts that the survey provides "a complete, up to date and accurate measure of the labour force." The department maintains (in a timely reminder to us about how this system affects our lives) that "labour force statistics are used by government, business, economists, social scientists, and many others in the study of our economy." The statistics provide "better information . . . to initiate appropriate policies."

The average housewife is expected to respond that she is not seeking work because of "family responsibilities." Evidently, "government, business, economists, social scientists, and many others" are not interested to know that she worked ninety-plus hours, without overtime, without pay; that she cannot remember when she last had a holiday; that she would prefer to work shorter hours; or that she has no suitable child care. The "average housewife" does not work, and the household is not a productive enterprise.

A Strategy for Making Change

Let me describe briefly the history of our pressure to change the census in New Zealand. In 1983, and in keeping with the practice in many countries, the Department of Statistics invited submissions on how the census might be altered. Two hundred and fifty-seven replies were received. Forty-four submissions requested the inclusion of a question on voluntary work; twenty-eight advocated a question on unpaid household work.

All labor force questions in the 1981 census had related to those in paid work but included unpaid relatives assisting in business and those unemployed and seeking work. Those not in these categories were required to check "nil" for hours worked, check "nil" for occupation, and check "not applicable" for the name of the employing organization, address of workplace, industry, and main means of travel to work. In the question on employment status, they had to choose between retired, full-time student, housewife, or other.

The submissions to the department advanced substantial reasons for the inclusion of a question on voluntary work. For example, voluntary work needs to be considered "real work" and recognized because pressure for shorter working weeks, job sharing, increasing unemployment, and other major societal changes will affect voluntary organizations in a variety of ways. A question on voluntary work in the census might assist organizations in their requests for government assistance. Statistics could ensure effective planning for the services and the number of volunteers needed. Voluntary work needs to be recognized, argued these submissions, as being as important as paid work in reaching a realistic measure of economic and social activity in society. And such information is needed for future planning; whether for road building or child care, transportation or social security, full details of the population and work force are needed, not just details on those in "paid work."

The growing political mobilization of women in New Zealand on this issue was reflected in the twenty-one women's forums held around the country late in 1984. It ranged from calls for society at large to acknowledge volunteers' contributions as "real work" to practical requests such as free job training, reimbursement for travel and other expenses, provision of child care, and tax recognition. These women argued that while the overwhelmingly male financial donations to charity are claimed as tax deductions, the overwhelmingly female capital donations of time, skills, and labor are not tax-deductible. Specifically, the women wanted their voluntary work to be taken into consideration as previous work experience when they move back into the paid work force.

The government, on advice from the chief statistician, decided that "voluntary work" would be a new and separate question and would not be included with any of the existing labor force questions. This, it was primarily (and patronizingly) argued, was so that respondents were not confused by an unfamiliar question. It was also because the UN Statistical Commission recommends that only the "economically active population" should be included in the labor force questions. Voluntary work—whatever the activity and however obvious its market value might be—is not considered economic activity.

In the evaluation of submissions on voluntary work, the department commented: "Asking respondents to write down the number of hours they spend on voluntary work does rely on memory recall. Some voluntary work is affected by seasonal variation."

Just like paid work, I respond. Or is the insinuation that it's only volunteers who have poor memories? Then the department claims that "no overseas countries are known to have included the unpaid sector of the labour force in their national accounts." OECD studies by Derek Blades and others refute this. But it is hardly the point: no other country had the suffrage, no other country had national superannuation,* no other country had a nuclear weapons–free policy.

But there was consolation for those of us who had worked hard to see active pressure applied on the department. In the end, the department commented, "The question is one of high public interest, and the absence of alternative information sources means that any census data would have many users."

The final decision saw a question on voluntary work included, but it did not examine the type of voluntary work undertaken nor the name of the voluntary organization.

Superannuation is a universal benefit system for all those aged sixty or more.

But a precedent was created for women involved in a similar battle in other countries. The exact wording of the question included in the 1986 New Zealand Census of Population and Dwellings was:

How many hours of voluntary work do you do on a regular weekly basis? For example, meals on wheels, sports administration, marriage counseling, Te Kohanga Reo [nurseries and child care centers where Maori, the language of indigenous New Zealanders, is taught and spoken].

☐ nil hours
☐ 1–4 hours per week
☐ 5–9 hours per week
☐ 10–14 hours per week
☐ 15 or more hours per week

The question still implies that volunteerism is institutionalized. From time to time with most of my married friends, I am involved in "marriage counselling." And I frequently cook for or deliver food to relatives or friends who are ill or in need of care. Such actions may well be a pleasure, but they are certainly not leisure, so they must be voluntary work. Women need to be reassured that that is indeed what they are doing when thus engaged.

Submissions asking for the inclusion of unpaid household work, however, were not so successful. The arguments used to justify inclusion had many parallels with the arguments for including voluntary work: to gain recognition and improve the status of those involved in unpaid household work and to provide base data for further research in the area. Submissions also pointed out the necessity of quantifying such work so that it can be included in the GNP and so that account can be taken of it when planning policies and services.

But when the question was included in pilot-testing, the department says, respondents had difficulty with it. There was an unacceptably high rate of nonresponse to the question.* The

---

*Proposed census questions must "be of a nature to promote public attitudes to cooperation in the census generally."

department did not explain if the nonresponse was overwhelmingly from men (nor did it notice the apparent inconsistency: the majority of the population makes no response to the questions on the labor force). A woman friend who worked in the office in charge of pilot-testing told me that interviewers reported a high degree of aggression encountered with male respondents. When men were asked this question in the pilot studies a typical response was "What do you want to know that for?" But in the evaluation published, the department made no mention of that. Instead, women respondents were blamed. The department reported conceptual problems: "There was difficulty differentiating between hobbies and household work, e.g., gardening and sewing." And, of course, there was the problem of those respondents who thought that caring for children was a twenty-four hour job!

It seems to me that where there is a market equivalent, where obvious skills are involved, where there is obvious production, and even where there is (heaven forbid) pleasure in the task, it is still work. Yes, for many respondents, activities overlapped or were carried out simultaneously, making their allocation difficult or inaccurate. But let's be clear. The "conceptual difficulties" and "problems of data collection" arose because *too many women did too much work*. The inadequacies were not those of the respondents, who could count the hours they worked, but those of the decision makers and their system, which could not fathom or refused to believe the answers given.

So a question on (unpaid) household work was not included in the 1986 New Zealand census. But a separate question on "main activity" was in. The exact wording was, "What is your main work or activity?" The possible answers were as follows:

1. home duties—looking after children
2. home duties—not looking after children
3. full-time student
4. retired

5. unemployed
6. paid job, business, farming, or profession
7. unpaid work in a family business
8. other (such as hospital patient). Please state _____

Well, answer that. Many women I know should check number 8 and write "1, 2, 5, and 7 of the above: 110 hours a week." That is, I suggest, one approach to such an inadequate perpetuation of general economic invisibility. Another possibility is to check only option 7—unpaid work in a family business.

In Summary

As we have seen, the concept of collecting data for use in public policy that might help to determine the well-being of the population is severely flawed in this system. The alienation experienced by many women respondents points to a major problem with the UNSNA. The women of New Zealand have shown how to challenge the system, at least in regard to unpaid productive work. But a woman still has no way of informing the census about her reproductive work.

Only a handful of economists find these issues to be problematic. There is a vast literature on the UNSNA and its difficulties. But except in feminist circles, the value of women's productive and reproductive work is not even a part of the discussion.

6. Villainy and Incompetence

Problems Economists See in Their Own System

Even if an economist has no regard for feminist concerns whatsoever, he or she will in all likelihood still be able to list several major problems with the UNSNA. In 1985, I asked a number of economists how they viewed the United Nations System of National Accounts and their own countries' systems of national accounts. The four men were all offered anonymity so that they might be encouraged to speak freely.

One of them, a former student of Sir Richard Stone, had the following comments to make.

National accounts are inaccurate even in things that are supposedly measurable. The world's balance of payments statistics contain hundreds of billions of dollars of errors or omissions. Much of this is on the invisible side; we can't get accurate figures for invisibles—shipping services, insurances, cost of short-term bank loans involved in imports.

In domestic national accounts, consumption is a series of residuals. Some countries are now producing quarterly GDP statistics, which are a bit of a joke because they are so inaccurate. If economists are honest, they will tell you that there is a lack of faith in econometric modeling. But the politicians don't like to be without something.

This man had been the chief economist with a nation's major banking group, a chief economist in a prime minister's department, and was then an economist in private consultancy.

Another to whom I spoke had been for a number of years a prominent writer on economics and head of a country's major institute for economic research. He said that the UNSNA had been developed to measure market employment and the inflationary gap.

It was developed as a management tool for answering questions and is rarely used in the welfare context, for it is recognized that here it does not provide for good measures. The system of national accounts also makes international comparison difficult, and, in any individual country's context, there are serious problems with realizing predictions. . . .

In assessing something like a superannuation or benefit system for the elderly, the national accounts are useful if they demonstrate that the introduction of such a scheme, or its furtherance, demonstrates that the elderly's consumption of GDP is rising, as the number of them as a percentage of the population is growing. In a microsense [the accounts] may also demonstrate, for example, that the investment plans that the nation's post office has forecast sees its revenue as doubling as a proportion of GDP every seven to eight years. This suggests that the investment assumptions are too high. The national accounts are also useful as an instrument in major debates about the amount of investment as a percentage of GDP that should be expended on major projects.

There is of course no intellectually reputable way of assessing and imputing the black market.

The third economist with whom I spoke had been an investment analyst for the city of London, had spent years with a multinational corporation in its head office, and was now the planning director of one of the largest multinationals in Australasia. Of the four economists, he was the most positive about the national accounts. He was also the only one of the four who had not, at any time, held a position of responsibility in a public policy sphere. And he was the only one who had been continually employed in the private business world. His support for the system was readily suggested by his handing to me the last report for the directors of his company, which he had written for his 1984–87 plan. The second paragraph, for example, demonstrates his dependence on GNP figures—which, remember, are the product of the UNSNA.

The OECD in general will move into the plan period in good shape, with the USA and Canada having slowed back to a rate of real GNP growth of perhaps 2%, the European economies beginning their recovery later and beginning to exceed that rate of growth at perhaps 3%, and Japan and Australia both dominated by export growth accelerating faster still at over 4% per annum. Such a forecast explicitly assumes that the fears of a world financial crisis continue to diminish, as falling real oil prices and rising economic activity hold the situation of most debtor countries at least stable. It assumes that OECD inflation will remain stable at about 5%, and that continuing real interest rates, as a result of substantial Government deficits, are regarded as being part of the normal order of things. It also assumes that there is no significant destabilising conflict, particularly in the Gulf area, to cause either a redistribution of purchasing power from one set of countries to another or a major change in consumer psychology.

Unfortunately for his predictions, as of October 1987, the United States had assembled in the Strait of Hormuz its largest naval fleet since Vietnam. Oil prices were rising, and assumptions based on an absence of conflict were undergoing a testing period. The U.S. Senate had voted unanimously to suspend 11 percent of its total oil imports, that quantity from Iran.

Economist number four had been economic advisor to a developed nation's major union movement and now worked as a consultant, both for the prime minister's department and privately. He told me that, when he reads that growth is forecast for this year and next year, this tells him that the economy may be tight, dependent on the country where growth is presumed to occur. He will look at the extent of industrialization and urbanization occurring and may recognize that unpaid work is becoming monetarized and so really there is no growth.

Economists are very afraid of being found out. I read GDP as a breakdown between incomes of companies and workers and even then with some skepticism. The Department of Statistics here recasts the figures with at least an 8 percent difference, and they are not precise. The economic definition of what contributes to the national welfare is extremely limited. Work could or should be enjoyable, and some leisure and recreation undeniably is productive.

We always value the reproduction of capital. Why don't we value the reproduction of labor? We could take the discipline on its own logic. For me, the system of national accounts demonstrates in the economic discipline the gap between villainy and incompetence.

The Problem of Pricing

In the previous chapter we examined aspects of the incompetence—and more is yet to come. But what is the nature of the villainy?

Present calculations suggest that when per capita income falls because of an increase in population relative to GDP, there is a decline in the welfare of the people. But the increase may well occur because of a decline in the death rate and increasing longevity—which is, of course, generally interpreted as a rise in welfare. National income accounting can't account for that, because the UNSNA's concentration on prices means that it must not allow any attribution for quality. Obviously, that is a major problem. But this fixation on prices raises another problem as well—which prices will be used when comparing two countries? What exchange rate will make their two currencies comparable?

National income statistics are compiled in local currency units. The usual way to derive figures to be used for cross-national comparisons is to use the exchange rate as a basis for converting GDP in local currency units to U.S. dollars. This is ludicrous, as Paul Samuelson noted:

One day in 1973 the United States moved from being decidedly the most affluent nation to being definitely below Sweden. Does anybody believe in such violent changes in relative real income? You must if you rely on official or market exchange rates for your purchasing power parity deflaters.[1]

Many of us have been in countries (in Western and Eastern Europe, in China, and in the developing world) where the difference between the official and the black market exchange rate has been multiples of anything up to twenty times what we were paid at the airport. The international system chooses "the official exchange rate method" rather than "purchasing power parity" because the second is costly and time consuming to work out.

In addition, this conversion rate is based on the relative prices of internationally traded goods. But many goods and services in least-developed countries, especially inexpensive food staples that are unstandardized and produced with labor-intensive methods, have no impact on the exchange rate, since they are not traded internationally. So the conversion of GDP into U.S. dollars at the existing exchange rate tends to understate the value of output of these goods and services. This distortion is greatest for low income countries, such as Papua New Guinea and Nepal.

Then there is something suspicious about estimates that show that several million citizens with least-developed-country per capita incomes of two hundred (U.S.) dollars per year can be compared with citizens of the United States who live with per capita (annual) incomes in excess of five thousand (U.S.) dollars. If this figure of two hundred dollars indicates that people are living on the quantity of goods and services that could be bought in the United States for two hundred dollars in a year, that poses substantial problems. If they were invited to do this in Manhattan, they would quickly die. Yet, if the data do not mean that these million people can or cannot live on what can be bought in the United States for so much a year or a day, it is not at all clear what they are supposed to mean.

There is significant debate on the question of the recording of commodity transactions at market prices and the particular problems of price statistics. Price statistics are used to deflate estimates at current prices, to estimate output at current prices from quantum data, and to calculate trade and transport margins by comparing producer and purchaser prices. Such statistics are often collected only in a nation's capital or in main trade areas. They do not account for seasonal fluctuations unless they are taken weekly. Data on such indicators as housing rentals are utterly unreliable. The whole question of the imputation of rent is somewhat ludicrous in the international situation. First, millions of people are homeless. That includes those who do not have a home to live in in their own country, those who are outside their country, and those who, because of war, are currently in flight from their country. That includes those who live in ditches, drainpipes, railway stations, or shelter under bridges, sacks, cardboard, newspaper, and corrugated iron in every country I have visited. Second, as Ron Fergie pointed out in establishing the national income accounts in Papua New Guinea, there are conceptual difficulties in imputing a home when a mud hut has a life expectation of only three to five years. Derek Blades, in his survey of developing countries, showed that different sorts of huts in different countries hold different lifetime expectations, ranging from a few years to over thirty.

Three Problems Acknowledged by Economists

Few economists will acknowledge openly the villainy and incompetence of the UN System of National Accounts. But many economic commentators do openly recognize three areas of difficulty in the UNSNA: the hidden economy, the integration of environmental pollution costs into accounting, and the measurement of leisure time. Let's now examine, in turn, each of these three generally acknowledged problem areas.

The Hidden Economy

In 1984, I visited Burma. What I saw there reconfirmed my own suspicions about the UNSNA's inability to accurately measure a country's economic well-being. In the Shan state in central Burma, the houses I saw were mostly made of thatch.

Often the living quarters were elevated above the pens housing brahma cattle or pigs or goats or poultry. Often the elevation was above rancid water. The average size for an extended family seemed to be about twenty square meters. The floors were earthen with bed mats on the floors or on a slightly raised, tightly woven base on a simple frame. The staples of rice, bananas, and tea grew in fine symmetrical rows along with cabbages, chiles, mustard, chocos, and avocados. Most members of the family left their homes at dawn. There was firewood to gather, tea to pick, goats and cattle to watch, rice to pound, nuts to rake and dry, fabric to weave, mules and oxen to work with yoke and wooden ploughs, areas to clear with small hand scythes, and, always, heavy loads to carry. Once a week, perhaps more frequently, a huge basket, which usually took two people to lift into position, would be carried for an hour or more on a woman's head over mountain slopes to market and there filled with dried, salted fish and other commodities for the family or village. The family might spend an average of three or four kyats, that is, fifty cents, a day.

Some days when the teacher made the hour's walk in from the nearest town, there would be school, but without pens or paper. The girls were unlikely to attend. If they had younger brothers or sisters, they were, at seven or eight, already the nurturers; otherwise, they were at work in the fields. At very young ages and for varying lengths of time, the children might be Buddhist monks or nuns.

If a family lived closer to a town, and particularly if near a road or railway line, the members might be involved in the constant preparation of food, boiled eggs, rice, chicken, vegetable simoses to sell to travelers, twenty-four hours a day. When my train drew into stations at 3 A.M. half the vendors selling such things and offering cups of mint tea through the window were aged under ten. Even if the national statisticians solved the conceptual difficulties of measuring such subsistence activities, these children would not be counted, for they are not deemed old enough to be "economically active."

The houses were bare but very clean. The water, unfortunately, was not, and this inhibited primary health care work. Many people were without access to basic medical care, although I often observed the Red Cross symbol above empty buildings. Some aid schemes worked: the United Nations Development Program pine afforestation scheme was observably effective. Others, too frequently, were disasters: there is not much point giving electricity to a hill village if the generator runs on diesel fuel that the village cannot buy and, anyway, the only way to get the fuel to the village is to carry it on someone's back for over an hour. Transportation links are horrendous and every vehicle is overloaded with people and produce.

It was obvious to me that Burma is a very poor country and that the largest sector of its economy is subsistence. Yet the United Nations noted in its 1984 World Economic Survey that Burma had "an average annual growth rate per capita GDP of 2.5 percent." How can this be? The answer is that Burma has a huge underground economy, probably the second largest sector of the economy, ensuring that the Burmese government comes under no pressure on its balance of payments. And what is this underground, hidden economy?

Burma's hidden economy consists of undeclared legal production of goods and services, production of illegal goods and services, and concealed income in kind, the sort of work that Mario the pimp and addict from chapter 1 was involved in.

For example, although the Burmese government prohibits imports, the streets are lined with marketeers of plastic and wind-up toys, the same as those being sold on the sidewalk outside Macy's in Manhattan. And it is quite obvious that there are imported cameras and radios and television sets in the country, owned by nationals. The importation of overseas currency and gold is also banned. But these are purchased on the street (at enormously marked-up prices) by representatives of the leaders of the three private armies that control the three borders of Burma. These armies are involved in carrying illegal imports across the borders and, of course, in the trade of drugs from the enormous production of these in the northern regions. This is the hidden economy of Burma. These are the kinds of activities responsible for the UN's rosy picture of "growth" in Burma.

Many countries try to include undeclared legal production in the GDP either by using only basic sources or by making explicit adjustments to sources that appear biased downwards. So assessments are made, for example, for tax avoidance. Illegal production in the United States in the black market would include narcotics, gambling, and prostitution. In Great Britain, there is a substantial literature on employee theft, or the use of facilities and commodities available within one's place of employ for one's own benefit when they are not understood as part of the wages and conditions of employment.

Thailand's economy is, in many ways, similar to Burma's. So when Thailand appears on the list of those countries experiencing growth, I wonder what percentage of that might be attributed to the international drug trade and what percentage of that might be attributed to the sexual slavery of women. It took me four days on my third visit to Bangkok to work up the courage to visit the prostitution area. I was accompanied by a friend, a black American male who at times in his diplomatic career had been seconded to the UN Commission on the Status of Women. He had investigated the conditions in these bars previously. No one else had ever asked him as a first question, "How old are these children?" We watched ten-, twelve-, and sixteen-year-old girls dancing in numbered swimming costumes, or in nothing at all, along cat walks. They are sold to these places by parents. They live, eat, and sleep here and are enslaved not only in theory. In 1984, when one of these bars burned down, the skeletons of six girls aged between ten and sixteen were found in the ruins, chained to the beds.

It is illegal under the Thai criminal code to work as a prostitute or to live off the earnings of a prostitute. Those guilty are supposedly punishable by a fine or imprisonment. But prostitution became institutionalized during the Vietnam war when U.S. troops were stationed there. And when they left, tourism took over. In 1981, reports estimated that, in Bangkok alone, 300,000 women and children worked in approximately 1157 places offering sex services, earning an average of $40 per month while sex-tour guides and hotel bar and brothel owners kept the profit.[2] This is Thailand's hidden economy.

What do economists say about the significance of such hidden economies? Economist Edgar Feige wrote in 1979 that the hidden economy in the United States was equal to 27 percent of America's GNP and could be growing at around 40 percent a year in nominal terms.[3] Partially in reaction to such accusations, an OECD study conducted by Derek Blades on the hidden economy and the national accounts warned:

If hidden activities are indeed being undertaken on such a scale and if national accountants omit them from their calculations, national accounts statistics would be irrelevant as overall measures of economic activity, and hopelessly misleading for purposes of economic analysis. Savings ratios would be biased, the size and growth of the economy would be understated, unemployment would be exaggerated, and on the plausible assumption that hidden output costs less than comparable output in the exposed community, inflation would be overstated.[4]

In other words, economists see enormous significance in the hidden economy of graft, greed, and sexual slavery. They warn that ignoring such activities could make national account statistics "irrelevant" and "hopelessly misleading." Yet these same economists conclude that women's unpaid work is insignificant, even though it is far larger than Feige's assessments of the hidden economy.

Women are also told it is difficult to value their work because of the conceptual inadequacies of measurement tools. But doesn't the hidden economy have conceptual measurement difficulties as well? And don't economists come up with numerous suggestions for measuring it?

Frey and Weck-Hanneman, for example, suggest that there

are four approaches to measuring the size of the hidden economy.[5] The first uses figures on tax evasion as a basis for evaluating the hidden economy's economic activity in terms of GNP. The second approach points out that independent estimates of the income and expenditure side of individual households as well as national accounts reveal that the expenditure side is larger than the income side. The initial discrepancy "can be attributed to the hidden economy." The third approach maintains that a decline in the participation rate of the official economy can be taken as an indicator of increased activities in the hidden economy. Finally, the most developed approach considers the changes and the demand for money brought about by changes in the hidden economy activities. This currency demand approach assumes that the hidden transactions are undertaken in cash in order not to leave any observable traces for the tax authorities. So it deduces, from the total quantity of money, what the size of total economic activity has to be. Subtracting official GNP from the thereby estimated total GNP gives an estimate of the GNP in the hidden sector. In 1978 the size of the hidden economy as a percentage of GNP was estimated by the OECD to be the following:

Sweden	13.2%	Canada	8.7%	Finland	7.6%
Belgium	12.1%	Germany	8.6%	Spain	6.5%
Denmark	11.8%	USA	8.3%	Japan	4.1%
Italy	11.4%	UK	8.0%		

Certainly, each of these approaches to measuring the hidden economy has enormous conceptual and measurement problems. But these are the same difficulties attributed to the measurement of women's work. If economists can devise ways to measure one, why not the other? Evidently the brotherhood will measure only the brotherhood's activity, wherever and however it occurs.

Environmental Pollution

Questions of physical or monetary measurements of pollution and destruction of the environment have been major concerns of mainstream commentators for some years. In 1975, Sir Richard Stone was commissioned by the UN to draft a System of Social and Demographic Statistics. He wrote:

Information about the environment is of obvious importance in connection with the subject matter of this report. Pollution of the air, sea and land and the disturbance of ecological balances are highly relevant to health, to feeding and otherwise providing for the world's rapidly growing population, to the acceptability of policies of unconstrained economic growth and to the choice of the techniques of production.[6]

Despite this acknowledgment of the importance of environmental considerations, the UNSNA still records no costs of poisoning the population and the earth—at least, not directly. In fact, it is quite clear that what many of us regard as the flagrant destruction of natural resources is recorded as growth and thus as part of our well-being. But when major cities in the world such as Bangkok and Bombay become uninhabitable for those with a propensity for bronchitis; when the rising temperature of the earth threatens to melt polar ice caps and force entire countries (for example, Bangladesh) to disappear under the sea; and when massive cleanup and decontamination methods are needed in the nuclear accidents at Three Mile Island and Chernobyl—are we supposed to accept these as indications that our well-being is improving?

U.S. environmentalist and commentator Lewis Regenstein has written that the United States is being inundated with chemicals sprayed from the air, spewed from chimney stacks, applied to the crop land, showered over entire forests, buried beneath the earth and sea, and added to the food and drink. It may be too late, he writes, for most citizens to find antidotes to these persistent chemical poisons. It is projected that 56 million Americans will contract cancer annually, much of it as the result of the chemicals that surround them. Other results of the poisons include vomiting, miscarriages, stillbirths, blindness, bleeding, insanity, and, mercifully in some cases, death.[7]

But with the exception of those poisonings that are undeniable, such as at Love Canal or Three Mile Island, these illnesses will not be visible to the UNSNA. They will be visible in the national accounts only as consumption of medical and other professional services and thus treated as *value-added* in national income accounting. While it might seem obvious to you and me that such costs should be *subtracted from expenditures* on Gross National Product, this is not the case. To get a net national product, all that is subtracted from GNP is the depreciation on the stock of capital goods, that is, the monetary equivalent of the reinvestments necessary to maintain the capital stock (such as, stockpiles of nuclear bombs). The idea is to "keep the capital intact." The goods and services involved in cleaning up an ecological disaster, just like cleaning up after a war, are said to be an expression of society's "preferences." In the case of goods and services exchanged in the market, this occurs automatically. Economists say that the market prices (of, for example, medical treatment) reflect actual wants. But this gets very convoluted. If our actual wants are for clear air, fresh water, and standing forests, we cannot possibly express such desires, for they cannot be expressed in the market. No one and nothing records the permanent damage to water, air, and ecosystems as an income accounting cost.

So in the case of the environment, the mechanism is inoperative. Since nature is not traded via the market, the effects on our fragile system remain unrecorded. National income provides for deficits in money but not deficits in natural resources—or deficits in the human character that perpetuates such destruction. Meanwhile growth releases its (literal) poisons.

While the manufacture of most poisonous insecticides has now been moved to the developing world, there is no lack of poisons destroying the environment in the northern hemisphere. The United States Environmental Protection Agency (EPA) estimates that U.S. industry, which works with more than four hundred highly toxic chemicals, annually produces more than a ton of liquid and solid hazardous waste per citizen. On a global scale, over sixty thousand synthetic chemical compounds are in commercial use, and a thousand new ones are created each year. Few have been tested to determine their harmful effect on the environment. Yet we are supposed to believe they are safe for the human species. The still unfolding tragedies of cancers and lung diseases caused by exposure to asbestos fifty years ago join the sagas of Love Canal and Three Mile Island. Poisoning the planet, and then containing the poison at "acceptable" levels, is now big business and adds to the national income.

This might occur in several ways. An industry's environmental protection investment and the current operating expenditures for its plants are now calculated. In the last few years in the United States, capital stock calculations for environmental protection have been introduced so that depreciation can be calculated. The data for expenditure on environmental protection includes all sectors and the government, and current operating costs are also recorded. These costs are almost always borne by a company and are thus regarded as an intermediate delivery with no value-added to national income.

But expenditure on treatment plants is usually financed by the government via charges. In accordance with national income accounting convention, this expenditure is entered as final delivery and consequently contributes to the growth of national income. Estimates put the current business in the hazardous waste area in the United States at between $3 billion and $6 billion annually.[8] Major multinational companies like Bechtel and Westinghouse are moving into the business, seeing that their past and present mining and nuclear power interests will give the "clean-up" companies years of business.

Pollution damage affects all of us, and it is not possible to avoid it. It will increase the output of service industries if we choose to use them (for example, the cost of extra cleaning of laundry and household goods), or it will increase the amount of housework that a woman must do. If we live close to an expressway or an airport, our property value will decrease, and we will have to pay more for freedom from noise.

If we live in Canada, whether we like it or not, we are victims of the effect of acid rain from the United States. If we live in Europe on the Rhine, then we are the recipients of all that our neighbors up river have poured into that body of water. But if we lived in Bhopal during the Union Carbide plant disaster, we were gassed. As Lester Thurow remarks in his book *Zero-Sum Society*, water pollution can be avoided by staying away from polluted water, but it is much harder not to breathe.[9]

During the 1970s, Sir Richard Stone worked on ways that social factors, such as environmental pollution costs, might be included in national accounting. He was impressed by the work of Wassily Leontief, another Nobel prize winner in economics and the founder of input-output analysis who in 1970 proposed

a means of handling pollution analytically within an input output framework. In principle the idea is a simple one. All that is needed is to expand the input output table for "regular" industries by adding a row and column for each treatment service designed to handle one of the pollutants. Each new column would contain the inputs needed to operate one of the treatment services and, on the assumption that industrial pollution is to be entirely eliminated, each new row would contain the quantity of the relevant pollutant omitted by each activity, whether a regular industry or a treatment service; and the omissions would provide a measure of the cost that must be incurred by the polluter. However it is not obvious that total elimination should be the target; it might be better to aim at partial elimination, thereby leaving more resources for the production of "regular" goods and services.[10]

While this may measure the rate and cost of current destruction, it is of little comfort. It is not a "conservation" policy and does not ensure any visibility for the remaining natural resources. My own conclusion is that the discipline of economics has not contributed at all to the enhancement of the environment. With Jonathan Porritt, director of Friends of the Earth, United Kingdom, I have more than a suspicion, indeed the experience, that "politicians feel pathetically insecure when they cannot promise growth." And in the international economic system, preservation does not add up to growth; it counts for nothing.

Leisure Time

In addition to the hidden economy and the value of the environment, the third area of major commentary for national income analysts has been the measurement of leisure or free time. For many years this gave me much difficulty because *I* could not see why such a measurement was a problem in income accounting. It was only some months ago that it hit me like a bolt out of the blue: *the reason that the measurement of free time was a problem for men was because they had free time.* In the average day of the average unpaid woman, there is seldom free time during which no productive activities take place. But the male commentators realized that they themselves had leisure time that they needed to account for. Never mind that women had no leisure time, and were invisible most of their lives in this system. Here was a part of male activity unaccounted for. It must be measured.

In commenting on Sir Richard Stone's acceptance of the Nobel prize in economics in 1984, the *New York Times* said that his two-story house was lined with books from floor to ceiling and that Sir Richard and his wife spent much time reading. It also said that Sir Richard was a patron of the arts and an avid theater-goer who had been known to invite whole casts back to his home for parties complete with Irish whisky, French food, and expensive cigars. Sir Richard obviously had leisure time. But Stone's consultancy report on social and demographic statistics for the UN says,

The first step is to classify activities (all of which require time) and then to select those which can be said to use free time. Evidently this cannot be done solely by reference to the activity itself; for instance, for a professional musician or music student instrumental practice represents work, whereas for an amateur it should be regarded as a leisure activity.[11]

Evidently, Sir Richard's own leisure time was not a problem for him, but *measuring* such time presents many difficulties.

U.S. economists Heilbroner and Thurow conceive of the problem in a similar way.[12] They write that leisure time is enjoyable and necessary to consume material goods and services. Nevertheless, they say economists are not able to find a good technique for measuring the extent of leisure or for placing a value on it. What, they ask, should be subtracted from the twenty-four hour day to indicate hours of leisure? Presumably leisure hours are those that give pleasure or utility. But, they ask, what about work? Work is considered to be pain and should be subtracted. (Remember Charlotte Perkins Gilman called this approach a particularly masculine "and pitiful conception of labor as a curse.") And what of leisure activities that are recommended as principles of preventive medicine—like recreation?

Yes, what about recreation. Lest we get bogged down in the economists' fretting over measurements, let's see what recreation can tell us about women and leisure. Recreation is an activity or nonactivity, freely chosen, that provides stimulation, pleasure, satisfaction, or other intrinsic rewards. Not surprisingly, there is little data on recreation. But a recent recreation survey conducted in New Zealand can help to give us some clues about women's lives.[13] In this survey, recreation was defined for respondents as "those things that you enjoy doing (for example, hobbies, sport, social or cultural interests) and in which you are some way involved." Three features in particular emerged with regard to women's recreation: home-based activities involved nine out of ten women compared to five out of ten men; cultural pursuits showed higher participation levels for women; and sporting activities showed higher participation levels for men. The general findings of the survey showed that children limited the recreational participation of women and that this was not the case for men, particularly with regard to sport: men's sporting involvement *increases* with the birth of children. This was a new and astounding revelation to me.

Wives and mothers laughed at my naivety and said, "But of course."

Leghorn and Parker in their excellent work *Women's Worth*,[14] pose an interesting question: If men are so keen to measure in terms of production, why don't they include in their statistics the production, by women, of leisure for men? The world over, they suggest, women are working harder to produce more leisure time for men.

In my own studies in New Zealand this would indeed seem to be the case. A principal of my local girl's high school said recently, "Leisure time is the time we have to spare when our commitments and work are completed." It is questionable indeed whether some women have any leisure at all. Another friend of mine in her master's thesis wrote, "The mind must be free of guilt feelings and ready to pursue any number of activities, with the sole purpose of enjoyment for its own sake, and not feeling that you should be doing something else."[15] If that is so, then I know women who have never been leisured in their lives.

It is occasionally recognized that women need a rest from whatever it is they do (which, the economists assure us, isn't "work"). In the Soviet Union, for example, compensation for such overwork is reflected in the number of free passes to sanitoriums distributed to women. For Russian women, the housework burden is substantial and occupies a large portion of women's "nonworking" time. Men generally have twice the amount of free time compared with women. A Leningrad study showed that 81 percent of women do the housework themselves, 70–75 percent do the shopping, and 68 percent say that they receive "not much" or "hardly any" help in chores. Eighty-five percent think that their husbands should share equally in the housework. A comparison with other studies shows that rural Soviet women carry an even greater work burden.

And when the Soviet family takes a holiday, mother doesn't. Forty-one percent of married people spend their holiday at home; 30.8 percent spend it at a relative's house; and 27.8 percent go to a resort. Any woman knows that having the family at home or going to stay with relatives increases the amount of domestic work to be done. During the summer, women have priority for passes to sanitoriums and rest homes in the Crimea. In 1969, they received 60 percent of the passes. In this way, "gratitude" is expressed to "mothers, wives, and sisters for their selfless work."[16]

In the report "A Profile of Filipino Women" prepared for the U.S. Agency for International Development (USAID), the authors write that "in relation to use of spare hours, it has been observed that rural women are generally time conscious and there is no such thing as spare hours for them." Ninety-five percent of men were involved in "political activities" during leisure hours, and the same proportion of women were involved in "economic" or "income-generating activities." Because of this, the report concluded, they hardly have any time left for recreation nor the opportunities to interact with outside issues.[17]

If the question of who has leisure is to be asked of the head of the household, women are again in trouble. In rural Bangladesh, aid project staff report speaking separately to the men and women of a prosperous, conservative farm family. The women, in response to questions about what they did, spoke about their chickens, vegetables, rice processing, and the like. The men, in response to questions about their women, said "they cook and sew quilts."[18]

While seeking to maintain an image of women at leisure, men's social pressure is to deny them any at all. Part of the reason for this is because women do not "work" and thus must be at leisure when the men aren't around. In Costa Rica, homemakers seemed to think they were expected to work all the time. They were very skilled in altering the pace of the work in relation to social pressures that they sensed. If the result of a task, such as sewing a button on a school blouse or cleaning rice before cooking, was needed at a particular moment, the women moved quickly. If the mending or food preparation task was needed for another day, the tempo was slowed and the women often joined a neighbor for conversation while carrying out the task. It their husbands appeared, the work activity increased and the conversation diminished. A subtle social pressure seemed to eliminate purely recreational activities for these homemakers.[19]

Social pressure combined with the stress of two full-time jobs ensures that employed women have less leisure time than employed men. And these employed men have *more* leisure time than housewives, because, as Leghorn and Parker contend, women create the leisure time for them. In a study of the average time budget of employed men, employed women, and housewives in twelve countries in 1975, the total free time per week for employed men was 34 hours, for employed women it was 14.5 hours per week, and for housewives it was 32.6 hours per week.*

The data about housewives is highly suspect since the statistical conspiracy is such that, when women are invisible as workers, then they can be told that they are at leisure when they are fulfilling unpaid domestic duties. If they are invisible as workers, then they will be invisible as targets for leisure activities. Many women are still frozen in an inability to recreate themselves, still needing to be told that they have a right to leisure time.

But that seems a sophisticated thought. Millions of women still need to be told that they have a right to a life free from fear of war, destruction, poison, starvation, hunger, illness, and homelessness. In the institutionalization of value through the UNSNA, the family of man avoids confronting the absence of well-being in the family of women. In 1982, eight-hundred mil-

---

*The countries included Belgium, Bulgaria, Czechoslovakia, France, the Federal Republic of Germany, the German Democratic Republic, Hungary, Peru, Poland, the United States, the Soviet Union, and Yugoslavia. The survey did not cover purely agricultural households whose members worked only on farms.

lion people in the Third World were living in absolute poverty: most of those affected were migrant workers and their families, youth, the disabled, and the aged—and the majority in all those categories were women. Approximately five-hundred million people suffer from malnutrition; the most seriously affected are children under five and women. Twenty million persons die annually of hunger-related causes, and one billion endure chronic undernourishment and other poverty deprivations; again, the majority are women and children.

The difficulties of measuring men's illegal and exploitative activities, the contamination of our planet's ecosystem, and the free time of those who have it consume the time of scholars, academics, multilateral institutions, and government treasuries. Meanwhile, women's work continues to be ignored.

As we have seen, women and children count for nothing. It is fascinating to see, next, what does count for something.

7. The Value of Death

How War, Poverty, and Poisons Help the Economy

While women, children, and the environment are counted as nothing, the entire international economic system calls war productive and valuable. The men who rule us are willing to perpetrate wars and mass destruction. The policy propaganda of national income accounting generates a belief that many economic problems—unemployment, underutilization of capital, lack of growth—are susceptible to improvement through military spending.

This is in spite of the fact that military spending allocates resources to unproductive endeavors. Military spending does not add to an economy's productive capital stock. A stockpile of nuclear weapons is not worth anything to anybody.

The economic position of war is still measured the way that Keynes, Stone, and Milton Gilbert developed the formula between 1939 and 1943, in terms of profit, production, capital, and "manpower." Nowhere is there an account for death, poverty, homelessness, refugee populations, ruined food sources, the enormous waste in investment in armaments, and an increasingly fragile and exploited environment.

As the world began the 1986 International Year of Peace, fifteen wars were being fought in the Americas, Asia, and Africa. World military expenditures were in excess of $800 billion, a new peak for a single year. These expenditures had risen more than 40 percent in the last decade. Five to six new nuclear bombs were made every day. More public money was spent by governments to defend citizens against the possibility of military attack than against the everyday ravages of ill health, disease, and injury. Meanwhile the most elementary health care systems were still lacking in many parts of the world. These are not the characteristics of a world that values life. How does the UNSNA influence this? What pictures emerge of what is valuable in this institutionalized ideology?

War and the Economy: Death Visible as Production

Bearing in mind that the system of national accounts had its origins in "how to pay for the war," it is important that we begin there—with war. Since the years immediately following World War II, the world's annual military expenditures have more than quadrupled. The total amount expended since 1945 is estimated to be $3–4 trillion on the nuclear arsenal alone. In the four years between the United Nations General Assembly sessions on disarmament, world military expenditures exceeded $1.6 trillion. This translates into $1 million spent on weapons every minute of every hour of every day in 1981.[1]

Militarization can be measured nationally as the share of GDP devoted to the production of military goods and services or as a military share of the nation's budget. Globally it can be judged by the military share of the global product and the arms' share of international trade.

From 1980 to 1984 world military spending grew from $564 billion to $649 billion (in 1980 prices), a growth rate of over 3.5 percent. Military spending in 1983 was over 5 percent of world output and twenty-seven times as large as all the overseas development assistance provided by the OECD countries in that year.[2] The bulk of global military spending remains concentrated among the industrialized countries. Global military expenditures in 1985 of $900 billion exceeded the income of the poorest half of humanity. In other words, military expenditures surpassed the combined GDP of China, India, and all African countries south of the Sahara. This is comparable to the combined Gross National Products of all the countries of Africa and Latin America.

The annual expenditure represents approximately 8 percent of total world output and is equal to 25 percent of all annual fixed investment. World military spending, on an annual basis, is more than the total value of gross fixed capital formation in all the developing countries combined and about the same as global public expenditure on education. Arms expenditure exceeds world spending on health by 28 percent. At 1982 prices and exchange rates, outlays on military expenditures now add up to $17 trillion—an amount six times as large as the annual income currently produced by the 3.6 billion people in the third world.

In current prices, world military expenditure per year amounts to more than $110 for every man, woman, and child on the planet. Our policymakers cannot boast the equivalent per capita expenditure on food, water, shelter, health, education, or ecosystem protection.

An important part of world industrial production is still preempted by military requirements, just as the needs of the civilian population were secondary to the British war effort in 1939–45. Estimates range up to 32 percent of world military expenditure as the value of industrial production given over to military use. In 1982, this represented an industrial output (at current prices) of roughly $180 billion.[3]

At any time, major percentages of a selected group of minerals are claimed for military consumption. Many are mined by multinationals (whose head offices are located in the northern hemisphere) and exported north from the developing countries for armaments manufacture. In the case of aluminum, copper, nickel, and platinum, estimated global military consumption for the first five years of this decade was greater than the demand for these minerals for all purposes in Africa, Asia (including China), and Latin America combined.[4] The military consumption of petroleum came close to 5 to 6 percent of the total world consumption; this is close to half of the entire consumption by all the developing countries (excluding China).

Real (or actual) expenditure on military research and development is estimated to have increased by under 1 percent a year from 1974 to 1980, by 5–8 percent from 1980 to 1983, and by more than 10 percent from 1983 to 1984. Research and development have increased as a percentage of military expenditure. The rise in real military expenditure has not been as high, on a percentage basis.

Global expenditure on military research and development is one-quarter of all expenditures of the world on research and development for all purposes. Approximately 20 percent of the world's qualified scientists and engineers, if not more, are engaged in military work. *Both of the superpowers*, the United States and the Soviet Union, devote twice the amount of public money to weapons research as they spend on research for all civilian needs combined.

More than seventy million people are estimated to be directly or indirectly engaged in military activities worldwide. This figure includes some twenty-five million persons in the world's regular armed forces. When paramilitaries, militarists, and reservists are added to this, we are able to conclude that there is one soldier for every forty-three people on earth. There are probably four million civilians employed in defense departments worldwide, over three million scientists and engineers engaged in military research and development work, and at least five million workers directly engaged in the production of weapons and other specialized military equipment.[5]

All of these people are economically active and productive, and, according to the economic system, they perform valuable work.

The two superpowers have 11 percent of the global population, spend more than half the world's military budget, spend 80 percent of the research and development military budget, export 53 percent of the arms they produce, control 97 percent of the world's inventory of nuclear weapons, and occupy military bases throughout the world. A rough estimate of $3–4 trillion spent on nuclear forces alone since the end of World War II is more than the superpowers spent in public funds over the same period for the health care of five-hundred million people.

The doubling of the United States' national debt, from $914 billion in 1980 to $1.841 trillion in 1985 is due more to the growth in military expenditures than to any other factor. Between 1980 and 1985, U.S. military expenditures climbed from $134 billion to $244 billion (in current dollars). This increase of roughly $100 billion dwarfs growth in all other major economic sectors including health, which increased $11 billion, and agriculture, which rose $15 billion.

The U.S. Department of Defense (DOD) is the largest centrally planned economy outside the Soviet Union.[6] In the capitalist, free market United States, this department's property— plants and equipment, land, inventories of war and other commodities—amounts to over $200 billion. This is equal to about 7 percent of the assets of the entire American economy. It owns 39 million acres of land, roughly an area the size of Hawaii; it rules over a population of more than 3 million—direct employees or soldiers—and spends an official budget of close to $100 billion, a budget three-quarters as large as the entire Gross National Product of Great Britain.

The DOD is largely responsible for pursuing administration policy to establish a web of dependency on militarism and the military-industrial base from state to state, industry to industry, and multinational corporation to multinational corporation. Lockheed aircraft, for example, makes in excess of 80 percent of its sales to the government.* The DOD also shows up as one of the largest marketing chains in the world, after Sears. It is a major factor in the housing industry, spending more for military housing in several decades than the total spent by the

---

*This is not unusual in the developed countries. In one of the other wealthy countries, the Federal Republic of Germany, the military shares 70–80 percent of the annual output of the aerospace industry.

federal government on all other public housing. It is estimated that in excess of twenty-two thousand firms in the United States are prime contractors with the DOD, although the widespread practice of subcontracting means that a much larger number of enterprises—perhaps one hundred thousand in all—look to defense spending for a portion of their income.[7]

If you are counting, what all this adds up to is that killing people, or being prepared to kill them, is considered very valuable. And it has become increasingly more valuable. In the United States since World War II, the price of an average automobile has gone up six to seven times; a portable typewriter, two to five times; a modest house, ten to twelve times. Since 1945, the average price increases for all goods and services on the consumer price index show a multiple of six. Yet escalation of two hundred times is not unusual for weapons. If comparable prices had occurred in civilian goods, the current price of an average automobile would be above three-hundred thousand dollars.

If a country develops an economic system that is based on how to pay for the war, and if the amounts of fixed capital investment that are apparent are tied up in armaments, and if that country is a major exporter of arms and its industrial fabric is dependent on them, then it would be in that country's interests to ensure that it always has a market. It is not an exaggeration to say that it is clearly in the interests of the world's leading arms exporters to make sure there is always a war going on somewhere. It has clearly been in the interests of the United States to sustain war and major political tension in the Persian Gulf region since the oil shock of 1974–75.

In the twentieth century, there have been 207 wars and 78 million lives lost. Two-thirds of the world's countries, representing 97 percent of the global population, have been in at least one war this century. There have been 120 wars since World War II, fought almost exclusively in the Third World. Between 1945 and 1985, 93 new nations were created, most following some degree of warfare. Many of these countries

have foreign bases or other military installations on their soil.*
Many of them have military rulers.

By 1985, 57 out of 114 independent developing states were
militarily controlled. There had been 138 successful coups between 1960 and 1985. Militarized political power means limitations on the right to vote, denial of the people's voice in
government, and violence, torture, brutality, disappearances,
and political killings. Despite this, not one country where
oppression was practiced failed to receive a substantial flow of
arms.

International trade in arms reached an estimated $39 million
in 1982. It has become a significant share of exports of some
developing countries as well as the developed countries. On
the supply side, the trade in arms has been dominated by six
industrialized countries: France, the Federal Republic of Germany, Italy, the Soviet Union, the United Kingdom, and the
United States. Brazil is now the largest third world exporter of
arms and is fast approaching the big six. Not far behind is
Israel, with 35 percent of arms exports going to South Africa,
Israel's largest single customer. The economic significance of
arms exports can be gauged from the fact that by 1978 such
exports accounted for more than half of the combined trade
surplus of the developed economies, helping to offset the increased costs of their oil imports.

In the international economic system, the arms race registers
death both as manufactured production and as our "desire" to
consume it as a government service. So death by war has a
mathematical value. Other death—by poverty, starvation,
thirst, homelessness, disease—is not of the same order. It is
not even registered as a deficit. These deaths do not enter the
market—their "value" is in registering no cost to the market.

I have been one of the generation born since 1945 who has
been told all my life that we were not at war and that one of

---

*The total number of countries or territories in the world that have foreign
bases or other military installations on their soil is, coincidentally, 93.

the reasons that we were not engaged in a war was because of the nuclear bomb. The *Concise Oxford Dictionary* defines war as "a quarrel usually between nations conducted by force, a state of open hostility, suspension of ordinary international law." Used figuratively, the word means "hostility or contention between persons"; used to describe a "war of nerves," its definition is "an attempt to wear down an opponent by gradual destruction of morale."

—Every minute, thirty children die from want of food and inexpensive vaccines. And every minute the world's military budget absorbs $1.3 million of the public treasury. This is war.

—The United States now devotes over $200 billion a year to military defense against foreign enemies. But 45 percent of Americans are afraid to go out alone at night within one mile of their homes. This is war.

—The cost of a single new nuclear submarine equals the annual education budget of twenty-three developing countries with 160 million school-aged children. This is war.

—In a year when U.S. farmers were paid to take nearly 100 million acres of cropland out of production, 450 million people in the world were starving. This is war.

—For every 100,000 people in the world, there are 556 soldiers but only 85 doctors. This is war.

—For every soldier, the average world military expenditure is $22,000. For every school-aged child, the average public education expenditure is $380. This is war.

War is marketable. War pays, literally. War contributes to growth and development. The economic system says so.

So what are the invisible costs—and how might they be assessed?

When War and Poverty Mix: Death Invisible as Debt

The arms race is villainous; so is poverty. When combined with incompetence, the result can be lethal. Here is a picture of what I mean.

I arrived in Addis Ababa, Ethiopia, in October 1984, immediately after the screening of a British Broadcasting Corporation film on famine in the country. Ethiopia has a population of 32 million. Fifty percent of the people are under age twenty. More than 6 million of them are in dire need of food at this moment. One thousand of them die from starvation each week. The conservative estimate for the number currently starving is 12 million; the majority of these are women and children.

In 1985, eleven African countries were suffering drought and receiving international aid; more were expected to be added to the list. None of them had the population of Ethiopia, but neither did any of them receive the "per capita aid" going to Ethiopia. The largest percentage of this aid (from the Soviet Union to the government, from Western nations to the rebels) was in the nature of military supplies, equipment, and advisers. Certainly many religious, charitable, governmental, and multilateral aid agencies assisted the starving and dying, but the civil war had priority. Somalia, Dijibouti, Rwanda, Burundi, Sudan, Chad, Niger, and the other countries are not perceived as having the strategic importance of Ethiopia, bordering the Red Sea, a short distance from Saudi Arabia. Ethiopia has now assembled the largest army in sub–Saharan Africa and spends 42 percent of its budget for military purposes. Nowhere else in Africa is the Soviet presence so visible.

When I arrived in Addis Ababa, I was welcomed by lavish decorations, still bright and prominent from the September celebrations of the tenth anniversary of the popular revolution and the installation of the Provisional Military Administrative Council. Huge billboards of Marx and Engels and vast concrete edifices of Lenin, "peace" signs that featured crossed machine guns, large colored signs featuring Comrade Mengistu Haile Meriam, chairperson of the workers party of Ethiopia, and the ever-present call of "Long Live Proletarian Internationalism" illustrated the truth of the rumor in the last year that well in excess of (U.S.) $150 million was spent on this commemoration.

The government had some cause to celebrate. The overthrow

of the old regime of Haile Selassie was the overthrow of feudal serfdom. The building of domestic dwellings and rehousing programs in Addis Ababa had been prolific, and the results were still much in evidence. Ethiopia had won international awards for its intensive literary campaigns. The language is Amharic, spoken only in Ethiopia, with very few books available, all of them heavily censored and generally full of rhetoric about "capitalists" and "imperialists" and "colonists."

Shortly before the revolutionary celebrations, every resident of Addis Ababa had to hand in their identification cards to receive new ones. Rumor had it that not enough new cards were printed. Each day, during my 1984 visit, I observed lines of patient people, many returning day after day, waiting to get an ID card. Without an ID card there was no ration card. Without a ration card, there was no bread, oil, sugar, spaghetti, or flour.

One day I walked quietly down one of the roads that leads into the city. I saw coming toward me a group of people dressed in rags. They were met on the road by armed and uniformed soldiers carrying stock whips, and they were beaten back down the road from whence they had come. It was explained to me that they would not have been carrying identification cards.

Selamta, the publication of Ethiopian airlines, informs the visitor that 60 percent of Ethiopia's land is arable but only 10.4 percent is presently cultivated. (For comparison, note that China is feeding 22 percent of the world's population on 7 percent of the earth's arable land.) The publication says that 90 percent of the population earns its living from the land, mainly as subsistence farmers. The exports are coffee, oil seeds, pulses, vegetables, sugars, and food stuffs for animals. The essay claims "a thriving livestock sector exporting cattle on the hoof and hides and skins."

Before the revolution, the experience was the feudal system of serfdom. Land reform was hailed as a vast improvement. The land is nationalized so that there is no title and no security of tenure. As a result, there is a major unwillingness on the part of the population to spend money on fertilizer, shelter, and other inputs into agriculture. Severe drought, poor soil, negative price policies for agriculture products, a decrease in demand for African agricultural products, and a poor allocation of resources for agricultural development have all taken a massive toll. The situation is exacerbated beyond relief by the total invisibility of the real farmers and food producers, for *it is in this part of the world that the concentration of women in agriculture is the highest*. And we know by now that the higher the proportion of women in agriculture in any country, the more poorly documented are their needs. Policy does not address their concerns.

The African continent has had the highest annual population growth rate in the world in the last two decades. It has a young population with 44 percent under age fifteen. The world's lowest life expectancies and the highest rates of child mortality are found in Africa. Ethiopia, along with Burkina Faso, Niger, Mali, and Guinea Bissau, has one of the world's highest crude death rates (that is, the total of those dying, not adjusted with the number of births). The estimated million lives lost in famine in Africa exceeds that of any conflict since World War II.

How is it that the real drama of famine in Ethiopia and Africa has been ignored for so long? How is it that this city of the headquarters of the Organization for African Unity and the Economic Commission on Africa, with diplomatic representation from over seventy countries, could be silent for so long in 1983 and 1984 about such devastation?

Western diplomatic representatives told me that warnings and protests to the Ethiopian government were met with the request not to meddle in domestic affairs. For over a year, while the government prepared for the tenth anniversary celebrations, all transportation priorities were given to the air, sea, and land movements of cement, signs, lighting, and military equipment needed for September 12, 1984. There was a stranglehold on every project not connected with the celebrations.

Aid project equipment for river diversion, hospital extensions, technical laboratories, and water supply contracts had no priority. Nor was priority given to the insufficient quantities of grain supplied by the European Economic Community (EEC). This was held up in backlogs at the ports because of inefficient handling and because transport was tied up in the revolution anniversary preparations.

The famine story broke just after Western governments, pioneered by the U.S. administration, found themselves "unable to guarantee the continued survival" of the International Fund for Agricultural Development, which had been prominent in assisting small-scale agriculture in poorer countries, including Ethiopia, in just the way that might make famine less likely in the future. The Reverend Charles Elliott, former head of Christian Aid Charity, claims that the American and British hostility to the Marxist regime was based on the hope that the famine would topple the government. Aware that the last famine brought about the collapse of the totalitarian regime of Haile Selassie, some hoped for another collapse in this famine.

Lip Service Is Generous

A large proportion of food producers in Africa are women— a fact that is widely acknowledged in bureaucratic documents from national governments and multilateral agencies. There is no doubt that in some countries and at some levels, policy rhetoric has given women some visibility. But an understanding of the sexual division of labor and resources stops at lip service.

In the last major Sahelian drought, USAID's program seriously damaged the nomadic women's economic and social position. Among the Fulani and Tuareg herders, the program reconstituted herds lost in the drought by replacing cattle only for men. Women's stock was not being replaced. This crippled their social system. Animals were unavailable for dowry and bride wealth payments, which, in turn, meant that women had lost their independent property. This was apparently the unintentional result of a government program that issued a card to the "head" of each family and replaced animals only to the family head.

In an effort to see if anything had been learned from that experience, I asked the director of the major agricultural multilateral agency involved in Ethiopia a question (shrouded in innocence): "But who are the farmers here?"

"Oh, I don't know anything about that," he replied, "I only know about coffee." In other words, female labor is not seen as important in intensive agricultural systems that are equated with modern technology and that are designed to maximize export productivity.

In a letter to the United Nations secretary general,[8] a group of experts on aid to Africa, appointed by the Bonn economic summit, reported that

increased agricultural and food production lies at the heart of the problem. . . . Emphasis should be therefore placed on the formulation and implementation of agricultural and food policies which would give priority to small holder farmers, particularly women who produce the vast majority of subsistence food crops. This also implies much improved institutions for extension, marketing and research, including encouragement for the non-Governmental and private sector.

In one of her series of superb reports, Ruth Leger Sivard writes, "It is now becoming clear that a factor contributing to Africa's food shortages is the way women have been systematically excluded from access to land and from control of modern agriculture.[9]

But the opinions of Ruth Sivard and the group of experts mentioned above receive minimal attention when compared with those of the World Bank. The bank's view, or lack of it, can be assessed in the following documents. In a recent best-selling World Bank publication called *Putting People First: Sociological Variables in Rural Development*,[10] which is described as "a culturally sensitive approach to the preparation, planning, and implementation of rural development projects," women are specifically mentioned once in 444 pages. This solitary reference reads:

Design in implementation problems related to the neglect of women's roles was mentioned in just six of the reports, too few for analysis. The Project Performance and Audit Report of a few West African projects, however, called attention specifically to socially incompatible assumptions about the roles and activities of women. Some recommendations in these audits can be reiterated: *if women are to be prominent agricultural producers*, female personnel should be drawn into the extension system; associations of female producers should be carefully investigated; and production and marketing units that exclude women will not function effectively in a cultural tradition or in a project that expects women to produce and sell. Neglect of women's roles are simply a corollary of the general lack of socially informed design and implementation strategy. *Specific discussions of men's roles was almost as rare as the mention of women* [my emphasis].[11]

In 1984, World Bank senior vice president Ernest Stern described the African situation as follows:

We along with other donors, I think it is fair to say, among all our achievements, have failed in Africa. We have not fully understood the problems, we have not identified the priorities, we have not always designed our projects to fit the agro-climatic conditions of Africa and the social, cultural and political frameworks of Africa. . . . We, and everybody else, are still unclear about what can be done in agriculture in Africa.[12]

Decades in literature detailing the dominant role of women in agriculture in Africa do not seem to have penetrated the fortress of the World Bank. This organization, you will recall, requires the establishment of national accounts in countries seeking aid and loans. This organization imposes economic policy changes, based on national accounts statistics, on recipient countries. The consequences are horrific.

Poverty and the Economy: The Unaccounted for Costs

In the late twentieth century, the greater number of the casualties and victims of war are not the military but "civilians"—

that is, overwhelmingly, women and children. In the late twentieth century, the greater number of casualties and victims of the market are not the workers but the "economically inactive"—that is, overwhelmingly, women and children.

Over 100 million people in sub–Saharan Africa suffer from hunger and malnutrition. Per capita food production has dropped by some 20 percent over the last twenty years. While the population increased annually by 3 percent, food production merely increased by 1.2 percent. Grain imports absorbed 20 percent of total foreign exchange earnings of sub–Saharan Africa.

Poverty kills. It kills faster and, currently, on a higher level than war and nuclear militarization. It kills more rapidly than the environmental devastation of the world and the polluted environments of workplaces around the world.

If there were to be nuclear war, it would be genocide. But we don't need nuclear war in order to experience genocide. Neglect of the people and the human condition by governments is, on its current scale, genocidal. And as in war, the largest number of poverty's victims are likely to be civilian women and children—the "use value" part of the population.

All too often in public opinion, I hear an easy assumption that, in countries such as Ethiopia, resources are diverted from meeting human needs because of a lack of democracy. Let's examine the figures from developed nations, the nations that set out to lead the world in democracy.

In the United States, twelve times as many poor children die in fires as do nonpoor children. Eight times as many poor children die of disease as nonpoor children. A study in the state of Maine, which is, incidentally, 98 percent white, says whatever cause of death you name, you will find that more poor children die of it, more often, than nonpoor children.

Theresa Funiciello, a welfare rights organizer in the United States, writes, "By almost any honest measure, poverty is the number one killer of children in the United States. Doctors don't say so, at least not in so many words, because poverty isn't a medical affliction—it is an economic and social one. But it kills just the same."[13]

In New York City, 40 percent of the children—700,000 of them—are living in families that the government classifies as poor. Among them, 10,000 do not have homes of their own and live in shelters for the homeless. Still others suffer from social disorders related to poverty: 3,000 children are born addicted to drugs each year, and 12,000 are removed to foster homes because of abuse or neglect. The greatest victims of poverty continue to be among minorities—blacks and Hispanics—and among single and unwed mothers.[14]

In 1985 the official estimate of the number of starving in the United States was 34 million people. The American Federation of State, County, and Municipal Employees claimed, in 1986, that polls showed the percentage of Americans who wanted medicaid for the poor to be protected or actually expanded was 91 percent. The comparable figures for medicare and student loans were 96 percent and 79 percent. Only 22 percent of the public wanted to see military spending increased.

An examination of the impact of public expenditure cuts under the Thatcher government in Britain looked at the objective impact of the reduction in public spending on men and women. The main findings were that the current social policy negatively affected women, as both public sector workers and consumers, more than men. The main social policy implication was that the restructuring of the welfare state hit women first and foremost. Effects of the cuts were assessed with reference to education, health, transport, and personal social services and, more generally, with reference to unemployment.[15]

Public expenditure cuts generally fall on the poor. In its summary of the survey of economic and social conditions in Latin America in 1985, the UN reports, "In many cases *the reduction of the fiscal deficit has been effected by making substantial cuts in social and economic development expenditure,* and in most of the countries real wages have gone down considerably (my emphasis)."[16]

These policies of austerity were followed to generate "growth," which would, in turn, generate "work" opportunities. This growth is not confined to the developed world. The UN World Economic Survey has forecast a "modest expansion" in the economic growth of a number of developing countries in the next few years. Burma and Thailand are among them—so is India.

The Other Benefits of Growth: Poisons and Pills

The worst industrial chemical accident in history occurred at the Union Carbide pesticide factory in Bhopal, India, in December 1984. We still do not know exactly what happened in Bhopal: the causes of the accident, the nature of the toxicological reaction to the gas, the utter inadequacy of treatment for victims.

The truth is that no one really cares. You see, not only were these people not productive (they weren't included in labor force statistics), but as far as the Indian government is concerned, they didn't even exist. The official death toll from Bhopal was about two thousand. Doctors on the site say the true figure was closer to ten thousand. Nearly half of Bhopal's residents lived in slum colonies called *bastis*. Ninety percent of the people affected by the gas at Bhopal were slum dwellers. They were also the most vulnerable population because of pervasive malnutrition and chronic disease.

Bhopal is the most visible of thousands of related catastrophes that have occurred around the world with the spread of modern technology and with the exploitation of the developing world by multinationals. The irony is, of course, that although the production of pesticide at the factory of Bhopal has ceased, the accident spins its web into the economy so that now large sums of money are paid in American and Indian courts (to people with not the least bit of interest in the victims of the disaster) to work out how much Union Carbide will pay, or pay off, or pay out, to local and central government in India.

It is quite clear that most of the victims of the Bhopal accident will never receive any form of settlement.

Bhopal is the tip of the iceberg. Thirty-eight percent of international trade in pesticides is with the Third World. More than 30 percent of all pesticides exported from the United States are not approved for use within that country. Approximately 20 percent of these have formally been registered but were suspended or canceled for most uses after dangers became apparent.

It is not simply war and environmental havoc that the developed countries successfully continue to export. Is it simply coincidence that the chief producers of legitimized pharmaceutical drugs also happen to be the three wealthiest countries in the world? The United States produces 34 percent; Japan, 20 percent; and West Germany, 13 percent of these drugs. During the 1970s, drug sales in the Third World increased by 20 percent per annum. However in 1980, of the 2,452 new drugs introduced in the year, only 4 percent were launched in the U.S. and Canada; more than 40 percent were launched in the Third World. In the South Pacific I have seen family-planning pills, some years old and now forbidden in the developed world, dumped as "aid" on the populations. In stalls in India and Nepal I have seen unlabeled international pharmaceutical products—that are available in the developed world only on prescription and under medical supervision—for sale for cash across a counter.

I cannot but note in passing that, while the "drugs" of the Western world are legitimate and counted in the market, the drugs of the developing world are illegal and forced into the hidden economy. But double standards are commonplace in this economic system.

The system also accommodates double standards in industrial practices. Manufacturing or industrial-led growth in the developing world may well create export-led growth in the GDP and may well create employment. A nation's system of national accounts will measure this. But it will not measure the environmental destruction in pollution caused by such factories, nor the enormous cost to the health of those employed.

Barry Newman of the *Wall Street Journal* recently investigated industrial practices in Malaysia. His stories are not unusual.[17] One finds similar or identical situations throughout Southeast Asia. Nipon Steel's mill ("which probably wouldn't be allowed to operate in Japan") was reputed to be the filthiest and most dangerous factory in Malaysia. A U.S. manager of a Diamond Shamrock arsenical pesticide plant in Malaysia had never seen the workplace standards for arsenic developed and enforced in the United States by the Occupational Safety and Health Agency (OSHA). But he blithely commented, "Hell, if OSHA walked in [here], they would probably close the place down." Malaysian government officials conceded that the overriding government policy was to attract investors. The first question asked by investors, according to one government doctor, is, "What regulations do you have and how well do you enforce them?" Another government official rejected the idea that sick and injured Malaysian workers should have the right to sue employers. "We believe the employer needs a little protection."

The ignorance of health authorities was appalling. A government occupational health specialist had never heard of Benzedrene, a drug commonly used to relieve respiratory trouble. Another found nothing wrong in a survey of an asbestos plant and postulated that "the Asian body is immune" to the dangers of the dust. Another government doctor lamented that some companies refused to divulge what chemical they were using, under the claim that they were protecting trade secrets.

What can be understood from such examples? It is not implicit that a country with a poor or negative growth rate should have such gross neglect of the "value" of human life and of the labor force. China is different—as different as one quarter of the world must be—as inscrutable as the cliché has it, but certainly different.

Looking for Alternatives

China's per capita income is less than (U.S.) $500 annually, yet levels of health and longevity are comparable to those in industrial societies. Ninety-five percent of Chinese children are enrolled in primary school, and the country's 80 percent literacy rate is among the highest in the Third World. Chinese women have a longevity expectation of sixty-nine. Relatively low real incomes do not mean that it is impossible to change the living standards of a population.

The "value" of life is certainly different in China; for me it was the most "foreign" experience I have ever had, and I questioned all my values. How could I reconcile the universal provision for the citizens of China of the five basic necessities— food, clothing, housing, medical care, and burial—with the inability of those same citizens to choose their employment, to choose to live alone, or to choose to get a passport and travel where and when they wanted to?

I saw only three beggars during my four weeks in China, a woman and her two small children outside the Shanghai railway station. Nowhere did I see the dereliction of human life that is apparent in New York City's Penn Station or that one sees any evening under the bridges on the banks of the Thames in London. Nor do those American and British citizens, it occurs to me, have the chance to choose their employment, to choose to live alone, or to choose to get a passport and travel where and when they want to.

Despite all the differences in China, something was universally familiar about women's lives—something tyrannous, something about the way in which they were "valued." Women do not have reproductive freedom: the right to choices regarding their own fertility. Female infanticide is well documented. Real wage rates differ markedly between the sexes; there is sex stereotyping in employment and discrimination in working conditions. Union workers call for women to go home to create job opportunities for men. Women do the housework and paid work. Prostitution, sexist advertising, and the reappearance of "maids" mark the transition to modernization.

But the transition is also marked by other decisions.

As recently as 1972, China was spending 14 percent of its GNP for military purposes. It began a systematic reduction in 1975 and, except for 1979, has reduced expenditure in all of the last eight years. By 1985, military spending had fallen to 7.5 percent of GDP. In July 1985, during the time of my visit to China, the government announced a plan to invest $360 million over two years to retrain one million soldiers to return to civilian life. This would cut the armed forces from 4.2 to 3.2 million, a reduction of 24 percent, and worldwide would reduce the number of men and women under arms by 4 percent.

New governments in Peru and Argentina also began pursuing reductions in expenditure for military purposes. These reductions were all being pursued independent of any negotiated reductions in neighboring countries. Japan spends under 1 percent of its GDP for military purposes, compared with 7 percent in the United States and 14 percent in the Soviet Union. The combination of negligible defense expenditures and high domestic savings has enabled the Japanese to invest heavily in modernizing plant and equipment. This, in turn, enhances the nation's competitive position enabling it to run a large foreign trade surplus even though it imports virtually all its oil and most of its raw materials. (It also has, incidentally, the lowest wage rate for women compared with men of any industrialized work force in the world.)

China, Peru, Argentina, and Japan are exceptions. The weight of propaganda still insists that war produces valuable growth. When the 1984 UN economic survey reports that "country by country comparisons over time for the period following World War II show that productivity growth was higher in periods with high military spending," my conclusion is, "But of course, that is what the national accounts system was organized to prove."

The system is mightily assisted in this by the language of

avoidance now employed by the military. Spending escalates to develop sophisticated weapons to "wipe out the opposition's nuclear forces." If you are trying to get a new budget through your government advisors, it is much more credible to develop a weapon to do this than to develop one that will "slaughter one-hundred million civilians in the opposing camp." Wars are now far more life threatening for civilians than for combatants.

The system of national accounts is not so much a tribute to logical coherence, as a reflection of the perceived social urgencies of the time of their development. The almost guaranteed continuation of war has induced analysts to agree to abide by the many conventions that the original war system demanded. Those who stand to gain from this—the superpowers, the arms exporters, the military dictatorships—are the key players on the world stage. They do not wish the system to change. Multinationals and politicians do not wish for a change. The incompetence and villainy is quite clear.

Since 1945, we have spent $4 trillion on nuclear weapons. This is enough to kill every person on earth twelve times over. Since the possibility of our dying more than once is slightly ridiculous, this means that for every living person on this planet there has been an expenditure of $700 million to effectively kill us once. The real expenditure on killing us has been that multiplied by twelve.

In this way we measure the value of death.

This does raise the question of the value of life.

8. A Value on Your Time

Women, Children, and the Economics of Reproduction

The previous chapter examined the high value men place on death. Now we will examine the value our society places on life—and on the women who give and bear life. In a sane world, it would seem, humankind would place a high value on life and those able to provide it. Given the world of the last chapter, however, we might fear the worst. Let's take a look at the economics of reproduction.

Women give birth. Women deliver human life to the world. Sometimes they are sold to men that they might bear children, and sons in particular, and they can be left or divorced if they fail in this. These are not market transactions—they are the economics of reproduction.

And what is the precise nature of reproduction? Has the concept ever been adequately defined? Is it, as suggested by Ron Fergie, the statistician in chapter 4, just another case of production? Is it, as social scientist and former midwife Mary O'Brien describes it, "about motherhood: despised, derided and neglected motherhood"?

It is about a great deal more, in fact—and in theory. And if we apply ourselves to some linear demarcated thinking, at least six facets of reproduction can be distinguished within an economic context.*

---

* It is not important for the lay reader to understand these terms. We recognize the descriptions which follow them. These "conceptual categories," expressed

Biological reproduction is the most obvious. Its characteristics are pregnancy, giving birth, lactation, and motherhood. Within economics, its only visibility is as welfare. This form of reproduction is conceptually different from the *reproduction of the labor force*. Reproduction of the labor force focuses, on the political and economic stage, on "fertility." Powerful patriarchs of legislative, religious, and cultural bodies deny women the right to control their own fertility, and thus to control the reproduction of the labor force.

Now if we remain with the interdisciplinary jargon of this exercise of conceptualizing reproduction, we next encounter the *reproduction of the relations of production*. In the traditional labor force theory interpretation, this concept leads to the exploitation of women's productive work (lower pay, lower status, few benefits, less job security). In the household, this is the reproduction of enslavement.

Enslavement also includes female infanticide, preference for sons, maternal mortality, the custom of women eating last or least, female sexual slavery, and marriage. These aforementioned are characteristics of the *reproduction of the relations of reproduction*.

You will begin to notice that "exchange" is current in all these facets of reproduction, but this seldom occurs in the market. It is no less true of the *reproduction of the social relations between women and men*, which includes the religious, legal, and cultural beliefs and practices that define women as the property of men. This is enslavement. And it is most definitely about economics.

Now, if production has a boundary, does reproduction? Most certainly—this is the categorization, and subsequent institutionalization, of who does (and doesn't) and/or should (or

in the words in which the male world has generally discussed reproduction, are here so that men might understand, for the first time, a participant observer's description of the multiple processes. It also serves as an example of a tiresome process for feminists, which is the need to "translate back" to the male world, through their obfuscated terms, the "simple and undisputable facts" of the female world.

shouldn't) reproduce. It is distinguished and characterized in the oppressions of ageism, classism, racism, "development," colonization, neocolonization, religious fundamentalism, and homophobia.

All six forms of reproduction can be observed in many markets and in a myriad of ways. In identifying some markets— the technological medical market, the legal market, the sexuality market, and others—we can observe the forms of economic activity characteristic of reproduction.

The Technological Medical Market

The black market for babies has *always* been operative, particularly in countries with restrictive adoption laws. The new "developments" in medical technology have opened new "markets" for babies, and a surrogate mother is an indispensable "worker" in one of these processes. Or is she?

Susan Ince applied to be a surrogate mother with a U.S. company that provides surrogates. She reports on the questions she asked the director of the company and the answers she received:

What happens if you don't become pregnant?

Artificial insemination is tried twice a month for six months. If the surrogate has not conceived, she is then removed from the programme and the father begins again with a different surrogate.

And she receives no money for her participation?

No. Look at it this way. We pay all the fees and medical expenses. What does it cost you? Unless you start putting a value on your time.[1]

Unless you start putting a value on your time?

Writing in *The Mother Machine*,[2] Gena Corea notes that, under one piece of proposed legislation governing surrogacy in the United States, if the surrogate mother miscarries prior to the fifth month of pregnancy, no compensation other than medical expenses will be paid. If she miscarries after this time, 10 percent of the fee plus medical expenses would be paid. Corea has written to me subsequently:

Of course this makes it clear that the baby is a product. You don't deliver the goods, you don't get paid. But there is another point to be made here. If the woman miscarries prior to the fifth month of pregnancy, does the physician who examined her not get paid? Does the physician who inseminated her not get paid? Does the psychiatrist who screened her not get paid? Does the lawyer who arranged the surrogate pregnancy lose out on his money? Not on your life.

They all get their money. But there is no need to pay the woman. And most people don't notice anything amiss in this arrangement. They really don't know what you are talking about when you object to it. You can't rent a *cow* in this country for five months for free. But you can rent a woman.[3]

In Britain, the "babies for sale" ban is being beaten by agencies that send surrogate mothers to the Continent for their pregnancies. Reproductive Freedom International pays women between £5,000 and £7,000 (U.S. $9,100 and U.S. $12,740) for "keeping a diary of their pregnancy as part of a serious research project and not for selling babies." The agency's boss, Ms. Lorrien Finley, says this is not illegal. "The surrogates are effectively being paid for working. It just happens that they need to get pregnant to get the job." The babies will go to couples who each pay Ms. Finley £13,000 (U.S. $23,660).

Lawyers, physicians, legislators, and ethicists who write of institutionalizing surrogate motherhood already have plans for reproducing the productive economic inequalities of the North-South dynamic in the field of reproduction.

Social commentator Vance Packard suggests that surrogacy would provide young women with an undemanding career.

It would help if the hired mother was of an easy going nature and enjoyed pregnancy and TV watching. The women would no doubt be free to take on a physically undemanding extra job. If the mother were to gestate an embryo conceived with another woman's egg, the job should not require much of the surrogate in the way of education, family background, good looks, or even skin colour. If the woman is simply to be an incubator, the price would certainly be lower than if she contributed half the baby's heredity. . . . In South Texas, pleasant, conscientious, Mexican American girls [sic] might leap at a fee of $5,000 for bearing a child and girls [sic] south of the border might leap at half that fee. If lawyers can arrange Mexican divorces for Americans, they surely can arrange Mexican gestations.[4]

These surrogates may be seen to be the "lucky" ones: that is, they get paid. For the men who run the surrogacy industry have a high expectation that women should be motivated by altruism to donate eggs, wombs, and their time to these medical experiments. While women's time retains a nil value, lawyer Noel Keane's fee for his services for arranging a birthing with an unpaid (euphemistically, a "volunteer") surrogate has risen from $3,000 in 1981 to $4,000 in 1986. The fees for the technodocs who work in reproductive biology have similarly risen. Their professional organization, the American Fertility Society, released a report in 1986 entitled "Ethical Considerations of the New Reproductive Technologies." It states that "surrogate motherhood offers the woman a chance to be altruistic." The medical and scientific membership of the society takes no such chance.

Louise Brown, the world's first test-tube baby, cost more than £1,000,000 (U.S. $1,820,000) to "produce." It was never suggested that too much had been paid to any of the medical practitioners to produce this child. The new reproductive processes are sold by the patriarchy, be it governments, the medical profession, or newspapers, as being a wonderful answer for the problem of infertile couples. Because of the mass emotional hysteria surrounding the question, women who do accept payment for surrogacy are seen as greedy, calculating, and heartless women extorting undeserved money from a poor, desperate, infertile couple.

In their book *The Reproductive Revolution: New Ways of Making Babies*,[5] Peter Singer and Dean Wells suggest it is best if women serve as surrogates for free, for no payment. Discussing those circumstances in which none of us women can be found to serve as unpaid volunteer gestators for couples who want babies, Singer and Wells write,

In these circumstances, the adoptive couple will be inadequately protected, they will put their money down but find themselves with a worthless contract which the courts will refuse to enforce. Some surrogates will take the money and run first to an abortionist. Others will gradually turn the screw on the adoptive couple as their longed for baby comes closer to its time of delivery.[6]

Singer and Wells advocate the formation of a state surrogacy board. Private surrogacy arrangements would be illegal. The board would encourage volunteer women to gestate babies for free. Failing that, it would set a fee for the women. One advantage of this procedure would be that

since the Board would act as a buffer between the couple and the surrogate it would make it much more difficult for the surrogate to extort additional money from the couple. . . . Most countries now recognise the need for laws to protect consumers. Are not childless couples who make surrogacy arrangements also consumers? If so, do they not merit protection?[7]

Note that the consumer (that is, the adoptive male parent specifically) needs protection—not the surrogate mother. There's a paranoid fear here of women claiming their reproductive power. It is demonstrated in the suggestion that the production of sperm is worth a great deal more than the production of eggs, as when Singer and Wells write:

There is every reason to expect an adequate supply of eggs for reproductive technology from voluntary donations as long as there are patients in IVF [in vitro fertilization] programs producing surplus eggs. A woman donating an egg can do so without inconvenience and without harming her own chances of becoming pregnant. We would expect most of these women to be very willing to donate surplus eggs to other infertile women. There would be no need to offer monetary incentive. . . .
Women undergoing tubal sterilisation can donate an egg without an additional inconvenient medical procedure. *If they are willing to have*

a hormone administered to stimulate the production of several eggs, more eggs can be obtained without additional risk. In Britain, eggs used for research purposes have already been obtained from such voluntary donations.

The weight of argument by the abstract and practical, is clearly in favour of setting up a voluntary system for egg donation. As long as IVF patients produce surplus eggs, it could be a purely voluntary system, for the patients do not suffer any inconvenience as a result of making the donation. Sperm donors, on the other hand, do have to give up their time to make the donations, and they have to put up with some inconvenience. (How much depends on their sexual habits.) A modified voluntary system, like that described earlier, is appropriate here.[8]

These boys conclude that sperm vending places a greater strain on the man than egg "donation" does on the woman. She only gets shot up with hormones and gets her ovaries grasped and twisted and eggs sucked out of her follicles, with what long-term effects on her we don't know—but he loses some of his valuable time. And apparently he long ago started placing a value on his time, so he should get some sort of compensation.

This is a strange treatment of the notion of scarcity. It is eggs, wombs, and surrogates that are in shorter supply, not sperm. The world needs a small proportion of its male population for its continued biological reproduction. This inversion of value is also realized in the market for animals. I saw an Angora buck sell in New Zealand in 1985 for $120,000: the top-priced doe was $40,000. Stallions change hands on the world bloodstock market for millions of dollars. But among the Turu people (whom I discussed in chapter 1 as exchanging bridewealth), cows, heifers, does, and ewes are more highly priced than their male equivalents, steers, bulls, bucks, or rams.

The Legal Market

The surrogate industry is one that prostitutes women's bodies for reproductive purposes. This is not the first time that bodies or parts of bodies have been seen as having a market or exchange value. The law courts provide us with some of the more extraordinary judgments on the value of reproduction.

In Lake Charles, Louisiana, in 1986, a jury awarded $4.92 million to the family of a toddler whose penis had to be amputated after it was severely damaged during a circumcision when he was two years old.[9] I have found it impossible to find any record of any tortious liability case where that amount of damages was awarded as a result of the *death* of a young girl, let alone the loss of a limb or of her reproductive function.

In regulations adopted under the Automobile Insurance Act,[10] the government of Quebec tried to be very fair about the compensation available for the loss of male or female genital organs. The loss of a penis is compensated at the same rate as the loss of a vagina. The loss of both testicles is compensated at the same rate as a woman's loss of her internal genital organs. Accident compensation schemes eliminate tortious liability, so you cannot sue in the courts for damages following death or injury. But the regulating bodies of the scheme set maximum payout limits for permanent injury. For those who are not in the paid work force at the time of their accident, this is their only compensation. So, because women are more often in the unpaid work force, they once again end up with less compensation than men.

There are insufficient cases for conclusive results in an examination of compensation for loss of reproductive capability under the accident compensation regime in New Zealand, so 1978 will serve as an example. There were two hearings on appeal for accident or injury to sexual and reproductive organs.[11] In the first case, a twenty-five-year-old woman, who was thirty-seven weeks pregnant, had a full-thickness ruptured uterus. The fetus was expelled into her abdomen and was asphyxiated. After a subtotal hysterectomy, she could no longer have children. The woman was married and a housewife. Her award was for (N.Z.) $8,000. This was the maximum amount payable at the time for permanent disability. In a second case,

in 1978, a forty-two-year-old married caretaker lost his left tes-
ticle. He had one month of continual pain before its removal
and has, the report says, "a worry of further accidents." There
is stress on his married life. He was awarded $500.

It is clear, then, that the market has found a way of "valuing"
the reproductive capability. But what "market" might be seen
to be operative for the "product" of that capability, namely,
children?

Children do have a price on their head. While in the nineteenth century in the United States, working class families in-
sured their children, today 74 percent of children in households
with incomes between $20,000 and $24,999 have some form of
life insurance compared with only 37 percent in households
with incomes below $6,000.[12] The nature of the value of chil-
dren has changed. In academic research and theories about fertility in developing countries, special attention is given to the
value of children as security assets.[13] In early compensation
cases for children in the United States, this was the basis of
awards. In *Munro v. Dredging* in California in 1890, consideration of a mother's sorrow was rejected by the court, but the
jury was instructed to determine the pecuniary value of the
"loss of comfort, society and protection," caused by a son's
death.[14]

Another principle for judgment, along with a clear statement
of the value of women's productive and reproductive work, is
found in a 1904 New Jersey decision. The case involved the
deaths of a sixteen-year-old boy and a nineteen-year-old girl,
both killed in a collision between a trolley car and a train. Initial
verdicts of $6,000 and $5,000, respectively, were contested as
excessive by the New Jersey Street Railway Company. In a new
decision, Judge Adams upheld the boy's $6,000 award but re-
duced the girl's to $3,000, declaring,

A woman may become a breadwinner; a man must be one. If she
devoted herself to the career as she . . . probably would if she had
not married, she could after a few years have earned, if very successful, at most about $110 a month . . . taking the most optimistic

view of Miss Werpupp's financial future, I think that Mr. Eastwood's expectations were at least twice as valuable.[15]

Ten years later, a New Jersey jury, in a legal suit against a manufacturer of condensed milk, awarded a father $2,000 for the death of his three-month-old son, but only $1,000 for the boy's twin sister.[16]

The conceptual frameworks of fertility theory in the developed world put great emphasis on the near-term costs of children to parents, often to the exclusion of later security concerns.[17] In 1960, in the Michigan case of *Wycko v. Gnodtke*, concerning the accidental death of a fourteen-year-old boy, Judge Smith upheld an award of some $15,000 to the boy's parents. Smith was totally condemnatory of the old "security" or "child labor" approach. He introduced a new alternative: the worth of a child should be determined by past parental investment in his or her upbringing.

Just as with respect to a manufacturing plant, or industrial machine, value involves the cost of acquisition . . . maintenance, service . . . and renovation, we must consider the expenses of birth, of food, of clothing, medicines, of instructions, of nurture and shelter.[18]

The law thus joined fertility and economic theories in implying that the cost of children is determined in advance just like the price of goods produced for sale in a competitive market. The neo-classical schools of economics, such as the Chicago School, claim that an increase in the price or cost of children leads to a decrease in the number of children demanded, all else equal. "All else equal" is an economist's assumption that overlooks the fact that parents can directly affect the cost of children by choosing how much money to spend on them and that children can directly affect their own price by choosing how much they will contribute to parental income. Some economists will grant that personal decisions, about birth control, for example, may affect bargaining power between family members. But the possibility that a woman's political struggle to control her own fertility might determine such decisions has never been conceded.

Sociologist Viviana Zelizer reports that the direct pricing of sentimental worth has now entered the argument. She writes:

The mother is the preferred lead off witness in child death cases followed by the father and any siblings. A suggested standard closing argument for the plaintiff's lawyer shows how such testimony is used: "You have seen and heard from the child's mother. You know about the deep concern she felt for this boy. . . . It is obvious to anyone who has seen these parents and heard them testify that they lived their lives for their children." Where recovery for moral pain is allowed, psychiatrists usually testify on parents' mental distress. In *Zeebord v. Gay*, for instance, an eminent psychiatrist testified in the death of a twelve year old girl, the youngest of five children, explaining: "A mother really invests a lot of herself into her children and especially into the baby of the family. . . . It is like investing in blue-chip stocks. . . . This is what a mother is going to give to society. . . . If anything happens to that child . . . you lost your investment. That is why (mothers) have this prolonged neurotic reaction and long grief . . . after such a loss.[19]

Zelizer comments, "While the economically useful child was legally 'owned' by the father, the 'priceless' child is considered the mother's sentimental asset."[20] She further notes, "In Russia, no death actions exist for unproductive minors." Both the Soviet Union and the Peoples Republic of China denounce compensation for nonpecuniary loss as the ultimate capitalist exploitation. "Only the Bourgeois think that mental suffering can be cured by money, and like commodities, can be exchanged by currency."*[21]

Australian Phillipa Gemmel Smith, pregnant with her first child, was curious about the cost of children. In 1986, in an article in a women's magazine, she estimated the total cost of food, clothes, entertainment, and holidays, child care, maternity furniture, and other costs of a child from the age of birth

---

* So much for the mental suffering of a rape victim.

to five years, at $41,220 (U.S. $29,728). For the years from six to twelve for the same items, she estimated the total cost at $41,780 (U.S. $30,132). This, of course, was extremely different from the minimum cost at that time defined by the Australian government in benefits, which totaled $31.70 (U.S. $22.86) a week for a supporting parent, in addition to a basic unemployment benefit of $97.90 (U.S. $70.61). In speaking to friends, Gemmel Smith reported that by the time she carried her child through the door of her home it would have cost about $1,500 (U.S. $1,082).[22]

This will be a wanted child. In the few wrongful birth cases that are brought to trial in the United States, "sentimental value" operates to diminish any chances of recovery for the parents. A wrongful birth case could, for example, concern a woman who believed herself to have been sterilized but who subsequently conceived and bore a child. Most plaintiffs settle out of court. According to one legal commentator, "the emotional susceptibility" of juries to the joys of parenthood remains a serious obstacle for wrongful birth plaintiffs. The parents in *Troppi v. Scarf*, for instance, accepted $12,000, considerably less than their original request for $250,000.[23]

In Great Britain the situation is a little different. The *Guardian* newspaper reported in 1979 that a woman who gave birth to a healthy baby boy after an unsuccessful abortion had been awarded nearly £20,000 (U.S. $36,400) in damages against the Harley Street doctor who carried out the operation.

The judge awarded her £3,500 (U.S. $6,370) for diminution of marriage prospects, £7,000 (U.S. $12,740) for loss of past earnings, and £7,500 (U.S. $13,650) for loss of future earnings in her job as an audio secretary. He also made an award of £750 (U.S. $1,365) for "pain and suffering" in childbearing and for the "anxiety, distress, and mental suffering" she had experienced. But, he argued, these matters had to be weighed against "the happiness motherhood has obviously brought . . . ." Mr. Justice Watkins said he rejected an argument by the defense that it was "wholly repugnant" and against public policy to regard the birth of a perfectly healthy child as a loss.

The Social and Cultural Market

Up to this point, I have concentrated our attention on the "markets" concerned with biological reproduction: that is, the capacity and willingness to reproduce human life, pregnancy, and giving birth. The reproduction is of a product—both a child and a potential member of the labor force. Within the labor force, the exploitation of women is reproduced by way of lower pay, lower status, fewer benefits, and less job security. This concept of reproduction—reproduction of the relations of production—includes the theoretical work of socialist feminists who have raised "reproductive labor" or "housework" to the status of a necessity equally as important to society as production. It also embraces economists Baran and Sweezy's conclusion that the functional reproduction of the U.S. economy would require less than half the human and natural resources actually used.

But within the household, the (unpaid) laborer reproduces, through housework, the social relations within the family.

Mary O'Brien was born in Scotland and practiced as a nurse and midwife in the slums of Glasgow for twenty-five years. She is now an associate professor of sociology and education in Ontario, Canada. In her book, *The Politics of Reproduction*, O'Brien writes that

an important element in the capacity of the ruling classes to exercise power over men lies precisely in the fact that no man is powerless. However exploited, however stupid, however brutal, however deceived, all men are potent in the realm of reproduction. No man is ultimately powerless. . . . The social relations of reproduction are relations of dominance.[24]

More explicitly, French feminist theorist Christine Delphy comments:

What makes "housework" is not each particular operation, nor even their sum total, but their particular organisation which is itself due to the relations of production in which the person doing them finds herself.[25]

Since the benefits which they receive have no relationship to the services which they provide, it is impossible for women to improve their own standards of living by improving their services. The only solution for them is to provide the same services for a richer man. This does not make [her] a member of that class. She herself does not own the means of production. Her standard of living does not depend on her class relationship to the proletariat, but on her serf relations of production with her husband.

To supply unpaid labour within the framework of a universal and personal relationship (marriage) constitutes precisely a relationship of slavery.[26]

The market (or lack of it) for the reproduction of women's enslavement is reinforced by the law in judgments on maintenance, custody, matrimonial property and tortious liability for causing death. It is clear that the general consensus, reproduced by different agents of the patriarchy, is that there is not much value on a woman's time.

Many women have an experience similar to that of Mrs. Murdoch, a woman whose married life began during 1943 in Alberta, Canada. Starting with few assets, the early years of the Murdoch's marriage were spent working as a couple on several ranches until they were in a position to obtain their own land. On property obtained by the couple, Mrs. Murdoch was deeply involved in both the domestic and commercial spheres of production. She told the court, "[I worked at] haying, raking, swathing, mowing, driving trucks and tractors and teams, quietening horses, taking cattle back and forth to the reserve, dehorning, vaccinating, branding, anything that was to be done. I worked outside with him, just as a man would, anything that was to be done."

Moreover, during most of their married life, her husband was working off the farm. Consequently, until a son was old enough to help, she did much of the work on her own. Upon marital breakdown in 1968, she sought to obtain a one-half interest in the assets that had accumulated during the years of the marriage and that were registered in the name of her husband. The rural judge dismissed this aspect of the case in 1974. Her appeals to both the appellate division in Alberta and to the Supreme Court of Canada were dismissed.[27] That is, twenty-five years of unpaid labor that was imbedded in farm capital was held to be the property of her husband. The judge said that her contribution in labor "consisted of no more than was to be ordinarily expected of a ranch wife" and, in effect, provided her with no legal basis to establish a claim to productive property.

Similarly, a U.S. housewife reported in 1981, "I came out of the divorce court with a cash entitlement of $2,500 and was told I was lucky to get it. I figured it out; 23 cents a day for 31 years of hard labor."[28]

A few may have the experience of New Zealand women, who receive at age sixty the full government superannuation, at the same level as men who have had a lifelong engagement in the paid work force. Matrimonial property acquired during a marriage must be divided fifty-fifty on divorce or death, unless such a division would be "repugnant to justice." But in the courts, the custodial parent, generally the mother, is unable to have the courts recognize the daily work of mothering and household maintenance in deciding the amount of child support the father is expected to pay. Most women and children are simply deserted, without recourse to courts. Yet they survive in lives of great value (if not economic worth) that defy every economic pigeonhole and proscription, and simply, systematically, disappear from the equations. Ruth Sidel, a professor of sociology at Hunter College, New York City, who has also been a psychiatric social worker, says that millions of women are only a divorce away from destitution.

In matters of divorce, custody, and maintenance, the courts place little value on women's lives.

But in tortious cases it might be quite different. In *Legare v. United States*,[29] the judge awarded the surviving husband $150,100 for the death and conscious suffering of his wife and mother of their six children. In 1961, judgment for the plaintiff in his own right was for $125,100 (including $98,838 for the loss of his wife's services; $25,000 for the loss of her companionship and consortium; and $1,200 for the funeral bill) and $25,000 as the personal representative of the wife's estate for her conscious pain and suffering. In the judgment the court held,

I conclude that the expense to the father of providing the children a home, the services of a suitable person to run the home and administer to the children's needs and the services of domestic help can be met by providing the plaintiff $8,500 per year for 18 years, compounded at 4%.

The value of children is as varied as that of mothers and wives. The children's value is often influenced by the reproduction of gender power relations.

The *New York Times* reported in 1986 that mothers virtually always get custody of their children if both parties to a divorce agree to that arrangement, but when couples disagree, an increasing number of fathers win custody especially if they remarry women who do not work outside the home.[30] Men have more money to pay for the enormous legal bill and so can use the suggestion that there will be a court battle as economic blackmail. According to Doris Jonis Freed, a New York matrimonial attorney, some fathers are raising the possibility of a custody fight as a bargaining tool to lower the amount of child support or other financial settlement they must pay to their former wives. Freed commented that more and more couples are opting for joint custody. However, support awards in courts do not take into account the fact that the parent who tends the child most of the time needs more money than the one who cares for the child just a fraction of the time.

The Labor Market

Male economists have recognized the "reproduction of social relations" as a characteristic of reproduction. But their terms are conceptually limited. For example, in their book *Monopoly Capital*,[31] economists Baran and Sweezy show racism and schooling as social mechanisms of control that socialize the vast mass of the population into a fearful complacency in which the only alternative world is one that is worse. This is part of the "reproduction of social relations." But Baran and Sweezy do not take the next step in observation: *information* and *conception*. The larger number of single households headed by women, the large number of black families in poverty, the continuing stereotyping in education that discriminates against women, all resulting in women employed in lower status and lower paid jobs, is reproduction of the major social mechanism of control—the ideology and practice of patriarchy.

John Kenneth Galbraith identifies the social mechanisms of control as the techno-structure—managers, executives, government employees, and trade union officials—who have power because they perform the vital role in modern production of ensuring the smooth flow of resources through complex processes.[32] Galbraith says that the techno-structure uses that power to reduce the influence of market forces to zero. Market forces, he says, are a textbook myth. The choice is not about a market system or a command system but about *who* will do the commanding. And while the techno-structure can be violent and wasteful, the major problem is that it is shortsighted and unenlightened. Galbraith sees advertising and military expenditure as rational activities for reproducing a fundamentally dysfunctional, irrational social system.

Galbraith describes the reproduction of the social relations of power. In overwhelming numbers, managers, executives, government employees, and trade union officials in the techno-structure in any country are male. It is the same in any legal

system, parliament, church hierarchy, military or police force—
and with devastating results.

Lucy Komisar reports of visiting shantytown brothels near
the U.S. military base at Palmerole where Honduran women
"serve" as prostitutes for Honduran and U.S. soldiers.[33] She
writes of young Honduran women, some just sixteen years old,
kidnapped and brought to the brothels as captives; of women
who escaped and were caught and returned by Honduran po-
licemen. The owners of the brothel-cantinas take much of the
prostitution fee. Many of the women have been drawn so
deeply into debt to the men who supply their food and minimal
housing that they can never pay off their debts and gain their
freedom. Komisar found that the local police, who were controlled by the Honduran military, acted as enforcers of the
prostitution system. The women's customers included enlisted
men and officers from the U.S. military. The U.S. involvement
in this enforced enslavement was explicit: U.S. army doctors routinely conducted medical examinations on Honduran
women working in brothels to ensure "safe" access to sex.

The Sexuality Market

You will remember that at the beginning of this chapter I
discussed the concept of the reproduction boundary. It is important at this point to distinguish who lies outside that boundary. There we find

1. *prepubescent people*, valued not in themselves but only as
   a long-term investment with accumulating interest (Becker
   and the Chicago School: the value of a child is its expected
   worth as an adult), and *old people*, in particular, postmenopausal women perceived as useless/worthless because
   they are postreproductive biologically, thus junk-heaped
   as obsolescent because these repositories of a culture's experience and wisdom are viewed as "a burden on society";

2. *celibate persons* who, unless living in a context *demanding* celibacy (religious or, in must cultures, the state of virginity for women or the state of widowhood), are otherwise considered repressed, sick, or "weird";

3. *any peoples* perceived as threatening because of the combination of their *poverty and/or enslavement*, their *capacity for revolt*, and their *number* (that is, entire peoples—largely Third World—who are forced outside the reproduction boundary toward/into extinction through forced sterilization, coercive population programs, deliberate destabilization of a region to encourage death by starvation or war or refugee crisis);

4. *heterosexual women who demand reproductive freedom*— through contraception and abortion rights. (This is threatening because it is, in effect, workers' control over their labor and because it makes it possible for a woman to cross the reproduction boundary at will, thus making the boundary, as it were, disappear); and

5. *same-sex lovers, but especially lesbian women*, who are seen as forsaking their womanly reproductive function ("barren lesbians"). This is why lesbian mothers in choosing fertilization—whether they become mothers prelesbianism or postlesbianism—are "privileged," in the sense of "heterosexual privilege." They have crossed the reproduction boundary to the inside; they have contributed a "product" and thus have reproductive validity (at least that taken-for-granted invisible "validity" shared by all women who reproduce biologically). However they have conceived, they are, in this particular, no longer threatening to the patriarchy. They are now "under control."

Notice that except for celibates (who are perceived as "nonsexual") and Third World people (who are perceived as *overly* sexual, nonstop breeders), *all* the other categories are seen as threatening because they can or do choose to separate sexuality from reproduction. Children's sexuality is regarded negatively (or denied outright) because it can't produce "the product"; affirmations of sexuality among the elderly are similarly regarded; obviously the same situation exists with heterosexual women vis-à-vis contraception and abortion. But the greatest opprobrium is reserved for lesbian women, because children might in time cross inside the boundary (are expected to); old folks are presumed to have already done their part (were expected to); the poor and peoples of color are at least reproducing as well as copulating (but more than they're expected to); the celibates aren't reproducing but at least are (perceived as) not having any fun not doing so; and the heterosexual woman using contraceptive or abortive means is seen as crossing the boundary *temporarily*, since she might always cross back and conceive (hence the operative euphemisms "family planning" or "spacing"). The lesbian woman, on the other hand, unless she has been or is a mother, is perceived as having placed herself deliberately outside the reproduction boundary, with two additional offences: she has done so during an age-overlap with fertility years (unlike children or elders), *and* she has separated sexuality from conception *permanently*, thus bringing down the whole house of cards. Finally, it is just possible that she may have seen through the whole process of the reproduction of enslavement, which is threatening to the masters and threatening to the enslaved, for the mirror she holds up to their lives may reveal too clearly for the powerless the extent of their co-option.

The Economics of Breast-feeding

At the outset of this chapter we examined six categories that can be conceptually separated for the purpose of defining reproduction. But for women, the process of reproduction often includes all the categories. Let us take, as an example, breast-feeding, for breasts and breast milk operate as a microcosmic example of all the forms of enslavement present in the concept of reproduction.

In Caracas, Venezuela, in July 1977, a journalist reported on the emergency ward of the large hospital de Niños, located in the center of the city.[34] Fifty-two infants lay inside. All were suffering from gastroenteritis, a serious inflammation of the stomach and intestines. Many were also suffering from pneumonia. According to the doctor in charge, roughly five thousand Venezuelan babies died each year from gastroenteritis, and an equal number died from pneumonia. The doctor further explained that these babies, like many who preceded them and those who would follow, had all been bottle-fed. He concluded, "a totally breast fed baby just does not get sick like this."

Studies of infant feeding patterns around the world indicate that breast-feeding generally is the most satisfactory food supply for infants, at least for the first four to six months of life. It has nutritional advantages over cow's milk, goat's milk, and infant formulas, is well packaged, and is obviously the cheapest, being of no market value. It also has household budgetary advantages over its two competitors. It does not require the direct visible costs of providing bottles, teats, etc., or the indirect costs (that is, if you put a value on your time) of the alternative forms of infant feeding. An inadequately fed infant is a cost to the health system (as the Venezuelan case illustrates), to the education system (because of brain development), and to society generally. A mother's energy and time spent in breast-feeding in the developing world certainly lowers a country's import bill and, as a preventive health measure, passes on the mother's immunities to the child.

Historically, breast milk has played its part in racism and classism through the work of wet nurses. While in the South of the United States, black women slaves were used as wet nurses and mammies, in Great Britain, working class women were "hired" for such duties. Today it is not uncommon in Africa and Latin America for women in village cultures to voluntarily spell one another with a baby at the breast if both women are lactating—another of those things women do to keep each other alive. It is thought to make a special bond between children, who are then "milk siblings" even if their mothers are not blood-related at all. In the hareem tradition, it wasn't/isn't uncommon for a woman to nurse another woman's child, either as a gesture of close friendship or from necessity if the child's mother is ill—or because the nursing woman is forced to because of being a "lower" wife.

Human milk has not usually been considered or classified as a food by planners or agronomists, as it is not grown agriculturally nor purchased in a processed container.[35] If the question had ever arisen in the system of national accounts, United Nations statisticians would probably have argued that it was conceptually difficult to measure the shadow price of breast milk. One could ascertain the "opportunity cost" in terms of the time that a woman takes for breast-feeding and in terms of the additional food for the mother. That presumes, of course, a value on the mother's time.

One could investigate the availability of alternative forms of milk for a child, its price, and the distance to the outlet for that alternative form. But this as a value measurement does not emphasize the fact that breast milk is better for an infant. We are, however, now well aware that the international economic system makes no distinction between creative (or life-enhancing) and destructive production and consumption. It cannot identify what is good for us.

In New Zealand, the costs of consumption of fresh milk versus dried (or evaporated) milk versus modified milk formulas have been calculated by Farmer Birbeck et al.[36] They put the cost of a liter of milk per day to feed a three-to-four-month-old infant at less than thirty cents (U.S. nineteen cents) for unmodified cow's milk but fifty-one to eighty cents (U.S. thirty-three to fifty-one cents) per day for the special infant formulas or adapted milk. They argue that "the cheaper food cannot be recommended ethically. No artificial food is a complete substitute for breast milk, but if breast feeding is not possible, the best alternative is a well tried adapted formula."

That is, if you have suitable water available, and most of the world's mothers are not that lucky.

If a child does not have solids introduced to its diet after the age of six months, it will not grow healthily. In many countries with high infant mortality rates, the practice is for women to breast-feed for up to two years. Often it is assumed that this is because the women do not understand the need for the child to be fed solid foods or are inexperienced and "stupid" and do not understand the nutritional needs of the child or are too poverty stricken to provide any alternative form of solid food. Rarely is it assumed that it is a decision that a woman is making to safeguard her own life or health from a series of rapid and fatiguing pregnancies, since empirical research has established that breast-feeding postpones the return of ovulation and men-struation after birth.

Two further reasons for prolonging breast-feeding may also be operative. Sometimes breast-feeding is a chance to "rest" for a few minutes without too much criticism. An old Irish proverb says something to the effect that "the only times a woman should be seen sitting down are in church or with a babe at her breast." And sometimes a woman prolongs breast-feeding because (for some, but not all) it is pleasurably erotic and may well be the first "pressure-free," self-controlled, genuine plea-sure she has ever experienced in her life. This is one reason why many mothers speak about children as sources of sen-suality.

Studies have shown that the use of the pill is a significant variable in breast-feeding. It can stop the likelihood that a woman will breast feed at all, though a woman with access to the pill is more likely to stop breast-feeding after three months and will add supplemental foods by the sixth month. Other studies show the following reasons for declines in breast-feeding:

1. Educated middle- or upper-class women in developing countries mimic what they perceive to be the Western ap-

proach to breast-feeding, that is, a move from breast milk to substitutes.

2. Bottle-feeding is more convenient, for mothers are now working outside the home. This points to a worldwide lack of consideration by employers to allow women to breast-feed while at work.

3. Birthing has moved into hospitals, where the institutional timetable insists on a schedule of breast-feeding that often creates stress for both mother and child.[37]

Women who do not breast-feed and women who breast-feed for "too long" or for "too short" a time are seen by health specialists in multilateral aid agencies as problems. Women who breast-feed in accordance with the best practice for the health of mother and child are simply expected to get on with it, to continue their valueless productive and reproductive activity in their own time.

But breasts do have their "productive" moments. Just as rape, in "reproducing" social relations between men and women, demonstrates that the lesbian's bid for freedom beyond the reproduction boundary is but partial, so too the decision not to lactate does not free a woman's breasts from exploitation. Advertising uses them to decorate objects for sale. Pornographers use breasts in films and publications for sexual stimulation. The prostitution "trade" contributes breasts to the hidden economy. The garment industry profits from the marketing of lingerie to flatten or exaggerate or reshape them ("high and thrusting," "pointed," or "low-slung, natural") according to changing fashion. And the medical profession performs so-called cosmetic surgery to rebuild women's bodies, and breasts in particular, to serve the male concept of how they should look.

Yet reproduction is of no value, and women are seen as worthless.

The Social Welfare Market

Gender previctimization, or the targeting of females while still in the womb, has already become a lucrative practice in India. According to Mona Daswani, a social worker in Bombay, doctors have set up businesses to detect female fetuses through amniocentesis. When a female fetus is found, it is aborted. Daswani estimates that 78,000 female fetuses were aborted this way between 1978 and 1980.[38]

In China, since the introduction of the one-child family policy, there has been an alarming rise in female infanticide resulting in a serious outnumbering of female infants by males. According to the *People's Daily*, "The phenomenon of butchering, drowning and leaving to die female infants and maltreating women who give birth to female infants is a grave social problem." On November 30, 1982, in a statement to the People's National Assembly, Premier Zhao Ziyang specifically condemned the "murder by drowning" of infant girls.[39]

If the murder does not occur at birth, it may occur soon afterwards. In the rural areas of Bangladesh, the mortality rate among girls under five is 35–50 percent higher than among boys because of the low standing of women and need to provide dowries.[40] And where food is scarce, the cultural practice of women and girl children eating last may see girls starve to death.

One billion people on the planet today are chronically undernourished: the majority of these are women and children. Deaths relating to hunger and starvation average fifty thousand a day: the majority of these are women and children. Chronic malnutrition exists in richer countries among the elderly and in families headed by unemployed women with dependent children.

Women's poor or poorer health or the neglect of women's health is deliberately reproduced by the economic and political system. The Economic and Social Council of the United Nations identifies the improvement of health and the advancement of the status of women as contributing most to an improvement in the well-being of populations. (It seems impossible for this patriarchy to imagine advancing women as a matter of justice and for the sake of women themselves.) The Economic and Social Council then comments:

Though committed to reducing morbidity and mortality, the Governments of many developing countries, faced with severe reductions in available resources, have found it necessary to make substantial cuts in essential health services. Similarly efforts to provide safe drinking water and basic sanitation have been slowed by deteriorating economic conditions.[41]

The World Health Organization raises the question of whether "the relatively low status and prestige accorded to primary health care stems from the fact that it is mainly women who provide it. Or rather are women the main providers of such care because it is still viewed by too many people and men particularly as unprestigious work and therefore to be left largely to women?"[42]

Answer: both.

One of the ways in which we women reproduce the conditions of our own existence is in health care. For many governments, a cut in health care shifts the burden from the government sector back to the household. But most health care is provided by women for women anyway and to children and men, too. Health (including childbirth, infant care, nutrition, contraception, and menstrual cramps) is for most women a matter to be met and dealt with at home by mothers, grandmothers, wives, daughters, friends, or neighbors. Even in the formal system, health care will be provided by women generally, who constitute the bulk of the labor force.

Women also reproduce social relations that have a deleterious effect on their health. It was mothers who bound feet; it is women who perform clitoridectomy and other forms of female circumcision on young girls. It is mothers who refuse to believe or else deny their daughters' reports of the father, uncle, brother, or neighbor's molestation. Many of us have friends who were raped, often within marriage, and never admitted it to themselves. We watch mothers who every day deny themselves, "blocking off" their own pains or desires, reproducing mental illness, consumed with guilt if they put themselves first.

We do not see our teas, herbal medicines, oils, massage, compresses, poultices, salves, social support, willingness to listen, counsel, offers of emotional support, and our empowerment of each other as activities that have no value. When they are performed by paid members of the medical profession or social workers or the clergy or pharmaceutical companies, by physiotherapists and other paramedics, they have a market or exchange value. When women do them for each other and for children and, of course, for the men we know, they are neither productive nor reproductive. Men seldom have these skills or undertake these tasks except when paid to reinforce a patriarchal ideology—as priest, as hospital social worker, as police officer. They have all the comfort and support they need from institutions that reinforce their power and gender culture, which ensures an enslaved comforter should their system fail them.

It is possible that health care is women's work not only because it is seen as subordinate but also in some way "dirty." There are many cultural and religious taboos associated with pregnancy, childbirth, and menstruation. Moral values combine with economic ones to ensure an enslavement to inadequate health. In the introduction to *Sisterhood Is Global*, feminist Robin Morgan writes, "Women everywhere suffer from the *absence* of contraceptive information and devices and the suppression of traditional women's knowledge of them, or from the *presence* of unsafe means of preventing conception. . . . Thirty to fifty percent of all "maternal" deaths in Latin America are due to improperly performed illegal abortions or to complications following abortion attempts. . . . Every ten minutes in 1980, an Indian woman died of a septic abortion. . . . Illegal abortion is the leading cause of female deaths in Caracas. . . .

In Peru 10 to 15 percent of all women in prison were convicted for having had illegal abortions."[43] In most cultures women also nurse the dying and wash the dead.

Our enslavement can also be ensured by addiction to chemical pharmaceuticals. The *Isis* International Bulletin in 1978 reported that 67 percent of psychoactive drugs are given to women. Each year, one-third of us over the age of thirty receive prescription tranquillizers, stimulants, and/or antidepressants. Coping with low paying, unfulfilling jobs, family and child care, and never-ending housework, women present doctors with vague complaints of pressures, frustrations, and anxiety. Since 90 percent of U.S. physicians are men, the doctor is usually unable to fully comprehend a woman patient's complaints. Biases of the male doctors are reinforced by advertising in the drug industry. And women are reproduced as chemical dependants, as depressives, and as "sick," in this way.[44]

Alternatively, women may be discouraged from perceiving themselves as ill. The relative needs of different members of the family may be closely related to a sense of priorities, that is, that the needs of males in general, and the head of the household in particular, are such that a higher standard of health must be expected and assumed for them.

Another clear example of the absence of value in the good health of a woman is demonstrated in the health studies that exclude women from the sample population when one wishes to obtain information about "people." U.S. feminist Karen Messing notes that

crucial data can be ignored. In a 1963 study of the effect of work on pregnancy outcome by the U.S. Public Health Service, the worker's husband's occupation was recorded, but that of the pregnant worker herself was not. This expensive study was thus useless for identifying working conditions that pose a risk to pregnant women and their fetuses, and the absence of such data has rendered protection for the women very difficult.[45]

The Propaganda Market

The functions of reproduction, overwhelmingly filled by and concerned with women and children, are the first to be formally excluded from the market system or government expenditure in times of recession. Despite evidence linking recession and its consequences to higher mortality and infant mortality, expenditure is invariably shifted from investment in human welfare to investment in productive capital. This is not only the policy of individual governments but tends to be the basis of "commandments" issued by such as the World Bank, the International Monetary Fund, and other major international banking agencies when they are financing or refinancing the debt of developing countries. Even though education of the mother has clearly been demonstrated as a major factor in attaining improvements in nutrition, health, infant mortality, and fertility, long-term beneficial effects of education are lost because girls are the first to drop out of, or be withdrawn from, school. Independent U.S. researcher Ruth Sivard is among those who have suggested that there is a relationship between national average literacy rates and infant mortality.[46] But the attainment of literacy usually involves school attendance.

Where attendance at primary school interferes with a need for child labor in a subsistence economy, then it will be the "least valuable" of the children who are withdrawn from school to carry out tasks. These are, of course, young girls.

The Economic and Social Council of the United Nations reports:

A major problem . . . in attaining and ensuring the goal of universal primary education is the low level of the enrollment ratio of females. Girls form the majority (often 75%) of children not enrolled in the primary school age group. Indeed that seems to be the core of the problem of universalisation of primary education in the developing countries . . . especially in South Asia.[47]

Governments never say, "Yes, we know women are educationally disadvantaged, and we know that if we improve their literacy standard both theirs and their children's health would improve. But frankly, we don't think that is as important an investment as other things, for example, the military and the (predominantly) male labor force." A class analysis by male theorists seldom draws attention to the gender of the poorest or of the world's children or of those most lacking in opportunity.

Generally, men excuse their deliberate policy of oversight and/or devaluation in evasive jargon. The United Nations is particularly good at this and will say things like, "Efforts to achieve equality of educational opportunity for women have been hampered by the need to make difficult choices among competing demands for limited and even declining resources."[48]

Even where education is provided, we have glaring demonstrations of the reproduction of both social relations between men and women and reproduction of the relations of production. The 1982 statistical yearbook of the UN Educational, Scientific, and Cultural Organization (UNESCO) shows the enrollment rates of male and female students in two fields of study: literature, religion, and theology on the one hand and engineering sciences on the other. In the fifty-seven countries for which data exists, whatever their level of economic and educational development, whatever the rate of participation of young women in higher education, whatever the school system or the socioeconomic system, the same trends occur: with few exceptions, women tend far more often to study literature than men. But above all, far fewer of them *without any exception* are enrolled in institutions that train engineers.

Thus the individual and collective investment represented by the education of women is turned to little practical account or it is subtly directed so that it serves only to give "added value" to what is expected of women as mothers and housekeepers.

Since 1983, the total spent by governments on the major social services including education, health, amenities, and housing has fallen below the level needed to maintain the status quo. The increase in absolute poverty is likely to be serious in the years to come, not only because of the lack of productive employment, but also because of the generally inadequate provision of the basics of reproduction—shelter, nutrition, health care facilities, safe drinking water, education, and transportation.

According to some commentators, these difficulties should be easily overcome because so much of the world's population has so much valueless time on its hands during which to fulfill these responsibilities. The General Assembly of the United Nations, representing our male rulers, reports:

> Women's productive and reproductive roles tend to be compatible in rural areas of low income countries, since family agriculture and cottage industries keep women close to the home, permit flexibility in working conditions and *require low investment of the mother's time*. . . . As the economic contribution of both children and women is of prime importance for the family, any remaining incompatibility between childcare and work is often resolved by *a woman's reducing her leisure time rather than her work time or family size* [my emphasis].[49]

This, of course, assumes that a woman has leisure time. It certainly assumes that she "places no value on her time." It does not suggest that her comparatively unproductive and inactive partner might use some of his leisure time to participate in child care or household activities—but then he puts a value on his time.

Wheeling and Dealing: The Power Politics of Reproduction

Power politics are not confined to the household, though the balance of power beyond the household simply magnifies the gender social relations of reproduction inside the household. Governments and parliaments, the overwhelming majority of which are male, regulate the reproductive lives of women throughout the world.

In an abortion debate in the U.S. House of Representatives on September 22, 1983, Representative Dannemeyer (R-CA) suggested that by prohibiting abortion future taxpayers "will be brought into the world in order to help pay off the national debt." In Dannemeyer's words, "If we are going to pay off the debt, somebody has got to be born to pay the taxes to pay it off. Now since 1973, the decline in the birthrate per fertile female has reached the point, where, as a civilization we run the serious risk of disappearing from the face of the planet."[50]

Dannemeyer's statement is nonsense. But that doesn't stop him and his brethren from making similar pronunciations annually in the institutions that govern us. When the operation of power relations within a household does not reproduce the old pattern, and there are discernible changes in fertility, Big Brother can intervene to redress the balance in favor of the patriarchy.

Deborah Bryceson and Ulla Vuorela have described the case of Finland to demonstrate this interaction. They write:

Demographic and welfare changes have begun to exert a tension in state policy. The low birth rate together with the improved health care and long life expectancy have modified the social formations age structure such that over the last twenty-five years the number of children under 15 has decreased, and people at retirement age at 65 and over have increased. The services for the aged and disabled have come to represent an ever larger part of social services. As a result the state has designed new policies to attract women to give birth to more babies. Children are again seen as old age security, but now through the mediation of the state who calculate children as future taxpayers. Thus the necessity of achieving a certain minimum rate of population growth defines human reproduction requirements in the biological and social sense at a national level. In turn the lives of women of child bearing age are affected as they are strongly encouraged by the new state family policy measures, to bear more children.[51]

Changes in the predominant ideology of the patriarchs in power can have major effects for the relations of reproduction. The Iranian revolution is a clear example of this. A former Iranian delegate to the UN Commission on the Status of Women, the Gaza Strip, some of the most horrendous health problems on the planet. In 1989, more than ten million people, mostly women and children, were living in refugee camps.

Fertility theories invite us to believe that the social relations of reproduction differ between the developed and the developing world. But how different are the practices of India, China, and Bangladesh in sex preference theory to the outrageous comments of Paul Samuelson, professor emeritus of economics at Massachusetts Institute of Technology and Nobel prize winner in economics? In a paper in the *American Economic Review*, under the heading "Frontiers in Demographic Economics," he wrote:

New techniques are making it possible to know in advance what will be the sex of a baby. With knowledge may come power to control. Thus if one learns by amniocentesis that an embryo is female, and if one prefers a male, an abortion might be decided on. If such customs become common, some far reaching sociological changes could occur. And these would have economic ramifications. . . .

Scarcity tends toward value. The more women there are, all things equal, the lower might be expected to be their relative wages and lifetime earnings. Feminists might therefore look with some approval upon a future trend toward more sons rather than daughters. . . . If some people indulge a strong enough preference for sons, that will skew the adult sex ratio upwards, tending to raise female wage rates and lower male rates. . . . One past reason for preferring sons may have been their superior earning power. Although daughters may perhaps be counted on to be more nurturing to you in your old age, sons may have the greater wherewithall to support you. Or the vanity of having the family name carried on may, under our patriarchial culture, be better served by sons. But now that the contrived scarcity of females raises their earnings, you have a new economic motive to indulge your preference for males less. . . .

Or the approach may be gradual in the fashion of adaptive expectations. To keep up with the latest fad, we could even fabricate a rational expectations model: in it, people make a best guess about what the future development of the sex ratio will be; they take account of what is implied by this for relative earnings of their sons, daughters,

Mahnaz Afkhami, writes that within a few months of Kho
eini's return to Iran in February 1979

a systematic and vigorous attempt began to reverse all the chang
we had achieved. Women were eliminated from all decision-makin
positions within the government. Those who remained at low level
were required to wear the veil. . . . The Family Protection law was se
aside. Childcare centres were closed. Abortion became illegal under
all circumstances. Women were ruled unfit to serve as judges. Adul-
tery became punishable by stoning. The Womens Organization was
declared a den of corruption and its goals conducive to the expansion
of prostitution. University women were segregated in cafeterias and
on buses. Women who demonstrated against these oppressive rules
were slandered, accused of immoral behaviour, attacked and imprisoned. Opposition grew. Executions became a daily occurrence.[52]

Women died, and die daily, as slaves to the reproduction of
patriarchy, and their "produce," their children, die, too. William Chandler expresses this powerfully when he writes: More
children die because they are improperly weaned than because
of famine. More children die because their parents do not know
how to manage diarrhea than because of epidemics. More children die because their mothers have no wells, hoes, or purchasing power than because of war. They die because their
mothers are exhausted from excessive childbirth, work, and in-
fection. And when children are stunted and retarded from dis
ease and malnutrition, then overburdened parents cannot gen
erate wealth, education, and development, and burgeonin
populations inadequately prepared for life add to the degr
dation of natural systems. These stresses perpetuate drougl
disease, and famine.[53]

Chandler further reports that about 17 million children d
each year from the combined effects of poor nutrition, diarrh
malaria, pneumonia, measles, whooping cough, and tetan
Two-thirds of these deaths are preventable. Children are m
at risk in war zones—including international and civil w;
border disputes, and the war-zone of domestic violence. S
fighting creates not just refugees, but as UNWRA evidence

grandsons and granddaughters, and in terms of this make their decisions; and, miracle of miracles, when all do this they together contrive what it is that they each expect.[54]

Samuelson seems to share his contemptuous ideology toward women with physicist William Bradford Shockley, who was awarded a Nobel prize for inventing the transistor. Shockley outlines several steps to a population control plan that reinforces the monogamous unit and strengthens male control. It begins by convincing people that population limitation is desirable and necessary for survival. The census bureau then calculates the number of children each woman may have (2.2, if one-third of a 1 percent increase is permitted each year). The public health department than sterilizes every girl as she enters puberty by a subcutaneous injection of a contraceptive capsule, which provides a slow seepage of contraceptive hormones until it is removed. When the girl marries she is issued twenty-two "deci-child certificates." Her doctor will remove the contraceptive capsule on payment of ten certificates and will replace it when the baby is born. After two babies, the couple may either sell their remaining two certificates (through the stock exchange) or try to buy eight more on the open market and have a third child. Those who do not have children have twenty-two certificates to sell.

Feminist writers Jalna Hanmer and Pat Allen comment, "In this scheme control of female reproduction passes largely to the state, and, to the extent that males are superordinate in society, to men in and out of the family."[55]

Fertility theories record the availability or nonavailability of family planning to women of the developing world, the form of contraceptive available, its various health hazards, and laws governing women's reproductive freedom. Often women are left with no alternative but prolonged breast-feeding. Often, as in the case of compulsory sterilizations, women are given no alternative. Women certainly do not have control in the reproductive sphere.

Naming the Market

The politics of reproduction is a politics of enslavement. Hanmer and Allen write:

> The reality is that men live in harmony with women by subordinating them. Control is generally exercised over women's sexual and reproductive capacities through customs that determine when and how we may have children, and through the appropriation of these children through kinship, inheritance, and marriage customs. In our society our sexuality is often devalued and denied. An ideology justifying the general devaluation of women is essential if material exploitation is to succeed; it lays the basis for adherence to social customs and rules that enable men successfully to exercise individual and collective power and authority over women.[56]

The general devaluation of women in both production and reproduction is sustained in the United Nations System of National Accounts. There is no conceptual characteristic of reproduction that at some time or some place has not been expressed in terms of a market price. But reproduction is invisible in Sir Richard Stone's system. Enslavement is assumed not to occur in the UNSNA. Perhaps the authors assumed that, since they believed men to be free, the rest of us are free. That is a polite interpretation. Men who win Nobel prizes are generally considered more observant than the rest of us.

You will recall that Joan Robinson suggested that "to learn from the economists regarded as scientists, it is necessary to separate what is valid in their description of the system from the propaganda that they make." She suggests that if the ideas of an economist make sense as a description of reality when they are turned on their heads, then there is something to be learned from them.

The description of reality in the female world may well force the disintegration of the traditional economic description of the system along with its ideology. If the elastic production boundary cannot be expanded to include imputations of all women's productive and reproductive work, it would suggest that we have run headlong into a system of propaganda.

9. The Eye of The Beholder

The UNSNA as Applied Patriarchy

Despite many years of token acknowledgment by the UN and other agencies of women's vital role in production and reproduction, and despite many women's real efforts to create awareness, the UNSNA and the countries and agencies that work with it have refused to include women in their statistics. What is it that the propaganda obscures? What occupies the time of these invisible women?

As an agent of sexist propaganda, economics does not operate in isolation. It is supported by and is part of the international gender conspiracy administered by political, religious, legal, administrative, and cultural hierarchies. It is part of the continuum that ensures women's invisibility and enslavement. How does this conspiracy operate, and what is the conceptual reality of the female world that is thus ignored? While the examples of this are as multiple and varied as our lives, in this chapter we will show how the ideology is institutionalized.

A well-meaning apologist might suggest that economists' propaganda may not be conscious. Such a suggestion implies that the discipline of economics is several decades behind the natural sciences in its approach to thinking and research. Neoclassical economic theory finds its origins in nineteenth century physics. Such foundations gave rise to the belief that there were certain "laws" of economics—the law of supply and demand, for example—that along with other equations and principles were fundamental, unquestionable, and measurable.

Albert Einstein and successive quantum physicists have put an end to all of that. Writing in *The Tao of Physics* in 1977, Fritjof Capra explains:

In modern physics a very different attitude has now developed. Physicists have come to see that all their theories of natural phenomena, including the "laws" they describe, are creations of the human mind; properties of our conceptual map of reality, rather than of reality itself. This conceptual scheme is necessarily limited and approximate, as are all the scientific theories and "laws of nature" it contains.[1]

The laws of economics and those that govern the UNSNA are creations of the *male* mind and do not reflect or encompass the reality of the female world. The conceptual models are limited to the world that the economist knows or observes, and housework is most certainly not part of that world.

Urban Housework

New subtleties in the argument about women's work have arisen in two forms. One argues that feminism has raised the consciousness of men, and, enlightened, they now share the responsibility for housework. This is promulgated along with the claim that labor-saving household appliances eliminate a great deal of the housework that women do. While some studies in the United States suggest that in the last two decades this may be the case, statistician Joann Vanek's work shows that, between 1920 and 1960, the time that women who were not employed outside the home spent in housework increased.[2] Her study covered a period when the urban population of the United States increased and the ownership of household appliances spread. In spite of the fact that rural women preserved food and did much more physical work than urban women, Vanek's investigation shows that urban housewives spent more time in housework than rural ones. One reason for the increase in the time spent in housework appears to be the decrease in the proportion of urban families that had domestic servants.

Middle-class women without servants found vacuum cleaners and washing machines an attractive investment. Although the appliances eliminated some of the more onerous aspects of housework, they did require someone to operate them. In the household without servants, the housewife became the sole domestic worker. Any decrease in the amount of domestic work in urban environments would now be presumed to be because of the greater use of service industries, like laundries, and because of an increased purchase of processed and prepared foods.

In her book *More Work for Mother*, Ruth Schwartz Cowan speaks of the deception of women in terms of twentieth-century household technology. The technology has led men, and frequently women, to believe that households no longer produce anything particularly important and that, consequently, housewives no longer have anything particularly time consuming to do. She writes:

Modern labour-saving devices eliminated drudgery, not labour. Before industrialisation, women fed, clothed, and nursed their families and prepared (with the help of their husbands and children), food, clothing, and medication. In the post-industrial age, women feed, clothe, and nurse their families (without much direct assistance from anyone else) by cooking, cleaning, driving, shopping, and waiting.[3]

Cowan shows that the nature of the work has changed, but the necessity for spending vast amounts of time on it has not. In studying the ironies of household technology, from the open hearth to the microwave, Cowan shows that technological systems, that might have eliminated the labor of housework, could have been built, but such systems would have eliminated the home as well. This is conceptual ideological and revolutionary change that Americans (and, generally, men everywhere) are consistently and insistently unwilling to accept.

And while some men have learned some housework skills, any change towards a sharing of responsibility for this work burden has been minimal. Whether or not women's time spent in housework has decreased may be debatable; what is not debatable is the fact that women work harder at home than men. In that much-vaunted doyen of liberalism and social democracy, Sweden, where legal changes and social presumptions effect a facade of male feminist sympathy, housework is still devalued. The Swedish Central Bureau of Statistics reports that 71 percent of Swedish men never clean the house, 52 percent of the men never shop, 73 percent of the men never wash clothes, and 64 percent of the men never do the dishes. Cathy Keeton, president of *Omni* magazine and coauthor with Yvonne Baskin of *Women of Tomorrow*, cites a 1984 survey that shows that 72 percent of American women do most of the house cleaning, 75 percent cook most of the meals, and only 40 percent say their partners share equally in taking care of the children. Since women did most of the work in the home, Keeton questioned the general assumption that women allocate less effort to paying jobs because of their family and household responsibilities.

She found an answer in the work of Denise and William Bilby, sociologists at the University of California at Santa Barbara, who studied the work women and men do in their jobs and the work they do in their homes. Their findings were (1) that women work harder than men at home and at their jobs; (2) that women give more time and attention to their jobs than men, despite the fact that women also spend more than twice as much time on household tasks; and (3) that more women than men reported having jobs that require a great deal of physical or mental effort and at which they do even more than is asked of them. The result is, of course, that women get very tired and cut back on sleep and leisure time to get everything done. Stressing that women do not reduce efforts in the workplace to meet family obligations, the sociologists concluded, "Now we know why women are fatigued. Physicians can talk about it, but now we have the evidence."[4]

Housework is essential, but it is not measurable by conditions that have been laid down in paid work, like an eight-hour day. Work that has an obvious measurable market equivalent is questioned as economic activity, especially when it is household confined. In 1978, the British feminist magazine *Spare Rib* reported that an industrial tribunal had ruled that a woman's bookkeeping and telephone work for her husband's business was "only an extension of her household duties." But in the same year a doctor's wife succeeded in winning her case that the work of wives in the doctor's surgery should be paid.[5]

Rural Housework

A significant amount of the research material on the working day of rural women concentrates on those who live in developing countries, and a significant amount of the debate on the tasks involved in housework are confined to studies of urban women in developed countries. Estimates of the amount of time spent in child rearing and homemaking, farm work and off-farm employment for rural women in developing countries are very large. The overwork of the rural women of Africa is such that the hours they spend in arduous activities affects their life expectancy. Table 8 shows the division of labor between men and women in rural areas of Africa. While the tasks differ, and the forms of life style, culture, and development are different, there is a consistency in the division of labor with rural women in the developed countries.[6] The UN Economic Commission on Africa (UNECA) notes that men take over responsibility for women's tasks as soon as they are mechanized or when they are transformed from subsistence into market production.[7]

There are few other instances in which African men can be expected to take over women's tasks. In her study of the management of multiple roles in the African economy, Achola Okeyo asked Kenyan market women "when you are away on business, who takes charge of caring for your husband and small children, minding the livestock and chickens, cleaning the house and fetching water?" The results, recorded in table

Table 8.

Division of Labor Between Men and Women, Rural Africa

Task	Men[a] (% of total labor)	Women[a] (% of total labor)
Land clearing	95	5
Turning the soil	70	30
Planting	50	50
Hoeing and weeding	30	70
Harvesting	40	60
Transporting crops from farm to home	20	80
Hoeing crops	20	80
Processing food crops	10	90
Marketing excess crops	40	60
Pruning tree crops	90	10
Carrying water and fuel	10	90
Caring for domestic animals	50	50
Hunting	90	10
Feeding and caring for children, men, and the aged	5	95

Source: UNECA Africa Training and Research Centre for Women, *Women of Africa, Today and Tomorrow* (Addis Ababa: 1975), 6.

[a]With or without help from children.

9, showed that, in every category of work involved, the labor of children is substituted. The presence of a husband at home does nothing to alleviate the burden of work: co-wives seldom substitute for market women's households.[8]

It is unlikely that the petty marketing of these Kenyan

Table 9.

Substitution of Labor for Performing Market Women's
Household and Related Tasks

Task	Substitute labor (number of respondents in each category)					
	Hired labor	Children	Spouse	Other relatives	Not applicable	No response
Child care	6	51[a]	5	10	12[b]	—
Housework						
Water portage	4	38	—	7	33[c]	2
Cooking	4	46	—	17	15[d]	2
Cleaning	7	37	—	11	26[e]	3
Tending livestock	11	32	23	8	6	4

Source: Achola Okeyo, "Women in the Household Economy: Managing Multiple Roles," *Studies in Family Planning* 10 (November–December 1979).

---

[a]This computation includes nine respondents who cite the babysitter (*japidi*) as the substitute labor. Babysitting is always performed by children under age fourteen and therefore counts as work done by children.

[b]Nine respondents have grownup children, and three have no children.

[c]Twenty-two said they fetch water themselves. Eleven have water tanks and therefore no longer have to fetch water.

[d]Six respondents are widows and therefore do not have a husband who has to be fed in their absence. Nine do their own cooking.

[e]These respondents said they have to do own their housecleaning.

women will be visible for the purposes of the national accounts. The census is likely to declare that they are housewives.

How Much Work Doesn't Count

The conceptual incapacity of statisticians and the UNSNA to define housework, and to recognize what is and is not labor, is exacerbated both by the great volume of work that women do and the fact that they do many chores at the same time. The Government Chief Statistician in New Zealand who reacted with such horror to pre-1986 census pilot studies where women answered that child care was a twenty-four hour job, would have a lot of trouble in Bolivia. In La Paz, women wait in line for up to twenty-four hours to have bottles of gas for cooking filled. In Guyana, "the food line . . . is the longest line you can find anywhere. . . . A man here, a man there, sometimes some children, but women from back to front. . . . We have to go and line up from three to four o'clock in the morning to attempt to get food."

In my research I have encountered the constant irony that some of the best sources for information about the work that women do is published by the international office of the International Labor Organization (ILO). This same ILO is responsible for the definition that concludes that the vast bulk of the labor performed by women is not work. One such publication, entitled *Women at Work*, reports the huge housework burden in the cities of Latin America.

In the overwhelming majority of cases, the hours of work at home far exceed those of women who work outside the home according to the surveys and other studies which support this evidence. Some examples are striking. In Argentina the home worker works on average 68.9 hours a week, that is almost ten hours a day. In low income families in Bolivia domestic work involves a total of 15.5 hours daily on average including Sundays and holidays. In the case of Chile whilst economically active women devote what is already the considerable time of 57 hours 19 minutes on average to work outside the home, home makers spend the amazing amount of about 99 hours each week on domestic tasks.[9]

In a refrain that is now very familiar to us, we recognize that these women are classified as "unoccupied." The refrain is echoed by Fatima Mernissi in her book *Beyond the Veil*, where she describes the 1971 Moroccan census as defining women working within the household as inactive. Two million eight-hundred thousand Moroccan housewives are considered to contribute nothing to society. As census takers admitted, "In rural areas women's participation and economic activity is confused with housework, and a certain reticence on the part of the husband to declare his wife active was noticed."[10] In 1960 the number of women whose labor was underreported in Morocco was estimated to be one million two-hundred thousand.

In Algeria, the number of women reported as unpaid family

workers in the 1956 census was ninety-six thousand; after a postcensus reevaluation of data, it was estimated that 1.2 million women working as unpaid family members had not been reported.[11]

This treatment of women is continually recommended and reinforced by international agencies, economists, statisticians, and commentators. In their 1970 publication titled *The Economics of Subsistence Agriculture*, Colin Clark and Margaret Haswell write:

The most *convenient* unit of measurement, where possible, is the number of hectares of cultivated land per adult *male* engaged in agriculture. Undoubtedly a good deal of agricultural work is done by women, and some by children, particularly in Africa. In some modern countries, including Japan, Germany, and France, every farmer's wife is recorded by the census as a full time agricultural worker. This appears to be largely for political reasons to enhance the *supposed importance* of agriculture in the national economy. As the method of recording women's labour varies so greatly between countries, the only statistically *safe* procedure is to work on male labour only [my emphasis].[12]

The "convenient" and "statistically safe" procedure involves that of the head of the household. The fiction of this concept can be described in the case of Lesotho. The national figures indicate that about half of the Lesothan men are absent from the country at any given time. Most of them work in the mines in South Africa. This has resulted in some major structural and sectoral changes that differentiate Lesotho from most other countries. There are twice as many literate women as men; more girls than boys graduate from primary school; and more women than men hold professional positions in the government and participate in local politics.[13] But agricultural training is still predominantly given to rural men who subsequently migrate to South Africa, while women are trained in home economics. Despite the fact that in most cases women perform all agricultural tasks and make all decisions, women are not viewed as independent farmers, although it is widely known that 60–70 percent of rural households are female headed.

The widely used statistics about female-headed rural households don't differentiate between legal female-headed households created through death or divorce and de facto female-headed households created through the husband's migration to South Africa. In the Thaba Bosiu area of Lesotho, 89 percent of legal heads of household were women. For development purposes, however, all rural female-headed households are viewed as the de facto type with temporarily absent husbands.

The widespread beliefs that we have already encountered in the concept of the head of household are all operative in the Lesothan case. There is an expectation that male migrant workers to South Africa plan to return home in time to perform such traditionally male agricultural tasks as ploughing and planting. It is also believed that Lesothan women do not make significant decisions regarding agriculture until their husbands come home on their annual home leave. It is felt that agricultural credit is not a necessity for female-headed farm households because they have access to migrant husband's remittances. In spite of the considerable decision-making power of adult women, in-depth village studies show that women are careful to maintain the appearance of deference to their husbands.

One of the universal results of the institutionalized invisibility of women and the concept of the head of the household is massive poverty. Female-headed households are a third of the total number of households in the Caribbean.[14] They are found in large numbers in the informal sector at the forefront of the problem of combining income earning and home maintenance activities. Poverty is the major problem. These women are more likely to be unemployed than their male counterparts and, if working, are more likely to be involved in lower paying occupations. They are also more unlikely to be trained for an occupation at all. As in most other countries these women depend on the networks that we have with other women to provide for child care, household duties, food or cash in emergency situations, and general emotional support.

Hilda Scott reports that there are five and a half million "displaced homemakers" in the United States. These are women who never held a job but devoted themselves to their families and then overnight found themselves the sole support of their children when they lost their husbands through death, divorce, or desertion. The fact that they do survive is in large part a tribute to the voluntary and unpaid work of their sisters extending assistance. Abandoned wives, widows, divorcees, and single mothers struggling against overwhelming odds to bring up a family and to earn a living for the family are, in fact, dependent on those in the same situation for their survival.

A 1984 ILO study reported that in many developing countries three in every ten households were now headed by women and that even this was likely to be a conservative estimate. The ILO report described patriarchal social structures and bias and access to education, training, credit, technologies, and productive resources as being responsible for the fact that, wherever they are found, most female-headed households fall, by all standards, below the poverty line.

Most female-headed households in sub–Saharan Africa, in some Asian countries, and about half of Latin America, are rural. Yet in a paper for International Women's Year in 1975, UNECA estimated that domestic science constituted more than 50 percent of all the nonformal education offered to women in Africa.[15] Agriculture was very rarely offered. Women comprised 100 percent of participants in home economics compared with 15 percent in agriculture and zero for trade and commerce.

In an effort to help agricultural productivity in Malawi, foreign aid programs instituted a two-pronged plan of attack. First, they set up agricultural demonstrations in the Malawi communities and invited all the men to attend. Second, they started home economics classes for the Malawi women and passed out recipes for cheap, nutritious food such as soy beans. The program flopped entirely. The men worked as laborers on large plantations, and women were the farmers raising the family's food. Since the women weren't invited to the farming classes, they didn't grow the soy beans and couldn't use the recipes. The men, who dutifully attended the farming classes, couldn't use the information because they weren't farmers.

According to the official educational policy in Saudi Arabia adopted in 1970, "the object of education of a girl is to bring her up in a sound Islamic way so that she can fulfill her role in life as a successful housewife, ideal wife and good mother, and to prepare her for other activities that suit her nature such as teaching, nursing and the medical profession."[16]

Making the Connections: Nutrition

The pressures of rural impoverishment have seen a worldwide urban migration in search of paid work. The goods and services that were formerly produced or provided, usually by women, in the subsistence economy of the village now have to be bought. This puts pressure on the level of consumption, even though wages are considerably higher in the town than in the country.

Ester Boserup shows that the family's earned income in the town is generally far higher than in the country, while the volume of goods and services that the family can afford (the level of consumption) is often smaller because many subsistence activities are no longer possible. When GNP is calculated, account is taken of the production of goods and services in the subsistence economy, but at local prices. These are lower than those in the market sector, so that incomes (levels of consumption) in developing countries are usually higher than GNP would indicate. This discrepancy increases with the size of the subsistence sector. As economic growth progresses, the goods and services produced in the subsistence sector account for an increasingly small proportion of total production. Monetary payment then has to be made for forms of service that were originally provided through the subsistence economy. Basic goods are often replaced by processed products, meaning that the processing of the products (for example, grain to flour to packaging) must also be paid for. This results in growth in incomes (levels of consumption) being lower than the growth in GNP would suggest.[17]

Migration also affects nutrition. In the Pacific, the movement of people from villages into towns where there is no adequate land available to grow their own food, has resulted in a decrease in subsistence agriculture and has made the people depend mostly on imported foods. Their traditional diet has therefore changed from root vegetables (such as cassava, taro, yam, and sweet potato), starchy fruits (such as cooking bananas and breadfruit), coconuts, nuts, fresh fish, and green leaves, to rice, bread, tinned fish and meat, and sugar. The major nutritional differences between the traditional diet and the Westernized diet include increases in calorie intake (energy), sugar, salts, animal fats, and alcohol, and decrease in the substance called fiber, which is necessary for general well-being. Major new health problems include obesity, diabetes, hypertension, heart disease, tooth decay, and cancer.[18]

It is not necessary for migration to occur for the GNP effect outlined by Boserup to be established. Work sponsored by the Consumer Nutrition Division of the U.S. Department of Agriculture and reported in 1985 discusses household demand for convenience and nonconvenience foods.[19] Convenience foods are described as "any fully or partially prepared food in which significant preparation time, culinary skills, or energy inputs have been transformed from the home maker's kitchen to the food processor and distributor." Nonconvenience foods are described as "fresh (unprocessed) foods, ingredient foods, or home produced, home frozen, home canned or home preserved food items."

The study showed that households in central cities and suburban areas allocate more shares of the food dollars to convenience foods, and households in nonmetropolitan areas allocate larger shares to nonconvenience foods. Black or other nonwhite households, and households where the manager is at least thirty-five years old, allot smaller shares to convenience foods and larger to nonconvenience relative to their counterparts. Female managers of households apportion larger shares to nonconvenience and smaller shares to convenience foods compared with male household managers. The same result is found with respect to unemployed household managers. Managers without college education spend more on non-convenience foods, while the primary users of convenience foods are white households with employed household managers less than thirty-five years old. It is this last group whose consumptive patterns are seen to contribute the most to the Gross National Product of the United States. It does *not* follow that they thereby contribute the most to the well-being of the community.

Commercial agriculture has often discouraged initiative for women's subsistence activities that provided the varied diet and some surplus for cash income. A report from western Colombia describes a situation where women headed many of the households and provided, even when married, cash income as agricultural laborers, in addition to crops from their gardens. They were driven out of production with the encroachment of cash crops introduced by Green Revolution technicians. "Whereas men saw their interests being improved by wage labour available in the mechanised farming sector, women lost control over the variety of crops that had been the mainstay of their subsistence activities and ensured their children food in the face of market values of monocrop cultivation. Some of their coffee trees were ruined by the insecticides dusted over tracks outside the commercial crop area by planes used in the commercial enterprises. In the male dominated society of rural Colombia where an attitude of irresponsible paternity prevails, the women, who had been the main providers for the family lost the margin of control they had exercised."[20]

The control over food and access to it gives political control. Starvation affects men and women differently. Physiologically, young adult men are the most resistant to extreme lack of food. Mortality rates suggest that the aged, pregnant and lactating women, and young children especially are most affected by communal starvation. In a paper presented in 1981 on famine in India, Gail Pearson explains that starvation is accompanied by a disintegration of personality, by mental apathy, irritability, and depression. Occasionally, individuals become extremely aggressive, and there are cases of cannibalism. Many suffer from the disruption of sleep by dreams and nightmares. Some individuals become totally indifferent to their surroundings. Others adopt a wandering habit and move about aimlessly in the search for food. Previously "moral" women turn to prostitution to obtain food.[21]

Making the Connections: Trade and Productivity

Control over the resources for the production of food also gives political control. In 1984, reports from The Gambia told of a $16.48 million project to make The Gambia more self-sufficient in rice. The bulldozers moved in over a ripened crop of fifteen hundred hectares of existing rice swampland to convert them to high-yielding crops. In 1984, compensation had still not been paid to the farmers nine months after they had lost their crops. Hundreds of women were ordered not to grow rice during the rainy season—rice they needed to feed their children and families. Food aid was promised for months while the women lived in helpless anxiety. Though women owned the farmland, the village headman had leased their land, along with unused swamp land, for fifty years to the government. Mariania Koita, a farmer affected, says, "I think this project will distribute all the fields to the men. It was the same with earlier projects when we helped build them—but they gave the men all the plots. It was the World Bank that gave the land to the men."[22]

While agriculture in Africa constitutes the major source of employment, food, raw materials for industry, and foreign exchange, its contribution to GDP has been steadily declining since the 1960s. The decline in food production in the past decade has been most marked in the production of staple food crops, where there was a drop in absolute terms in the production of millet, sorghum, rice, and maize by most of the producers south of the Sahara. Only in cassava production was there no decline. The average African now has 10 percent less homegrown food than a decade earlier. More and more emphasis has been placed on enhancing agricultural exports rather than increasing food production. In most countries, more resources have been devoted to research into cash crops than has been put into research, agricultural extension, statistical and other farm services for food crops. Emphasis has been placed on large-scale irrigation projects and not enough on small-scale ones and the digging of wells that can help the small farmer.

Food crops tend to be the subsistence agricultural activities and are primarily carried out by women. Since these farmers are not seen to be contributing to the market economy, they are not given improved tools. The stereotyping is not limited to agriculture. Since women frequently do house construction, improvements related to water conservation, drainage, sanitation, and building of methane tanks for fuel, as well as improved food storage facilities, do not lie outside their range of competence. But they are generally excluded from advisory committees or from training schemes connected with these projects.

In 1980, a review by the Food and Agricultural Organization (FAO) commented that for years aid agencies had complained of "serious constraints" where male extension workers were not permitted to communicate directly with the women working the fields. It didn't ever seem to occur to the aid agencies that in those instances the answer was to train and to send women extension workers. It was not as if African women did not know what they wanted. By 1980, women's groups had already identified training in food preservation, simple drip irrigation techniques, animal diseases, and access to wells and two-wheeled carts for transporting water and firewood as their priorities.[23]

Nor was this scenario confined to Africa. The world price of sugar soared in the early 1970s. In Belize in Central America, more and more land was put into sugar cane. More and more men took jobs in the sugar industry, and more and more small holdings were planted with cane. Local food production steadily declined. In one year alone, consumption of local maize and rice declined 15 percent, and wheat imports rose 62 percent. Soon there was a national shortage of staple foods. "In the old days," says Maya Indian villager, Dona Ettelvina, "we were poor but there was plenty of food. Now, we have money but nothing to eat."

In Belize, women again have paid the heaviest price. Food crops used to be bought into the family and jointly owned by the family. The preparation, storage, and distribution were the responsibility of the woman and formed the basis of her social and economic role. Part of the crop she stored to be eaten in the months before the next harvest. Another part she sent to needy female relatives as insurance against the time when the harvest failed and she herself would need similar help. Part of the crop that was spoiled by mold or parasites would be fed to pigs, turkeys, chickens, and pigeons. These animals not only provided food but also provided economic power for the women who owned and tended them. Now canned meat is imported. The loss of food crops and animals has left women like Dona Ettelvina almost entirely dependent on men. The sugar cash that has replaced food belongs to men, yet their incomes have not risen enough to pull families out of poverty. Although the illusion of prosperity is widespread, persistent high child malnutrition shows it is only an illusion. In the eyes of economists, development has come to this corner of Belize. Income per capita has undoubtedly risen. But who has benefited?[24]

Making the Connections: The Laws of Property and Ownership

One of the tools assisting economics in its universal propaganda has been the law. The global litany of the legal system operating as one tool of oppression is never ending. In marriage, domicile, custody; in the English Common Law, the Code Napoleon, the Hindu Code of Manu, in Shari'a law; in the cosmetic legal guarantees of sexual equality; in constitutions; in inheritance and land laws: legal systems reinforce the patriarchal economic system. In Kenya, Lesotho, Nigeria, Togo, and Ethiopia, women are, for the most part, prohibited from owning and exercising proprietary rights over real property. Further restrictions are found in discriminatory customary laws in the areas of inheritance, property rights within and upon dissolution of marriage, and legal capacity.

Female heirs are not allowed to inherit property or else may only receive smaller shares than male heirs under the customary law of the Hindu, Mitakshara, Parsees, and various Christian sects in India, Thesani law in Sri Lanka, and Islamic law in the various countries of Asia where Muslims reside.

Laws limiting the legal capacity of married women to administer property and act in commercial matters exist in at least three Latin American countries—Brazil, Bolivia, and Peru. Peru serves as an example of the negative effects of land reform on rural women. While women owned the land in most peasant communities, the Peruvian land reform legislation denies married women, or women who have never been married, access to their own parcels of land. This is the result of the use of the head of the family concept in land reform legislation.

Some governments have a more explicit policy of male preference in land distribution embedded in laws and in legislation with agrarian reform. In the Colombia Agrarian Reform Law of 1971, lands were distributed to the "needy," defined as men eighteen years and over. In some countries, women lose control over their property on marriage, a common practice in Chile. In Nepal, daughters are denied the right to inherit leasehold granted to deceased fathers, although sons can inherit. In that country (as I have described in chapter 4) 70 percent of all agricultural work is done by women.

These land reform programs that we hear so much about in development programs in Central America, do nothing to ensure a fair distribution of the titles to land among men and women, despite the fact that women perform at least half of all the agricultural production.

When women do control their land, profitability may be limited due to small size, allocation of marginal pieces, and/or lack of access to technology. Almost all the training and technology in development programs for improving agriculture is given to men.

The gradual shift from the subsistence to the cash economy appears to be at the expense of women. In predominantly Muslim Senegal, women's personal plots, on which they grow groundnuts, are less than a third of the size of men's. When mechanical sowers and weeders were introduced, women were the last to have access to them, virtually guaranteeing lower yield.

Even in socialist countries, land reform programs often continue to work against women. A 1976 study of Tanzania discovered that women were worse off in these settlements than previously, when they had had their own crops and access to land.[25] Under the new schemes, all rights to land were allocated to the men and proceeds of the land belonged to the men. Women lost their rights to land and independent income, thereby becoming more dependent on their husbands.

"Natural" law has proved an equally effective tool of oppression. The universal experience of women is to be mother and worker, producer and reproducer. Though the economic system may change, for women everywhere this experience does not change. But institutionalized within the family, the serfdom is complete.

Making the Connections: Fertility

Not only do women not have rights to ownership and control of land, but they are precluded, again by customary and civil law, from rights to the control (and ownership) of their own fertility. Melphy Sakupwanya, a social worker and development officer in Zimbabwe, says, "Women know they can benefit from smaller families but their men don't think that way, and their attitudes are encouraged by their families. As women receive more education and hold careers, things change. But the pressures on them are enormous. Our men still feel that they are not marrying for themselves but for their families. A husband and wife may want to space their children or buy a house first, but this kind of planning is disturbed by the husband's relatives, who expect children in return for the bride price. Never mind the cost of living, it is felt that you are richer if you have more children."[26]

More than ignorance of birth control, or lack of access to contraceptives, large families reflect the powerlessness of people. Where poor families are pitted against each other for survival, another child is sometimes seen as an asset—a means of bringing in additional income and a source of security in old age. Large families are then a rational choice for survival. Moreover, given poor nutrition, sanitation, and medical care, parents realize that they must have large families to ensure the survival of even one son to adulthood. Perdita Huston reports from interviews conducted in Asia, Latin America, and Africa that large families also reflect the special powerlessness of women.[27] Even when a woman realizes that the gain from having an additional child has become small or nonexistent, she may hesitate to use birth control for fear of rejection by her husband on whom she is dependent.

If women have access to contraceptives, they cannot be sure that it will not further undermine their health. Depom Provera, which is banned in the United States (but not in New Zealand where it is used to control the fertility of psychiatric patients), is widely dispensed to Third World women. Intrauterine devices alter bleeding patterns and are often inserted without proper sanitation or aftercare. Female sterilization is particularly hazardous when forced upon women or performed in anything but first-rate medical and hygienic conditions.

When a child is born, there is a universal code operating for son preference. It may not be so overt in the developed world but is nonetheless present. A dear friend of mine who had just given birth to her second child, and second daughter, tells me of receiving congratulatory cards, while still in the maternity hospital, that said "better luck next time." In the Arab world, commentator Anny Bakalian observes, the birth of a son is the cause of joyous celebration. Girls are tolerated as a firstborn, but this toleration diminishes with each successive birth. As lactating mothers are less likely to become pregnant, a daughter is weaned quickly to ensure another conception that, the parents hope, will produce an heir. Boys are often pampered, "kept noticeably cleaner, better dressed, and groomed," and "male children are more likely to be taken to the doctor in cases of illness, while with girls greater reliance is placed on home remedies and folk medicine."[28]

Fatima Mernissi explains that the classical Islamic concept of sex sees female sexuality as more "natural" and more powerful than that of the male. The control of this power, it is argued, requires greater powers of reasoning and strength of character than women possess. Men, believed to be superior to women morally, intellectually, and physically, are "naturally" vested with authority over women and are charged with their protection. The codes of female modesty, veiling, and seclusion are thus all seen as solutions to the need to "protect society from the possible consequences of female sexuality."[29]

Universally, female sexuality does need protection—not by men, but *from men*. Whether it is because of their continual and usually unadmitted victimization and rape as married women and their abuse in pornographic publications, films, and videos or in their abuse in prostitution, women need the power to protect themselves and each other. In 1982, more than one million Japanese tourists visited Thailand, the Philippines, South Korea, Taiwan, and Hong Kong on tours called "trips for men only" that explicitly include visits to brothels. An estimated 60 percent of two million tourists visiting Thailand each year are allegedly drawn by bargain price sex.[30]

Chattels do not have choices. The chattel relationship is established very quickly by way of sexual obligation. Rape was, you will recall, a law relating to the violation of one man's property by another. And universally, it still is. Since you cannot violate your own property, the international brotherhood may rape their wives with impunity.

Publicly, people take only what belongs to them, but as the worldwide experience of sexual harassment tells us, women are common property. Andrea Dworkin points out that this fact was acknowledged, with no recognition of its significance, by the scholars of the Institute for Sex Research (the Kinsey Institute) who studied sex offenders.

If we labelled punishable sexual behaviour as a sex offence, we would find ourselves in the ridiculous situation of having all of our male histories consist almost wholly of sex offenders, the remaining few being not only non-offenders but non-conformists. The man who kisses a girl in defiance of her expressed wishes is committing a forced sexual relationship and is liable to an assault charge, but to solemnly label him as a sex offender would be to reduce our study to a ludicrous level.[31]

Chattels do not have choices. They are forced into marriages; they are veiled and secluded; they are the victims of polygamy, prostitution, wife battery, incest, and honor murders.

In her book, Kathleen Barry writes, "Female sexual slavery is present in all situations where women and girls cannot change the immediate conditions of their existence; where regardless of how they got into those conditions they cannot get out; and where they are subject to sexual violence and exploitation."[32]

For some women, there is never an escape. In the United States, the FBI estimates that wife battery occurs at three times the rate of rape (excluding that within marriage, we presume), and a rape is reported every six minutes.[33]

In the Amazon valley, the highlands of Papua New Guinea, and in New Zealand, women are frequently kept in their place by gang rape when the ordinary mechanisms of masculine intimidation prove insufficient.

And Many More Connections

What subtle forms all this oppression takes. The tenets of "natural law" and sexual slavery unite in that sphere of "for her own good," which we are most familiar with as "protective legislation." Used to exclude us women from equal participatory opportunities (e.g., night work), it has not been used to keep us from our "natural" duties (e.g., nursing at night). Even when allowing women into paid work, the effort has ensured that they stay with the domestic and nurturant professions.

Protection of women's reproductive function is one of the primary motives behind much protective legislation for women, and the pregnant worker does indeed present a special case. It is essential, however, that the temporary circumstances of pregnancy be treated as temporary. The reaction of employers, unions, and governments alike has too often been to treat all women as if they were all pregnant all the time.

More subtleties permeate the Church. Religious institutions absorb women whom they assign free-of-charge to work in hospitals, orphanages, asylums, and homes. As in the context of marriage (to God), it is in exchange for their upkeep and not in exchange for a wage that the sisters or nuns do this work. And it is not a question of religious charity, since when men are grouped together in these institutions, they do not undertake tasks involving maintenance of humans.

There is no end to the forms of oppression perpetuated against women by men regardless of economic system, stage of development, religion, culture, race. The instruments and their effects differ. Habits of speech sustain attitudes. Reference is made to female social actors by their sex as a matter of priority, so that Fidel Castro, that paragon of virtue in the eye of women who've been coopted by the Left, can say of the Batista regime, "They killed tens of thousands of workers, students, and women." So, I am asked to conclude, women are not workers or students?

In fighting for their liberty, women cannot so easily take to the hills and apply for arms to a superpower as an independence movement. They cannot withdraw their labor. It is unthinkable for a woman to stop feeding her child, caring for the truly dependent. Women's indispensability sees her less able to fight for her rights, not because of so little power, but because of so much responsibility.

That powerlessness and that responsibility can give women extremely poor self-images and also inhibit them from participation in political life.

The intense amount of time taken in our work (and the fact that women believe that it is valueless) are among those burdens that make it so difficult for women to be active politically. Carollee Bengelsdorf, in her paper "On the Problem of Studying Women in Cuba," points to this as the difficulty for women to gain access to the party.

For such access requires not simply their presence in the workforce, but the kind of active participation in the workforce which might distinguish individual women as potential candidates. For women who are chiefly responsible for both home and children, such active and time consuming participation is often simply impossible. This is nowhere more starkly captured than in a survey done by the party after the 1974 Popular Power election in Matanzas which served as a forerunner to the establishment of Popular Power on a national scale. In that election, only 7% of those nominated and only 3% of those elected as base level delegates were female. When women were asked whether if nominated they would have agreed to run, some 54.3% said no, overwhelmingly because of domestic obligations. And similarly in a party survey of 211 workplaces, 85.7% of the women said that domestic obligations inhibited greater participation on their part.[34]

It is "back home" that women in the paid work force are expected to go when development or modernization become part of a country's economic policy. Over the past several years, as unemployment has reached new levels in China, the "back to the home" argument has become more visible. When I was there I read of union delegates' comments on making places in the work force for young men by getting rid of women from their positions. There is evidence that state and collective enterprises prefer to hire men. Management argues that female employment involves additional costs and contributes to inferior work quality. The employment of women commits enterprises to the provision of expensive facilities, such as nurseries, women's toilets, and maternity leave. Managers argue that the costs of these facilities are not balanced out by women's productivity, since their efficiency is adversely affected by family duties. Women cadres have argued that "women are too often overlooked when it comes time for promotion. The common view is that women do inferior work to men because of demands made on them by their domestic responsibility."[35]

The enslavement of women is not a secret. It is not difficult to see examples every day of women bought, sold, raped, traded, in marriage and in the courts, in childbirth and in paid work. In a letter dated May 5, 1986, from the chargé d'affaire of the Permanent Mission of Israel to the United Nations, addressed to Secretary General, the following appears:

Israel's policy to the employment and training of Arab women has been sensitive to their tradition and social obligations. The Ministry of Labour offers vocational training programmes and subjects for which there is demand by the population and in the labour market. Those courses are offered free of charge, and the graduates have no obligation to use their newly acquired skills by taking a job, *if the latter goes against the wishes of the woman's father, fiance, or husband.*

The report attributes the phenomenon of irregular workers

to the generally difficult living conditions in the occupied territories and family needs. In fact it is for reasons of tradition that many families prefer to send their women folk to work in Israel through a "Rais" (local contractor), who is held responsible for the girl's honour. The "Rais" contacts employers directly and *usually pays the women's wages to male members of her family* [my emphasis].[36]

These lives and the lives of the women in this chapter are found nowhere in the abstract quantitative models of the contemporary economists. Nowhere are we visible primarily as women in the UNSNA. Our presence is a record of our vicarious relationship to men. The propaganda and realization of "growth" and "development" occur literally over our backs and at our expense.

It seems to me that the propagandistic models of Sir Richard Stone are in a profound conceptual crisis. While the numbers of those who agree with me are relatively few in the fields of economics, statistics, or government, there are some—and they are increasingly joined by those from other fields and disciplines. The reasons for calling for change vary, but the sense of urgency for change is shared. Physicist Fritjof Capra writes:

The social and economic anomalies that can no longer address global inflation and unemployment, maldistribution of wealth, and energy shortages, among others are now painfully visible to everyone. The failure of the economic profession to come to terms with these problems is recognised by an increasingly sceptical public, by scientists from other disciplines, and by economists themselves. It is within the scope of economic theories to include qualitative distinctions which are crucial to the understanding of our lives and the planet.

Capra says of the new science of quantum physics,

The universe is no longer seen as a machine, made up of a multitude of objects, it has to be pictured as one indivisible, dynamic whole whose parts are essentially inter-related and can be understood only as patterns of a cosmic process.[37]

Is this too bold a view for economics? Is it asking too much of a conceptual change of a discipline to expect it to contribute to an interrelated universe?

If economics and its tools, such as the United Nations System of National Accounts, are to have any pretensions towards science, then this is the universe that must be reflected. An integral part of that universe is our planet's ecosystem. How do we value that?

10. "Your Economic Theory Makes No Sense"

Economics and the Exploitation of the Planet

One day in a nuclear age
They may understand our rage
Build machines that they can't control
And bury the waste in a great big hole.
Power was to become cheap and clean,
Grimy faces were never seen,
But deadly for twelve thousand years
is carbon fourteen

—STING

Have you ever drunk pure fresh water from a waterfall or mountain stream? The best champagne I've tasted could not compete for taste, bouquet, or crispness. Have you seen the orange/yellow/red/ochre/cream/green/turquoise of algae gathered on silica on volcanic shelves older than recorded history? No raku pottery glaze can imitate the beauty of color, texture, or design.

The pottery and the champagne are of value. But the water and silica are thought of as the free gifts of nature, simply there in abundance, or as community resources that will always be available. As an invisible factor in the economic universe, they might be labeled the "nonmarketed goods and services provided by the natural environment," along with shelter, clean air to breathe, food, fiber, and heating fuels. These also include the services that soil, water, and climate provide for agriculture, for waste disposal, for recreation, and for the contemplation of aesthetic beauty. They include the ecosystem checks and balances provided by all forms of life.

The exploitation of natural resources for economic gain has become an inherent part of development and has led to the realization by some people that these resources, whether rain forests, fish stocks, or fresh water, are no longer abundant and are in short supply. The global gifts of production have been widespread soil and coastal erosion, desertification, and deforestation. Water and air pollution are inherited by each generation as a result of past economic activity. Many consequences of this exploitation, the dangers to human health and animal and plant resources, will be unknown for decades. The conservation and resource management strategies adopted as a response to this situation have tended to be expensive, "growth" producing, and concerned with maximizing the exploitation of resources. So-called growth strategies, along with life as we know it on this planet, are not sustainable on this level and with this approach.

The treatment of Mother Earth and the treatment of women and children in the system of national accounts have many fundamental parallels.

Petra Kelly, Green party parliamentarian in West Germany, has written: "There is no essential difference between the rape of a woman, the conquest of a country, and the destruction of the earth. The his/story of the world records the gender of the rapists, conquerors and destroyers."[1] And as rape is legitimized by men in marriage, and murder legitimized in war, the plunder of the earth is legitimized if the resource has a market and can be owned, like the slave woman.

When nature reproduces itself in its own form, without intervention, and in a way that contributes to the well-being of the community, it is of no value. When nature produces a harvest, which can be processed for the market, it counts for something. When nature has a market value, destruction other than for the market gives rise to legal suit; when nature's function is invisible and valueless, it can be destroyed at will.

If Counting Were the Answer

If our object was to make an argument for imputing measurements of the conservation or destruction of natural resources in the national accounts, we would immediately confront difficulties.

The best known forms of pollution can be categorized. Air pollution includes the discharge of noxious gases and solid particles into the atmosphere from automobiles, trucks, utility generating plants, steel mills, chemical factories, paper mills, and other manufacturing. Water pollution involves the discharge of organic and inorganic wastes into streams and lakes. This is mainly industrial pollution or municipal pollution which involves inadequately treated sewage. Accumulation of solid wastes occurs as pollution in automobile junkyards and the trash of cans, bottles, and other disposables. Noise pollution includes jet engines, plus motor traffic, construction activity, industrial machinery, and radios. And, of course, there is the pollution of radioactivity and the pollution of nuclear wastes.

Physical measurement of environmental pollution may take three forms:

1. Measures of the state of the natural environment—air, water, and soil—and, by repeated monitoring, of changes in that state. Such measures have been made for a long time.
2. Measures of the quantities of discharge of substances regarded as pollutants.
3. Measures of the consequences of pollution for human health; for animal, bird, and marine life; and for plant contamination.[2]

Efforts have been made to collect or impute data for monetary measurements of pollution. These fall into three broad classes:

1. Statistics of actual expenditures on abatement or control of pollution. This data exists but is not necessarily identified separately in the accounts of enterprises and public authorities.
2. Estimates of the hypothetical costs of achieving given physical standards in purity of air, water, and soil.
3. Estimates of various kinds of damage caused by or resulting as a consequence of pollution.[3]

It is clear that some natural resources, like forests, are renewable over time. Some, for example, minerals, are depleted through use. Some, like natural silence, are unknown to billions of people in their lifetime. Yet noise is the most endemic and one of the most intractable of environmental problems, imposing stress, disturbing sleep, reducing efficiency, causing severe annoyance, and, in some occupations, being a major cause of deafness. Some resources are degradable through various forms of pollution or mismanagement—land or water or the atmosphere. Others when not in use are instantly renewable. Because we cannot see these so clearly, we tend not to think about them as natural resources. Included in this group would be the electromagnetic spectrums that are part of the natural environment of earth and space. These make possible radio and television communications with moving vehicles on land and sea, in the air, or in outer space. This resource is not depletable, but it is rare or scarce. It is always available in infinite abundance except for that portion that is being used, and when that portion is not in use, it is instantly renewable.

While few of our resources fall into that category in terms of use, the electromagnetic spectrum demonstrates a clear characteristic of natural resources. They do not recognize national boundaries.

What Counts on This Boundary of Production

In July 1976, an explosion caused by the faulty operating of the *only* safety valve at the ICMESA chemical plant in Seveso, northern Italy, spread a huge noxious black cloud over the area. After twenty days, forty-six people had been hospitalized, and at the end of two months an area of nearly 350 hectares was declared contaminated, and more than two thousand people were evacuated. It was announced that the poison that had escaped was dioxin, one of the most dangerous chemicals in the world, used by the U.S. army as a defoliant during the Vietnam war.* The effects of dioxin are slow and long lasting, sometimes only becoming evident after one generation. It penetrates the skin, the blood, the liver, the kidneys, the stomach, the lungs, and the central nervous system. It causes cancer and genetic mutations. It also attacks pregnant women and their unborn babies. Several women from Seveso managed to get abortions in spite of the antiabortion law then in force in Italy. Other pregnant women were prevented from having abortions by the church. One woman gave birth to a stillborn baby without a brain, and children born since have suffered stomach abnormalities.[4]

Twelve years later, the town is still deserted. The full effects of this contamination will only be known after twenty to twenty-five years. By that time, the possibility of a successful legal suit for damages would be remote, since establishing a direct causal link for cancer, for example, would be difficult. ICMESA is a subsidiary of Givandan, a Swiss chemical and cosmetic manufacturer owned by Hoffman–La Roche, the biggest pharmaceutical company in the world, best known for its top-selling tranquilizers, Librium and Valium. Three Swiss firms, Hoffman–La Roche, Sandoz, and Ciba–Geigy account for 15 percent of the world's sales of pharmaceuticals.

Sandoz has among the top ten market turnovers in the world, a turnover bigger than Upjohn, Bayer, and Bristol–

---

*Large amounts of dioxin also escaped in the Bhopal disaster in India.

Myers. Sandoz was responsible, in November 1986, for the massive pollution of the Rhine, rapidly turning it into a dead river in the heart of Western Europe. The contaminated water resulted from a spillage after a fire at the Sandoz chemical plant near Basle on November 1. The Swiss failed to adequately warn about thirty tons of toxic waste, mainly dyes and mercury, that flooded into the Rhine, sending pollution to levels six times above those normally measured. Stretches of the Rhine in Germany were biologically dead, and Dutch farmers were advised to keep livestock away from the river's banks. Sluices and locks on the extensive Dutch inland waterway system had to be closed to prevent pollution entering domestic water supplies. The waste then flowed into the North Sea where it contaminated fish supplies. Inland fishermen were halted from fishing in the Rhine, and the European public was warned against consumption of the river fish. No drinking water was available to be drawn from the river for at least a week. After the spillage, several hundred kilograms of insecticide settled on the floor of the Rhine bed and had to be removed with suction machinery. Dioxin again escaped. The devastation might have been far more extensive if there had been rain during the period.

The technical chief of Sandoz reportedly denied allegations by the West German environmentalist Green party that Sandoz had been presented with an insurance company report five years ago that criticized its safety provisions. He said that Sandoz had invited the Zurich Insurance Company to analyze any dangers at the plant in 1981, but no "formal" report had ever been presented, as Sandoz had transferred coverage to another insurance firm offering lower premiums. The Sandoz chief said, all *"justified"* compensation claims would be paid, while the general manager of Sandoz said the company had assumed complete moral responsibility for the accident.[5]

The question then arises as to what would constitute a "justified" compensation claim. The market system will undoubtedly look to compensate fishermen, local authorities who have had to make other water supply accommodations, and perhaps farmers. It is unlikely that Sandoz will pay out in twenty or thirty years for any major medical results that might be attributed to the spillage. And to whom might one pay for the environmental and ecological devastation that has wrought havoc on the ecosystem of the river itself. For without proof that a market utility was interfered with, it will be argued there can be no justification for compensation. Such is the barrenness of the national income valuation approach.

The pollution of the Rhine waterway is not a new concern. The European Economic Community—which does not include Sandoz's home country of Switzerland—established rules on the basis of an equality standard approach. These rules state the quality required of surface water intended for the extraction of drinking water, of water intended for human consumption, and of water for bathing. Chloride pollution, thermal pollution, and sewage water are not covered.

The European council directive of May 4, 1976, "Pollution Caused by Certain Dangerous Substances Discharged into the Aquatic Environment of the Community," covers all surface waters. It is an example of an agreement that is possible beyond national boundaries, where a natural resource is shared, and where characteristic standards are able to be met without the need for market indices. The law, government regulations, and the prospect of major penalties imposed by the courts are used to police these directives. But the world's wealthy multinational pharmaceutical companies housed in Switzerland are not subject to these penalties. They may pay compensation for "proven market losses or costs"—identifiable and "justifiable"—but who "pays" for the poisoning of the water?

The Treatment of Water

We are now familiar with the treatment of water in the UNSNA as a natural resource, which is a free gift of nature continually renewed at an acceptable health level. This ensures no worth for water unless it is "employed" by the productive process. But the devaluation of water also occurs because of the key role that women play as acceptors, users, managers, and educators in matters of water and sanitation.

Along with food, shelter, and clean air to breathe, nothing can be deemed to be more important to the "well-being of a community" than the supply of fresh water. While some water is now bottled and marketed, this amount is miniscule. Fresh water is absolutely necessary for the maintenance of life and health. Its nonavailability causes enormous sickness, disease, and death, not simply for human beings, but also for animal and plant life. The vast amounts of pollution vomited into our air, the raising of the earth's temperature, the deforestation in many regions all lead to changes in the hydrological cycle. The "production" of water conceptually lies outside the boundary established for national income accounting. The disappearance of access to safe water is not recorded as a cost to the planet, ecosystem, or a nation's welfare. Water is not amenable, as a "commodity," to either qualitative or quantitative measurement for the purposes of cost-benefit analysis or income accounting, and so, like the unpaid work of women, it disappears from the public policy arena.

The World Health Organization (WHO) estimates that water-related diseases claim as many as 25 million lives a year and cause untold illness. The UN International Children's Emergency Fund (UNICEF) calculates that 15 million children die every year before reaching their fifth birthday. Half of them could be saved if they had access to safe drinking water. According to WHO, approximately 80 percent of all sicknesses and diseases can be attributed to inadequate water or sanitation. Typical of these illnesses are diarrhea, trachoma, parasitic worms, and malaria. In India, water borne diseases are responsible for the loss of 73 million working days every year. The analysis of this in terms of medical treatment and lost production shows costs of approximately $600 million annually. But these costs, you will recognize, include only the effects on those who are deemed to be economically active.

Table 10.

Service Coverage by Region in 1983

Population Covered (%)		
Region	Water	Sanitation
Africa	38	29
Asia and the Pacific (excluding China)	51	21
Latin America and the Caribbean	73	60
Western Asia	76	63

Source: United Nations Development Program (UNDP). *Decade Watch* 5 (April–June 1986).

Less than 40 percent of the sub–Saharan population of over 400 million people have access to safe drinking water and an even smaller number enjoy adequate sanitation (see table 10). Water-related diseases and sicknesses are responsible for the deaths of most of the 5 million children under five who die annually in Africa. Only 8 percent of the world's water supply is fresh or potable. Projections under the International Drinking Water Supply and Sanitation Decade (1981–1990) program estimate that approximately $600 billion is required to provide clean water and adequate sanitation during the ten-year period. Sixty billion dollars annually is a modest sum compared with annual military budgets.

This resource, so frequently taken for granted by those who have it in abundance (and who also happen to be those who make the rules about the UNSNA and have major military programs), has every functional utility imaginable.

A woman peace worker in Paraguay reported:

In one particular colony area the only water supply for at least ten to fifteen kilometres was a large puddle of clear water. Other than just swamp water, there were no wells of any sort. In this one puddle of water there were women washing clothes, women washing babies, numerous pigs wallowing, several boys washing their horses, girls drawing water and the local malaria control team washing out their DDT spray can.[6]

It is not only in the developing world that the resource of fresh water is being lost to us. A 1983 nationwide survey conducted by the U.S. Environmental Protection Agency found that trace levels of toxic chemicals were present in nearly 30 percent of the municipal water supplies serving more than ten thousand people. Ground water, the drinking water source for about half of the U.S. population, has become seriously contaminated by leaking chemical wastes and other substances.[7]

In the Republic of Korea in recent times, average annual increases in GNP have amounted to between 8 and 12 percent. In Seoul, which planned and provided for a population increase of 6 million people between 1955 and 1980, administrators failed to provide for either domestic or industrial sewage and sewage treatment during urbanization. Now the Han River is heavily polluted below the city and can no longer be used for either domestic water supply or irrigation. Eight tributaries to the Han River running through the city are heavily contaminated with industrial wastes and may never be reclaimed for uses other than waste disposal.[8] But we are told (and it is "conclusively" proven by national income figures) the "living standards" of the population of Seoul have improved dramatically.

In Milan, Italy, in December 1986, thousands of people were lining up daily with bottles and buckets to draw drinking water from tanker trucks because of pollution in the Po, Italy's longest river. A state of emergency was declared when levels of atrazine in the water reached ten times the allowable limit. The poisons, a residual of agricultural herbicides and pesticides, were washed into the river by rains.

Eventually rivers are cleared of the poisons. But our inland waters, rivers, and lake systems are our means of transport— our pollution canals to take our waste to the sea. What goes

into the sea stays there. Forever. And not "for good" but
for bad.

The Market for Trees and Crops

Grasslands, fisheries, and soil are also being rapidly depleted
and exploited "for bad," but perhaps the most visible current
depletion is of forests. Dead and dying forests are now plainly
visible in West Germany, Norway, Canada, Czechoslovakia,
and Poland. Previously stable forests in the temperate zone are
now suffering from air pollution and acid rain. The world's
tropical forests are disappearing at a rate of 2 percent a year
and far faster in West Africa and Southeast Asia, where moist
tropical forests may well disappear by the end of the century.[9]

The effect of smoke pollution on plants had been noticed as
far back as 1691, when the evergreens of Lord Devonshire's
London garden were remarked upon as being "smutty from
smoke." In 1722, Thomas Fairchild published *The City Gardener*,
the first book to deal with urban gardening, which showed that
by this time the major problem to be combated was the smoke
from coal fires in London and the fumes from the new factories
in the provinces.[10] Few consequences of ecological deterioration
can now be confined within national geographical boundaries.

In any meeting between the Canadian prime minister and
the president of the United States, the effect of acid rain on
Canadian forests as a result of pollution in the United States
is always a major agenda item. Sissel Roanbeck, Norway's minister for the environment, points out that Norway's pollution
problem is British industry.[11] Britain has the fourth largest
emission of sulphur into the air of any country on earth. Most
of it falls on Norway as acid rain. A study by the Czechoslo-
vakian Academy of Sciences, reported in 1984, estimated annual damage from acid rain to be at least $1.5 billion with the
loss of forests accounting for most of the total. With this academy report, Czechoslovakia became one of the first countries

to recognize the effect of air pollution and acid rain on farm productivity, linking fossil fuel combustion and agricultural output.[12] In West Germany in 1983, the Bavarian Agricultural Ministry estimated the loss of trees in southern Germany at $1.2 billion. In the short run, damage to German forests is expected to increase harvesting and reduce timber prices. Over the longer term, however, timber prices will rise as the forested area dwindles and trees become scarce.[13]

A forest can be viewed as an economic resource, as a sociocultural amenity, and as an ecosystem. The economic resource may be for forestry or fuel or achieved through tourism. As a sociocultural amenity, we may tramp or bushwalk or birdwatch or simply marvel at the beauty of a forest. All over the world, species of plants, birds, and animals function in life-supporting forest systems whose balance is disturbed and frequently destroyed by human intervention. To adequately portray these three dimensions of resources would require quite different "measures," bearing in mind the conceptual problems of measurement already mentioned. But neoclassical economics and national income accounting afford us only one view of the world.

The results of this are inevitable. Vera Massundra reports from Asia that current attempts at "social forestry," in spite of stated objectives to the contrary, tend to promote the planting of trees that benefit large industries, that is, the market.[14] The needs of rural households—for food, fodder, fuel, and a livelihood—could be met by forests with planned management, but these needs are generally ignored. Forest policies, forest sciences, and forest management are invariably in the hands of men, whose eyes are set on the revenue and high income—profit offered by large industry. Planned attempts at afforestation—on forest fringes, along sides of highways and village roads, on waste land, and including social forestry projects supported by international aid—seem to be becoming a monopoly for eucalyptus and similar plants, which offer nothing to women, while depriving them of food, fodder, and fuel. The market and public policy work hand in hand to ignore the needs of the community and the community's environment.

Journalist Gail Omvedt reports that the government of India, backed by the policies of the World Bank, has promoted mono-crop plantations of lumber trees that are useless to local people and actually destructive to local ecologies.[15] In 1970, for instance, a USAID report recommended that the Indian government replace much of its mixed tropical forests with plantations of pine, eucalyptus, and teak and then utilize the "invaluable asset" of woodcraftsmen, "working for one of the lowest wages in the world," to produce furniture and paper for export. USAID is providing over $50 million to the governments of states like Maharashtra for the development of social forestry. Although officials talk glibly of planting every kind of tree, the emphasis is on eucalyptus. Its use is enthusiastically adopted by rich farmers who find it a very profitable crop. However, the tree is useless to villagers except as lumber, while it uses enormous amounts of water in the semiarid regions where it is usually planted.

Omvedt reports that when the World Bank programs instituted teak planting in the southern tribal areas of the Bihar state, the people began to cut down the teak trees, understanding that they were replacing the highly useful sal tree. In the resulting trouble, police fired on demonstrators, killing dozens of people. Now, this is not supposed to happen. Remember the national accounts system treats government expenditure separately because its public policy motives are supposed to be different from those of the market. But the police of Bihar demonstrate that the motives of patriarchy are similar wherever the patriarchs are found.

What is wanted in Bihar are indigenous tree species that are adapted to local conditions and have multiple uses offering usable bark and roots, edible leaves, nuts or fruits, and shade. These primary services are seldom marketed and so seen by policy planners to have no value. Development policies that carry forward such indigenous traditions require both significant grass roots participation and control and also major changes in the entire economic model. This is something that no section of bourgeois political leadership in the government of India or the World Bank or USAID or anywhere else is prepared to encourage, in spite of the rhetorical bows in this direction.*

Forests are also destroyed at an alarming rate to make room for agricultural crops—and, generally, export-oriented monocrop production. In exceptional cases, women and children win a political battle to *conserve* a community resource, but it is a rare occurrence.

In the remote Himalayan village of Dungari-Paitoli, six hundred kilometers north of New Delhi, the local women have not allowed the men to sell off the nearby community forest to the government to turn it into a farm for seed potatoes. If the forest had been cut down, the women would have had to spend several more hours every day to fetch the family's daily requirement of fuel and fodder. Women in these parts walk an average of ten kilometers on three days out of four, for an average of seven hours at a time. They bring back about twenty-five kilograms of wood with each load. All women, young, old, and even pregnant, participate in this activity. The women discussed the men's argument that the establishment of the farm would bring all the fruits of development, a road, a health clinic, and maybe even a high school. This, they said, was of less importance than the forest, which met the families' basic needs, for which the women were responsible.[16]

---

*A USAID publication on women in development, for example, reports: "Women have a large stake in reafforestation projects which can provide fuel, food, fodder and medicines as well as a cash return. Rural women have been shown to be very knowledgeable about the attributes of both familiar forest products and new rapid-growing trees for forest plantations. Women, however, cannot be expected to care for the seedlings and young trees if the primary benefits accrue to others. Only if women share the control of forest product distribution will they have the incentive to participate in reafforestation."

The monocrop (one species) forestry approach is succored and encouraged by national income accounting. Policies encourage export cropping and market income. Women farmers concentrate on subsistence cropping and feeding people. Many of the characteristics of their traditional agri-ecosystems are socially, environmentally, and economically much more desirable than those of monocrop systems. In general, intercrop (mixed cropping) systems are more productive. They utilize soil resources and photosynthetically active radiation more efficiently. They resist insect pests and plant pathogens in weeds better. They produce a more varied diet. They better utilize local resources and nonhybrid, open-pollinated, locally adapted, insect-resistant seeds. They contribute to (subsistence) economic stability. Although in much of Africa today the women farmers are generally confined to farming low quality marginal soils with little capital or government support, their systems are compatible with their environment and can provide valuable information for the development of additional yield sustaining systems.

Anyone of us who has gardened for a short time can learn to rotate crops, to keep different vegetables apart and fennel right out of the way, to plant garlic for insect control, to allow grasshoppers and ladybugs to keep aphids and spiders under control naturally, to utilize marigolds at every opportunity, to make compost, and to collect and dry seeds. We *choose* to do this, even when the market is saturated with processed manures, herbicides, insecticides, and sufficient seedlings for our own monocrop production. We do it because we love and respect the earth and the planet. We do it because it makes sense. We do it because we understand our disruption and wish it to be as unobtrusive as possible.

The inability to attribute a market value to a part of the ecosystem does not mean that it is not *worthy* of consideration in the public policy equation. Yet the treatment of the environment in the national accounts, and in public policy, reproduces the arrogant ideology that only money is of value, that the market is the only source of knowledge. It suggests that all of life can be condensed to this narrow and soulless view, which precipitates us, at an ever increasing pace, towards the destruction of all forms of life on the planet.

What Am I Bid for a Giant Panda?

In this context, just how does one "value" a species of wildlife? Several years ago in New Zealand a bird called the Chatham Islands robin was reduced to fewer than a dozen birds. The New Zealand Wildlife Service found a small island with the appropriate ecosystem for the bird. It carried out a rapid program of vermin elimination on the island and transferred the remaining robins to that island for the breeding season. It was a success story, and that species now gains in number. The kakapo, the world's strangest parrot, and a creature that nineteenth century ornithologist John Gould called "the most wonderful, perhaps, of all living birds," may yet be saved with similar treatment. Once believed extinct, the total number is now believed to be about one hundred. The heaviest parrot in the world, weighing up to six pounds, it nests in holes in the ground instead of in trees. It may breed only twice in a decade. The wildlife service in New Zealand is now spending $100,000 (U.S. $64,140) a year to save the kakapo. Four islands are being cleared of predators in the hope that separate populations of this bird might breed. The fact that New Zealand is the home to more endangered bird species than any other country in the world is an illustration of the human population's determination to sustain the lives of these species. The impetus to save such species seems to be one that springs from popular public pressure for the government to act in this way. Reports of surveys carried out internationally would tend to suggest that the motives of New Zealanders are, in this respect, at odds with those of much of the rest of the world.

In an exclusive survey of leading conservation strategists from sixty-five nations reported in *International Wildlife*,[17] authors Jonathon Fisher and Norman Myers report the conclusion that "wild resources must pay their own way." In this most controversial and contested theme of their survey, the experts called for a doctrine of utilization: to treat wildlife in most cases as an economic resource to benefit people. According to 46 percent of those responding, the following activities "usually help" the cause of conserving wild species: hunting, fishing, tourism to observe wildlife, ranching for meat, medical experimentation, and other controlled exploitation that kills or uses individual animals. Only 5 percent of the experts think that these activities "usually hurt." At the same time, 27 percent say that protection of individual animals on humane or ethical grounds "usually hurts" the cause of conserving wild species, while only 17 percent say it "usually helps." Traditional wildlife managers, as well as others who favor "use," argue that animal species can best be saved if a continuing supply makes them economically viable and beneficial to people, especially in the populated Third World. That way, according to their view, humans who share living space with wildlife have a self-serving reason for saving the resource. The kakapo and the Chatham Islands robin wouldn't have had much of a chance elsewhere, it appears.

One academic paper I read recently, entitled "A Model for Valuing Endangered Species," focused on one particular economic argument for preserving some endangered species. Value was to be ascertained according to the use of the species, directly or indirectly, to obtain expected improved medical, agricultural, or manufactured goods. (Endangered species would then have more value than surrogate mothers "used" to "obtain" medical goods.)

How much is an endangered species worth? is not only an impossible question but also an inappropriate one. Who can accurately determine a price tag for the giant panda?

Yet in the United States, when a decision must be made on a proposed dam, officials are asked to estimate the value of wildlife that would be affected. Since more than $40 billion changed hands in 1980 because of wildlife (according to a U.S. Fish and Wildlife Service survey), economists use these figures to calculate the value of wildlife that would be lost by damming a river. They use a concept called Wildlife Fish User Days (WFUD)—the amount of money that an individual would spend in twelve hours in pursuit of the animals. The forest service estimates that an elk is valued at $16–$25 per WFUD. Fish tip the scales at $14–$21 per WFUD, while waterfowl are valued at $19–$32.[18]

Such an approach gives no value at all to the environment or to its ecosystem. It is simply a matter of weighing one market utility—namely, a silt-producing, ecologically damaging, "productive" dam—against another—namely, income from the legitimized violence of men against animals, euphemistically called leisure.

The marketability of such leisure pursuits was seen clearly in the colonial era with the establishment of game parks in Africa. Here fences were erected around areas where "dangerous" animals ranged, so that European hunters could be flown in on safari to slaughter them. In the meantime, wandering tribes, who for centuries had systematically grazed their animals and gathered their own food and water across that land, were kept from it by the fences. The ecosystem balance, which had been achieved by them with their environment, was lost, along with their self-sufficiency, independence, culture, and way of life.

But the most dangerous of creatures to humans is not imprisoned in a game park, and it is far from being an endangered species. And this most dangerous of creatures acts in a superbly efficient way to save major remaining ecosystems from human destruction.

In terms of the number of people killed each year throughout history, the title of the most dangerous jungle creature goes to the mosquito. Mosquitoes have been around for at least 50 million years and have evolved some twenty-seven hundred species of which only a few threaten humans. But those few cause havoc. The World Health Organization estimates that in sub–Saharan Africa alone, more than a million children die every year from malaria, just one of the many mosquito borne diseases.

American naturalist David Quammen points out the irony that the mosquito has been a powerful force for the preservation of the world's tropical forests.[19] "Clear the vegetation from the brink of a jungle water-hole," he says, "move in with tents and animals and jeeps, and *anopheles gambiae* not normally mated there will arrive within a month, bringing malaria. Cut the tall timber from five acres of rain forest, and species of *aedes*—that would otherwise live out their lives in the high forest canopy passing yellow fever between monkeys—will literally fall on you and begin biting you before your chainsaw has cooled." Thus, says Quammen, "the forests are elaborately booby-trapped against disruption."

Now just what sort of cost-benefit analysis might be made concerning the mosquito? The distinguishing feature of cost-benefit analysis is the attempt to quantify and assign a monetary value to all the cost and benefit components. Thus aggregate comparisons are established, and the size of surplus costs or benefits estimated, and on the basis of these, recommendations are made to decision-makers.

In economic terms, the creature itself is worth nothing. The malarial deaths it causes have no market value in and of themselves, but international aid transfers, the payments to multinational drug companies for medicines, and the payment of medical teams and technicians working in the field, all form part of national income accounting.

No analysis is available of just what a cleanup of the world's water resources might do to the mosquito. This would not suit the interests of the powerful lobbyists in the multinational pesticide industries, whose other major contracts are with defense departments for the supply of defoliants and chemical weapons such as napalm. Nor can we factor in the benefit to the globe of the superb guard mounted by the mosquito to preserve tropical jungle forests, major agents for precipitation. Up to half the world's genetic diversity in wild plant and animal species is concentrated on 6 percent of its land surface in tropical rain forests. At our present rate of destruction (called growth and development) it is believed one million of these species could be extinct by the end of the century. The mosquito is their, and our, last line of defense in the preservation of these forests.

Meanwhile, as we pursue the mosquitoes with poison, which takes a slow toll everywhere as it enters our food chains, contaminates our water, affects pregnancy and reproduction—the results of the manufacture and use of pesticides—the mosquito has rapidly developed resistance to every pesticide deployed against it and has adapted to living in man-made environments. And the development of pesticides to rid the world of mosquitoes has left its legacy in the chemical poisons that have infected our air, water, and our bodies.

Growth's Legacy—War's Waste Material

The wastes of the nuclear industry have a toxic life that exists the length of recorded history. The question of how to safely and economically dispose of nuclear reactors and their wastes at the end of their lifetimes is still completely unanswered. Radioactivity builds up each year the plant operates, and all the contaminated plants and equipment must be securely isolated from people and the environment.

There are now over 500 nuclear power plants operating or under construction for completion in fifty-six countries. In addition there are 375 research reactors. Table 11 establishes the number of such reactors in 1984.

During the seven years between the Three Mile Island accident and the Chernobyl disaster we were invited to acquire the impression that nuclear power was dying. This was principally because in this period not a single new nuclear plant was ordered in the United States, 48 on order were canceled, and half a dozen went broke. In the same period, Sweden voted to

Table 11.

Nuclear Reactors as of December 31, 1984

Country	Power reactors	Research reactors
Argentina	3	5
Australia	0	3
Austria	1	3
Belgium	8	5
Brazil	3	3
Bulgaria	6	1
Canada	25	12
Chile	0	2
China	3	4
Colombia	0	1
Cuba	2	0
Czechoslovakia	10	4
Denmark	0	2
Egypt	0	1
Finland	4	1
France	64	21
E. Germany	7	5
W. Germany	27	32
Greece	0	1
Hungary	4	4
India	10	5
Indonesia	0	2
Iran	0	1
Iraq	0	2
Israel	0	2
Italy	6	12
Japan	40	22
N. Korea	0	2
S. Korea	9	3

Table 11 continued

Country	Power reactors	Research reactors
Libya	0	1
Malaysia	0	1
Mexico	2	2
Morocco	0	1
Netherlands	2	4
Norway	0	2
Pakistan	1	1
Peru	0	1
Philippines	1	1
Poland	2	5
Portugal	0	1
Romania	3	3
South Africa	2	1
Spain	14	4
Sweden	12	3
Switzerland	5	5
Taiwan	6	1
Thailand	0	1
Turkey	0	3
United Kingdom	42	16
United States	130	127
Uruguay	0	1
USSR	61	23
Venezuela	0	1
Vietnam	0	1
Yugoslavia	1	3
Zaire	0	1
Total	516	375

Sources: Based on Lester Brown, *State of the World 1986* (Washington, DC: Worldwatch Institute); Cynthia Pollock, *Decommissioning Nuclear Power Plants* (New York: W. W. Norton & Co., 1986), 120–36.

phase out its nuclear industry by the year 2010, and the Danish parliament voted not to include nuclear power stations in future public energy plans.

Yet this was a period in which some nations—the Peoples Republic of China, for example, which until that point had been nuclear-free—signed their first contracts to proceed with nuclear power. It was also a period in which commercial nuclear power in the United States grew substantially. When the alarm went off at Three Mile Island in March 1979, 70 commercial power reactors were in operation in the United States. By 1986, 99 commercial reactors were licensed to operate in the country, and 33 more were under construction. In 1984, nuclear plants produced 13 percent of the electricity consumed in America. By 1986 they produced 16 percent, and more was on the way.

Other countries maintained an even faster pace of nuclear development. In 1986 France drew 65 percent of its electricity from the atom; Belgium, 60 percent; West Germany, 30 percent; Japan, 27 percent; and Britain, 19 percent.

The economics of bombs and electricity are heavily intertwined, as evidenced by the fact that all things nuclear in the United States, civilian and military, come under one federal department, the presumably civilian Department of Energy.[20]

Of all the estimates of the cost for decommissioning power plants, the lowest is about $50 million and the highest is about $3 billion per plant.[21] Cynthia Pollack writes that

Much of the nuclear decommissioning bill is to fall due in a single decade, from the year 2000 to the year 2010. Given current policies, most of this bill will be paid by a generation that did not take part in the decision to build the first round of nuclear power plants and that did not use much of the power generated. [Not a single large commercial power unit has ever been dismantled.] Decommissioning is waste management on a new scale. There are, it is thought, three courses that might be followed. The first is to decontaminate and dismantle the facility immediately after shutdown; the second to put it into storage for fifty to a hundred years to undergo radioactive decay prior to dismantlement; and the third is simply to erect a permanent tomb around it. Each option involves shutting down the plant, removing the spent fuel from the reactor core, draining all liquids, and flushing the pipes. Under the immediate dismantlement scenario, the radiated structures would be partially decontaminated, radioactive steel and concrete disassembled using advanced scoring and cutting techniques, and all radioactive debris shipped to a waste burial facility. The site would then theoretically be available for unrestricted use. Plants to be mothballed would undergo preliminary cleanup, but the structure would remain intact and be placed under constant guard to prevent public access.

Entombment, the third option, would involve covering the reactor with reinforced concrete (as has been done in Chernobyl) and erecting barriers to keep out intruders.

Whatever method is chosen, decommissioning a nuclear plant is a task without precedent. Because of the dangers involved for all who work on or near the site in such a venture, productivity is unavoidably low, less than half what it could be in nonradioactive environment. The volume of solvents used must be carefully regulated because the effluent used becomes radioactive, and spills during either operation or cleanup can result in contamination of the surrounding soil. Keeping waste volumes to a minimum is an illusive goal. Each piece of machinery and every tool that comes into direct contact with a contaminated surface must be decontaminated or added to the radioactive waste pile.

Decommissioning experience is very limited. A twenty-two megawatt Elk River plant in Minnesota is the largest that has been fully decontaminated and dismantled. The U.S. Department of Energy (DOE) completed this three-year project in 1974 at a cost of $6.15 million. Cleanup costs at Three Mile Island are projected to pass $1 billion before decommissioning itself is even contemplated. Swiss studies estimate that decommissioning a retired nuclear plant would cost one-fifth as much as the facility originally cost to build,[22] and independent analyses in the United States predict that decommissioning will cost as much as the original contribution in constant dollars.[23] Since a retired and highly radioactive nuclear plant is not likely to be regarded as secure collateral for borrowing, and since, when a reactor stops producing power, it also stops earning money for its owner, it is not clear who will pay the market cost of decommissioning nuclear power plants. What is clear is that these "costs" will be value-added to the national income. What is clear is which generation will pay the true "cost" of having this form of energy proliferate throughout the globe.

No country currently has the capacity to permanently dispose of the high level wastes now stored at a single reactor. No country has really solved the problem of where to dump its wastes. We in the Pacific are faced with the prospect of having northern hemisphere nations dump their fallout material in our ocean, as if it were their backyard sewer. They argue that they can do this because it is safe. If it is safe, we argue, then they should dump it in their own backyard. But our argument, of course, still avoids the point. There is nowhere on this small planet that it is safe to dump these highly toxic wastes. In the long term, if the global community has to dispose of more than five hundred nuclear power plants, the total bill will amount to an excess of $500 billion. This does not mean that they will disappear.

Nuclear power plants are the prime source of fuel for the nuclear armaments industry. To meet increased material needs the U.S. Department of Energy has almost doubled its annual rate of plutonium tritium production since 1979. At the same time the objective of a five-ton reserve of plutonium was established. The Department of Energy spent over $15 billion for nuclear weapons in the fiscal year 1984–85. Eight warhead types were in full-scale production during this period.[24]

Betty Reardon argues that the war system itself has been sustained through the matricide of Mother Earth in the exhaustion of resources and the pollution of the atmosphere resulting from the production and testing of weapons. She writes:

Ecological destruction is at its base misogynist. It is not, as some feminists claim, an example of the notion that masculine forces are death courting and feminine life giving. Rather it is simply another result of the masculine drive to control and dominate the feminine—a drive at work in most men, and in some women, that is projected by male rule into the larger society. The rape of the earth is a most apt metaphor for this defilement, a process that has led to the capacity to bring about the death of the ravaged planet.[25]

Reardon argues that more than any other world order issue, the threat to ecological balance demonstrates the destructive consequences of the dichotomy between men and nature, through which the human species has been led to wage literal war against the natural environment.

Now the greatest threat to global and national security is ecological devastation. National defense establishments are useless against these new threats. Neither highly sophisticated weapons systems nor bloated military budgets can halt deforestation or arrest the soil erosion now affecting so many Third World countries. Blocking external aggression may be relatively simple compared with stopping the deterioration of life support systems.

The fact that no natural resources are amenable to income accounting does not stop the economic theorists and practitioners attempting their forced consistency. In an area of imputation where guesstimates exceed any of the "conceptual and data gathering difficulties" inherent in assessing values for women's unpaid productive and reproductive work, governments and international agencies back the experts in their cost-benefit analyses. There is no subtlety in the direction of their work. There is no subtlety in the direction of their concern—which is not to assess the effects on the planet of this rape and pillage but to assess market values for resources yet to be exploited.

11. If Counting Were the Limit of Intelligence

My Search for an Alternative to the UNSNA

It is neither impossible nor difficult for a particular class or caste to enslave others. Though generally frowned upon, this enslavement is rarely contested if shown to be "scientifically valid" and if it seems "conceptually impossible" to function in any other way. The propaganda that supports the patriarchal ideology is loaded with such "objective," "logical" characteristics, and as we have seen, they are demonstrably invalid.

Occasionally even liberals within the patriarchal tradition have seen difficulties and have sought reform. Before I move to the suggestion of a totally different model on which to base public policy formation, I want to traverse the work of some of the reformers. This will demonstrate the adaptability of tools and concepts currently operative in the UNSNA. It will also show you how I arrived at my conclusion that we need a different model entirely, and it traces my own path as a politician and activist in the search for another way.

Stage One: Imputing a Value for Women's Work

As a fledgling politician, desperate to create a visibility for my sisters in a public policy context, I believed the answer to the problem of our exclusion lay simply in the imputation of a value for women's unpaid productive work. This is conceptually and statistically possible *now*. As has been evident throughout this book, our lack of inclusion is ideological. As John Kenneth Galbraith described it, "The servant role of women is critical for the expansion of consumption in the modern economy."[1]

Feminist writer Hilda Scott points out that if business had to replace with commercial services all the merely material functions women perform, at rates the average working man could afford, or finance them in the public sector, the wages and tax bill would put the U.S. budget deficit to shame. Business would have to hire more people, presumably women, to provide these additional services.[2]

Payment or replacement is not the point of issue. We are looking to determine the worth of these services.

In June 1970, Lisa Leghorn wrote to the public relations department of the Chase Manhattan Bank concerning a survey conducted with the families of Wall Street employees to determine "what a wife was worth." The bank replied, "The information contained below [see table 12] was derived from an informal survey of Wall Street employees and their families which we believe demonstrates that maintaining a household often requires as many or more skills as required in jobs outside the home."

Leghorn then demonstrated that by multiplying that figure by the number of weeks in a year and the number of housewives in the United States, one arrives at a figure of between $5 billion and $650 billion per year, which was (at that time) over half the declared Gross National Product of approximately $1 trillion, five to six times the military budget, and twice the total government budget.[3]

A survey by the American Council of Life Insurance, to determine the cost of replacing the services of a full-time homemaker in the event of her death or total disability, was published in 1982. Based on data from reporting employment agencies and state employment departments, the national av-

Table 12.

Chase Manhattan Bank Survey: What Is a Wife Worth?

Job	Hours per Week	Rate per Hour	Value per Week
Nursemaid	44.5	$2.00	$89.00
Housekeeper	17.5	3.25	56.88
Cook	13.1	3.25	42.58
Dishwasher	6.2	2.00	12.40
Laundress	5.9	2.50	14.75
Food buyer	3.3	3.50	11.55
Gardener	2.3	3.00	6.90
Chauffeur	2.0	3.25	6.50
Maintenance man	1.7	3.00	5.10
Seamstress	1.3	3.25	4.22
Dietician	1.2	4.50	5.40
Practical nurse	0.6	3.75	2.25
Total	99.6		$257.53

Source: Leghorn and Warrior, *Houseworker's Handbook* (Cambridge, MA: Women's Center, 1973).

erage annual salary for a live-in housekeeper was $8,500; for a live-out housekeeper the average salary was $8,900. Costs in the cities were higher. Using the 1981–82 prices for a substitute homemaker and assuming a mother replacement for sixteen years, the total salary (adjusted for a 5 percent annual inflation) to be paid to a live-in substitute homemaker in an urban area was $246,000.[4] In the same year, the U.S. Social Security Administration estimated the value of basic homemaking, not including all roles, at between $9,200 and $12,600 annually.[5]

At this point, economists and statisticians can be relied upon to scream loudly that these figures are not empirically or scientifically based. Yet they are decidedly more sound than the measurements of the hidden economy or the statistical discrepancy used in the UNSNA. The problem is, that this contribution is so large that the neat little models and precedents established by the patriarchs cannot cope with the magnitude of change required to impute this production and consumption.

The magnitude of the value of unpaid work in these examples is utterly comparable with measures in the studies that have been undertaken in accordance with the rituals of the scientific method.

In her book *Unpaid Work in the Household*,[6] Luisella Goldschmidt-Clermont reviews seventy-five evaluations of the household sector undertaken since 1960 in industrialized countries. These estimates, of the contribution by the household sector to GNP, range from 25–40 percent. Goldschmidt-Clermont argues that the transformation of natural resources (for example, agricultural products into goods ready to satisfy human needs) is a chain of successive production processes that does not change in nature when passing the border line of monetary exchanges. She writes:

[T]he border line between production and consumption, as drawn in economics, is only a conventional line, convenient for distinguishing between relatively easy to measure monetary transactions on the one hand, and nonmonetary production for exchange or self consumption on the other.[7]

While it is clear that the methods evaluated by Goldschmidt-Clermont have been used in the *developed* world, and on *housework*, it is quite clear to me that they can, and should, be developed to encompass *all* unpaid work that women do.

The value of unpaid work is generally derived from market wages. The basis for imputation might be one of six methods. Briefly, these methods would use

1. the wages of substitute workers who could be hired for performing productive activities in the household (substitute workers could be either polyvalent: domestic ser-

vants, housekeepers, family aids; or specialized: cooks, launderers, babysitters);

2. the wages of workers performing functions equivalent to household production functions (as in, for example, the Chase Manhattan Bank survey);

3. the wages of workers performing tasks requiring qualifications similar to those required by household tasks;

4. wages foregone in the market by those engaged in unpaid household work (that is, "the opportunity cost" of their time;

5. the average wages of market workers (sometimes differentiated by sex, age, education, residential area, legal minimum wages, and so on); and

6. wages in kind, that is, noncash benefits (housing, board, clothing, medical care, food).

In a major study of the estimate of the value of household work in Canada in 1961–71, Adler and Hawrylyshyn used three methods to estimate the imputed dollar value of household work in relation to GNP.[8] The first method, based on "wages for market-equivalent functions," gave a result of 41 percent of GNP if based on female wages, but 53 percent of GNP if based on male wages. One of the obvious difficulties with this method is that it perpetuates unequal pay and does not include any concept of comparable worth. In addition, the market equivalent functions of so many of the characteristics of mothering and household work are sex-segregated or sex-stereotyped jobs, which are filled by women and lower paid. In assessing the dollar value of housework by using a "wage for a substitute household worker," the distortion in GNP was only 34 percent. The opportunity cost method gave a result of 40 percent of GNP.

Dependent on the form of valuation chosen, the percentage contribution of women to the GNP varies a great deal across definitions. The opportunity cost approach is the economist's ideal. It is based on the assumption that women make an economically rational decision about whether to do an additional hour of housework or go out and seek paid employment. Given the socialization of women to see themselves as mothers, the social pressures for them to fulfill this role, and the lack of support services to enable any option, this assumption is invalid. In addition, measuring potential wage rates is fraught with computational problems. Generally, the average hourly wage, by sex, of full-time civilian workers, less income tax, is the assumed opportunity cost. This has several difficulties. Marianne Ferber and Carole Greene write:

Evidence derived from data on young married women suggests that full time homemakers frequently are unable to provide estimates either of their potential earnings or of the lower wage they would accept to enter the labour market, and that such estimates as they do provide are not soundly based. We also found that using wages of women in the labour force market to estimate the value of the home time of full time homemakers involves upward bias. We conclude that there are good reasons for caution in using the opportunity cost approach.[9]

Washington economist Gar Alparovitz pointed out to me that Ferber and Greene's approach to opportunity cost could be seen to be very conservative.[10] Opportunity cost might readily be imputed in terms of Milton Gilbert's rationale for the U.S. war budget. Wages for a textile worker should be imputed, not at the rate for sewing silk stockings, but at the rate for sewing parachutes. Unskilled homemakers who, like "Rosie the Riveter," became engineers and mechanics in a matter of weeks in the mobilization for war, might well claim that the rates for those skills were their opportunity cost.

The replacement cost alternative, that is, paying another person to carry out all the housekeeping or homemaking or mothering tasks, generally lowers the estimate of production since these categories of workers are deemed to have the lowest amount of skill in the workplace. The 1965 edition of the *Dictionary of Occupational Titles* published by the U.S. Department of Labor listed and assessed 21,741 salaried occupations. The assessment of the levels of worker function are ranked 1–8 with regard to data, people, and things. A marine mammal handler was ranked at .328, a hotel clerk at .368, a dog trainer at .228, and a dog pound attendant at .874. It is impossible to code a job at lower than .878. Included in this category are maid,* teacher (nursery school), nurse aid, home health aid, practical nurse, and foster mother. Wages generally bear some relationship to skill in regard to data, people, and things. Replacing a housekeeper would be expected, in accordance with the dictionary, to be cheaper than replacing a dog trainer. Estimating the cost of each function of housework is difficult because several things are often done at once; child care and shopping, or meal preparation and homework supervision.

A further consideration is the necessity to impute double and triple time for the activities that fall outside the traditional forty-hour week. Time budget data are required, whatever method is used. There is no conceptual or measurement problem; it is just that such data are not considered necessary for calculating the GNP. The data could be collected by adding a time budget survey to any country's household budget survey. One might then be able to respond "scientifically" to Ronald Schettkat of the International Institute of Management in Berlin. Commentating on time budget studies, he writes: "It is . . . questionable whether the measured time (spent in housework) relates sensibly to output. It is possible that time inputs over estimate the necessary time for production because time is not used effectively in an economic sense."[11]

Schettkat referred to Joann Vanek's work to demonstrate that full-time housewives spent a lot more time in household production than wives engaged in both sectors.[12] Vanek's explanation for this difference was that full-time housewives were demonstrating their economic value to the family more by the amount of time units than by the effective use of each unit of time. Schettkat comments, "In other words it may be assumed that a part of the time spent in housework by full time house-

---

*For job description, see appendix 3.

wives is wasted in a strictly economic sense." This is *not* what Vanek said. You will recall in the discussion of leisure that study after study demonstrates that women who labor (paid or unpaid) beyond the household, work more hours and have less leisure time than any other population group. Their hours in household production are fewer because they run out of time!

Schettkat has a lot in common with a USAID evaluation report on a water program in Kenya. A well had been built so that the time the women carried water per day dropped from two or three hours to less than thirty minutes. The officials would not presume success for the scheme because, they reported, the assumption that the women would use the time saved "productively" was highly speculative.

This comment is not only patronizing but also typically neo-colonialist. Time-saving devices *may* create leisure opportunities for those in the developed world but not in the developing world, where any form of imputation of women's work is likely to involve a larger distortion of GDP than those suggested in the earlier mentioned studies of housework in the Western world. Such imputations can most certainly be made. Raj Krishna, a consultant with the Asian and Pacific Development Council, has written:

Every bit of quasi-productive work can be valued at the rate at which hired workers would do the same or similar work. For every transitional, semi-feudal, semi-commercial economy, almost every kind of unpaid quasi-productive labour is purchased and paid for in some nearby commercialized subsector. The wages received per unit of time by paid cooks, maids, nurses, sweepers, washermen, fishermen, hunters, gardeners, tailors, weavers, dairy-workers, poultry workers, woodcutters, water carriers, cattle watchers and porters can be ascertained and used to value the time devoted by women to unpaid work similar to the work of these categories of wage earners. For any residual unskilled activities for which a specific market wage is not available the general wage rate for unskilled labour in the area per unit of time can be used for computing the value of time absorbed by them. The part of the net output of tangible goods collected or produced (fuel, fish, meat, clothes, fruits, vegetables, milk and milk products, etc.) which is not already included in the national product, can also be valued at their market prices. . . .

Many components of the national product are currently imputed by national accounts statisticians with similar or worse procedures. Indeed, all estimates of income generated in unregistered and/or unorganized sectors are imputed in one way or another. Therefore, there should be no objections to another exercise in imputation to assess women's economic contribution more appropriately. When such assessment becomes a regular feature of national accounting, surveys to conduct the time allocation data and wage data required for imputation, will also be designed better and conducted more frequently.[13]

In the international statistical community, the resistances to change are still those outlined by Ron Fergie in my discussions with him in 1981. These reflect (1) a belief in the current system, (2) a respect for precedents, (3) an unwillingness to tackle the technical problems associated with the introduction of change, and (4) a lack of knowledge or awareness of recent developments in statistical collection.

Economists Marianne Ferber and Bonnie Birnbaum comment:

It is likely that our failure to assign a price for the services of the homemaker has tended to convey the impression that they are valueless rather than priceless. . . . The failure to set a value on household work places the homemaker at a disadvantage with regard to inheritance taxes and property settlements in divorce cases. Reliable estimates of the value of housework are needed for injury cases, life insurance, etc.[14]

Public Policy Implications

Ferber and Birnbaum are correct as far as they go. The public policy implications of imputing women's work into the national accounts are vast. First, per capita GDP would change markedly. A more reliable indicator of the well-being of the community would be available, because all caring services, subsistence production, and that vast range of life-enhancing work would be visible and counted. And priorities would change.

The needs for credit facilities, fertilizers, seeds would be clear for subsistence agricultural producers. The realistic per capita production would change the nature and scope of government inputs, in all countries, into agriculture. The needs for training and retraining the unpaid work force would receive attention as a policy priority. Unpaid workers could make a realistic claim on the public purse as opposed to being condemned to "welfare." *Every decision made* by a government would be influenced in a profound way.

Of course as long as men rule women there can be no real expectation of change, but the women in elected and bureaucratic office would be empowered in their lobbying and work. And the information would empower the powerless—to change governments, leaders, and the nature of economic power.

In rural communities, and particularly those in the developing world, the policy implications are enormous. Comparing the household to a productive unit, and not restricting it to a consuming unit, is conceptually founded. Households do, and have at all times, combined labor, capital goods (land or reproducible fixed assets), and intermediate goods to produce what is required to satisfy their needs when the market fails to do so. In times of crisis, when markets are disrupted, household production largely substitutes for organized market output.

I proceeded, for reasons which I will outline, to see that this imputation, while invaluable for the feminist policymaker, and while immediately possible, was conservatively reformist. It accepted the basic principles of the current system. It was a form of co-option. It would certainly be better than no reform at all. And yet the possibility of its realization terrifies the patriarchs.

While conceding that GDP is not a good indicator for welfare, but continuing to use it as a measure for welfare, economists and statisticians have responded to efforts to impute a value for women's unpaid work by suggesting that another form of indicators be assembled so that the market orientation of GDP is not distorted. This would ensure that policy decisions continued to be focused on economic activity by men in the marketplace as if it reflected all forms of value in the world. In addition, the UN Statistical Commission reports that users of statistics are in great need of internationally comparable data from as many countries as possible.[15] In the light of our previous discussion of the concept of household and the other forms of statistical data that defy cross-cultural comparison, international users must be in great difficulty. But such use of the national accounts ensures that the UNSNA serves the multinational military marketplace. The opinions of a statistician such as Richard Barkay, who saw the primary importance of the national accounts in Nepal for *national* planning, are completely ignored.[16]

Problems with Imputing Women's Work

The first difficulty I had with the imputation of unpaid productive work as the whole solution was the subject of chapters 8 and 9. As an answer, this reform perpetuated the invisibility of reproduction. And while the patriarchal procedures of the law, government, medical technology, and the workplace have "paid" for reproduction, such imputation was anathema to me. If reproduction was to include all reproductive work in addition to all productive work, then the concept of reproductive work would need to encompass all the functions of reproduction outlined earlier.

I could not avoid the "facts of everyday experience," where I observed women combining a myriad of unpaid productive and reproductive skills in their tasks. I knew, too, another reality, one that I expressed in introducing the notorious New Zealand amendment at the UN half-decade conference for women, in Copenhagen in 1980. Then, I said, "Women's exclusive association with the domestic or reproductive sector is at the crux of women's subordination and its perpetuation. Men don't die in childbirth. Maternal mortality is the leading cause of the low life expectancy among women in developing countries, just as anemia and malnutrition are the causes of their chronic fatigue. Women continue to satisfy the basic human need to reproduce human society, and continue to see reproduction unpaid, undervalued, unacknowledged."[17]

While I knew that reproduction should not be imputed, I also know that we must insist that it be. (Feminist academic input is urgently required in this sphere to ensure that reproductive work is not confined by definition to the biological function of giving birth.) Joan Robinson's words kept coming back to me: If the system did not make sense when we stood it on its head, it would be exposed as propaganda. Since the system is sold to us as a public policy instrument to establish the well-being of the community and since its authors boast a flexible boundary of production, a value-free system would withstand imputation and inclusion of all unpaid work that women do. If, as Ron Fergie insists, reproduction is just another form of production, then we should insist on its inclusion.

By now you will recognize that such a system would be both completely transformed, and in terms of its current usage, totally dysfunctional. This in itself would be quite an achievement, but causes me great discomfort. While I shall insist that we work to transform the system in this way, and use all its tools to do that, we must not rest there. With all its immediate relief and distinct policy possibilities, we would still be left with a system that reduced women's lives to statements of mathematical formula.

The Environment

And, at last, I began to see (for this took me some years) that our global ecosystem, our environment, all other species, our Mother Earth was still exposed to rape and exploitation by the national accounts, and the creation of visibility for women changed nothing here. In my slow, dogged way I began the process of working through this problem.

In 1975, Sir Richard Stone was commissioned by the United

Nations to draft a System of Social and Demographic Statistics. He wrote:

It would be possible to construct an estimate of the gross domestic product in which pollution was accounted for. Whether or not this measure would fall on the introduction of an anti-pollution policy would depend on how the services of reducing pollution were treated. If they were treated as intermediate product the gross domestic product would measure the output of commodities in the conventional sense, and so would *tend to fall* at constant prices since some of the resources previously used to produce conventional commodities are diverted to the reduction of pollution.

As a consequence of this treatment the new policy will show itself in a rise in the price of conventional commodities.[18]

As an example of what might be measured, he cited the comprehensive estimate of the total damage costs of air and water pollution made for Italy as long ago as 1969 (see table 13, p. 289). The purpose then was, not only to establish the existing annual damage cost, but to extrapolate those costs to 1985 on the assumption that no substantial changes in the policy and legislation relating to polluting activities would occur.

The total damage cost in 1970 was equivalent to slightly under 1 percent of GDP. Damage was expected to increase by 1985 (on the assumption of no policy change and at 1968 prices) by 3.2 times, or 8 percent a year. The assumed growth rate of the economy of Italy was not forecast to be nearly so great.

This exercise may give an estimate of the percentage of GNP contributed by pollution. But that was not the point of my problem. Countries with substantial resources would still find such pollution a relatively minor contributor to GNP. As Richard Goodland from the Office of Environmental Affairs at the World Bank writes, GNP is used to reflect what *society* prioritizes. (In such contexts it often helps if one reads *patriarchy* for *society*.) Resource rich countries, or those with unemployed carrying capacity, can more afford to maximize GNP as long as throughput is viewed as a flow from a near infinite source to a near infinite sink. This sink concept treats our planet

Table 13.

Italy: Environmental Damage Costs by Air and Water
Pollution (Billions of Lire, 1968 Prices)

	1970	1985
1. Health	130	490
2. Cultural assets	42–43	134–58
3. Agriculture and zootechnics	12–13	35–46
4. Tourism and free time	67	120
5. Water: industry and drinking	24	83–84
6. Ecological assets	47	91
7. Other damages	44–165	143–602
Total	366–489	1,096–1,591
Rounded total[a]	400–578	1,120–1,615

Source: UN Statistical Office, *Towards a System of Social and Demographic Statistics,* F no. 18 (1975).

Notes:

Line 1. Treatment costs, loss of wages, loss of housewives' services, premature deaths (present value of future income).

Line 2. Deterioration of archaeological assets, works of art, monuments, books, and records. Based largely on hypothetical costs of a program for conservation and restoration.

Line 3. Proportion of net output of certain products in areas affected by water pollution.

Line 4. Variety of estimates.

Line 5. Estimates for 1968 and 1981. Based mainly on additional treatment costs.

Line 6. Estimates for 1968. Loss of fish and timber and wild life.

Line 7. Estimates for 1967—a variety of losses: deterioration of buildings, clothes, cars, consumer goods, and "various activities." The wide range is based on classification of population into "black zones" (most affected by pollution—with about 4 million people) and "polluted" zones (about 14 million people).

[a]As given in source: presumably allows for updating items for which data given relate to earlier years.

as an endless sewer. Goodland suggests a greater role for government control. (But governments are controlled by the brothers of the men who control the corporate businesses, so governments are unlikely to decide optimally.) Since the environment is no longer a free good, Goodland argues, it must be accounted for as an asset, or generator of services to society in scarce supply, in demand, and *therefore competed for*.

What kind of mind could write that about the weather, I asked myself. Probably nothing affects national income accounts quite like the weather, and nowhere is that visible in the GNP. But just who is going to force consistency on the weather, measure its supply and demand, the services rendered, and the competition for it?

Yet, I did understand the sincerity and deep-seated concern of other commentators who saw one of the only possibilities of slowing the rape of the planet to be founded in incorporating environmental indicators into national income accounting. I was among them. Many who care about the planet cannot see any alternative to forcing decision makers to consider the planet's plight except by imputing data for national income accounting purposes. The hundreds of policymakers and government officials that I have met from all political blocs persuade me to echo that conclusion. I have encountered many men with manifestly myopic worldviews, a dependency on economic data that they clearly don't fully understand, and with hopelessly inadequate personalities that would not lend themselves to the vulnerable position of defending a forest or unpolluted river if the treasury's cost-benefit analysis recommended "development." So were there alternatives?

E. F. Schumacher, in his classic book *Small Is Beautiful*, criticized the custom of treating fossil fuels and living nature as income instead of as part of the total capital we are using, and by far the larger part at that. He wrote: "If we treated them as capital items we should be concerned with conservation. We should do everything in our power to try to minimise the current rate of use. It is inherent in the methodology of economics to ignore man's [*sic*] dependence on the natural world."[19]

Economics, he argued, should distinguish between those manufactured goods made from renewable resources and those based on nonrenewable resources. Cost, to a manufacturer, is the same whether he uses five dollars worth of oil or five dollars worth of coconuts. And his decision will be rational if he makes the choice that brings the greatest profit. To the rest of us, the two costs are not the same. Since oil supplies cannot be renewed, the overexploitation should be counted as *disruptive growth*.

By now I had begun to think that perhaps an answer lay in dividing both the income and expenditure columns of the national accounts into "creative" and "destructive" production, consumption, and services. Certainly it would involve establishing a demarcation between the two but not one that required any more experience or observation than the boundary of production. I would be willing to do it. Guidelines would be reasonable. For example, anything concerned with giving birth to, nurturing, sustaining, or conserving life—all life—would be creative. Anything specifically designed to kill life—there would be no corrupt euphemisms like "peace keeping" or "balancing power" involved here—would be destructive. Again the effect would be to expose the values of the men who rule us everywhere, to empower the powerless to transform the system. I found others who had thought this way.

Stage Two: Economic Welfare

In the 1960s, William Norhaus and James Tobin developed the Measure of Economic Welfare (MEW). Under this system, GNP is adjusted by subtracting those items that do not contribute to economic welfare and adding those items that do contribute but are currently not counted. So all unpaid labor and unpriced benefits (housework and recreation) would be added and all unpriced goods and harmful and wasteful products (pollutions, cigarettes, bombs, most advertising) would be subtracted.

This is a tempting conception, and was, during the early years of my thinking on this whole issue, the goal that I thought might be pursued. In particular I recognized that the national accounts (as represented in table 1, chapter 2), recast in this way, would have been a treasure trove of *power* (information) for a feminist in government—not the personal power "over" of the male world, but power for the previously invisible; power to work for change where wealth was directed to destruction. There is *no* reason why these accounts cannot be formulated in this way *now*, not just to empower office holders, but to empower the public voting constituency.

If the environment were to be treated in national income accounting, Dr. Christian Leipert of the International Institute for Environment and Society had outlined two categories of "defensive" economic activities.[20] Costs would be subtracted from GNP figures as opposed to being recorded as growth. In the first category are those defensive expenditures induced by the overexploitation of environmental resources in the general course of the economic growth process. This includes the following:

1. investment in and running costs of environmental protection in both the manufacturing industry and government
2. expenditures as compensation for damage that environmental pollutants have caused to:
   a) domestic and commercial buildings, production facilities, roadway and railway bridges, high voltage pylons, historical monuments, works of art, and the like
   b) exposed surfaces and objects (necessary cleaning of windows, textiles, and cars, for example)

c) crops and forests
d) human health

The second category of defensive expenditures are those inducted by spacial concentration, centralization of production, and associated urbanization (additional costs that agglomeration imposes on occupational pursuits and the achievement of income and consumption goals). This includes

1. rising costs of getting to work (car use, accidents, and public transportation, for example);
2. the rising costs for recreation;
3. increasing expenditures on rents, housing, and land use; and
4. rising costs of public and private security.

Other categories are defensive expenditures induced by the negative effects of cars, transport, unhealthy consumption and behavior patterns (for example, smoking, unhealthy nutrition, excessive consumption of alcohol, the use of drugs), poor working conditions (industrial diseases and accidents), and increased risks generated by the maturation of the industrial system.

I entertained an amalgam of these possibilities for some time. But our interdependencies for survival and well-being are not confined by national boundaries and neither are the effects of our destruction on the environment. An argument that most nations cannot afford the resources to undertake such surveys falls flat on its face in that context.* Sea-ice distribution, forest cover, and radioactive fallout levels are not situation-specific in their effects and in the global ecosystem interaction. And there

---

*Priorities for establishment of environmental indicators were outlined by the UN Environmental Program in 1984. Indicators are statistics that can be used to show significant trends in the state of the environment. Relationships between human intervention and natural resources are not indicated, but the list of qualitative measurements currently recorded is very extensive and is included in appendix 2.

was a hole in the sky south of New Zealand that would be invisible if this was the answer.

The sustained manufacture (recorded as growth) of chlorofluorocarbons for spray cans, air conditioners, and foam is depleting the atmosphere's protective ozone layer. This is a major cause for concern. If allowed to continue, the world's weather processes will change and animals and plants will be weakened from radiation damage. Already a massive expanding hole, equivalent to the area of the United States, has appeared over the Antarctic. Ultraviolet radiation is already acting there as a stress, killing aquatic life. If the hole were to spread, it would diminish crop yields and produce cancers.

The initial report of the hole by British scientists in March 1985 was generally dismissed by the international scientific community. But later in that year scientists in the National Aeronautics and Space Administration (NASA) produced satellite data confirming the British findings and showing how big the hole was. Scientists at NASA found that the depletion of ozone was so severe that the computer analyzing the data had been suppressing it, having been programmed to assume that deviations so extreme must be errors.

The relatively pollution-free environments near Antarctica are likely to find their people the guinea pigs of scientists studying the phenomenon before any international action is taken. If you live in New Zealand and read the *New York Times* that's how it feels. "It's like rolling dice," said Michael B. Mackleroy of Harvard University's Center for Earth and Planetary Physics. "The big money question is if what's happening in Antarctica is likely to be a foretaste of what might happen in the northern region."

But the UN Statistical Commission's rejection of proposals such as Leipert's is not based on the understanding that our planet's destruction now knows no national boundaries. In a report written for the UN Environment Program, Edward Teiler writes:

The compilation of alternative aggregates to GNP has generated a strong negative reaction among the international community of statisticians. Thus the Statistical Office of the U.N.'s Department of Economic and Social Affairs has questioned the value of an alternative aggregate on the grounds that the cost required to reach international agreement on its content and meaning might exceed the benefit desired. . . . The U.N. Statistical Commission has expressed its opposition to the opening of the national accounts to an additional element of subjectivity which would result from the introduction of new imputations.[21]

Well, we wouldn't want their accounts disturbed by a "subjectivity," would we? So the leading liberals in the debate offered a compromise. Roefie Hueting, head of the department for environmental statistics in the Netherlands, wrote in 1983:

It is on theoretical grounds not possible . . . especially in the most important cases, to correct national income for environmental deterioration. . . . In some cases—expenditures on compensation and elimination costs—correction is possible. . . . *New Scarcity* [by Roefie Hueting] emphatically does not recommend presenting the figures corrected in this way as a new national income. For the correction is marginal and the risk that the public will regard the corrected figures as perfect is very great indeed. *New Scarcity* stresses the following: starting from the subject matter of economics, economic growth can mean only one thing: increase in welfare. Welfare is dependent on a number of factors such as: produce goods and services, scarce environmental goods, time, income distribution, working conditions, employment, the safety of the future. Since it proves to be impossible in most cases to construct shadow prices for environmental functions, produce goods and environmental goods cannot be placed under the same denominator. The market price of a produced good gives only an indication of its marginal utility in respect of other marketable goods, but does not provide the slightest indication of its utility in respect of unpriced goods.[22]

As a result of the work by Hueting and others, the UN Statistical Commission noted in April 1987 that environmental and natural resources accounting "could be linked to the [UNSNA] by means of a framework of satellite accounts."[23] Some countries have attempted to establish an environmental accounting system to operate as an appendage to national accounts. The Japanese "green accounts" are such an example, as is the Norwegian system, which divides resources into renewable, "conditionally" renewable, and nonrenewable. Renewable resources are reserved as a description for the great cycling systems of nature—that is, the hydrological air mass and solar radiation systems. "Conditional" as a description is ominous—the forewarning of humanity's potential to inadvertently set off irreversible processes in biological resources and the quality of life-support systems. Nonrenewable includes the conventional view with regard to minerals and fossil fuels, further divided between those that can be recycled and those permanently degraded by use. The Norwegian system is not well designed to depict a holistic perspective on the relationship of human activity and environmental change.

In the Norwegian system (see figure 2), notice the continued centrality of the national accounts: despite the euphemistic "human (economic) activity," this is the world of men, markets, and the military. In accordance with the recommendations for a building block approach to the treatment of women's unpaid productive and reproductive work, we should visualize yet another box revolving around the male world labeled "housework" or some such thing. The range of environmental indicators that might be measured are found in appendix 2. The Norwegian sketch allows for the fact that the environmental resources are not generally *consumed* by the production process. The most important aspect is that the *quality* of the resource is changed and that this alters the suitability for other uses.

It's a better picture, but I still don't see the lens in focus. The environment as an ecosystem is clearly missing in the overall schema.

Figure 2.
National Accounts

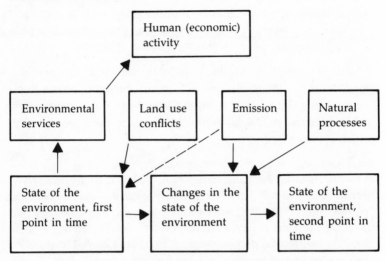

Source: Statistisk Sentral byra. *RessursregnesKap* (Oslo: 1981), 35.

Stage Three: Coming Full Circle

I had come full circle again. I could squeeze, push, frame this ecosystem I knew and loved into that system. I would fight, argue, harangue, and act to see that it did become visible in that way, because the visibility would transform the system and empower that which has no voice and no vote. But neither my intelligence nor my imagination would let me settle there. My difficulty was E. F. Schumacher's:

To press non-economic values into the framework of the economic calculus economists use the method of cost benefit analysis. This is generally thought to be an enlightened and progressive development as it is at least an attempt to take account of costs and benefits which might otherwise be disregarded altogether. In fact, however, it is a procedure by which the higher is reduced to the level of the lower and the priceless is given a price. It can therefore never serve to clarify the situation and lead to an enlightened decision. All it can do is lead to self deception or to the deception of others; for to undertake to measure the immeasurable is absurd. . . . The logical absurdity, however, is not the greatest fault of the undertaking: what is worse and destructive of civilisation is the pretence that everything has a price or, in other words, that money is the highest of all values.[24]

"Values" are those of the participant observer. So would a possible approach to the resolution of my dilemma be demonstrated by the current scientific approach of quantum physics? I thought of Niels Bohrs's theory of complementarity, which Robin Morgan describes:

Even if it is impossible to determine both the velocity and the position of an electron at the same time, nonetheless each (separately) is needed to gain a full picture of the atomic reality—just as both the "particle picture" and the "wave picture" are two complementary portrayals of the same reality, even if they can't be charted at the same time. In other words, despite one's *methods* being limited to either/or, one's *conception* can embrace both, and glimpse the whole.[25]

If our econometric modelers, our statisticians, our bureaucrats, our representatives, and our rulers were to accept the conceptual and intellectual challenge, two "complementary portrayals of the same reality" would inform their decisions.

How, then, might it be possible for economics to "glimpse the whole"?

12. Glimpsing the Whole

A New Model for Global Economics

A need or desire to glimpse the whole has never found its place in the disciplinary mainstream of economics. The majority approach is entrenched, reactionary, and, at best, strictly reformist. In the context of the UNSNA this is characterized by the "building block" approach, which argues that the stability and longitudinal comparability of statistics in the existing system should not be disturbed. This ensures a continued vicarious and second class relationship of "the maintenance of well-being in the community" to the continued primary importance of "winning the war" and of "the market."

My discomfort with the notion that, for the "forced consistency" of the accounts, everything had to be reduced to a market price, led me to the alternative concept of U.S. environmentalist Hazel Henderson.[1] A diagram of a layered cake (see figure 3) illustrates that the unmeasured, nonmonetary section of the economy and environmental degradation were not some peripheral part of the economy, a satellite or a building block. And not a slice of the whole, but a whole layer of the whole.

This was better, but my well-founded paranoia was uncomfortable with layers. I could be sure that, in the hands of the UN Statistical Commission, the top layer (with the icing) would be the market, which would trickle down any surplus goodies through the environmental layer to the household on the bottom layer—bearing the weight of the whole cake.

My search continued and was shared.

Figure 3.
The Economy as a Layered Cake

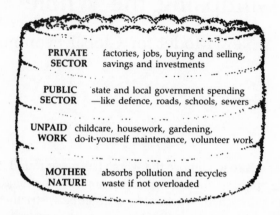

PRIVATE SECTOR	factories, jobs, buying and selling, savings and investments
PUBLIC SECTOR	state and local government spending —like defence, roads, schools, sewers
UNPAID WORK	childcare, housework, gardening, do-it-yourself maintenance, volunteer work
MOTHER NATURE	absorbs pollution and recycles waste if not overloaded

Source: The Politics of the Solar Age: Hazel Henderson, Anchor/Doubleday, New York, 1981.

Pietilä's Alternative

Hilkka Pietilä is a Finnish feminist activist whom I first met in 1980. It was her visual conception of the national economy, in a paper prepared for the forum at the UN end-of-decade conference for women in Nairobi in 1985, that most glimpsed the whole.[2]

Pietilä's diagram (see figure 4) describes the nonmonetary part of the economy as the *free economy*, since it consists of the work and production that people do voluntarily for the well-being of their families and for pleasure without requesting or receiving pay. The *protected sector* consists of production and work for the home market as well as public services (such as food production, construction of houses and infrastructure, administration, schools, health, transport, and communication). This sector is, in most countries, protected and guided by legislation and official means, and thus the prices and other terms can be determined independently without too much pressure from the world economy. Large scale production for export is usually called the open economy. Pietilä calls it the

Figure 4.
Pietilä's Concept of the National Economy (using Finland as example)

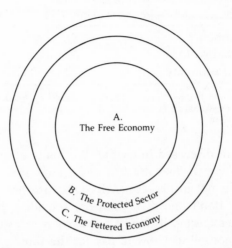

A.
The Free Economy

B. The Protected Sector

C. The Fettered Economy

Proportions in Finland 1980:		Time	Money
A.	The free economy, informal econ.	54%	35%
B.	The protected sector	36%	46%
C.	The fettered economy	10%	19%

fettered economy, since this is fettered to the world market. The terms of this sector, the prices, competitiveness, demand, and so on are determined by the international market. Pietilä writes that, in terms of the UNSNA, the whole life of society is geared to support this sector, while it accounts for a quite modest proportion of the total production in any one nation and in the world. In addition, Pietilä recognizes that money payment is not the sole criterion for the assessment of work. Work can also be assessed by *volume*: in terms of the labor power involved in the process (the number of workers) or the work time absorbed (number of hours). Volumes of input or output can be expressed in physical units or in the number of people cared for. (See table 14 for the way Pietilä lists the proportion of time and money in Finland in 1980.)

This concept would be anathema to Milton Gilbert, the

Table 14.

Assessment of Work in Finland's Economy, 1980

	Time (%)	Money (%)
The free economy	54	35
The protected sector	36	46
The fettered economy	10	19

Source: "Tomorrow Begins Today," (Paper presented by Hilkka Pietilä at the ICDA/Isis Forum Workshop at the UN End-of-Decade Conference for Women, Nairobi, July 1985).

economist we discussed in chapter 2. This is not his *structure* of the economy. It does not *force consistency*. It *is* useful *pedagogically*—but not in his terms. (Its great use here is to teach us what we don't know!) It does not provide a *framework* to improve the *estimates*. It does not *measure* nearly every item.

It would not tell us "how to pay for the war."

It would be of much greater use to governments for *real* policy analysis. And, yes, the resources to present such a picture would be available. If the *market* wants GDP figures, then, in the tradition of Friedman, the *market can pay for them*. The market, after all, supports the principle of user pays. The free resources can then be diverted to the service of the free and protected sectors, as much to tell us what we do not know as to tell us the policy implications of the new statistics.

Political and economic policies flow from the narrow agendas of political elites, and their decisions on the data they choose to collect are utterly inadequate. And while we can collect more data, goals and priorities should flow, not from assemblages of statistics, but from values. Our *values*—the values of centuries of enslavement.

We will still need data for guidance, as many of the examples in this book demonstrate. In the area of the ecosystem, for example, renewable and nonrenewable resource depletion can be distinguished. For renewable resources, environmental stress and the potential for permanent damage occurs when "the exploitation of these resources is greater than their carrying capacity measured by their natural rate of regeneration."[3]

For both renewable and nonrenewable resources, the notions of equity and conservation demand another policy principle. One environmental economist, John G. Riley, has suggested that a given rate of depletion is "excessive" or "unjust" if it results in relatively diminished levels of well-being for future generations.[4] The clear-cutting of the world's rain forests obviously falls into this category. So does the extraction of uranium, since it cannot sanely be argued that the end result of poisonous waste products—that will contaminate our globe for twelve thousand years—will enhance the level of well-being for future generations.

Ralph D'Arge writes that a reasonable inference is that a depletion rate is "excessive" in the physical dimension when it results in a level of extraction that exceeds the combined assimilative capability of the natural environment and the recycling capacity of the human environment.[5]

What matters in terms of measurement are the *qualitative* indicators and our interaction with them. This is conceptually determined by policies. For example, Pietilä's model allows for the conceptual integration of all these approaches and more. The forms of integration between sectors, and the policy consequences, will be demonstrated by many of the traditional forms of data collection but with their concentration redirected. This has been done often before, particularly where there has been a concern about nutrition.

Between May 1976 and April 1977, the Central Bank of the Dominican Republic conducted the first nationwide survey of household income and expenditure ever undertaken in the country. Because the Dominican Republic is largely rural and agricultural and because, at median income levels, food accounts for slightly more than 60 percent of total spending for a typical household, particular care was taken to obtain reliable and complete information on food expenditure and consumption. There were two important points about this survey. First, domestic production as well as market purchases were included in *every* food category, and estimates were obtained for the quantity of food, whether purchased or not, as well as for the value. Second, the availability of data on both value and quantity made it possible to estimate unit value, or price, for every purchase or consumption. The survey was conducted for a whole year to account for seasonal and geographical price variation.

This demonstrates how visibility and information may affect policies. Take, for example, milk, which is controlled at producer level. Producers were requesting an increase in price support. The government was reluctant to use the price of a food whose consumption it wishes to stimulate (especially among young children) and unsure about the costs and benefit of a subsidy. The study showed consumption is extremely sensitive to income changes but responds very little to changes in price. Holding down the price will not affect consumption, but may affect production. It is more efficient to arrange direct distribution of milk to poor children.

The use of the model is limited only by our imagination or fear of reality. The UNSNA model limits our imagination and reinforces the world's fears—of annihilation, of poisoning, of death. But there is, currently, little prospect of change. The UN Statistical Commission has announced that the next years for the conclusion of a census in every country are 1990–91. Along with other UN agencies under pressure to reform their data bases, the Statistical Commission is intransigent. I believe our aim should be international adoption by the powerless of the strategy described in chapter 5 and now part of the program of such feminist think tanks as the Sisterhood Is Global Institute.[6] Before I proceed to a call for action, let me update you on the most recent reasons for inaction by the patriarchy.

Reasons for Inaction: Patriarchy's Perspective

Some argue (always privately, so as not to offend) that illiterate rural women in the developing world would not be able to answer these surveys, that these women would simply not have available the amount of time needed to collect data, and that they would not be willing participants. (This, of course, conflicts with the presumption that since women do not work they have time to spare.) Yet the World Fertility Survey Individual Core Questionnaire was conducted with these same women, even though it took considerable time to administer. Any respondent might have been asked up to one hundred questions. But the basic documentation released since the survey shows that it is one of the most extraordinarily accurate forms of census that any UN agency has ever undertaken.[7]

The Living Standards Measurements Survey (LSMS), undertaken by the World Bank, has begun testing a questionnaire that takes four to six hours to administer, is spread over one or two visits to a household, and involves many household members. When it was first circulated, most members of the International Statistical Commission called it complex and un-administrable. Field operations in Peru and the Ivory Coast since then prove otherwise. With appropriate and intensive training, interviewers are capable of administering such a questionnaire. Data from the questionnaire has more than passed conventional tests for quality. The LSMS consultants have indicated that refusal rates in the Ivory Coast are less than 5 percent; in Peru, less than 4.5 percent, including both the first and second round visits.[8]

Another argument claims that statistics collected on women will not be as accurate as those collected on men. This completely misses the point. Helen Ware, a consultant with the International Research and Training Institute for the Advancement of Women (INSTRAW), has written a paper entitled "The Role of Household Surveys in Improving Statistics and Indicators on Women." In the opening paragraph she writes:

All officially published data should be as factually accurate as possible. Any statistical picture in which women's concerns are not adequately covered and depicted is quite simply false. A portrait of the world in which men and their concerns figure as larger than life whilst women and their interests are diminished and reduced in size is inevitably false and inaccurate. Data which do not accurately reflect the situation of women should not be accepted.[9]

If we women begin simply to fill in all census surveys and questionnaires as full-time workers (although unpaid) we will be assisting the acceptability of making data nonsexist. At the end-of-decade conference in 1985 in Nairobi, the following recommendation was contained in the document entitled "Forward Looking Strategies for the Advancement of Women":

The remunerated and, in particular, the unremunerated contributions of women to all aspects and sectors of development should be recognized, and appropriate efforts should be made to measure and reflect these contributions in national accounts and economic statistics and in the gross national product. Concrete steps should be taken to quantify the unremunerated contribution of women to agriculture, food production, reproduction and household activities.[10]

This was a considerable conceptual step for a UN document, and I never know whether to be cynical or amused when I see the word *reproduction* in such a paragraph. Clearly (meaning it is clear if you are a woman who attends these conferences), the *women* delegates mean by reproduction something beginning to approach the concept in chapter 8. This is an indisputable fact of observation as is the equally clear observation that the men at these conferences, particularly the male representatives of UN multilateral agencies, see reproduction as birthing and condescend not to make a fuss about its inclusion in a UN women's document.

This is because they know that they will be able to omit the conception, or narrow it to theirs, in any document that would emanate from a higher level (remember Fergie), more objective forum. The UN's treatment of the *demand* from the world's women to be statistically visible is a perfect example of either villainy or incompetence, which was the effect of the UNSNA suggested by one of the economists in chapter 6.

The incompetence is illustrated in the myriad stories of aid schemes that ignored women, of aid schemes that *caused* malnutrition, of aid schemes that changed climatic conditions and rainfall expectations, of aid schemes that left women without fuel, or aid schemes that were culturally imperialistic; the list is never ending. The incompetence is demonstrated in the breathtaking ignorance and insensitivity of statements made by UN officials such as Stern of the World Bank, on the situation in Africa, which you will remember from my comments on famine. The apparent lack of cohesion between agencies shows itself when data produced by one, calling attention to women's enslavement in the so-called development process, is ignored by another.

The UN Food and Agriculture Organization (FAO) has recently concluded that agricultural development agencies face major constraints when they try to reorient their plans of work and initiate new programs to take account of the involvement of women in rural production. On the lack of data about women, the information note says:

One US Department of Labour statement held that only 5% of the women in Africa work. . . . One way to make available more reliable information about women in agriculture is to ensure that collection methods and criteria reflect the work that women do. Another is to compile agricultural statistics according to sex. Finally, more attention must be given to information about activities that fall outside conventional surveys, for example, time spent by women on various domestic and related chores.[11]

The other problem seen by FAO is "a dearth of professional women in international, national and local agencies." And just what is a "professional" woman? We know in the international feminist network scarcely a position in a multilateral agency for which a suitable woman candidate could not be found. But we also know that feminist women are not welcome.

Ignoring the calls from the women's conferences and their other agencies is part of the villainy and mirrors precisely the response of governments to the demands of their female population for change. Since governments are generally represented on the UN Statistical Commission by their national statisticians, this should come as no surprise.

For several years INSTRAW has been holding conferences and receiving consultancy reports on measuring women's household activity and their participation in the informal sector. This work has had the effect of formally introducing to the UN network the concepts and information that women writers (such as Ester Boserup or Selma James)[12] have been publishing for many years. But INSTRAW is safely out of the way—an underfunded agency in the Caribbean—not in the UN mainstream.

In addition, irrespective of INSTRAW's findings and recommendations, the Statistical Commission has decided it will have no part in change. The proposal that nonmonetary economic activity should be included in national accounts estimates was brushed aside as a welfare issue by the Expert Group on Welfare Orientated Supplements to the National Accounts and Balances and other Measures of Levels of Living, which met in New York in 1976. According to the report of the expert group, the UN Statistical Commission "stressed that work on welfare measurement should not be allowed to disturb the [UNSNA] and MPS. Measures of welfare should be developed as supplements to the national accounts and balances, not as revisions to them."[13]

Despite the conclusion of the INSTRAW expert group in 1983 that "collection of data in a form that misrepresented the situation of women should not be justified solely on the grounds of maintaining comparability of historical time-series,"[14] the UN Statistical Commission, meeting at its twenty-fourth session in March 1987, noted that "the [UNSNA] definition of economic activity should not be revised to include value added by homemakers but that such activities should be covered in separate, supplementary estimates."[15]

At the same meeting, recommendations were made about the underground or hidden economy. In clarifying the UNSNA production boundary, such activity can disturb the UNSNA and MPS. The commission recommended that the value added by activities that produce goods and services for sale that are not reported or registered "should be included in the gross domestic product (GDP) along with the value added by similar activities in the 'open' or 'formal' economy."[16]

Ben and Mario, the "workers" we met in chapter 1, are primarily productive. Cathy and Tendai's activities are merely "supplementary" and "welfare." Pedantically speaking, their activities *are* welfare: none of us fare well by Ben or Mario's economic activity.

Some months before their 1987 meeting, I met in New York with Jan von Tongeren, head of the UN Statistical Commission. We discussed the work in progress on the UNSNA in league with the OECD, the International Monetary Fund (IMF), the World Bank, and the EEC. He explained that the commission was not developing a lot of data. The emphasis was on what to do with the data that was being collected and how to organize it. In response to my questions on the unpaid work of women, environmental pollution, and the hidden economy, he said that it was difficult to satisfy everyone in definitions and that when they had sufficient detail, then they might change their concepts. He agreed that the dominance of statisticians and economists who believed in the U.S. orientation of a system of national accounts inside the international agencies meant that any possibility of progress in developing further indicators was limited. He agreed that in the GDP the production income generating aspects show developed countries as better than they are and gave us as an example the fact that no deduction is made for costs to the environment or for the depletion of natural resources. In response to my questions on the inclusion of invisible work, he argued that such work should not be included as production because to do so would be to do a disservice to the unpaid. This needs to be shown on the distribution side of the accounts, he said, because good expert breakdowns show that much invisible work results in capital formation and not in consumption. An entry such as he suggested would make explicit how badly off the poor really are. He led me to believe that his own personal preference was to develop separate indicators and alternative measures as a satellite system for the GDP.

The results of the March 1987 meeting show that sufficient detail is available for imputing the hidden economy but not for imputing unpaid work, in spite of "good expert breakdowns" of the activity being available. Since it can be assumed that no conceptual changes will take place in the practices of the Statistical Commission between March 1987 and the 1990 round of censuses, let me consider briefly the other proposed recommendations of most interest to women.

On the clarification of the production boundary, following the proposal to include the hidden economy, the commission recommended that

the types of production for own consumption that should be included in GDP should be specified in detail in the revised [UNSNA]. The existing rules are not well understood and are interpreted differently from one country to another. The revised [UNSNA] should provide a comprehensive list of all such activities that may be included.[17]

Oh, goodie . . . a *comprehensive* list. If I were a betting woman, I'd lay out a mint on that list *not* including most of Cathy and Tendai's economic activity. Women everywhere should be lobbying central governments now about what they consider should be included in that list. In fact, every one of the following recommendations deserves a loud, vigorous, and angry response. Concerning the subsectoring of the household sector in the UNSNA, the commission proposed:

The possibility of using such subsectoring to more adequately distinguish at least some types of informal activity should be carefully considered. For example, farm and non-farm households might be distinguished, and farm households could be further divided between those whose income is mainly consumption from own production and those whose main income comes from cash sales; non-farm households could be further divided into those whose main income is from formal activities and those who are mainly dependent on earnings from informal activities.[18]

No, the motive is *not* to include the unpaid subsistence activities of women. The subsectoring is a move to ensure that even if some of women's unpaid production muddies the production boundary waters by being included as production for own consumption, those activities—not being cash activities and, therefore, being of no interest to First World governments, bankers, and multinationals—can be detected, if not eliminated. The possibility of distinguishing sectors so that some hitherto unknown altruism might direct policies towards the poorest of the poor has no place here and is no part of the motive.

Let's examine briefly three more such proposals.

The Group proposed that countries should regularly estimate home-makers' value added in such activities as minding and educating children, caring for sick and elderly family members, preparing meals, house-cleaning, repairing and washing clothes and health care. These estimates should not be included in GDP as defined in [UNSNA] but, rather, estimates of home-makers' value added should be added to GDP to obtain a measure of "expanded GDP." The implication is that home-makers' value added should be valued in accordance with [UNSNA] principles. Gross output of home-makers' services and their intermediate consumption should therefore be valued using market prices for similar services and goods. In practice, it would usually be necessary to approximate the required measure using the wages of paid workers producing similar kinds of services.[19]

So, if the production boundary is not expanded, it is not necessary to collect these figures. Governments "should," not "shall"—so they won't. And if they do, it will be an "expanded GDP."

Birth is excluded.

Guidelines and special analytical studies should be prepared on economic output by sex. This would require various assumptions about the sex division of non-wage components of value added and thus goes beyond national accounting as normally defined. A similar sex division should be worked out for expanded GDP; namely, GDP plus the value of housework.[20]

If the "assumptions" are to be made by the same sort of people who have thus far "informed" the UNSNA—Stone, Robbins, Gilbert, Fergie—we are in real trouble here, in a situation where we should feel there's been a minor victory.

Women are under-counted in the labour force for various reasons. The same *may* be true for the inclusion of women's contribution in the national accounts. The methods used by national accounts to estimate GDP *may* discriminate by sex either in the sense that certain informal activities are more likely to be omitted if they are performed by women rather than by men or in the sense that the informal activities usually performed by women are more likely to be omitted than the informal activities usually performed by men. These questions should be investigated by examining the estimation procedures at present used by a sample of countries [my emphasis].[21]

The same *may* be true? GDP *may* discriminate by sex? I know UN documents are notoriously polite, but this is ridiculous. These questions *should* (not will) be investigated by a *sample*? It's not proven yet?

And just one more quick flag for activists before I leave the commission's proposals. In regard to the calculation of Gross Domestic Product by sex, the commission "noted the great relevance in this respect of the current revision of the International Standard Classification of Occupations."[22] Well, I note it, too, and await the sleight of hand that will endeavor to classify the multiple unpaid roles of women's work as housework—and thus only in the "expanded GDP."

In Summary

Every discipline has its visionaries, and Simon Küznets was certainly one in the field of the national accounts. Thirty years ago he wrote:

It does seem to me, however, that as customary national income estimates and analysis are extended, and as their coverage includes more and more countries that differ markedly in their industrial structure and form of social organization, investigators interested in quantitative comparisons will have to take greater cognizance of the aspects of economic and social life that do not now enter national income measurement; and that national income concepts will have to be either modified or partly abandoned, in favour of more inclusive measures, less dependent on the appraisals of the market system. . . .

The eventual solution would obviously lie in devising a single yardstick that could then be applied to both types of economies—a yardstick that would perhaps lie outside the different economic and social institutions and be grounded in experimental science (of nutrition, warmth, health, shelter, etc.).[23]

In an interview in May 1985, just months before he died, Küznets told Dr. Christian Leipert that his entire career as a research economist had been based on the premise that economic activity must serve the needs of man (sic). When applied to the concept of GNP, this meant for him that GNP should be a criterion for the *net production* of the society, which has a *positive value* in the light of *human needs*. When asked why, from the early 1950s, he had given up on the topic of revising the calculation of GNP to give it a welfare orientation, Küznets emphasized that he had underestimated the logical and causality-related difficulties inherent in the analysis.[24] He did not have any assistance at the time with his work. Until the late 1960s, he remained almost the sole prominent economist to insist on a substantial final product orientation of the concept of GNP. The adherents to Richard Stone's "how to pay for the war" GNP were always found in the front ranks of the critics of the Küznets model, which they regarded as suspect because of the "excessive" number of its arbitrary assumptions and estimates. Conceiving that legitimized murder is valuable and marketable is not, apparently, suspect, arbitrary, or an assumption with which the rest of us disagree.

This original approach did not value leisure, the hidden

economy, or environmental pollution either, and the conceptual and measurement difficulties involved in these questions
are exceedingly arbitrary. Since the effect of imputing values in
these three fields is to create an even greater visibility for the
male world, statisticians and economists have been able to cast
aside their arguments of arbitrariness to work on these calculations.

Hilkka Pietilä's concept offers us an alternative, one that, as
a legislator and policy maker, I would have found invaluable.
It offers us the opportunity for assessing data by way of quality,
and quantity, by way of hours and money invested. It invites
us to consider interactions. It permits use of all advanced statistical mechanisms. It exposes propaganda in the place of a
lack of knowledge or where inconsistencies abound. Its great
value is in its application for domestic policies for a nation's
government and in the adaptation that can readily be made for
a regional or global picture.

Yes, it would work. Can you imagine the nation's annual
budget becoming a realistic description of the well-being of the
community and its environment, a reflection of real wealth and
different values? The budget would answer all of the following.
Who does what work and where—paid and unpaid? What is
the position of the nation's children and the aged? Who is not
housed adequately? Who has the poorest health? What changes
have occurred in water and air quality levels and why? What
is the nature, cause, and region of pollution, and what are the
health costs? What national resources have been harvested or
conserved? Who relieves the state of the burden of care and
dependency of others? What is the scope of subsistence production, and what are the nutritional results? At what price
does the nation currently value war?

Yes, it is a prospect that would terrify politicians—and their
patriarchal triumvirate with economists and statisticians. But
some of them have already abandoned that ship.

Herman Daly of the Louisiana State University in Baton
Rouge stresses the need to develop new concepts to replace

the old, even if it is not yet possible to point to concrete ways to apply them empirically. He told Christian Leipert:

[I]s not even the poorest approximation to the correct concept always better than accurate approximation to an irrelevant or erroneous concept[?] It is admittedly an exaggeration to say that GNP is worse than nothing, but I suspect that the world could get along well enough without it, as it did before 1940. We must face the question of what you would put in its place, but without letting its operational difficulty be concreted into an argument for staying with the (misleading) GNP.[25]

So we are not alone in seeing the need for change. We may be alone in making it. For the sake of our earth and ourselves, we must. What men value has brought us to the brink of death: What women find worthy may bring us back to life.

Epilogue

A Call to Action

If information empowers, and if power is the capacity to act, then I hope these few hundred pages have begun a process for many people. So what can we do?

The capacity to act takes many forms, and the options available are limited only by our fear, our lack of imagination, or a belief that specific "politically correct" strategies must be followed. While there exists a capacity to act, there is the possibility of change.

Australian philosopher and feminist Elizabeth Reid counsels that expanding the UNSNA to include our ecosystem and the unpaid work of women may see us co-opted. If the UNSNA, as it is currently structured, were to continue with environmental and social statistics vicariously related, as is the direction of international change, then I agree. But if inclusion is the strategy, then the system could not stand the pressure and would be transformed by the additions to something that might resemble Pietilä's model of the national economy. It may resemble something else, but her vision, more than any other I have found, enables us to glimpse the whole.

This debate has analogies with the battle for suffrage. The vote for women could be seen to be a strategy that co-opted women into an implicit endorsement of and support for patriarchal government. The euphemisms of the "democratically elected representatives of the people" are used to persuade women that this describes the process they participate in. Yet we know—not scientifically, not empirically, but in our guts and hearts, in our women's knowledge—that when more than half of the elected representatives are women, the institutional *structure* of government will change: the impact of women's culture in those numbers will see the hierarchy transformed. We don't know precisely how, and that's not really important. We know that the notion of power and its use would be transformed; we know that the substance of what is valued would be transformed. But since none of us know the capacity of women freed from centuries of enslavement, none of us can demarcate the route or conceive the end result of such freedom. There is no one way feminism on this road.

We're up against the world, literally, if we want change. Less than one hundred years ago those women in New Zealand who fought successfully to be the first to gain the suffrage must have felt much the same way. And while the vote does not address all our oppressions, we would not be without it. I *know* (as a "fact of everyday experience") that many of the reforms and legal equalities offered to women in Finland, Norway, and New Zealand, and the conservation consciousness of the governments in those countries, is a reflection of an involved, informed, active participation by the vast majority of women in the electoral process.

This is not the general experience, not because women are not interested, but because they are too busy surviving. Frequently, it is one major incident that changes lives.

Tragedy springing from environmental breakdown is often a significant mobilizer for women, who until that point have been co-opted and convinced by the system. Lois Gibbs was president of the Love Canal Home Owners' Association and was in large part responsible for the August 1978 declaration of the health emergency there. At a speech at the Women and Life on Earth Conference in 1980 she said,

The women of Love Canal are much like myself—housewives, mothers. Most have a high school education. We are lower middle class families with our biggest investment our home and our most precious asset our children. A majority did not work but remained home tending to houses, gardens and growing children. Since the Love Canal exposure this way of life has changed. Women are no longer at home because it is unsafe; we are not allowed to go near our gardens. The decisions have changed too, from normal everyday questions such as: What are we going to have for dinner? Where are we going on vacation? What colors shall we paint the walls? Now the decisions are, how can we afford a new home, will my baby have leukemia, will my daughter ever have a normal baby, what will we do with our sick child? We can't move and we can't stay here. . . .

The truth of the matter is that *we did not believe we were affected. The families had a blind faith in the government. We refused to believe* the Board of Education would build an elementary school *or that the city would allow us* to build our homes in a dangerous area. We knew there were strong odors, black gunk and other strange substances on the canal, but did not realize the dangers they represented[1] (my emphasis).

Many of us have our moments of blind faith. Friends who have been environmental political activists for years were shocked to silence, having at first been disbelieving, when I explained how national income accounting treated these things that we love and work to preserve.

Pat Smith lived in Newbury township, not far from Three Mile Island. Until the Chernobyl fire, this was the worst accident in the history of commercial nuclear power. Pat Smith said in an interview in 1980:

Exactly twelve months ago I was a homemaker, I was a mother. I was golfing five days a week. I had the ideal part-time job. I had the perfect life, I was always happy, bubbly. Now such a seriousness has taken over my life. God knows I would give anything to go back to the lifestyle I had, but I can't—if I want to sleep at night. Anything is less important than closing down Three Mile Island.

They tried to tell us we are emotional. Yeah, I am emotional about the whole thing. It's been hell living there for twelve months. If my kids come down with leukemia, I can't say what I am going to do. I might do something irrational if my kids are jeopardized.

If God made a nuclear accident happen, we swear he made it happen to us for a specific reason—*to wake us up. I am guilty, I am guilty.*

*I didn't do anything before this. More people have to get involved. We can't let the Government jam it down our throats.*² (my emphasis)

Pat Smith and Lois Gibbs reap the results of planning based on potential profit with no form of environmental accounting and no concern for such end results. They had bought into the propaganda. But then they led women *and men* out of that trap.

Undoubtedly women are working through the structured and legitimate channels for change and will always be there. After leading the Australian delegation to the first UN Conference for Women, in Mexico City, Elizabeth Reid wrote:

The only possible weapons to hand for us are proven ability and persuasion. We must become skilled in negotiating, lobbying and the preparation of resolutions, documents, legislation, etc. We must gain in extensive understanding of the workings of the system, be well briefed, well acquainted and visible. The art of persuasion lies in insuring that all claims are properly documented, analyses penetrating, strategies clearly and tellingly presented and the method of presentation must take into account the prevailing blindness and the probability of an initial response either of fear or boredom. These are the only means we have of gaining respect in those arenas, international or national, where we must work.³

These may well be the only means of gaining respect, but the question is whether or not respect is what we wish to gain. I spent nine years in the New Zealand legislature working in the way Reid describes—and yes, we need to be there, doing all that she suggests. But the more effective one's work, the more one gains, not respect, but loathing. The people, my constituency, *for* whom I worked, respected me; the male colleagues *with* whom I worked, grew to fear me. This work is slow, deliberate, exacting, and must continue—*at the same time* as we pursue strategies that the system never dreamed of.

I have a little dream that in 1990–91, which is the next period designated by the United Nations for a census to be held in every country, all women claim unpaid worker as their designation. Since housework is nowhere defined, it would seem totally legitimate, and they should insist on such a designation in all labor force and household surveys as well. If any government were to contest such a strategy through the civil courts, we can rely on the Bella Abzugs of the world as legal counsel. But if millions of women everywhere behaved in this way, the government *could not afford* to block up their legal system with contested suits. And, I conclude, understating my case, that the result of such a strategy would have a major transformative effect on a country's national accounts, particularly if there is a continuing refusal to split GDP contribution by gender.

Such a strategy would be assisted by a major consciousness-raising exercise. While pressure must be continued in international and national forums, it is too late to change anything of consequence structurally by 1990. So our energies must be directed towards the women's world. Our mainstream international organizations, such as the International Council of Women or the International Federation of Business and Professional Women's Clubs, should be lobbied from their country branch organizations to adopt such a strategy and assist in its publicity. The international women's think tank, the Sisterhood Is Global Institute, has adopted this strategy. *Of course* it occurs to me that women, particularly those who are the graduates of the process that Galbraith spoke of, or those whose job security depends on perpetuating the current system, would oppose such a move. Women opposed the suffrage; women oppose pornography censorship; women oppose nuclear disarmament. We must not find the energy we need to spread the message diverted to respond to them: that is an old and familiar trap, and the patriarchy loves its results.

This is the grass roots response available, in kind, to all women. And while it may be seen as a reformist policy, it is an action of cultural creativity and ultimately a vision of a new concept of value.

Which brings me to the role of women in elected office, in the bureaucracies of multilateral agencies, or in academic positions. For, in the old cliché, if they are not with us, they are against us. If they are sufficiently sold out and compromised to do nothing else, they can still release all the information they have: where to lobby and when; what the points of vulnerability are in a government's argument or a theory; and at what point to tackle them. They can release timetables, draft reports, details of strategies, even if they publicly and personally are seen to do nothing. I know, since I have been there, that all of this is possible. If they have more commitment, they can use the status of their office to be part of the consciousness raising; they can empower women constituents by example. If academics, they can change their course structures, encourage critical analyses that reflect some observation of, as Susan George termed it, "how the other half dies." No woman should find herself, when aware of the contents of this book, speaking of a labor force that does not include the unpaid productive and reproductive work of women. In our work, we, like the women of the suffrage movement, can expect to lose respect, jobs, publishers, lovers, friends, and security in such strategies: our sisters, without such relative comforts and freedoms, are losing their lives.

There are many other strategic alternatives, and some may become confused in translation from one language or one culture to another. Here, as in all our work for global feminism, there is the possibility of cultural insensitivity realizing yet another form of neocolonialism. But I am heartened to hear from Dr. Ian Pool, a UN consultant demographer, that the small African country of Burkina Faso, led by a woman chief statistician, has simply altered their census to record the unpaid work of women.

This is not the only form of innovation in that country. UNICEF reports that severe water shortages often faced the Mossi people, where rains are infrequent and the water sinks rapidly into the dry earth. Women, who are responsible for growing their family's food, suffer especially from this water shortage. Despite their central (and invisible) role in the village economy, Mossi women traditionally have had little voice in community affairs.

In Saye, the village women's local *haam* group (a *voluntary* organization) decided on a solution: build small earthen dams that would collect water during the rainy season. The men were skeptical, but *as a group* the women demanded that the dams be built, threatening to return to the villages of their birth if the village would not cooperate. In 1981, the women's *haam* group, working with the entire village population, built the first "women's dam." Not only was the dam successful, but it *cost only a fraction* of what the government spends on similar projects, and the villagers can maintain these dams by themselves. Which is a roundabout way of repeating what I maintained in the first chapter—not only do women *work*, but also women are *economical*.

Women working for multilateral agencies need to *insist* that *small scale* development is pursued. We don't need any more international agency reports that note and promote and recognize and encourage and all those other favorite weasel-words that make no commitment to anything at all. We should be *immediately* suspicious of any document containing such rhetoric and not waste too much energy on pursuing change in that direction.

We need to take care, too, that we understand the subtleties of strategies undertaken by others. Take, for example, the criticism of Maria della Costa's campaign of wages for housework. The writers of the Latin American collective work *Slaves of Slaves* attacked the proposal as both "reformist" and "economistic," and so it is. But Italian feminist writer Lucia Chiavola contends that these writers do not understand what della Costa was saying, as the English translations of the writer lose the original humane wit. Not, said della Costa, wages for the unpaid work of housewives because wages may sedate women in the house, but emphasis on the unpaid labor of the housewife as a lever for a "higher degree of subversion" in the women's movement. Della Costa's campaign helped to have feminist issues understood by 12 million Italian housewives—which is no mean feat.

Some things are changing. The *Los Angeles Times* reported on April 20, 1986, that eleven of the top seventeen employers in the greater Los Angeles area recognized volunteer experience in hiring. They include Los Angeles County, the Los Angeles Unified School District, Los Angeles city government, UCLA, Rockwell International, Pacific Bell, TRW, Bank of America, Security Pacific National Bank, Kaiser Permanente, and All Carter All Ale Stores. The California Department of Fair Employment and Housing, for example, carries the following as a regulation on prior work experience: "If an employer or other covered entity considers prior work experience in the selection or assignment of an employee, the employer or other covered entity shall also consider prior unpaid volunteer work experience."

Ms. magazine reported in November 1986 that, in Finland, a group of women are using their reproductive work to political ends. In June of that year more than four thousand Finnish women decided to go "no natal for no nukes." Led by Marjo Liukkonen, the women presented the minister of trade and commerce with a petition declaring their resolve not to bear children until Finland changes its pronuclear energy policy.

On October 24, 1985, women in twenty-two countries organized either "time off for women" activities or full-scale strikes to let governments know we want all women's work, including our unwaged work, made visible in the Gross National Product.

And some things never change. In November 1986, a report from Chicago showed that medical costs for a lumpectomy (an operation for breast cancer that removes only the lump) was 37 percent more expensive than mastectomies, or complete breast removal. The medical profession has ensured a financial incentive for major mutilation of the female body, in a situation where a lumpectomy would generally be better for the patient.

In December 1986, reports from southern Africa showed extremely high use of potent and highly toxic pesticides to protect livestock and boost beef *exports* to European and other countries. Dieldrin, a powerful pesticide chemical related to DDT and manufactured by Royal Dutch Shell in South Africa, is banned for use in agriculture in that country. It has been banned for use within the borders of most northern hemisphere countries. Production is still allowed for export to the developing countries that do not yet ban it. Now some southern African mothers' milk is so polluted with dieldrin that this most healthy and natural of human food would not be allowed on a supermarket shelf.

In January 1987, West German officials were struggling with three thousand tons of radioactive powdered milk, a legacy of the Chernobyl disaster. The milk, from Bavaria, was found in 150 railroad cars in Bremen and Cologne, on its way to processing plants to be turned into animal feed for delivery to developing countries, via Egypt.

In February 1987, Kathy Rarua, second secretary for education in the Pacific island country of Vanuatu, told a *New Zealand Herald* journalist on her visit to New Zealand: "We have a lot of problems with girls' education because traditionally they are regarded as not accounting to much, just as child-bearers. They are somebody who can help the husband or his family build wealth and status by working the land, breeding the pigs and so on."

The traditional exchange of marriage gifts between in-laws has been manipulated to excuse "selling off" girls for as much as possible. Rarua says, "In Vanuatu there is a sort of joke about girls: they are called 'Toyotas' because the market price for a young bride equals a new car for her family." Though men value a car, a woman is worth nothing. But not for much longer, if we each start taking action.

We will, in our communities and our countries, have to use our judgment and our collective women's wisdom to discern the best alternative strategies. In the course of our work, we will also find men whose work is invaluable to us. Politics makes for strange coalitions, and I have tended to welcome allies wherever they might be found. Among the theorists, for example, Kenneth Boulding, professor emeritus of economics at the University of Colorado at Boulder, writes:

I have been gradually coming under the conviction, disturbing for a professional theorist, that there is no such thing as economics—there is only social science applied to economic problems. Indeed, there may not even be such a thing as social science—there may only be general science applied to the problems of society.[4]

Environmental statistician Christian Leipert, agonizing over the backwardness of his fellow disciplinarians, has written that their

methodological scruples condemn adherents of GNP to inactivity in this (welfare) area. . . . Without the conviction . . . of the need for an indicator of net national welfare for qualitative questions, it is impossible to mobilize the intestinal fortitude to display vulnerable calculations concerning the difficult problems of delimitation.[5]

In other words, they are afraid to say they can't do it and afraid to say they don't know how. If a concept or tangible object that is part of our universe can be number-crunched, economics will colonize it with impunity. If it cannot be adapted by such treatment, they will pronounce it beyond their sphere.

In the media, I have often found male reporters utterly reliable in pursuing stories on destruction of our ecosystem, on pollution, on poisoning, on toxic wastes. And undoubtedly such preservation of our environment and wildlife species as can be celebrated has been the result of people working together.

But no liberal-minded male is waiting onstage to change the institutionalized value of women's work. That becomes the task for each of us in all that we do. What we can do, without committing any form of violent psychological or physical atrocity to any other person, is inhibited only by our imagination. (It might even be fun. Friends of mine go camping on census night to upset the statistics by claiming that they have no fuel, water, electricity, or windows.)

We women are visible and valuable to each other, and we must, now in our billions, proclaim that visibility and that worth. Our anger must be creatively directed for change. We must remember that true freedom is a world without fear. And if there is still confusion about who will achieve that, then we must each of us walk to a clear pool of water. Look *at* the water. It has value. Now look *into* the water. The woman we see there counts for something. She can help to change the world.

Appendix 1.
The Material Product System

The quantitatively most important difference between the UNSNA and the MPS is that of the boundary of production. In the UNSNA with a few exceptions (e.g., illegal transactions) virtually all activities relating to the production of goods and the provision of services are treated as "productive." Only activities that are not conventionally remunerated (housewives' services) are excluded from the production concept. In the MPS the production concept is limited to (1) goods and (2) services related to the production, repair, transportation and distribution of goods (usually referred to as material services).

There are two aspects to the processes in the Material Product System or the System of Balances of the National Economy, as it is sometimes called.

The productive character of labour is the criterion delineating the sphere of material production. The final result of the activity in the material sphere is material goods including material services.

The non-material sphere embraces activities directed towards rendering non-material services in order to meet social, cultural and communal needs of individual members of the community and of the community as a whole. The input of social labour into this sphere, though of a socially beneficial nature, does not increase the total quantity of material goods at the disposition of the community. In the non-material sphere takes place the process of use and redistribution of material goods and incomes produced in the sphere of material production.

Material production is primary in comparison with the human activities creating non-material services. The rendering of non-material services depends on the production of material goods, since it would be impossible without the consumption of such goods. The wealthier a community is, the more material goods it produces, the greater is

328 / APPENDIX 1

the share of those goods which it can make available for the rendering
of non-material services.

Source: United Nations, *Comparisons of the System of National Accounts and the
System of Balances of the National Economy, Part One: Conceptual Relationships, Studies
in Methods*, Department of Economic and Social Affairs, Statistical Office, Series
F, No. 20 (ST/ESA/STAT/SER.F/20), (New York, 1977).

Appendix 2.
Environmental Indicators

Atmosphere

CO_2 concentration

Sulphur dioxide
   emissions
   concentrations

Nitrogen oxides
   emissions
   concentrations

Precipitation chemistry
   wet deposition
   dry deposition

CO emissions

O_3 concentrations
   stratosphere
   troposphere

Particulate/smoke
   emissions
   concentrations

Chlorofluorocarbon
   emissions

Precipitation and
   meteorology

Marine Environment

Sea-ice distribution

Physical oceanographic
   mean sea level
   sea surface temperature
   deep water temperatures
   deep water salinites
   CO_2 in sea water

Fish
   catches
   stocks
   mariculture

Marine mammals
   catches
   stocks

Discharges to the sea from
   rivers (selected
   pollutants)

Dumping of wastes

Accidental oil spills

Pollutant concentrations
   organochlorines
      polynuclear
   aromatic
   hydrocarbons
   heavy metals

Mangrove exploitation

Inland Waters

Abstractions
for domestic, industrial,
and agricultural
purposes

Nitrate and phosphate
concentrations in rivers,
reservoirs, and ground
waters

Biological oxygen demand
and dissolved oxygen
measurements in rivers

Acidity

Fish stocks and catches,
lakes, rivers

Concentrations of monitored
pollutants

Aquaculture production

Extent of permanent snow
and ice, including
glaciers

Floods: areas and damage
mariculture

Lithosphere

Extractions of sand, gravel,
and rock

Reserves, resources, and
extractions of nonfuel
minerals (especially
major metals)

Coal and oil production data

Number and scale of
earthquakes and volcanic
eruptions

Quantities and types of
wastes disposed of
(radioactive wastes
itemized separately)

Terrestrial Environment

Areas of protected habitat
(national parks and
conservation areas)

Status of threatened and
endangered species

Status of major species

Desertification (extent of
arid, semiarid, and
subhumid land plus
selected defined classes
of land use, e.g., range
land, irrigated land, etc.)

Forest cover (disaggregated
by major biome type—
separate data for natural
and plantation forests
and for forest use)

Wetland extent and rates of
drainage

Land use, including
agriculture, forestry, and
urbanization patterns
conversions

Agriculture and Forestry

Food production
(disaggregated by main
crop)

Timber production

Domestic livestock
(numbers and types)

Production and use of
pesticides and fertilizers
(disaggregated by type)

Mechanization

Postharvest crop losses

Area irrigated

Agricultural labor

Soil degradation

Population

Total population

Birthrate

Deathrate

Distribution by age and sex

Migration (international and
national)

Rate of change in population

Human Settlements

Settlements (size, density)

Urban and rural areas and
resident populations

Percentage of public having
access to clean water
supply (urban and rural)

Percentage of public served
by sewage treatment
systems (urban and
rural)

Population exposed to noise

Health

Life expectancy

Infant mortality
(first year and up to five
years)

Availability of medical help
(number of doctors and
hospital places)

Environmental diseases
(malaria, schistosomiasis,
onchocerciasis, etc.)

Infectious disease mortality

Prevalence of cardiovascular
disease

Nutritional status

Environmental health (e.g.,
industrial exposure to
carcinogens)

Industry

Percentage of GDP accounted
for by agriculture and
services

Index of industrial
production

Energy

Energy consumption and
production by type of
fuel (including offshore
oil, fuel wood)
disaggregated by type of
economy

Hydro, wind, wave, and
biofuel energy
production

Nuclear energy
(installed capacity)

Transport

Number of road vehicles

Number of miles traveled by
road, rail, air, and sea
passengers

Road accidents

Road coverage

Number and type of aircraft

World shipping fleet
(disaggregated by major
registrations)

Total oil transported

Tourism

International tourist arrivals

Environmental Awareness

Number of courses and/or
teachers

Legislation (number of bills
passed)

Peace and Security

Military expenditure

Trends in radioactive fallout

Source: United Nations Environmental Program (UNEP), *State of the Environment
1984*, UNEP/GC.12/11/ADD.2.

Appendix 3.
Dictionary of Occupational Titles

Definition of a Housemaid

MAID, GENERAL (dom. ser.) 306.878. **housekeeper, home.** Performs any combination of the following duties in keeping private home clean and orderly, in cooking and serving meals, and in rendering personal services to family members: Plans meals and purchases foodstuffs and household supplies. Prepares and cooks vegetables, meats, and other foods according to employer's instructions or following own methods. Serves meals and refreshments. Washes dishes and cleans silverware. Oversees activities of children, assisting them in dressing and bathing. Cleans furnishings, floors, and windows, using vacuum cleaner, mops, broom, cloths, and cleaning solutions. Changes linens and makes beds. Washes linens and other garments by hand or machine, and mends and irons clothing, linens, and other household articles, using hand iron or electric ironer. Performs additional duties, such as answering telephone and doorbell, and feeding pets. Is usually only worker employed. When employed in motherless home, may be designated HOUSEKEEPER, WORKING; or when employed by welfare agency to take charge of home because of illness or for working mother, may be designated HOMEMAKER.

Source: *Dictionary of Occupational Titles*, U.S. Department of Labor, Employment and Training Administration (Washington, DC: U.S. Gov't. Printing Office, 4th ed., 1977).

Notes

Prologue

1. Frederick Engels, *Anti-Dühring* (London: Lawrence and Wishart: Marxist-Leninist Library, 1936. Vol. 1).
2. Ibid., 180.
3. Ibid.
4. Ibid., 183.
5. Ibid., 203.
6. Maria della Costa with Selma James, *The Power of Women and the Subversion of the Community* (Bristol, England: Falling Wall Press, 1980).
7. For titles, see Bibliography.
8. Daniel P. Moynihan, *The Politics of a Guaranteed Income* (New York: Random House, 1973), 17.
9. Mary O'Brien, *The Politics of Reproduction* (London: Routledge & Kegan Paul, 1981), 196.
10. Albert Einstein, *Ideas and Opinions* (New York: Dell Publishing Company, Fifth Laurel Printing—1981), 153.
11. For titles, see Bibliography.
12. World Bank, *LSMS Working Paper No. 10: Reflections on the LSMS Group Meeting*, 15.
13. Katherine Mansfield, *The Journal of Katherine Mansfield*, ed. J. Middleton Murray (London: Constable & Co., 1954), 333; October 14, 1922.

Chapter 1.

1. J. M. Keynes, *The General Theory of Employment, Interest and Money* (London: Macmillan, 1965; New York: Harcourt Brace Jovanovich, 1936).
2. Lionel Robbins, as quoted in Tjalling C. Koopmans, *Three Essays on the State of Economic Science* (New York: McGraw-Hill, 1957), 140–42.
3. Sheila Rowbotham, *Woman's Consciousness, Man's World* (Baltimore: Penguin Books, 1973), 32–34.
4. Norman Lewis (editor), *The New Roget's Thesaurus of the English Language in Dictionary Form* (New York: G.P. Putnam's Sons, 16th Imp, 1964), 165.
5. Paul A. Samuelson, "Modes of Thought in Economics and Biology." *American Economic Review* 75 (May 1985): 167.
6. Ulrike Von Buchwald and Ingrid Palmer, *Monitoring Changes in the Conditions of Women—A Critical Review of Possible Approaches.* UNR15D/78/C.18, Geneva, 19.
7. L. C. R. Robbins, *An Essay on the Nature and Significance of Economic Science.* London: Macmillan, 1969.

8. Matthew 10:29-31 (KJV).

9. Sir Richard Steele, *The Tatler*, 203.

10. John Addison, *The Spectator*, 477.

11. William Hazlitt, *"Essays On the Clerical Character."*

12. Adam Smith, *The Wealth of Nations* (New York: Random House, 1965), 14.

13. Joan Robinson, *An Essay on Marxian Economics*, 2d ed. (New York: St. Martin's Press, 1966), 20.

14. Joan Robinson, *Economic Philosophy* (London: Watts, 1962), 39.

15. Joan Robinson, *An Essay on Marxian Economics*, 20.

16. Alex Preminger, ed.; Frank J. Warnke and O. B. Hardison, Jr., assoc. eds., *Princeton Encyclopedia of Poetry and Poetics* (Princeton, NJ: Princeton University Press, 1965), 259-67.

17. M. W. Jones-Lee, M. Hammerton, and P. R. Phillips, "The Value of Safety: Results of a National Sample Survey," *Economics Journal* 95 (March 1985): 49-72.

18. John Broome, "The Economic Value of Life," *Economics* 52, University of Bristol (August 1985): 281-94.

19. "If an activity is of such a character that it might be delegated to a paid worker then that activity shall be deemed productive." Margaret G. Reid, *Economics of Household Production* (New York: Wiley, 1934).

20. Ralph T. Byrns and Gerald W. Stone, *Economics*, 2d ed. (Glenview, IL: Scott, Foresman, 1984), 5.

21. Smith, *The Wealth of Nations*.

22. Charlotte Perkins Gilman, *The Man-Made World or Our Androcentric Culture* (New York: Johnson Reprint Corp., 1971), 232-36.

23. Katherine Newland, *Global Employment and Economic Justice: The Policy Challenge* (Washington: Worldwatch Paper, 28).

24. Louise A. Ferman, "The Work Ethic in the World of Informal Work," Industrial Relations Research Association Series: *The Work Ethic—A Critical Analysis* (Madison, WI: Industrial Relations Research Association, 1983), 211.

25. *New York Times Book Review*, April 20, 1986, p. 12.

26. Frederick Engels, *The Origin of the Family, Private Property and the State* (London: Lawrence and Wishart, 1940 [1884]), 1-2.

27. "Female Farmers—the doubly ignored," *Development Forum* (September 1986), 7.

28. D. J. Casley and D. A. Lury, *Data Collection in Developing Countries* (New York: Clarendon Press), 440.

29. International Encyclopedia of Social Sciences, s.v. "labor force."

30. Robin Morgan (ed.), *Sisterhood Is Global* (Garden City, NY: Doubleday, 1984), 700.

31. Lester C. Thurow, *The Zero-Sum Society* (New York: Penguin Books, 1980), 106.

32. Harold K. Schneider, *The Wahi Wanyaturu Economics in African Society* (Chicago: Aldine Publishing, 1970).

33. Quoted in Kathleen Jones, "Housework," *Isis International Bulletin* (October 1977): 34-37.

34. Quoted in Joann Vanek, "Time Spent in Housework, Market Work, Homework and the Family," *Scientific American* (November 1974): 82–89.
35. Gwen Wesson, "The De-Skilling of Women in Relation to the Production, Processing and Preservation of Food" (Unpublished paper).
36. John Kenneth Galbraith, *Annals of an Abiding Liberal*, ed. Andrea D. Williams (New York: New American Library, 1980), 41.
37. Joan Robinson, *Collected Economic Papers*, Vol. V (Cambridge, MA: The M.I.T. Press, 1980), 211.
38. Gary S. Becker, *A Treatise on the Family* (Cambridge, MA: Harvard University Press, 1981).
39. Bonnie G. Birnbaum and Marianne A. Ferber, "The 'New Home Economics': Retrospects and Prospects," *Journal of Consumer Research* 4 (June 1977): 19–28.
40. Robert A. Pollack, "A Transaction Cost Approach to Families and Households," *Journal of Economic Literature* 23 (June 1985): 581–608.
41. Donald N. McCloskey, "The Rhetoric of Economics," *The Journal of Economic Literature* 21 (June 1983): 481–517.
42. Han Suyin, "The Woman Revolution," *UNESCO Courier* (July 1982): 30–34.
43. Ester Boserup, *Women's Role in Economic Development* (New York: St. Martin's Press, 1970).
44. Christine Delphy, *The Main Enemy: A Materialistic Analysis of Women's Oppression* (London: Women's Research and Resources Centre Publications, 1977), 11–12.
45. Berit Ås, "A Five-Dimensional Model For Change: Contradictions and Feminist Consciousness," *Womens Studies Quarterly* 4, p. 109.
46. Joan Robinson, *Collected Economic Papers*, vol. 2, pp. 1–17.
47. Ruth Hubbard, "Should Professional Women Be Like Professional Men?" in *Women in Scientific and Engineering Professions*, ed. Violet B. Haas and Carolyn C. Perrucci (Ann Arbor, MI: University of Michigan Press, 1984), 211.

Chapter 2.

1. United Nations, Department of Economic Affairs, Statistical Office, *A System of National Accounts and Supporting Tables, Studies in Methods*, no. 2 (ST/STAT/SER. F/2) (1953).
2. Ibid., par. 5, p. 1.
3. Ibid., par. 6, p. 1.
4. Joseph W. Duncan and William C. Shelton, *Revolution in United States Government Statistics* (U.S. Department of Commerce, Office of Federal Statistical Policy and Standards, October 1978).
5. *International Encyclopedia of Social Sciences*, s.v. "national income."
6. Smith, *The Wealth of Nations*, 14.
7. Ibid.
8. Karl Marx, *Capital* (London: Lawrence and Wishart, 1967).
9. Alfred Marshall, *Principles of Economics* (London: Macmillan, 1980).

10. Quoted in B. P. Haig and S. S. McBurney, *The Interpretation of National Income Estimates* (Canberra, Australia: Australian National University Press, 1968), 76.

11. Duncan and Shelton, *Government Statistics*, 78.

12. Simon Küznets, assisted by Lilian Epstein and Elizabeth Jenks, *National Income and Its Composition 1919–1938* (New York: National Bureau of Economic Research, 1941).

13. Simon Küznets, *National Income and Industrial Structure* (London: Economic Change, 1954) 177–78.

14. E. A. G. Robinson, "John Maynard Keynes 1883–1946," in *Keynes General Theory: Reports of Three Decades*, ed. Robert Lekachman (New York: St. Martin's Press), 67.

15. Ibid., 68.

16. Duncan and Shelton, *Government Statistics*, 84–86.

17. J. Viner, *International Trade and Economic Development* (Oxford: Clarendon Press, 1953), 99–100.

18. Morgan (ed.), *Sisterhood Is Global*, 387.

19. *Encyclopaedia of Economics* (Guilford, CT: DPG Reference Publishing Co., 1981), 55.

20. United Nations, *Studies in Methods*, Series F, no. 2, par. 136.

21. Ibid.

22. Ibid., par. 169–74.

23. Ibid., par. 182.

24. Ibid., par. 141.

25. Morgan (ed.), *Sisterhood Is Global*, 697.

26. United Nations, *Studies in Methods*, Series F, no. 2, par. 8.

Chapter 3.

1. Meena Acharya, "Time Use Data and the Living Standards Measurement Study," *LSMS Working Paper No. 18* (Washington, DC: World Bank Development Research Department, July 1982).

2. Suha Hindiyeh, "Social Change and Agriculture in the West Bank 1950–1967: Aspects of Sharecropping and Commercialisation" (Ph.D. diss., University of Kent, 1985), 155.

3. Elise Boulding, "Measures of Women's Work in the Third World, Problems and Suggestions," *Women and Poverty in the Third World* in Maya Buvinic, Margaret A. Lycette, and William Paul McGreevey, eds. (Baltimore, MD: Johns Hopkins Press, 1983), 286.

4. United Nations, Studies in Methods, Series F, no. 2, par. 19.

5. Ibid., par. 24.

6. Ibid., par. 26.

7. Ibid., par. 27.

8. Ibid., par. 28.

9. Ibid., par. 30.

10. Ibid., par. 31.

11. *Report of the Working Group on the Treatment of Non-Monetary (Subsistence) Transactions within the Framework of the National Accounts*, E/CN 14/60, Addis Ababa, June 27–July 2, 1960.

12. United Nations Statistical Office, *A System of National Accounts*, Studies in Methods, Series F, no. 2, revision 3 (1968), par. 5.13 and 6.19–24.
13. United Nations, Studies in Methods, Series F, no. 2, par. 54.
14. Kathleen Newland, *The Sisterhood of Man* (New York: W. W. Norton, 1979), 129–30.
15. United Nations, Economic and Social Council, UN Statistics Council Commission, *Demographic and Social Indicators:* Report of the Secretary-General, E/CN.3/1983/18 (March 7–16, 1983), par. 51.
16. Harold Copeman, *The National Accounts: A Short Guide; Studies in Official Statistics No. 36* (London: Her Majesty's Stationery Office, May 1981).
17. Draft unpublished paper, Interdepartmental circulation, 1981.
18. Derek W. Blades, *Non-Monetary (Subsistence) Activities in the National Accounts of Developing Countries* (OECD, October 29, 1975), 53–54.
19. Eva Alterman-Blay, "The Case of Brazil in Women at Work in the Labor Force and at Home," *Research Series No. 22* (General International Institute for Labour Studies, 1976): 109.
20. Maria Mies, "Housewives Produce for the World Market—The Lace-Makers of Narpassur" (Geneva: ILO, 1980).
21. Personal communication in a conversation with Ron Fergie, 1981.
22. Casley and Lury, *Data Collection in Developing Countries*, 187.
23. Svetlana Turchaninova, "Women's Employment in the USSR," in *Women, Workers and Society* (ILO, 1976), 151.

Chapter 4.

1. United Nations, Economic and Social Council, *Meeting User Needs For, and Improving the Dissemination of International Statistics*, Report of the Secretary General (E/CN-.3/1985/1).
2. Ramesh Chander, Christiaan Grootaert, and Graham Pyatt, "Living Standards and Surveys in Developing Countries," *LSMS Working Paper No. 1* (Washington, DC: World Bank Development Research Department 18–138, October 1980), 16.
3. Kathryn E. Walker and Margaret E. Woods, *Time Used: A Measure of Household Production of Family Goods and Services* (Washington, DC: American Home Economics Association, 1976).
4. United Nations, Economic and Social Council, *Meeting User Needs For, and Improving the Dissemination of International Statistics*, Report of the Secretary General (E/CN.3/1985/2).
5. Morgan (ed.), *Sisterhood Is Global*, 454.
6. Meena Acharya, "Time Use Data and the Living Standards Measurement Study." *LSMS Working Paper No. 18*, Washington DC: World Bank Development Research Department 1982.
7. Richard M. Barkay, "National Accounting with Limited Data: Lessons from Nepal," *Review of Income and Wealth*, series 28, no. 3 (September 1982), 306.
8. Ibid.
9. Ibid.

Chapter 5.

1. Personal communication in a letter from Senator Janine Haines.
2. Casley and Lury, *Data Collection in Developing Countries*.

3. United Nations, Department of International and Social Affairs, Statistical Office, *Handbook of Household Surveys, Studies in Methods*, Series F, no. 31 (ST/ESA/STAT/SER.F/31) (1984), par. 13.15.
4. *Women in Rural Life: The Changing Scene* (Ontario: Ministry of Agriculture and Food).
5. Carolyn E. Sachs, *The Invisible Farmers: Women in Agricultural Production* (Totowa, NJ: Rowman & Allanheld, 1983), 39.
6. Rachel Rosenfeld, *Farm Women: Work, Farm and Family in the United States* (Chapel Hill: University of North Carolina Press, 1985), 267.
7. United Nations, *Handbook of Household Surveys*, par. 1.12.
8. Casley and Lury, *Data Collection in Developing Countries*, 17.

Chapter 6.

1. "Analytical Notes on International Real Income Measures," *Economic Journal* 84 (September 1978): 595–608.
2. Morgan (ed.), *Sisterhood Is Global*, 670.
3. Edgar Feige, "How Big is the Irregular Economy?" *Challenge* (November-December 1979).
4. Derek Blades, *The Hidden Economy and the National Accounts* (Paris: OECD, 1982), 28–45.
5. Bruno S. Frey and Hannelore Weck-Hanneman, "The Hidden Economy as an Unobserved Variable," *European Economic Review* 26 (1984): 33–53.
6. United Nations, Department of Economic and Social Affairs, Statistical Office, *Towards a System of Social and Demographic Statistics*, Studies in Methods, Series F, no. 18 (ST/ESA/STAT/SER.F/18) (1975).
7. Lewis Regenstein, "America the Poisoned: How Deadly Chemicals Are Destroying Our Environment, Our Wildlife, and How We Can Survive," *Acropolis* (1983).
8. *New York Times*, March 23, 1986, special feature.
9. Thurow, *The Zero-Sum Society*, 124.
10. Sir Richard Stone, "Political Economy, Economics and Beyond," *Economic Journal* (December 1980): 731–32.
11. United Nations, *Towards a System of Social and Demographic Statistics*, F, No. 18 par. 15–19.
12. Robert L. Heilbroner and Lester C. Thurow, *Understanding Macroeconomics*, 5th ed. (Englewood Cliffs, NJ: Prentice-Hall, 1975).
13. Lesley Middleton and David Tait, *Are Women Given A Choice? An Assessment Based on Information from the N.Z. Recreation Survey* (Wellington, New Zealand: Department of Internal Affairs, 1983).
14. Lisa Leghorn and Katherine Parker, *Women's Worth: Sexual Economics and the World of Women* (Boston, London, and Henley, England: Routledge & Kegan Paul, 1981).
15. Diana Jones, "What Price Equality? A Case Study of Government Funding in Sport," *New Zealand Journal of Health, Physical Education and Recreation* 16 (1983): 2–7.
16. William Moskoff, *Labor and Leisure in the Soviet Union: The Conflict between Public and Private Decision-Making in a Planned Economy* (New York: St. Martin's Press, 1984).

17. Maya Buvinic, Margaret A. Lycette, and William Paul McGreevey, eds., *Women and Poverty in the Third World* (Baltimore, MD: Johns Hopkins University Press, 1983), 35–61.
18. Sondra Zeidenstein, "Learning about Rural Women," *Studies in Family Planning* (Population Council) 10 (1979): 345.
19. Linda Nelson, "Household Time: A Cross Cultural Example" in *Women and Household Labor*, ed. Sarah Fenstermaker Berk (Beverly Hills, CA: Sage Publications, 1980), 186–87.

Chapter 7.

1. United Nations, Department for Disarmament Affairs, *Economic and Social Consequences of the Arms Race and of Military Expenditures* (Study Series 11, 1983).
2. UN General Assembly, Development and International Economic Cooperation, *Long Term Trends in Economic Development*, A /40/519 (August 23, 1985), 24.
3. United Nations, *Economic and Social Consequences of the Arms Race and of Military Expenditures*, 24.
4. Ibid.
5. Ibid.
6. Heilbroner and Thurow, *Understanding Macroeconomics*.
7. See Helen Caldicott, *Missile Envy* (New York: Murrow, 1984), an outstanding contribution to understanding the interdependencies of the U.S. economy and its military machine.
8. United Nations, *Critical Economic Situation in Africa*, A/40/724 (1986).
9. Ruth Leger Sivard, *Women . . . A World Survey* (Washington, DC: World Priorities, 1985).
10. Michael M. Cernea, *Putting People First: Sociological Variables in Rural Development* (New York: published for the World Bank by Oxford University Press, 1985).
11. Ibid., 350.
12. Ernest Stern, "The Evolving Role of the Bank in the 1980s," presented to the Agriculture Symposium, World Bank, Washington, DC, January 13, 1984.
13. *The Dirtiest Word in the English Language*, a book proposal and outline by Theresa Funiciello.
14. N. Nissim, "Poverty among Children in the United States on the Rise," *UNICEF* 1 (1986): 5.
15. Stephen Edgell and Vic Duke, "Gender and Social Policy: The Impact of the Public Expenditure Cuts and Reactions to Them," *Journal of Social Policy* (1983): 357–78.
16. United Nations, Economic and Social Council, *Summary of the Survey of the Economic and Social Conditions in Latin America 1985*, ECOSOC E/1986/63, April 30, 1986.
17. Barry Newman as reported in New Internationalist 129 (November 1983).

Chapter 8.

1. Susan Ince, in *Test Tube Women*, ed. Rita Arditi, Renate Duelli Klein, Shelley Minden (London: Pandora Press, 1984), 101.

2. Corea, *The Mother Machine*.
3. Personal communication, September 5, 1986.
4. Vance Packard, *The People Shapers* (New York: Bantam, 1979), 268–69.
5. Peter Singer and Dean Wells, *The Reproductive Revolution: New Ways of Making Babies* (Oxford: Oxford University Press, 1984).
6. Ibid.
7. Ibid.
8. Ibid., 83–84.
9. *Waikato Times* (New Zealand), May 28, 1986.
10. Government regulations, Quebec. A-25, r. 1. to r. 13., updated to June 4, 1985.
11. Accident Compensation Commission, New Zealand, September 1978, no. 2, section 120, quantum of awards.
12. Viviana A. Zelizer, *Pricing the Priceless Child: The Changing Social Value of Children* (New York: Basic Books, 1985).
13. Mead Cain, "Women's Status and Fertility in Developing Countries—Son Preference and Economic Security," *World Bank Staff Working Papers Number 682*, Population and Development Series No. 7 (Washington, DC: 1984).
14. Zelizer, *Pricing the Priceless Child*, 154.
15. Ibid., 155.
16. Ibid., 156.
17. Cain, "Women's Status and Fertility."
18. Zelizer, *Pricing the Priceless Child*, 158.
19. Ibid., 159.
20. Ibid., 159–60.
21. Ibid., 161.
22. "The Cost of Children," *Good Weekend* (1986): 6–9.
23. Zelizer, *Pricing the Priceless Child*, 167.
24. Mary O'Brien, *The Politics of Reproduction* (Boston: Routledge & Kegan Paul, 1953), 8.
25. Christine Delphy, *The Main Enemy: A Materialist Analysis of Women's Oppression* (London: Women's Research and Resources Centre Publications, 1977), 56.
26. Ibid., 15.
27. Murdoch C. Murdoch [1975] IR. C. S. Canada Law Reports, Supreme, Vol. 1, p. 423.
28. Quoted in Rae André, *Homemakers: The Forgotten Workers* (Chicago: University of Chicago Press, 1981), 150.
29. U.S. District Court, 195 F. Supp. 557 (S.P. Fla. 1961).
30. "The New Economics of Custody Suits," *New York Times*, Sunday, April 6, 1986.
31. P. A. Baran and P. M. Sweezy, *Monopoly Capital* (Harmondsworth, England: Penguin, 1968).
32. John Kenneth Galbraith, *The New Industrial State* (Harmondsworth, England: Penguin, 1974).
33. Lucy Komisar, "The Bloom Is off Alan Garcia," *Nation* 243 (September 6, 1986), 174–78.
34. Leah Margulis, "A Critical Essay on the Role of Promotion in Bottle Feeding," *PAG Bulletin* 8 (1977): 73–83.

35. D. Jelliffe and P. Jelliffe, *Human Milk in the Modern World* (Oxford: Oxford University Press, 1978).

36. R. H. Farmer, Birbeck *et al*, "Artificial Feeding of Infants," *New Zealand Medical Journal* 90: 390–92.

37. Nancy Pollock, "Mother's Milk, Its Contribution to the Household Budget in Various Pacific Islands," unpublished paper, Department of Anthropology, Victoria University of Wellington, January 1982.

38. Personal communication with Mona Daswani, Bombay, October 1984.

39. Morgan (ed.), *Sisterhood Is Global*, 145.

40. Janet Zollinger Giele, Audrey Chapman Smock, eds, "Bangladesh: A Struggle with Tradition and Poverty" in *Women, Roles and Status in Eight Countries* (New York: Wiley, 1977).

41. United Nations, Economic and Social Council, "Action by the United Nations to Implement the Recommendations of the World Population Conference, 1974: Monitoring of Population Trends and Policies," *Concise Report on Monitoring of Population Trends and Policies. Report of the Secretary-General Addendum*, E/CN.9/1984/2/Add.1 10 (December 1984).

42. "Women as Providers of Health Care," *WHO Chronicle* 37 (1983): 134–38.

43. Morgan (ed.), *Sisterhood Is Global*, 6–7.

44. "Women and Health," *Isis International Bulletin* (Spring 1978).

45. Karen Messing, "The Scientific Mystique" in *Women's Nature: Rationalizations of Inequality*, ed. Marion Lowe and Ruth Hubbard (New York, Oxford: Pergamon Press, 1983), 79.

46. Sivard, *Women . . . A World Survey*.

47. UN Economic and Social Council, *General Discussion of International Economic and Social Policy*, E/1986/64, 6.

48. Ibid.

49. United Nations, General Assembly, Development and International Cooperation: Long-Term Trends in Economic Development, "Overall Socioeconomic Perspective of the World Economy to the Year 2000," report of the Secretary-General, A/40/519/8/23/1985.

50. As reported in *Feminist Connexion* of Madison, WI (December 1983): 6.

51. Deborah Bryceson and Ulla Vuorela, "Outside the Domestic Labor Debate: Towards a Theory of Modes of Human Reproduction," *Review* of *Radical Political Economics* 16 (1984).

52. Morgan (ed.), *Sisterhood Is Global*, 336.

53. William Chandler, *Investing in Children*, Worldwatch paper no. 64 (Washington, DC: Worldwatch Institute, June 1985), 7.

54. Paul A. Samuelson, "Modes of Thought in Economics and Biology," *American Economic Review* 75 (May 1985).

55. Jalna Hanmer and Pat Allen, *Feminist Issues* (Spring 1982): 57.

56. Ibid., 67.

Chapter 9.

1. Fritjof Capra, *The Tao of Physics* (New York: Bantam Books, 1977).

2. Joann Vanek, "Time Spent in Housework: Market Work, Homework and the Family," *Scientific American* (November 1974): 82–89.

3. Ruth Schwartz Cowan, *More Work for Mother* (New York: Basic Books, 1983), 100.

4. *The Citizen* (Chicago), April 4, 1986.
5. Marsha Rowe, "Housework," in *Spare Rib Reader*, ed. Marsha Rowe (Harmondsworth, England, 1983), 131.
6. See, for example, Carolyn Sachs's research, as mentioned in chapter 5.
7. UNECA African Training and Research Centre for Women, *Women of Africa, Today and Tomorrow* (Addis Ababa, Ethiopia: 1975), 6.
8. Achola Okeyo, "Women in the Household Economy: Managing Multiple Roles," *Studies in Family Planning* 10 (November-December 1979).
9. Women at Work, Geneva, I.L.O., (1) 1985.
10. Fatima Mernissi, *Beyond the Veil* (Cambridge, MA: Schenkman Publishing, 1975), 74.
11. Lourdes Beneria, ed., "Accounting for Women's Work," in *Women and Development: The Sexual Division of Labor in Rural Societies* (New York: Praegar, 1982), 123.
12. Colin Clark and Margaret Haswell, *The Economics of Subsistence Agriculture* (New York: St. Martin's Press, 1970), 116.
13. Constantina Safilios-Rothschild, "The Persistence of Women's Invisibility in Agriculture: Theoretical and Policy Lessons from Lesotho and Sierra Leone," *Economic Development and Social Change* 33 (1985): 299–317.
14. Joycelin Masscak, *Women as Heads of Households in the Caribbean: Family Structure and Feminine Status* (UNESCO, 1983).
15. UNECA, "The Role of Women in African Development," E/Conf 66/BP18 (1975), 18–20.
16. "New Roles for Saudi Women," *People* 9 (1982).
17. Ester Boserup and Christina Liljencrantz, *Integration and Women in Development: Why When How* (New York: UNDP, May 1975).
18. "Pacific Women's Resource Bureau," *Women's Newsletter* 2 (January 1984).
19. Oral Capps Jnr et al., "Household Demand for Convenience and Non-Convenience Foods," *American Journal of Agricultural Economics* 67 (November 1985).
20. Anna Rubbo, *The Spread of Rural Capitalism—Its Effects on Black Women in the Canoa Valley, Western Colombia* (Estudies Andinos, 1974).
21. Gail Pearson, "Famine and Female Militancy in India" (Paper presented at Women and Food Conference, Sydney, Australia, February 1982).
22. Sarah Hobson, "Bulldozed," *New Internationalist* (January 1984): 21–22.
23. "Women in Rural Development: Recommendations and Realities," *FAO Review on Agriculture and Development* 13 (May-June 1980): 15–22.
24. Olga Stavrakis, "Sugar Cane Blues," *New Internationalist* (July 1980): 12.
25. Sachs, *The Invisible Farmers*, 131.
26. Reported in *Development Forum* (February-March 1985): 7.
27. Perdita Huston, *Message from the Village* (New York: Epoch B. Foundation, 1978).
28. Anny Bakalian, "Women the Vulnerable Sex?" *People* 9 (1982).
29. Mernissi, *Beyond the Veil*, 53.
30. Thanh-Dam Trnong, "The Dynamics of Sex Tourism: The Case of Southeast Asia," *Development and Change* 14 (April 1983).
31. Andrea Dworkin, *Pornography: Men Possessing Women* (New York: Putnam/Perigree, 1981), 52.

32. Kathleen Barry, *Female Sexual Slavery* (Englewood Cliffs, NJ: Prentice-Hall, 1979), 11.

33. Morgan, *Sisterhood Is Global*, 21.

34. Carollee Bengelsdorf, "On the Problem of Studying Women in Cuba," *Race and Class* 27 (Autumn 1985): 44–45.

35. Jean C. Robinson, "Of Women and Washing Machines: Employment, Housework and the Reproduction of Motherhood in Socialist China," *The China Quarterly* (March 1985): 32–57.

36. Letter to the Secretary General from the Charge d'Affaire of the Permanent Mission of Israel, May 5, 1986.

37. Fritjof Capra, *The Tao of Physics* (New York: Bantam Books, 1977).

Chapter 10.

1. Petra Kelly, personal communication, August 1986.

2. United Nations Statistical Commission, The Feasibility of Welfare-Oriented Measures to Supplement the National Accounts and Balances: A Technical Report, F, No. 22 (1977), par. 130.

3. Ibid., par. 135.

4. "Women and Health," *Isis International Bulletin* (Spring 1978).

5. *New Zealand Herald*, November 11, 1986.

6. United Nations Development Program, *Decade Watch* 5 (April-June 1986).

7. Ibid.

8. Lester Brown, *State of the World 1984* (Washington, DC: Worldwatch Institute, 1984).

9. Lester Brown, *State of the World 1986* (Washington, DC: Worldwatch Institute, 1986), 10.

10. *Complete Book of the Garden* (Readers Digest Assoc., Sydney, 1967), 28.

11. *The Guardian*, June 11, 1986.

12. Brown, *State of the World 1986*, 30.

13. Ibid.

14. Vera Massundra, "Another Development with Women: A View from Asia," *Development Dialogue* 1–2 (1982): 65–73.

15. Gail Omvedt, "On the Road to Environmental Armageddon," *The Guardian*, April 1986.

16. Anil Agarwal and Anila Anand, "Ask the Women Who Do the Work," *New Scientist*, 4 November 1982, 302.

17. See *International Wildlife* (May-June 1986), an exclusive international survey of leading conservation strategists from sixty-five nations.

18. *National Wildlife* (April-May 1986).

19. David Quammen, "Man Against Nature," *International Wildlife* (January-February 1986).

20. "Resource Paper on the U.S. Nuclear Arsenal," *Bulletin of Atomic Scientists*, 1984 supplement.

21. Brown, *State of the World 1986*, 119–20.

22. Ibid.

23. Ibid.

24. *Bulletin of Atomic Scientists*, 1984 supplement.

25. Betty A. Reardon, *Sexism and the War System* (New York: Teachers College Press, Columbia University, 1985).

Chapter 11.

1. John Kenneth Galbraith, *Annals of an Abiding Liberal* (Boston: Houghton Mifflin, 1979), 41.
2. Hilda Scott, *Working Your Way to the Bottom: The Feminization of Poverty* (Boston: Pandora Press, 1985).
3. Lisa Leghorn and Betsy Warrior, *Houseworker's Handbook* (Women's Center, 46 Pleasant Street, Cambridge, MA 02139; December 1973).
4. *The Economic Value of a Housewife* (Report of a survey by the American Council of Life Insurance, Washington, DC).
5. Scott, *Working Your Way to the Bottom*, 59.
6. Luisella Goldschmidt-Clermont, *Unpaid Work in the Household* (Geneva: International Labour Organization, 1982).
7. Ibid., 1.
8. Hans J. Adler and Oli Hawrylyshyn, "Estimates of the Value of Household Work—Canada, 1961 and 1971," *The Review of Income and Wealth* (December 1978): 333–55.
9. Marianne Ferber and Carole A. Greene, Housework v. Marketwork: Some Evidence How the Decision Is Made, Journal of Human Resources, xx. 1. 1985.
10. Gar Alparovitz, personal conversation with author, Washington, DC, April 1985.
11. Ronald Schettkat, "The Size of Household Production: Methodological Problems and Estimate for the Federal Republic of Germany in the Period 1964–1980," *Review of Income and Wealth* (September 1985): 309–21.
12. Joann Vanek, "Time Spent in Housework: Market Work, Homework and the Family," *Scientific American* (November 1974): 82–89.
13. Raj Krishna, *Women and Development Planning: With Special Interest to Asia and the Pacific* (Kuala Lumpur, Malaysia: Asian Pacific Development Conference [APDC]).
14. Marianne Ferber and Bonnie Birnbaum, "Housework: Priceless or Value-less?" Bureau of Economic and Business Research, Reprint 381 (Urbana-Champaign: University of Illinois), 387–400.
15. UN Statistical Commission, *Report of the Commission to the Economic and Social Council*, E/CN.3/1987/L.4/Add.1.
16. Richard M. Barkay, "National Accounting with Limited Data: Lessons from Nepal," *Review of Income and Wealth* (September 1982): 305–23.
17. Marilyn Waring, *Women, Politics and Power* (Wellington, N.Z.: Allen & Unwin/Port Nicholson Press, 1985), 64.
18. United Nations Statistical Office, *Towards A System of Social and Demographic Statistics*, F no. 18 (1975).
19. E. F. Schumacher, *Small Is Beautiful* (New York: Harper & Row, 1974).
20. Christian Leipert, "Environmental Damages, Defensive Expenditures, and Measurement of Net National Welfare," (Unpublished paper, 1986).
21. *The Use of Environmental Accounting for Development Planning*. A report written by Edward Teiler, U.N.E.P./WG. 85/Inf.2. (January 1983).

22. Roefie Hueting, "Results of an Economic Scenario that Gives Top Priority to Saving the Environment and Energy instead of Encourgaging Production Growth,"(Paper prepared for Research Symposium, Stockholm University, August 9–11, 1983).

23. UN Economic and Social Council, *Environment Statistics*, E/CN.3/1987/L.4. Add.10.

24. Schumacher, *Small Is Beautiful*.

25. Robin Morgan, *The Anatomy of Freedom, Feminism, Physics and Global Politics* (Garden City, NY: Anchor Books/Doubleday, 1984).

Chapter 12.

1. Hazel Henderson, *Creating Alternative Futures: The End of Economics* (New York: Berkley Pub. Corp., 1978).

2. Hilkka Pietilä, "Tomorrow Begins Today" (Paper presented at the ICDA/ISIS workshop in forum at the UN end-of-decade conference for women, Nairobi, July 1985), 9.

3. David Rapport and Arthur Friend, *Towards a Comprehensive Framework for Environmental Statistics: A Stress-Response Approach*. A Report Prepared by Statistics Canada (Ottawa: Minister of Supply and Services, 1979), 13.

4. John G. Riley, "The Just Rate of Depletion of a National Resource," *Journal of Environmental Economics and Management* 8 (December 4, 1980): 291–307.

5. Ralph D'Arge, "Essay on Economic Growth and Environmental Quality" in *The Economics of the Environment*, ed. Peter Bohm and Allen V. Kneese (London: Macmillan, 1974), 42.

6. A feminist think tank originated with the contributors to Robin Morgan's *Sisterhood Is Global*.

7. United Nations, *World Fertility Survey: Basic Documentation—No 2.1 & 10, Core Questionnaire and Modifications* (London, 1975 and 1977).

8. United Nations Economic and Social Council, *Technical Co-operation*, Statistical Commission, E/CN.3/1987/20.

9. Helen Ware (Paper prepared for expert group meeting on measurement of women's income and their participation and production in the informal sector, Santo Domingo, October, 1986), INSTRAW/AC.3/3 ESA/STAT/AC.29/3.

10. "Forward Looking Strategies for the Advancement of Women" (Report of the World Conference to Review and Appraise the Achievements of the United Nations Decade for Women: Equality Development and Peace, Nairobi, July 15–16, 1985), chap. 1, sec. A. par. 120.

11. Food and Agriculture Organization, Rome. Information Note on Women in Agriculture 1985.

12. See Selma James, *The Global Kitchen: Housewives in Dialogue* (London: 1985).

13. United Nations Statistical Commission, *The Feasibility of Welfare-Oriented Measures to Supplement the National Accounts and Balances:* F no. 20 (1977).

14. INSTRAW, Expert Group on Improving Statistics and Indicators on the Situation of Women, ESA/STAT/AC.17/9 (1983).

15. United Nations Economic and Social Council, report of the Secretary-General, *Updated Information on the Work of the Statistical Office of the U.N. Secretariat*, E/CN.3/1987/23.

16. Ibid., par. 26(a).
17. Ibid.
18. Ibid., par. 26(b).
19. Ibid., par. 26(c).
20. Ibid., par. 26(d).
21. Ibid., par. 26(e).
22. Ibid.
23. Simon Küznets, "Towards A Theory of Economic Growth," *Economic Growth and Structure* (New York: W. W. Norton & Co, 1965), 172–3.
24. Christian Leipert, Report on his visit to the United States (unpublished paper).
25. Ibid.

Epilogue

1. *Heresies*, no. 13, Feminism and Ecology, 40.
2. Ibid., 42.
3. Elizabeth Reid, "The Forgotten Fifty Per Cent," *Populi Special* 43-1 (1977): 19–35.
4. Quoted in Christian Leipert, "A Critical Appraisal of GNP, the Measurement of Net National Welfare and Environment Accounting" (Unpublished paper, May 1985).
5. Christian Leipert, "A Critical Appraisal of GNP," 20.

Bibliography

Adler, Hans J. "Selected Problems of Welfare and Production in the National Accounts." *Review of Income and Wealth* 29 (June 1982): 121–31.

Adler, Hans J. and Oli Hawrylyshyn. "Estimates of the Value of Household Work, Canada, 1961 and 1971." *The Review of Income and Wealth* 24 (December 1978): 333–55.

Asian and Pacific Centre for Women and Development (APCWD). *Notes on Data Collection with Special Reference to Women.* Women in Development Series. (Bangkok: APCWD, June 1980).

Baran, P. A. and P. M Sweezy. *Monopoly Capital.* (Harmondsworth: Penguin, 1968).

Barkay, Richard M. "National Accounting with Limited Data: Lessons from Nepal." *Review of Income and Wealth* 28 (September 1982): 305–23.

Barnett, Lincoln. *The Universe and Dr. Einstein.* 2d rev. ed. (New York: Bantam and William Morrow and Company, 1980).

Barry, Kathleen. *Female Sexual Slavery.* (Englewood Cliffs, NJ: Prentice–Hall, 1979).

Bauer, Michael. *Federal Republic of Germany: Status Report on the Promotion of Women in Developing Countries Under German Development Policy.* (Bonn, Germany: January 1981).

Baxandall, Rosalyn, Linda Gordon, and Susan Reverby. *America's Working Women.* (New York: Vintage Books, 1976).

Becker, Gary S. *A Treatise on the Family.* (Cambridge: Harvard University Press, 1981).

Beechey, Veronica. "On Patriarchy." *Feminist Review* Vol. 1, No. 3. (1979) 66–82.

Beneria, Lourdes. "Accounting for Women's Work." *Women and Development: The Sexual Division of Labour in Rural Societies.* (New York: Praeger, 1982).

Beneria, Lourdes. "Reproduction, Production and the Sexual Division of Labour." *Cambridge Journal of Economics* 3 (September 1979): 203–25.

Beneria, Lourdes and Anita Sen. "Accumulation, Reproduction and Women's Role in Economic Development: Boserup Revisited." *Signs.*

Bernard, Jessie. *The Female World.* (New York: Free Press, 1981).

———. *The Future of Marriage.* (New York: World Publishing Company, 1972).

Bertin, Leonard. "Nuclear Winter." *Canadian Institute for International Peace and Security.* (March 1986).

Birnbaum, Bonnie G. and Marianne A. Ferber. "Housework: Priceless or Valueless?" *BEBR.* Reprint No. 381, 387–400.

Birnbaum, Lucia Chiavola. *Liberazione della donna feminism in Italy.* (Middletown, CT: Wesleyan University Press, 1986).

Blades, Derek W. *Non-Monetary (Subsistence) Activities in the National Accounts of Developing Countries.* (OECD, 29 October 1975), 3–100.

Blades, Derek W., Derek D. Johnston, and Witold Marczewski. *Service Activities Based on National Accounts.* (OECD 1974).

Blau, Francine D. and Marianne A. Ferber. *The Economics of Women, Men, And Work.* (Englewood Cliffs, NJ: Prentice-Hall, 1986).

Böhm, David. *Wholeness and the Implicate Order.* (London: Routledge and Kegan Paul, 1980).

Boserup, Ester. *Women's Role in Economic Development.* (New York: St. Martin's Press, 1970).

Boserup, Ester and Christina Liljencrantz. *Integration and Women in Development: Why, When, How.* (New York: UNDP, May 1975).

Boulding, Elise. *The Underside of History: A View of Women Through Time.* (Boulder, CO: Westview Press, 1976).

Brandt Report. *North-South: A Programme for Survival.* (London: Pan Books, 1980).

Branson, William H. *Macroeconomic Theory and Policy.* (New York: Harper & Row, 1972).

Bratic, Elaine B. "Healthy Mothers, Healthy Babies Coalition—A Joint Private/Public Initiative." *Public Health Reports* 97 (1982): 503–8.

Brown, Lester. *State of the World, 1984.* Washington, D.C.: Worldwatch Institute.

Brownmiller, Susan. *Against Our Will: Men, Women, and Rape.* (New York: Bantam Books, 1976).

Bryceson, Deborah and U. Vuorela. "Outside the Domestic Labor Debate: Towards a Theory of Modes of Human-Reproduction." *Review of Radical Political Economics* 16 (1984): 137–166.

Burgmann, M. "Black Sisterhood: The Situation of Urban Aboriginal Women and Their Relationship to the White Women's Movement." *Politics*, 17 (1982): 23–37.

Bush, Corlann G. "The Barn is His, The House is Mine. Agricultural Technology and Sex Roles." *Energy and Transport*. (San Mateo: Sage Publications, 1986), 235–59.

Buvinic, Maya, Margaret A. Lycette, and William Paul McGreevey, eds. *Women and Poverty in the Third World*. (Baltimore: Johns Hopkins University Press, 1983).

Byrns, Ralph T. and Gerald W. Stone. *Economics*. Second Edition. (Glenview, IL: Scott, Foresman and Company, 1984), 5.

Cain, Mead. "Women's Status and Fertility in Developing Countries Son Preference and Economic Security." *World Bank Staff Working Papers Number 682*. Population and Development Series Number 7. (Washington, D.C., 1984).

Campioni, Mia and Elizabeth Gross. "Love's Labours Lost: Marxism and Feminism" in Judith Allen and Paul Pattern, *Beyond Marxism? Interventions Beyond Marx*. (Sydney: Intervention Publications, 1983).

Canada Treasury Board. *Guide to the Policy and Expenditure Management System*. (Ottawa: Queen's Printer, 1980).

Capra, Fritjof. *The Tao of Physics*. (New York: Bantam Books, 1977).

———. *The Turning Point: Science, Society and the Rising Culture*. (New York: Simon and Schuster, 1982).

Carson, Rachel. *Silent Spring*. (Harmondsworth: Penguin, 1979).

Casley, D. J. and D. A. Lury. *Data Collection in Developing Countries*. (New York: Clarendon Press).

Chodorow, Nancy. *The Reproduction of Mothering: Psychoanalysis and the Sociology of Gender*. (Berkeley: University of California Press, 1978).

Clark, Colin. "The economics of housework." *Bulletin of the Oxford Institute of Statistics* No. 20 (May 1958): 205–11.

Clark, Colin and Margaret Haswell. *The Economics of Subsistence Agriculture*. (New York: St. Martin's Press, 1970).

Copeman, Harold. *The National Accounts. A short guide. Studies in Official Statistics No. 36*. (London: Her Majesty's Stationery Office, May 1981).

Corea, Gena. *The Hidden Malpractice: How American Medicine Treats Women as Patients and Professionals*. (New York: William Morrow, 1977; New York: Jove Publishers, 1978).

———. *The Mother Machine*. (New York: Harper & Row, 1984).

_____. "Unnatural Selection." *The Progressive* 52 (January 1986): 22–24.

Cowan, Ruth Schwartz. *More Work for Mother.* (New York: Basic Books, 1983).

Crawford, Neta. "Summary of Soviet Strategic Nuclear Warheads." Unpublished paper. Institute for Defense and Disarmament Studies, Boston, MA, 1986.

Croll, Elisabeth. "Women in Rural Development—The People's Republic of China." (ILO, Geneva, 1979).

Daly, Mary. *Gyn/Ecology.* (Boston: Beacon Press, 1978).

Daniels, George H. and Mark H. Rose, eds. *Energy and Transport: Historical Perspectives on Policy Issues.* (Beverly Hills, CA: Sage Publications, 1982).

Davidson, Caroline. *A Woman's Work is Never Done: A History of Housework in the British Isles 1650–1950.* (London: Chatto & Windus, 1982).

Davies, Mirranda. *Third World—Second Sex: Women's Struggles and National Liberation.* (London: Zed Press, 1983).

Davies, Paul. *Superforce: The Search for a Grand Unified Theory of Nature.* (New York: Simon and Schuster, 1984).

Davies, Elizabeth Gould. *The First Sex.* (New York: Putnam, 1971).

de Beauvoir, Simone. *The Second Sex.* (Paris: Gallimard, 1949; New York: Avon Books, 1979).

Deere, Carmen Diana and Magdalena Leon de Leal. "Peasant Production, Proletarianization, and the Sexual Division of Labor in the Andes." *Signs* 7 (Winter 1981): 65–93.

Delphy, Christine. *Close to Home: A Materialist Analysis of Women's Oppression.* Translated and edited by Diana Leonard. (Amherst: University of Massachusetts Press, 1984).

_____. *The Main Enemy: A Material Analysis of Women's Oppression.* (London: Women's Research and Resources Centre Publications, 1977).

Dobb, M. *Theories of Value and Distribution since Adam Smith.* (Cambridge and New York: Cambridge University Press, 1973).

Dorian, T. F. and Leonard Spector. "Covert Nuclear Trade and the International Non-proliferation Regime." *Journal of International Affairs* 35, 1 (1982): 29–69.

Dreifus, Claudia, ed. *Seizing Our Bodies: The Politics of Women's Health.* (New York: Vintage Books, 1978).

Duncan, Joseph W. and William C. Shelton. *Revolution in United States Government Statistics.* U.S. Department of Commerce, Office of Federal Statistical Policy and Standards, October 1978.

(Dutch) National Advisory Council for Development Cooperation. *Recommendation on Women in Developing Countries: Aspects of Development Policy.* (Netherlands, May 1980).

Dworkin, Andrea. *Pornography: Men Possessing Women.* (New York: Putnam/Perigree, 1981).

Einstein, Albert. *Ideas and Opinions.* (New York: Dell, 1981).

Eisenstein, Zillah. *The Radical Future of Liberal Feminism.* (New York: Longman, Inc., 1981).

el Saadawi, Nawal. *The Hidden Face of Eve: Women in the Arab World.* (Boston: Beacon Press, 1982).

Encyclopedia of Economics. (Guilford, CT: DPG Reference Publishing Co., Inc., 1981).

Engels, Frederick. *The Origin of the Family, Private Property and the State.* (London: Lawrence and Wishart, 1940 [1884]), 1–2.

Fenstermaker Beck, Sarah. "Women and Household Labor." *Sage Yearbooks in Women's Policy Studies* 5 (1980).

Fergie, Ron. "Case Study on Design of a System of National Accounts—Papua New Guinea." Unpublished paper (Australia, 1981).

Firestone, Shulamith. *The Dialectic of Sex.* (New York: William Morrow, 1970).

Fiscal Planning Services, Inc. *Three Scenarios of Budget Cuts Under Gramm-Rudman* (Washington, D.C.: 1985).

Fisher, Jonathan and Norman Myers. "What We Must Do To Save Wildlife." *International Wildlife* Vol. 16. (May–June 1986), 12–15.

Folbre, Nancy. "Exploitation Comes Home: A Critique of the Marxian Theory of Family Labour." *Cambridge Journal of Economics* 6 (London: Academic Press Inc., 1982).

————. "Of Patriarchy Born: The Political Economy of Fertility Decisions." *Feminist Studies* 9 (Summer 1983).

Fong, Monica. "Victims of Old-Fashioned Statistics." *FAO Review on Agriculture and Development* 13 (May–June 1980).

Galbraith, John Kenneth. *The Affluent Society.* (Boston: Houghton Mifflin, 1974).

————. *The New Industrial State.* (Harmondsworth: Penguin, 1974).

————. *Annals of an Abiding Liberal.* Edited by Andrea D. Williams. (New York: New American Library, 1980), 38–46.

Garabaghi, Ninou K. "A New Approach to Women's Participation in the Economy." *International Social Science Journal* 35 (1983): 659–82.

Gelber, Sylvia M. "The Labour Force, the GNP and Unpaid House-keeping Service." *Labor Developments Abroad*. (Washington, D.C.: U.S. Department of Labor, August 1970), 12–15.

George, Susan. *How The Other Half Dies*. (Harmondsworth: Penguin, 1980).

Gilman, Charlotte Perkins. *The Man-Made World or Our Androcentric Culture*. (New York: Charlton Co., Johnson Reprint Corp., 1971).

———. *Women and Economics*. (New York: Harper Torchbooks, 1966).

Goldschmidt-Clermont, Luisella. *Unpaid Work in the Household*. (Geneva: International Labor Office, 1985).

Gordon, Robert J. *Macroeconomics*. (Boston: Little, Brown, 1981).

Gould, Carol C. and Marx W. Wartofsky, eds. *Women and Philosophy: Towards a Theory of Liberation*. (Toms River, NJ: Capricorn Books, 1976).

Grinspoon, Lester. *The Long Darkness*. (New Haven: Yale University Press, 1986).

Haig, B. P. and S. S. McBurney. *The Interpretation of National Income Estimates*. (Canberra: Australian National University Press, 1968).

Hannan, Michael T. "Families, Markets and Social Structures: An Essay on Becker's *A Treatise on the Family*." *Journal of Economic Literature* 20 (March 1982): 65–72.

Hawrylyshyn, Oli. *Estimating the Value of Household Work in Canada*. [L'estimation de la valeur du travail ménager au Canada]. (Ottawa: Statistics Canada, 1978).

———. "The Value of Household Services: A Survey of Empirical Estimates." *Review of Income and Wealth* 22 (June 1976): 101–32.

Heilbroner, Robert L. and Lester C. Thurow. *Understanding Macroeconomics*. 5th ed. (Englewood Cliffs, NJ: Prentice-Hall Inc., 1975).

Helzner, Judith F. *Evaluating Small Grants for Women in Development*. Distributed by Office of Women in Development Agency for International Development. (Washington, D.C., January 1980).

Hirschleifer, Jack. "The Expanding Domain of Economics," *The American Economic Review* 75 (December 1985): 53–68.

Hobbes, T. *Leviathan*. (Harmondsworth and Baltimore: Penguin, 1968).

Hobson, Sarah. "Bulldozed." *New Internationalist* No. 131. (January 1984): 21–22.

Hueting, Roefie. *New Scarcity and Economic Growth: More Welfare Through Less Production?* Translated by Trevor Preson. (Amsterdam, New York: North–Holland Publishing Co., 1980).

——. *Use of Environmental Data in the Economic Decision-Making Process Contribution of the Netherlands Bureau of Statistics.* U.N. Environment Program (UNEP/W.G.85/INF.11) February 25, 1983.

Hunt, E. K. "Joan Robinson and the Labour Theory of Value." *Cambridge Journal of Economics* 7 (1983): 331–42.

Huston, Perdita. *Message from the Village.* (New York: Epoch B. Foundation, 1978).

Hutchins, Grace. *Women Who Work.* (New York: International Publishers, 1952).

Independent Commission on Disarmament and Security. "The Consequences of Nuclear War." *Unesco Courier* 36 (August–September 1982): 44–47.

Jacobs, Sue-Ellen. *Women in Perspective: A Guide for Cross-Cultural Studies.* (Chicago: University of Illinois Press, 1976).

James, Selma. *The Global Kitchen.* (London: Housewives in Dialogue, 1985).

Kahn, Robbie Pfeufer. "The Language of Birth." *Socialist Review* Vol. 15 (1985): 185–98.

Kapp, Louise, ed. "American Woman: What Price Liberation" in *New Generation.* National Child Labor Committee, 1501 Broadway, Rm. 1111, New York, NY 10036 (Co-Sponsor: National Committee on Employment of Youth).

Kendrick, J. W. "The Historical Development of National Income Accounts." *History of Political Economy* (Vol. 2. (2) 1970. 284–315.

Keynes, J. M. *The General Theory of Employment, Interest and Money.* (London: Macmillan, 1965; New York: Harcourt Brace Jovanovich, 1936).

Keynes, John Neville. *The Scope and Method of Political Economy.* 4th ed. (Clifton, NJ: A. M. Kelley, 1973).

Koopmans, Tjalling. *Three Essays on the State of Economic Science.* (New York: McGraw–Hill, 1957).

Kuhn, Annette and Anne Marie Wolpe, eds. *Feminism and Materialism—Women and Modes of Production.* (Boston: Routledge & Kegan Paul, 1978).

Kuhn, T. S. *The Structures of Scientific Revolution.* (Chicago: Chicago University Press, 1962).

Küznets, Simon. *Economic Growth and Structure.* (London: Heinemann, 1966).

_____. *National Income and Its Composition, 1919–1938*. Assisted by Lillian Epstein and Elizabeth Jenks. (New York: National Bureau of Economic Research, 1941).

Langer, Susanne K. *Philosophy in a New Key*. (Cambridge: Harvard University Press, 1942).

Lapidus, Gail Warshofsky, ed. "Women, Work and the Family in the Soviet Union." *Problems of Economics: A Journal of Translations*. Seventeen articles translated by Vladimir Talmy from various Russian sources, 1975–1979. 24 S.N. (1981): 3–311.

Latin American and Caribbean Women's Collective. *Slave of Slaves: The Challenge of Latin American Women*. Translated by Michael Pallis. (London: Zed Press, 1980).

Lederer, Laura, ed. *Take Back the Night: Women on Pornography*. (New York: William Morrow, 1980).

The Legal Status of Rural Women. FAO Economic and Social Development Paper, No. 9, 1979.

Leghorn, Lisa and Katherine Parker. *Women's Worth: Sexual Economics and the World of Women*. (Boston, London, and Henley: Routledge & Kegan Paul, 1981).

Lekachman, Robert, ed. *Keynes' General Theory: Reports of Three Decades*. (New York: St. Martin's Press, Macmillan & Co. Ltd., 1964).

Lerner, Gerda. *The Creation of Patriarchy*. (New York: Oxford University Press, 1986).

Liklik Buk. *A Rural Development Handbook Catalogue for Papua New Guinea*. English ed. (Lae, Papua, New Guinea: Liklik Buk Information Centre, 1977).

Lovell, Michael C. *Macroeconomics: Measurement Theory and Policy*. (New York: John Wiley, 1975).

Luxembourg, Rosa. *Selected Political Writings*. (New York: Monthly Review Press, 1971).

Malos, Ellen, ed. *The Politics of Housework*. (London: Allison & Busby, 1980).

Marks, Elaine and Isabelle de Courtirroa, eds. *New French Feminisms*. (New York: Schocken Books, 1981).

Marshall, A. *Principles of Economics*. (London: Macmillan, 1980; Philadelphia: Porcupine Press, 1947).

Marx, K. *Theories of Surplus Value*. (London: Lawrence and Wishart, 1970; New York: Breekman Publications, 1969).

_____. *Capital*. Volume One. (London: Lawrence and Wishart, 1967; New York: International Publishers' Co., 1970).

_____. *Capital*. Volume Two. (London: Lawrence and Wishart, 1967; New York: International Publishers' Co., 1970a).

———. *Capital.* Volume Three. (London: Lawrence and Wishart, 1967; New York: International Publishers' Co., 1972).

Meiksins, P. "Productive and Unproductive Labor and Marx's Theory of Class." *Review of Radical Political Economics* 13 (1981): 32–42.

Meillassoux, Claude. *Maidens, Meal and Money Capitalism and the Domestic Economy.* (New York: Cambridge University Press, 1981), xii, 46–61, 98–103.

Mernissi, Fatima. *Beyond the Veil.* (Cambridge, MA: Schenkman Publishing Co., 1975), 74.

Mill, J. S. *Principles of Political Economy with some of their Applications to Social Philosophy.* (London: J. W. Parker and Co., 1965; Toronto: University of Toronto Press, 1852).

Millett, Kate. *Sexual Politics.* (New York: Avon Books, 1971).

———. *The Prostitution Papers.* (New York: Avon Books, 1973).

Mishan, E. J. "GNP—Measurement or Mirage?" *National Westminster Bank, Quarterly Review* 16 (November 1984): 2–13.

Morgan, Robin. *Going Too Far: The Personal Chronicle of a Feminist.* (New York: Random House and Vintage Books, 1978).

———. *Sisterhood Is Global.* (New York: Doubleday, 1984).

———. *Sisterhood Is Powerful.* (New York: Vintage Books, 1970).

———. *The Anatomy of Freedom, Feminism, Physics and Global Politics.* (Garden City, NY: Anchor Books/Doubleday, 1984).

Moskoff, William. *Labor and Leisure in the Soviet Union: The Conflict Between Public and Private Decision-Making in a Planned Economy.* (New York: St. Martin's Press, 1984).

Murphy, Martin. "Comparative Estimates of the Value of Household Work in the United States for 1976." *Review of Income and Wealth* 28 (March 1982): 29–37.

———. "The Value of Nonmarket Household Production: Opportunity Cost Versus Market Costs Estimates." *Review of Economic Wealth* 24 (September 1978): 243–55.

Myrdal, Gunnar. *Asian Drama: The Poverty of the Nations.* (New York: Allen Lane, 1968).

———. *The Political Element in the Development of Economic Theory.* (London: Routledge and Kegan Paul, 1969).

Nelson, Linda. *Women and Household Labor.* Edited by Sarah Fenstermaker Berk. (Beverly Hills, CA: Sage Publications, 1980), 186–87.

Newland, Kathleen. *The Sisterhood of Man.* (New York: W.W. Norton, 1979).

Noumea, Simi and Pamela Thomas. "The New Samoan Business-woman." *Pacific Perspective* 11 (1982): 5–12.

Oakley, Ann. *Subject Women.* (New York: Pantheon Books, 1981).

O'Brien, Mary. *The Politics of Reproduction.* (Boston: Routledge and Kegan Paul, 1983).

Okin, Susan Moller. *Women in Western Political Thought.* (Princeton University Press, 1979).

Omvedt, Gail. *We Will Smash This Prison.* (London: Zed Press, 1980).

Organization For Economic Co-Operation and Development. *Working Party No. 6 on the Role of Women in the Economy Single Parent Families.* MAS/WP6(84)2 (Paris, 27 February 1984).

Pagels, Heinz R. *The Cosmic Code, Quantum Physics as the Language of Nature.* (New York: Simon and Schuster, 1982).

Palmer, Ingrid. *The Nemov Case. Case Studies of the Impact of Large Scale Development Projects on Women: A Series For Planners.* (New York, September 1979) Working Paper No. 7, The Population Council, One Dag Hammarskjold Plaza, New York, NY 10017.

Papers on Patriarchy. (Brighton, U.K.: Women's Publishing Collective, 1976).

Perry, Ralph Barton. *General Theory of Value; Its Meaning and Basic Principles Construed in Terms of Interest.* (New York: Longmans, Green and Company, 1926).

Peterson, Jeannie, ed. *The Aftermath: Human and Ecological Consequences of Nuclear War.* (New York: Pantheon Books, 1983).

Pietilä, Hilkka. *Tomorrow Begins Today.* ICDA/ISIS Workshop in Forum 1985, Nairobi. (July 10–19, 1985).

Popper, K. R. *The Open Society and Its Enemies, Vol. 2, The High Tide of Prophecy: Hegel, Marx and the Aftermath.* (London: Routledge & Kegan Paul, 1966).

————. *The Poverty of Historicism.* (London: Routledge & Kegan Paul, 1977; New York: Harper & Row, 1969).

Quarterly National Accounts. OECD (June 18, 1979).

Reed, Evelyn. *Woman's Evolution.* (New York: Pathfinder Press, 1979).

Regenstein, Lewis. "America the Poisoned: How Deadly Chemicals Are Destroying Our Environment, Our Wildlife, And How We Can Survive!" *Acropolis* (1983).

Reid, Elizabeth. "The Forgotten Fifty Per Cent." *Populi Special* 4.1 (1977): 19–35.

Reynolds, Lloyd G. *Microeconomics: Analysis and Policy.* (Homewood, IL: Richard D. Irwin Inc., 1976).

Ricardo, D. *On the Principles of Political Economy and Taxation.* Edited by R. M. Harthell. (Harmondsworth, U.K.: Penguin, 1972; New York: Dutton and Co.).

Rich, Adrienne. "Compulsory Heterosexuality and Lesbian Existence." (London: Onlywomen Press, 1981).

———. "Of Women Born." (New York: Norton, 1986).

———. "Oh Lies, Secrets, Silence." (New York: Norton, 1979).

Robbins, Lionel. *An Essay on the Nature and Significance of Economic Science.* (London: Macmillan, 1969; New York: St. Martin's Press, 1932).

Robinson, E.A.G. "John Maynard Keynes 1883–1946" in *Kayes General Theory.* Reports of Three Decades. Robert Lekachman, ed. (New York: St. Martin's Press, 1964).

Robinson, J. *Economic Philosophy.* (London: Watts, 1962).

Robinson, J. and J. Eatwell. *An Introduction to Modern Economics.* (London and New York: McGraw-Hill, 1973).

Robinson, Joan. *An Essay on Marxian Economics.* 2d ed. (New York: St. Martin's Press).

———. *Collected Economic Papers.* Vol. 5. (Cambridge, MA: The M.I.T. Press, 1980).

Rogers, Barbara. *The Domestication of Women.* (London and New York: Tavistock Publications, 1981).

Rosenfeld, Rachel. *Farm Women: Work, Farm and Family in the United States.* (Chapel Hill: University of North Carolina Press, 1985).

Rowbotham, Sheila. *Woman's Consciousness, Man's World.* (Baltimore: Penguin Books, 1973).

Rowe, Marsha, ed. "Housework and History of the Housewife." *Spare Rib Reader.* (Harmondsworth, England: Penguin, 1982).

Rush, Florence. *The Best Kept Secret: Sexual Abuse of Children.* (New York: McGraw–Hill, 1980).

Sachs, Carolyn E. *The Invisible Farmers: Women in Agricultural Production.* (Totowa, NJ: Rowman & Allanheld, 1983).

Sagan, Carl. "Nuclear War and Climatic Catastrophe: Some Policy Implications." *Foreign Affairs* 62 (Winter 1983/84): 257–92.

Samuelson, Paul A. *Economics.* 10th ed. (New York: McGraw–Hill Inc., 1976).

Schreiner, Olive. *Women and Labour.* (London: Virago, 1978).

Schumacher, E. F. *Small Is Beautiful.* (New York: Harper & Row, 1974).

Schumpeter, J. A. *History of Economic Analysis.* (Oxford and New York: Oxford University Press, 1954).

Scott, Hilda. *Working Your Way to the Bottom: The Feminization of Poverty.* (Boston: Pandora Press, 1985).

Seidman, Ann. *The Roots of Crisis in Southern Africa.* (Trenton, NJ: African World Press, 1985), 13–27.

Sen, Gita and Caren Grown. *Development, Crises and Alternative Visions: Third World Women's Perspectives.* (New Delhi: Development Alternatives with Women for a New Era (DAWN), 1985).

Shamseddine, Ahmed Hassum. "The Value of Housewives' Activities in the United States." *Economics and Business Bulletin.* (Philadelphia, Summer 1968).

Sherman, Howard J. and Gary R. Evans. *Macroeconomics: Keynesian, Monetarist and Marxist Views.* (New York: Harper & Row, 1984).

Silk, Leonard. *Economics in Plain English.* (New York: Simon & Schuster, 1986).

Sills, David L., ed. *International Encyclopedia of Social Sciences.* (New York: Macmillan, 1968–1979).

Singer, Peter and Dean Wells. *The Reproductive Revolution: New Ways of Making Babies.* (Oxford: Oxford University Press, 1984).

Sivard, Ruth Leger. *Women . . . A World Survey.* (Washington, D.C.: World Priorities, 1985).

––––––. *World Military and Social Expenditures 1974.* (New York: Institute for World Order).

––––––. *World Military and Social Expenditures 1983.* (Washington, D.C.: World Priorities).

––––––. *World Military and Social Expenditures 1985.* (Washington, D.C.: World Priorities).

Smith, A. *The Wealth of Nations.* (Harmondsworth and New York: Penguin, 1974).

Stone, Byrns. *Economics.* 2d ed. (Glenview, IL: Scott Foresman & Co., 1984).

Stone, Sir Richard. "Political Economy, Economics and Beyond." *The Economic Journal* 90. (December 1980): 731–32.

Strasser, Susan. *Never Done.* (New York: Pantheon Books, 1982).

Strobel, Margaret. *Muslim Women in Monbasa 1890–1975.* (New Haven, CT and London: Yale University Press, 1979).

Studenski, Paul. *The Income of Nations.* (Washington Square, New York University Press, 1958).

Tadesse, Zenebeworke. *Women and Technological Development in Agriculture: An Overview of the Problems in Developing Countries.* Science and Technology Working Papers Series, No. 9 (New York, 1979).

Tagle, Dr. Maria A. *The Role of Women in Post-Harvest Conservation of Food*, UNITAR Seminar on "Creative Women in Changing Societies." Oslo (July 9–12, 1980).

Te Awekotuku, Ngahuia. "He Wahine, He Whenua: Maori Women and the Environment." *N.Z. Environment* 33 (Autumn 1982), 30.

Thanh-Dam, Tmong. "The Dynamics of Sex Tourism: The Case of Southeast Asia." *Development and Change* 14 (April 1983).

Theys, J. "Environmental Accounting and Its Use in Development Policy." Unpublished paper. Proposals based on the French Experience, January 1984.

Thompson, Dorothy, ed. *Over Our Dead Bodies—Women Against the Bomb*. (London: Virago, 1983).

Thurow, Lester C. *The Zero-Sum Society*. (New York: Penguin Books, 1980).

Tinker, Irene and Michele Bo Bramsen, eds. *Women and World Development*. (Washington: Overseas Development Council, 1976).

United Nations. *A System of National Accounts and Supporting Tables.* Studies in Methods, No. 2, Department of Economic Affairs, Statistical Office (ST/STAT/SER. F/2) New York 1953.

United Nations. *A System of National Accounts and Supporting Tables.* Statistical Office of the U.N. Studies in Methods. Series F, No. 2, Rev. 1. 1960, 1968.

United Nations. *Climatic Effects of Nuclear War Including Nuclear Winter.* Report of the Secretary-General. A/40/44. September 17, 1985.

United Nations. *Comparisons of the System of National Accounts and the System of Balances of the National Economy. Part 1, Conceptual Relationships.* Studies in Methods, Department of Economic and Social Affairs Statistical Office, Series F No. 20 (ST/ESA/STAT/SER.F/20) (New York 1977).

United Nations. *Compiling D Social Indicators on the Situation of Women.* Department of Economic and Social Affairs and INSTRAW, Studies in Methods, Series F., No. 32 (New York 1984).

United Nations. *Comprehensive Study on Nuclear Weapons.* Disarmament Study Series 1. Department of Political and Security Council Affairs, UN Center for Disarmament. (New York 1981).

United Nations. *Concepts and Definitions of Capital Formation.* Studies in Methods. Series F, No. 3 (New York, July 1953).

United Nations. *Consequences of the Arms Race and Military Expenditures.* Department for Disarmament Affairs, Economic and Social (New York, 1983).

United Nations. *Demographic and Social Indicators.* Economic and Social Council, Statistical Council Commission, Report of the Secretary-General (E/CN.3/1983/18). March 7–16, 1983.

United Nations. *Feasibility of Welfare-Oriented Measures to Supplement the National Accounts and Balances: A Technical Report.* Statistical Commission. Series F No. 20 (New York 1977).

United Nations. *Future Direction of Work on Social Indicators.* Economic and Social Council, Special Issues. Report of the Secretary-General (E/CN.3/1985/3) November 30, 1984.

United Nations. *Handbook of Household Surveys.* Studies in Methods, Department of International and Social Affairs, Statistical Office, Series F, No. 31 (ST/ESA/STAT/SER.F/31) (New York 1984).

United Nations. *Improving Concepts and Methods for Statistics and Indicators on the Situation of Women.* Department of International Economic and Social Affairs Statistical Office and International Research and Training Institute for the Advancement of Women. Studies in Methods. Series F, No. 33 (ST/ESA/STAT/SER.F/33) (New York 1984).

United Nations. *Legal Status of Rural Women: Limitations on the Economic Participation of Women in Rural Development.* FAO Economic and Social Development Paper, Profile 9. Rome, Italy, 1979.

United Nations. *Meeting User Needs for, and Improving the Dissemination of, International Statistics.* Economic and Social Council, Special Issues. Report of the Secretary-General (E/CN.3/1985/2) September 27, 1984.

United Nations. *National Accounts and Balances: System of Balances of the National Economy.* Economic and Social Council, December 21, 1985.

United Nations. *Overall Socio-economic Perspective of the World Economy to the Year 2000.* General Assembly, Development and International Economic Co-operation: Long-term Trends in Economic Development. Report of the Secretary-General. (A/40/519/8/23/1985).

United Nations. *Progress on the Development of Statistics of Mineral Resources.* Economic and Social Council, Report of the Secretary-General. E/CN.3/1985/9.

United Nations. *Progress Report on National and International Work on Social Indicators and on Related Concepts and Classifications for General Use.* Economic and Social Council, Demographic and Social Statistics: Social Indicators and Links Among Social, Demographic and Related Economic and Environment Statistics. Report of the Secretary-General. (E/CN.3/1983/18) May 3, 1982.

United Nations. *Progress Report on the Review of the System of National Accounts (SNA).* Economic and Social Council, Report of the Secretary-General (E/CN.3/1985/5) October 31, 1984.

United Nations. *Reduction of Military Budgets.* Disarmament Study Series 10. (New York 1983).

United Nations. *Relationship between Disarmament and Development.* Disarmament Study Series 5. (New York 1982).

United Nations. *Report of the First (Economic) Committee.* Economic and Social Council, Statistical Questions (E/1985/90/22/5/85).

United Nations. *Report of the World Conference to Review and Appraise the Achievements of the U.N. Decade for Women, Equality, Development and Peace.* A/Conf 116/28.

United Nations. *Special Problems of the Statistically Least Developed Countries.* Economic and Social Council, Report of the Secretary-General (E/CN/3/1985/16). September 10, 1984.

United Nations. *Technical Co-operation in Statistics Rendered by the Organs and Organizations of the United Nations System, Other International Organizations and Countries.* Economic and Social Council, Statistical Commission, Report of the Secretary-General (E/CN.3/1985/13).

United Nations. *Towards A System of Social and Demographic Statistics.* Studies in Methods, Department of Economic and Social Affairs, Statistical Office, Series F. No. 18 (ST/ESA/STAT/SER.F/18) (New York 1975).

United Nations. *World Economy Survey 1984: Current Trends and Policies in the World Economy.* Department of International Economic and Social Affairs (E/1984/62) (ST/ESA/151) (New York 1984).

United Nations. *World Population and Housing Census Program, 1985–1994.* Economic and Social Council, Report of the Secretary-General, Demographic and Social Statistics: Population and Housing Censuses. (E/CN.3/1985/12) November 9, 1984.

United Nations Children's Fund. *The State of the World's Children.* (New York: Oxford University Press, 1982).

United Nations Development Plan, Divison of Information. *A Long Hard Climb.* (1982–1983).

United Nations Economic Commission for Africa (UNECA). *Women of Africa, Today and Tomorrow.* (Addis Ababa: African Training and Research Center for Women, 1975), 6.

United States Agency for International Development. *Women in Development.* (Washington, D.C., October 1982).

United States General Accounting Office. *Report to the Chairman, House Committee on Government Operations.* Budget formulation. (Washington, D.C.: GAO, 1980).

Von Buchwald, Ulrike and Ingrid Palmer. *Monitoring Changes in the Conditions of Women—A Critical Review of Possible Approaches.* UNRISD/78/C.18 (Geneva:), 19.

WagMag. *A Newsletter for Women in Agriculture.* 14 (February 1985).

Waring, Marilyn. *Women Politics and Power.* (Wellington, New Zealand: Allen and Unwin/Port Nicholson Press, 1985).

Zeidenstein, Sondra, guest ed. "Learning About Rural Women." *Studies in Family Planning.* 10 (The Population Council, 1979).

Zelizer, Viviana A. *Pricing the Priceless Child: The Changing Social Value of Children.* (New York: Basic Books, Inc., 1985).

Index

Abortion: after chemical poisoning, 254; death from, 213; of female fetuses, 211, 220; illegal, 213, 214; sexuality market and, 205, 206; taxpayers lost by, 218

Abzug, Bella, 320

Account maintenance, housework including, 100

Accounts, national. *See* National accounts

Acid rain, 158, 260–65

Adams, Judge, 195–96

Addison, Joseph, 21

Adler, Hans J., 280

Advertising: breasts used in, 210; sexism in, 185

Afforestation, 151, 261–62, 263n

Afkhami, Mahnaz, 219

Africa: agriculture in, 29–30, 176–78, 179, 232–33, 234–35, 238–39, 264, 307; aid in, 173, 234–35, 239, 307; breast-feeding in, 207–8; child mortality in, 175, 258, 268; deforestation in, 260; drought in, 173, 176; family size in, 243; female-headed households in, 232–33, 234; game parks in, 267; life expectancy in, 175; malnutrition in, 173, 179; pesticides in, 323–24; sexual division of labor in, 228–29, 234–35; women's work in, 79, 81, 176–78, 232–33, 234–35, 239, 264, 307. *See also individual countries*

Ageism, 189

Agrarian Reform Law, Colombia, 241

Agriculture, 19, 29–30, 35, 50, 100; African, 29–30, 176–78, 179, 232–33, 234–35, 238–39, 264, 307; census of, 130–36; commercial cash-crop, 237, 238, 239, 242, 263, 264; deforestation for, 263; in Ethiopia, 174–75; female labor in, 24, 30, 74–79, 131–35, 175, 176–78, 228–42 passim, 264, 307; and International Fund for Agricultural Development, 176. *See also* Subsistence production

Aid, foreign, 12, 87–88, 173, 234–35, 239, 306–7

Aid to Families with Dependent Children, U.S., 72

Air pollution, 32, 158, 251, 252, 257–69 passim, 288, 289

Algeria, 231–32

Alienation, from economics, 46–47

Allen, Pat, 221, 222

Alparovitz, Gar, 281

Amazon valley, 245–46

American Council of Life Insurance, 277–78

American Economic Review, 220–21

American Federation of State, County, and Municipal Employees, 180

American Fertility Society, 191

American Home Economics Association, 101

Amharic, 174

Amniocentesis, 211, 220

Animals: market for, 193; raising, 101

Antarctica, 294

Anxieties, economics, 46–47

Aotearoa, 13. *See also* New Zealand

Argentina, 84, 185, 231

Armed forces: of Ethiopia, 173; world's, 168. *See also* Military expenditures; Wars

Arms race, 140, 166, 171–72. *See also* Nuclear weapons

Arms trade, 170, 171

Arsenic industry, 183

Ås, Berit, 42–43
Asia: deforestation in, 260, 261; family size in, 243; female-headed households in, 234; Islamic law in, 241. *See also individual countries*
Asian and Pacific Development Council, 283–84
Australia, 51, 116–17, 133n–34n, 146, 198
Australian Bureau of Statistics, 116–17
Austria, 51
Automobile Insurance Act, Quebec, 194
Awekotuku, Ngahuia te, 11

Babies: black market in, 189; and breast-feeding, 207; chemical poisoning and, 254; mortality rates of, 215; murder of female, 184, 188, 211; of surrogate mothers, 189–92; test-tube, 41, 189–91
Bakalian, Anny, 244
Bangladesh, 74, 81, 162, 211
Banking agencies: and recession, 215. *See also* International Monetary Fund; World Bank
Baran, P. A., 199, 203
Barkay, Richard M., 111, 112–14, 286
Barry, Kathleen, 245
Baskin, Yvonne, 227
Beauty, environmental, 250
Becker, Gary, 37–38, 204
Belgium, 154, 163n, 272
Belize, 240
Beneria, Lourdes, 7
Bengelsdorf, Carollee, 247
Bentzel, Rajnar, 48
Benzedrene, 183
Beti people, 29–30
Beyond the Veil (Mernissi), 231
Bhopal, India, 158, 181–82
Bible, 21
Bihar, India, 262–63
Bilby, Denis, 227
Bilby, William, 227
Biological determinism, 28–29, 38
Biological reproduction, 28–29, 188, 287
Birbeck, Farmer, 208
Birds, 265
Birnbaum, Bonnie, 38, 284

Birth control. *See* Contraception
Birth rates, 121n–22n, 218
Birth: wrongful, 198–99. *See also* Reproduction
Black market. *See* Hidden economy
Blacks, American, 31, 122n, 180, 207
Blades, Derek, 83–84, 140, 149, 153
Bohrs, Niels, 298
Bolivia, 230, 231, 241
Boserup, Ester, 7, 41–42, 235, 236, 308
Boulding, Elise, 75
Boulding, Kenneth, 325
Boundary: of reproduction, 188–89, 204–6, 210. *See also* Production boundary
Brazil, 84–87, 171, 241
Breast cancer surgery, 323
Breast-feeding, 206–10, 221, 324
Breasts, exploitation of, 210
Bride prices, 108, 324
Britain: arms trade of, 171; English Common Law in, 241; and Ethiopia, 176; government spending in, 180; hidden economy in, 152, 154; Keynes and, 36, 54–55; national accounts begun in, 49–50, 51, 54–55; nuclear power in, 272; pollution of, 260; surrogate motherhood in, 190; wet nurses in, 207; wrongful birth in, 198–99
Broome, John, 24–25
Brown, Louise, 191
Bryceson, Deborah, 218
Bulgaria, 51, 163n
Burkina Faso, 175, 321–22
Burma, 149–52, 181

California Department of Fair Employment and Housing, 323
Cameroon, 29–30
Canada: censuses of, 118–30, 132, 133; divorce and unpaid work in, 200–201; drugs launched in, 182; GNP of, 146; hidden economy in, 154; household work value in, 280; national accounts begun in, 51; pollution in, 158, 260; Quebec Automobile Insurance Act, 194
Capital gains, 53

Capital investment, 63–64
Capra, Fritjof, 225, 249
Caracas, Venezuela, 207, 213
Carson, Rachel, 11
Cash generating capacity: of
    countries, 3. See also Money value
Casley, D. J., 130, 137, 138
Castro, Fidel, 246–47
Celibate persons, sexuality market
    and, 205, 206
Censuses, 8, 74–75, 117–43, 304,
    319–20; agriculture, 130–36; and
    handicraft workers, 75, 87, 91; and
    housework, 8, 74, 89–91, 122,
    141–42, 231–32, 319–20; New
    Zealand, 115, 122n, 138–43;
    population, 117–30; production
    units in, 88; strategy for making
    change in, 138–43; topics
    recommended for, 117–18, 131
Central America, 84, 240, 241–42.
    See also individual countries
Chase Manhattan Bank, 277–78
Chemicals: pollution by, 19, 156,
    158, 181–82, 183, 254–55, 259, 269,
    323–24. See also Drugs
Chernobyl, 32, 155, 269, 273, 318,
    324
Chiavola, Lucia, 322
Chicago School, 37–38, 196, 204
Childbearing. See Babies; Birth;
    Reproduction
Child care, 28–29, 30, 31, 90;
    institutional, 91; and leisure time,
    217; time for, 230
Children, 251; in Burma, 150;
    censuses and, 118, 121n–22n, 131;
    custody of after divorce, 202;
    death of, 43, 172, 175, 211, 215,
    219, 237–38, 257, 258, 268; Fergie's
    Papua New Guinea report and,
    105; as future taxpayers, 218;
    health of, 172, 215–16, 219–20,
    257, 258, 268 (see also Death);
    insurance on, 195; in international
    economic system, 31; in labor
    force, 30n; malnutrition of, 164,
    172, 211, 237–38; Nepalese
    working, 111–12; and parents'
    recreation, 160–61; in poverty,
    179–80; prostitute, 152–53; rural
    labor of, 228–29; scientific method

and, 40; sex preference in choice
    of, 184, 188, 211, 220–21, 243–44;
    sexuality of, 204, 205–6; value of,
    3, 38, 195–99, 202, 204, 243. See
    also Babies; Child care; Girls
Chile, 231, 241
China, 174, 183–85, 197, 211, 247–
    48, 272
Christianity, 106n, 241
Ciba-Geigy, 254
Circumcision, female, 212
City Gardner (Fairchild), 260
Clark, Colin, 232
Classism, 189, 207
Clitoridectomy, 212
Clothing, care of, 100
Code Napoleon, 241
Colombia, 237, 241
Colonization, 49, 102, 189. See also
    Neocolonialism
Commerce. See Markets
Commission on the Status of
    Women, UN, 152
Communications systems, 253
Community work. See Volunteer
    work
Comparable worth, 37, 280. See also
    Pay
Conceptual difficulties, 114, 249,
    313–14; in agricultural data, 130;
    in hidden economy data, 153–54,
    314; in home imputation, 149; in
    housework data, 141–42, 230–31;
    and unpaid work by men, 105; in
    visibility of women's work, 80, 91,
    101, 153
Concise Oxford Dictionary, 172
Conference for Women, UN, 319
Consciousness raising, 320–21
Conservation, 3, 8, 265–66, 268–69,
    290–91, 317, 325
Consistency, forced, 57, 302
Conspiracy, international gender,
    224
"Constant dollar" terms, 116
Consumer price indexes, 115, 116,
    136, 137, 170
Consumption, 235; food, 107, 236–
    37, 304; military, 167–68; in
    national accounts, 51–52, 55, 59–
    62, 78, 89, 144; pollution
    connected with, 156; production

for own, 51–52, 78, 79, 107, 310–11 (*see also* Subsistence production); in rural areas, 76–77, 136. *See also* Shopping
Contraception, 205, 206, 209, 213, 221, 243
Control: over fertility/sexuality, 28, 188, 205, 222, 242–46; over food, 237–38; by technostructure, 203–4. *See also* Power
Cooking, 30–31, 100–101, 150
Copeman, Harold, 82
Corea, Gena, 29, 189–90
Corporate profits, in national accounts, 69
Cost: of decommissioning nuclear power plants, 273–74; of drinking water supply and sanitation, 11, 258; of environmental protection, 292; of getting to work, 293; of housing, 121, 293; of medical treatment, 190, 191, 257; of milk, 208; of nuclear power plants, 272; pollution damage, 288, 289, 292–93; of public and private security, 293; of recreation, 293. *See also* Spending; Value
Costa Rica, 162–63
Cost-benefit analysis, 268, 297–98
Cowan, Ruth Schwartz, 226
Crime. *See* Hidden economy
Cuba, 246–47
Cultural market, and reproduction, 199–202
Cultural recreation, 160
Custody, of children after divorce, 202
Czechoslovakia, 163n, 260, 261

Daly, Herman, 314–15
Dam, "women's", 322
Dannemeyer, Representative, 218
D'Arge, Ralph, 303
Daswani, Mona, 211
Data collection, 105, 115–43, 147–149, 304–12; difficulties of, 80, 91, 108–9, 113, 116–17, 142; on household work, 8, 74, 89–91, 113, 116–17, 122, 141–42, 230–35, 277–84, 319–20. *See also* Censuses
Daughters, sons preferred over, 184, 188, 211, 220, 243–44

Death: abortion-caused, 213; in Bhopal, 181; of children, 43, 172, 175, 211, 215, 219, 237–38, 257, 258, 268; "destructive" production and, 291; and reproduction, 213, 219; value of, 8–10, 165–86
Death rates. *See* Mortality rates
Debt, U.S. national, 169
Defense. *See* Armed forces
"Defensive" economic activities, 292–93
Deference, to men, 233
Deforestation, 251, 257, 260–65, 275
della Costa, Maria, 7, 322–23
Delphy, Christine, 42, 199–200
Demand: in national accounts, 58–69, 306; for nuclear weapons, 70–71
Democracy, and poverty, 179
Denmark, 154, 272
Department of Agriculture, U.S. (USDA), 134, 136, 236
Department of Commerce, U.S., 55, 72, 134
Department of Defense (DOD), U.S., 9, 169–70. *See also* Military expenditures
Department of Energy, U.S., 9, 272, 273–74
Department of Labor, U.S., 281–82, 307
Department of Statistics, New Zealand, 4, 115, 116, 138
Depom Provera, 243
Depression, 1920s, 52
Desertification, 251
Determinism, biological, 28–29, 38
Developed countries: rural and urban housework in, 228; and social relations of reproduction, 220; statisticians and, 114
Developing countries: double standard of West toward, 182–83; and drugs (legitimate), 182, 243; ecological devastation in, 275; GNP and GDP in, 71–72; military in, 170–71; pesticide trade with, 182; rural housework in, 228; sexuality market and, 205, 206; and social relations of

reproduction, 220; statisticians and, 114
"Deviant work activities", 27. *See also* Hidden economy
Devonshire, Lord, 260
Diamond Shamrock, 183
Dictionary of Occupational Titles, 281–82, 333
Dieldrin, 324
Diet, 54, 236. *See also* Nutrition
Dioxin, 254, 255
Disarmament, 140, 166
Discrimination, sex, 224, 242–49, 312; in advertising, 185; in censuses, 118; in education, 203; in labor force, 37, 184, 247–48; in legal system, 240–42, 246; in pay, 37, 184, 220, 280; statisticians and, 98–99
Diseases. *See* Illnesses
Displaced homemakers, 233–34
Divorce, 200–201, 202
Domestic work. *See* Housework
Dominance: in environment, 275; in social relations of reproduction, 199. *See also* Control; Patriarchy
Dominguez, Loreto M., 48
Dominican Republic, 303–4
Double standards, for West and developing world, 182–83
Drought, African, 173, 176
Drugs: contraceptive, 209, 243; illegal, 152; legal, 182, 214, 254–55
Dühring, E. K., 5
Duncan, Joseph W., 53, 55
Dungari-Paitoli, Himalayas, 263
Durable goods, in national accounts, 59
Dwellings. *See* Housing
Dworkin, Andrea, 245

East European countries, 33, 34, 89, 163n. *See also individual countries*
Econometric modeling, 144
Economic activity, definition of, 25–27, 41, 113, 122–23, 131, 140, 308
Economic and Social Council, UN, 93, 211–12, 215
Economics, 325; Chicago School, 37–38, 196, 204; classical, 47; Marxist, 29, 37, 42; neoclassical, 39, 196, 224, 261; patriarchal nature of, *see* Patriarchy; Pietilä's model of, 300–304, 314, 316; of reproduction, 10, 187–223; scientific method in, 39–43, 91, 97, 249; teaching of, 36–39; terminology in, 17–29, 41, 46–47, 58–73. *See also* International economics; Markets; Value
"Economics anxiety", 46–47
Economics of Subsistence Agriculture (Clark & Haswell), 232
Economists, 17–20, 47, 144–64, 222, 309, 314. *See also* Keynes, John Maynard; Robinson, Joan; Statisticians
Education: agriculture, 234; in Burma, 150; in China, 184; domestic science, 234; of girls, 215–16, 235, 324; war costs compared with, 172; of women, 203, 215–17, 234
EEC (European Economic Community), 93, 176, 256, 309
Einstein, Albert, 10–11, 225
Elderly: income of, 58; sexuality of, 204, 206; superannuation for, 140, 145, 201
Electricity, nuclear power and, 272
Electromagnetic spectrums, 253
Elliott, Charles, 176
Emerson, Ralph Waldo, 22
Employment. *See* Labor
Encyclopaedia of Economics, 59–60
Endangered species, 265–69
Engels, Frederick, 5–6, 29
England. *See* Britain
English Common Law, 241
Enslavement. *See* Slavery
Entombment, of nuclear power plants, 273
Environment, 11, 250–75, 287–91, 302–3, 316, 317–18, 325; colonization of, 40; conservation in, 3, 8, 265–66, 268–69, 290–91, 317, 325; indicators, 329–32; in international economic system, 14, 20, 25, 31–33, 49, 83; in national accounts, 3, 8, 49, 65, 158, 256–65 passim, 275, 287–96, 309 passim; public policy and, 1–2, 262, 264–65, 303. *See also* Minerals; Pollution, environment

Environmental Program, UN, 293n, 294–95
Environmental Protection Agency (EPA), U.S., 156, 259
Epstein, Lilian, 52–53
Erosion, 251, 275
Essays (Montaigne), 21
Establishment (production unit), in New Zealand national accounts, 88
"Ethical Considerations of the New Reproductive Technologies" (American Fertility Society), 191
Ethiopia, 173–76, 241
Ettelvina, Dona, 240
Eucalyptus, 261–62
Europe: East, 33, 34, 89, 163n; pollution in, 158. *See also individual countries*
European Economic Community (EEC), 93, 176, 256, 309
"Everyday experience", Robbins and, 18, 19
Exchange rates, 147–48
Expenditures. *See* Spending
Expert Group on Welfare Orientated Supplements to the National Accounts and Balances, 308
Exports: arms, 170, 171; Ethiopian, 174; in national accounts, 68; pesticide, 182; pesticide-protected, 323–24

Fairchild, Thomas, 260
Families: care of, 100 (*see also* Child care); custody of children after divorce in, 202; defined, 89; "new home economics" and, 37–38; sex preference in, 184, 188, 211, 220–21, 243–44; size of, 243; in transaction cost approach, 38–39. *See also* Marriage; Mothers
Famine: in Africa, 175–76. *See also* Starvation
FAO. *See* Food and Agriculture Organization, UN
Fathers, child custody by, 202
Federal Republic of Germany. *See* West Germany
Feige, Edgar, 153
Females. *See* Girls; Women

Feminists, 10, 93–103, 199, 225, 304, 307, 322–23
Ferber, Marianne, 38, 281, 284
Ferge, Zsuzsa, 34
Fergie, Ron, 4–5, 94–103, 114, 149, 187, 284, 287, 312
Fertility: control over, 28, 188, 222, 242–46. *See also* Birth rates; Reproduction
Fertility theory, 196, 220, 221
Fettered economy, in Pietilä's diagram, 300–301
Filipino women, spare time of, 162
Finances. *See* Aid, foreign; Banking agencies; Cost; Insurance; Investment; Money value
Financial investment: in recession, 215; vs. capital investment, 62–63
Finland, 154, 218, 302, 323
Finley, Lorrien, 190
Firewood gathering, 79, 81–82, 101, 107–8, 110, 263
Fisher, Jonathon, 266
Food and Agriculture Organization (FAO), UN, 43, 93, 130, 131, 239, 307
Food, 5; for babies, 206–10; consumption of, 51–52, 107, 136, 236–37, 304; convenience, 236–37; distribution of, 79; in Dominican Republic, 303–4; Ethiopia and, 175–76; growing of, 35, 100 (*see also* Agriculture; Gardening); imported, 236, 240; nonconvenience, 236–37; preparation of, 30–31, 100–101, 150; processing of, 79, 81, 84, 91, 100, 113; production of, 51–52, 107, 174, 179, 237–40 (*see also* Agriculture; Subsistence production); shortage of, 175–76 (*see also* Malnutrition); storage of, 79; transportation of, 79. *See also* Nutrition
Food line, 230–31
Forced consistency, 57, 302
"Force" theory, 5
Forests, 151, 251–69 passim, 275, 303
"Forward Looking Strategies for the Advancement of Women", 306
France, 51, 163n, 171, 232, 272

Freed, Doris Jonis, 202
Free economy, in Pietilä's diagram, 300
Free time, 149, 159–64, 217, 283
Frey, Bruno S., 153–54
Friedman, Milton, 36, 302
Friends of the Earth, 158
"Frontiers in Demographic Economics" (Samuelson), 220–21
Fuel, 51–52; in Burma, 151; collection of, 79, 81–82, 91, 101, 107–8, 110, 113, 119–21, 230, 263; in Nepal, 110–11
Fulani herders, 176–77
Funiciello, Theresa, 179–80

Galbraith, John Kenneth, 36, 39, 203, 277, 320
Gambia, 19, 238
Game parks, 267
Gardening, 136, 237, 260, 264
Garjer, W. H., 101
Garment industry, breasts used in, 210
GDP. *See* Gross Domestic Product
General Assembly, UN, 93, 166, 217
General Theory (Keynes), 36
Genital organs, legal market and damages to, 194–95
Genocide, 179
George, Susan, 321
German Democratic Republic, 163n
Germany: East, 163n; pre-split, 51. *See also* West Germany
Gibbs, Lois, 317–18, 319
Gilbert, Milton, 55–57, 66, 165, 281, 301–2, 312
Gilman, Charlotte Perkins, 26, 37, 160
Girls: education of, 215–16, 235, 324; murder of infant, 184, 188, 211; prostitute, 152–53, 211
Givandan, 254
GNP. *See* Gross National Product
Goldschmidt-Clermont, Luisella, 279
Goodland, Richard, 288, 290
Gould, John, 265
Government accounts, New Zealand, data collection from, 116
Government income, national income vs., 49

Government regulation: environmental, 290; of reproduction, 217–18, 221
Government responses, to women, 307–8
Government spending, 55, 65–68, 262; in Britain, 180; on capital goods, 63; and poverty, 180; in recession, 215; on social services, 72, 180, 215, 216–17. *See also* Military expenditures
Grain, 176, 179
Great Britain. *See* Britain
"Green accounts", Japanese, 296
Greene, Carole, 281
Greenham Common, 11
Green party, West German, 251, 255
Green Revolution, 237
Griffin, Susan, 11
Gross Domestic Product (GDP), 71–72, 87, 302, 309–12, 320; of Burma, 151; calculated by sex, 311–12; census among sources for, 117; conversion to exchange rates, 147–48; and environment, 288, 309; food production in, 238–39; hidden economy in, 152, 309; quarterly statistics on, 144; superannuation and, 145; and well-being, 47, 71–72, 284, 285–86
Gross National Product (GNP), 8, 55–58, 71–72, 146, 313, 323, 324; and consumption, 235–36, 237; and environment, 156, 259, 288–90, 292; hidden economy in, 154; housework value in relation to, 101, 280, 282, 284; and Measure of Economic Welfare, 291–92
Growth, 32–33, 57–58, 70–72, 146, 181; in Burma, 151–52, 181; environmental destruction and, 49, 158–59, 251, 291; militarism as, 49; in Thailand, 152
Guardian, 198
Guinea Bissau, 175
Guyana, 230–31

Haile Selassie, 174, 176
Haines, Janine, 116–17
Haiti, 84
Handicrafts, 75, 81, 84, 87, 91
Hanmer, Jalna, 221, 222

Hansen, Kurt, 48
Han Suyin, 41
Haswell, Margaret, 232
Hawrylyshyn, Oli, 280
Hazardous waste business, 157
Hazlitt, William, 21–22
Head of household, 100, 119, 123–
30, 137–38, 211, 232–34, 237
Health: of children, 172, 215–16,
219–20, 257, 258, 268; mosquitoes
and, 268; and nutrition, 236 (see
also Malnutrition); and pollution,
155–56, 257; of women, 211–14,
215–16. See also Death
Health care, 151, 166, 212; vs.
military expenditures, 169, 172;
pollution connected with, 156,
257; and reproduction, 189–93,
211, 220–21; U.S., 169, 180, 214;
by women, 213–14. See also
Medical profession
Heilbroner, Robert L., 160
Henderson, Hazel, 299
Hidden economy, 8, 16, 27, 149–54,
308–9, 310, 313–14; baby market
in, 189; breasts in, 210; drugs of,
182. See also Prostitution
Hindu Code of Manu, 241
Hispanics, American, 122n, 180
History, of national accounts, 49–58
Hobbes, Thomas, 22
Hoffman-La Roche, 254
Holders, in censuses, 130
Holdings, in censuses, 130, 131
Holy See, 4
"Home-based activities", 27. See also
Household production
Home-based recreation, 160
Homeless people, 149, 180
Homemakers: displaced, 233–34. See
also Housewives
Homes. See Housing
Homophobia, 189
Homosexuals, sexuality market and,
205, 206, 210
Honduran prostitution, 204
Hong Kong, 244
Household appliances, labor-saving,
225, 226
Household labor force surveys, 136–
38, 304–6, 320

Household production, 8, 12, 74–91,
116–17, 310–11. See also
Handicrafts; Housework;
Subsistence production
Households: accounting methods
used by, 97, 102; in censuses, 118,
119, 123–30, 131, 138; defined, 88–
90, 137; female-headed, 100, 211,
232–34, 237; head of in statistics-
gathering, 119, 123–30, 137–38,
232–34; management of, 37, 100;
surveys of, 116–17, 136–38, 304–6,
320. See also Household
production
Housemaids: in China, 185;
definition of, 333
House of Representatives, U.S., 218
Housewives, 12; Fergie's Papua New
Guinea report and, 108;
housework by, see Housework; in
labor surveys, 138; national
accounts excluding, 46, 74–91; on
tax forms, 134n; value of, 41, 200–
202, 277–87, 311
Housework, 19, 25–26, 25–35
passim, 27, 28–29, 41, 46, 74–101
passim, 114, 230–35, 296, 310–12;
data collection on, 8, 74, 89–91,
113, 116–17, 122, 141–42, 230–35,
277–84, 319–20; defined, 34, 100,
333; and job effort, 227; and
leisure time, 161–62, 217; men
doing, 99–101, 225, 226–27; rural,
225, 228–30, 231, 232, 285;
servants for, 185, 225–26, 333; and
social relations of production, 199,
200, in Soviet Union 89–90, 161–
62; urban, 225–28; value of, 41,
277–87, 311; wages for, 7, 277–78,
280–81, 322–23; women's unpaid
work beyond, 99–100, 101 (see also
Subsistence production; Volunteer
work). See also Child care
Housing, 59; in Burma, 149–50, 151;
censuses and, 119–21; construction
of, 59, 113; cost of, 121, 293;
ownership of, 59, 113, 121; rental,
14–15, 51–52, 59, 69, 121, 149;
U.S. military, 169–70
"How to Pay for the War" (Keynes
& Stone), 54–55
Hubbard, Ruth, 45

Hueting, Roefie, 295
Hume's Fork, 40
Hungary, 163n
Hunger. See Malnutrition
Hunting, 267
Huston, Perdita, 243
Huts, in national accounts, 149

ICMESA chemical plant, 254
Identification cards, Ethiopia, 174
Ideology: and invisibility of women, 95, 96, 277; of patriarchy, 44, 95, 96, 276
Illegal market. See Hidden economy
Illnesses: mosquito borne, 268; pollution-caused, 155–56, 257, 258. See also Health
ILO. See International Labor Organization
Imports: food, 236, 240; in national accounts, 68; oil, 171
Imputation, 7, 52, 78, 82, 83; of contributed unpaid labor, 68–69, 106–7; of firewood gathering, 107–8; of food production for own consumption, 51–52, 78, 107; of hidden economy, 16, 310; of rental housing, 14, 51–52; of reproduction, 223, 286–87; of unpaid men's work, 105; of unpaid work, 7, 11–12, 68–69, 78, 82, 102, 105, 106–8, 223, 276–87; 310; of women's work, 7, 11–12, 82, 107–8, 223, 276–87
Ince, Susan, 189
Income: government vs. national, 49. See also National accounts
Incompetence, 147, 172–73, 186, 306–7
India, 4, 87, 158, 181–82, 211, 238, 241, 257, 262–63
"Inductive verification", 90
Industrial production, 167, 182–83
Infanticide, female, 184, 188, 211
Infants. See Babies
Informal sector, 8, 26–27, 312. See also Hidden economy; Volunteer work
Insecticides, 156
Institute for Sex Research, 245
INSTRAW, 82, 305, 308

Insurance: and chemical accidents, 255–56; on children, 195
Interest, in national accounts, 70
International Civil Aviation Organization (ICAO), 93
International Council of Women, 108, 320
International Decade for Women (1975–85), UN, 41–42
International Drinking Water Supply and Sanitation Decade, 258
International economics: introduction to, 14–45; new model for, 299–315; war valued in, 165. See also Trade; United Nations System of National Accounts
International Encyclopedia of Social Science, 31, 53
International Federation of Business and Professional Women's Clubs, 320
International Fund for Agricultural Development, 176
International Institute for Environment and Society, 292
International Institute of Management, Berlin, 282
International Labor Organization (ILO), UN, 14, 30, 82, 88, 89–90, 93, 231, 234
International Monetary Fund (IMF), 2, 93, 215, 309
International Research and Training Institute for the Advancement of Women (INSTRAW), 82, 305, 308
International Standard Classification of Occupations, 312
International Wildlife, 265–66
International Women's Year, 234
International Year of Peace, 165
Intrauterine devices, contraceptive, 243
Inventory changes, investment as, 64–65
Investment, 55, 62–65, 145, 215
Invisibility, 144, 309–10; of environmental bounty, 250–51; of female-headed households, 233; of men's unpaid domestic work, 99; of reproduction, 222, 286; of women in censuses, 118, 122–23, 130, 132–36, 143; of women in

household surveys, 137, 163; of women in national accounts, 2, 49, 53, 61, 78, 81–91, 94–102, 105, 249; of women's work, 2, 7, 42, 53, 78, 81–91, 94–102, 105, 163, 175
Invisible Farmers (Sachs), 133–34
Iran, 81, 146, 218–19
Isis International Bulletin, 214
Islam, 241, 244
Israel, 171, 248
Italy, 51, 154, 171, 254, 259, 288
Ivory Coast, 305
Izvestia, 34

Jaffe, A. J., 31
Jamaica, 84, 94, 100, 103
James, Selma, 308
Japan: agricultural labor in, 232; brothel-visiting tourists from, 244; drugs produced by, 182; export growth in, 146; GDP and well-being in, 47; "green accounts" of, 296; hidden economy in, 154; income of elderly in, 58; military expenditures of, 185; national accounts begun in, 51; nuclear power in, 272; Third World industry of, 183
Jaszi, George, 48
Jobs. *See* Labor force
Jordan, 75, 81

Kakapo, 265
Kapital (Marx), 50–51
Keane, Noel, 191
Keeton, Cathy, 227
Kelly, Petra, 251
Kelvin's dictum, 40
Kenya, 11, 228–30, 241, 283
Kerensky government, 51
Keynes, John Maynard, 17, 23, 36, 47, 73, 90; Papua New Guinea accounts and, 104; and war, 54–55, 66, 165
Keynes, John Neville, 73
Khomeini, Ayatollah, 219
King, Gregory, 50
Kinsey Institute, 245
Koita, Mariania, 238
Komisar, Lucy, 204
Krishna, Raj, 283–84

Küznets, Simon, 36–37, 52–54, 55, 57, 58, 312–13

Labor: agricultural, 24, 30, 74–79, 131–35, 175, 176–78, 228–42 passim, 264, 307; definition of, 25–27; domestic, *see* Housework; Engels on, 5, 6; in international economic system, 42; productive (defined), 50; sexual division of, 228–29, 234–35, 311–12. *See also* Labor force; Unpaid work
Labor force: costs of participation in, 293; defined, 27; pregnancy in, 246; reproduction of, 188, 199, 220; sex discrimination in, 37, 184, 247–48; surveys, 136–38; 304–6; in technostructure, 203–4; women counted out of, 29–31, 312; women in paid, 37, 42–43, 184, 227, 246, 274–78. *See also* Pay
Lacemaking, 87
Lake Charles, Louisiana, 194
Land reform, 174–75, 241–42
Language: of economics, 17–29, 41; of Ethiopia, 174
La Paz, Bolivia, 230
Latin America: breast-feeding in, 207–8; discriminatory laws in, 241; family size in, 243; female-headed households in, 234; female labor in, 75, 231; government spending in, 180; housework in, 231; "maternal" deaths in, 213. *See also* Central America; *individual countries*
"Laws", 225; of economics, 224–25; of political economy, 74
Lawyers, pay for, 190, 191
Layered cake diagram, of economics, 299, 300
Left, 246–47. *See also* Marxist economics; Socialism
Legal system: and census data, 320; discriminatory, 240–42, 246; and reproduction, 193–99
Legare v. United States, 202
Leghorn, Lisa, 161, 163, 277
Legislatures, national, women in, 1, 44
Leipert, Christian, 292–93, 294, 313, 315, 325

Leisure, 149, 159–64, 217, 267, 283, 313–14
Lenin, Vladimir Illich, 34
Leontief, Wassily, 158
Lerner, Gerda, 28
Lesbians, sexuality market and, 205, 206, 210
Lesotho, South Africa, 232–33, 241
Life: "creative" production and, 291; value of, 3–4, 7, 8–10, 24–25, 166 184, 186, 187–223, 286–87. *See also* Health; Reproduction
Life expectancy: in Africa, 175; in China, 185; and housework time, 228
Life insurance, on children, 195
Literacy, 43, 174, 184, 215–16. *See also* Education
Liukkonen, Marjo, 323
Living Standards Measurements Survey (LSMS), World Bank, revw tr, 305
Lockheed aircraft, 169
Los Angeles Times, 323
Love Canal, 155, 157, 317–18
Lumber, 261–62
Lumpectomy, 323
Lury, D. A., 130, 137, 138

McCloskey, Donald N., 39–40
Mackleroy, Michael B., 294
Maids: in China, 185; definition of, 333
Maine, 179
Malaria, 268
Malawi, 81, 234–35
Malaysia, 183
Males. *See* Men; Sons
Mali, 175
Malnutrition, 164; in Africa, 173, 179; of men, 237–38; in U.S., 180; and war, 172; of women and children, 164, 172, 211, 237–38
Mansfield, Katherine, 13
Markets, 302; domestic work, 98; environment and, 251–52, 261–67, 275; illegal, *see* Hidden economy; Keynes on, 36; moral value vs. value in, 23, 24; and public policy, 217–21, 262, 264–65, 285–86; reproduction and, 189–223. *See also* Labor force; Trade

Marriage, 188; battery within, 245; "new home economics" and, 37–38; and property rights, 201, 241; rape within, 213, 244, 245; and social relations of production, 200–201; in transaction cost approach, 38–39; value of wives in, 41, 200–202, 277–87, 311
Marshall, Alfred, 23, 47, 51
Marxist economists, 29, 37, 42
Marx, Karl, 5, 23, 29, 50–51
Massundra, Vera, 261
Mastectomies, 323
Material production: in MPS, 51, 327–28. *See also* Markets; Production
Material Product System (MPS), 33, 34, 35, 51, 89, 308, 309, 327–28
Mathematics of economics, 17
Measure of Economic Welfare (MEW), 291–92
Measurement, 8; of environmental factors, 149, 154–59, 252–53, 314; of hidden economy, 8, 149–54, 314; of leisure time, 149, 159–64; and militarism, 56, 166; Pietilä's diagram and, 302; of subsistence production, 34–35, 54, 107–8, 232; of women's work, 34–35, 107–8, 153–54, 230–31, 232. *See also* Conceptual difficulties; Data collection; Statisticians
"Measuring National Income as Affected by the War" (Gilbert), 55–56
Medical market: and pollution-caused illnesses, 257; and reproduction, 41, 189–93, 211, 220–21. *See also* Drugs; Health care
Medical profession: and breasts, 210, 323; and health of women, 214; payment to, 190, 191, 257; socioeconomics in, 45
Men: and agriculture/subsistence production, 30, 107, 131, 228–40 passim; allies, 324–25; Beti, 30; and breasts, 210; Chicago School and, 38; child custody by, 202; and consumption in national accounts, 61; dominance of, 199 (*see also* Patriarchy); economic decisions made by, 3–4; economic

value granted to, 17–18, 19, 23; and education for women, 216; and environment, 261, 275; Fergie's Papua New Guinea report and, 105, 108; food chosen by, 237; and health care, 213; "higher level activities" of, 101; household surveys and, 137–38; housework done by, 99–101, 225, 226–27; and housework questions in censuses, 142; and laws of economics, 225; and leisure time, 159–63, 217; in medical profession, 45; Nepalese working, 111–12; and public policy 285–86; and religious charity, 246; and reproduction, 94, 99, 188n, 192–93, 199, 217–18, 220–21, 222, 243, 306; scientific method and, 40; and sexuality protection, 244; in Soviet Union, 161–62; and surrogate mothers, 191; in technostructure, 203–4; Turu, 33; UNSNA begun by, 48; UN statistics administered by, 92; UN statistics used by, 93; voluntary organizations financed by, 27; work conception of, 26

Mengistu Haile Meriam, 173
Mental suffering, cost of, 197
Mernissi, Fatima, 231, 244
Messing, Karen, 214
Metaphysics, value and, 23–24
Mexico, 84
Michigan, 196
Mid-Decade Conference on Women, UN, 4, 286–87
Migration, 235, 236
Milan, Italy, 259
Militarism: UNSNA and, 49, 54–58, 166, 286. See also Armed forces; Wars
Military equipment: international transfers of, 68. See also Arms trade; Nuclear weapons
Military expenditures, 3, 54–58, 65, 66–68, 165, 185–86; Argentina, 185; China, 185; Ethiopia, 173; global, 43, 165–68, 172; Japan, 185; Peru, 185; Soviet, 168–69, 185; U.S., 9, 16, 55–56, 72, 168–69, 172, 180, 185, 274. See also Arms trade

Milk, 206–10, 304, 324
Mill, John Stuart, 50
Minerals, 167–68, 253, 303. See also Oil
Ministry of Agriculture and Food, Ontario, 133
Ministry of Foreign Affairs, New Zealand, 4
Minnesota, 273
Miscellaneous corrections, in national accounts, 70–71
Missiles, U.S. economy and, 19–20
Missions, Papua New Guinea, 105–7
Mitchell, Wesley C., 53
Mitkshara, 241
"Model for Valuing Endangered Species", 266
Molestation, 212–13. See also Rape
Money value: in national accounts, 102. See also Markets; Nonmonetary activities; Pay; Prices; Rent
Monopoly Capital (Baran & Sweezy), 203
Montaigne, M. E., 21
Moral value, vs. market value, 23, 24
More, Thomas, 22
More Work for Mother (Cowan), 226
Morgan, Robin, 213, 298
Morocco, 231
Mortality. See Death
Mortality rates: in Africa, 175, 258, 268; of children, 175, 211, 215, 219, 237–38, 257, 258, 268; and recession, 215; starvation-caused, 237–38
Mosquitoes, 267–69
Mossi people, 321–22
Mother Machine (Corea), 29, 189–90
Mothers, 4; child custody by, 202; education of, 215–16; lesbian, 205, 206; and sentimental worth of children, 197; surrogate, 189–93. See also Reproduction
Moynihan, Daniel, 8
MPS. See Material Product System
Ms. magazine, 323
"Much Ado About Nothing" (Shakespeare), 21
Muckherjee, Moni Mohan, 48
Munro v. Dredging, 195

Murder, of females, 184, 188, 211
Murdoch, Mrs., 200–201
Myers, Norman, 266

Narsapur, India, 87, 88
NASA, 19–20
National accounts, 1–3, 47–48, 94, 297, 309, 320; in China, 184; demand in, 58–69, 306; in Dominican Republic, 303–4; economists' views of, 144–64; and environment, 3, 8, 49, 65, 158, 256–65 passim, 275, 287–96 passim, 309; hidden economy in, 8, 16, 149–54, 308–9, 310; Kuznets on, 52–54, 57, 58, 312–13; measurement difficulties in, *see* Measurement; and military, 3, 49, 54–58, 65, 66–68, 165, 185–86, 286, 313; Nepal, 112–14, 286; New Zealand, 1; Papua New Guinea, 94, 103–8, 149; pricing in, 147–49, 156; production boundary in, *see* Production boundary; and rural/urban income differences, 235–36; sources for, 115–43 (*see also* Data collection); supply in, 69–73; and total wealth of country, 63n; UNSNA governing measurement of, 1, 3, 44; and welfare measurement, 8, 47, 54, 55, 57, 71–72, 145, 284, 285–86, 308, 313; women's work value imputed in, 7, 11–12, 82, 276–87; World Bank requiring, 178. *See also* Gross Domestic Product; Gross National Product; United Nations System of National Accounts
National Aeronautics and Space Administration (NASA), 294
National Bureau of Economic Research (NBER), U.S., 51–53
"National Income and Expenditure of the United Kingdom" (Keynes & Stone), 54–55
National Income and Its Composition 1919–1938 (Kuznets), 53
Natural resources: "conditionally" renewable, 296; nonrenewable, 253, 291, 296, 302–3; renewable, 253, 291, 296, 302–3. *See also* Environment; Minerals

Nature, 11; reproduction as, 29. *See also* Environment
Neoclassical economics, 39, 196, 224, 261
Neocolonialism, 78, 106n, 189, 283, 321
Nepal, 108–14, 241, 286
Netherlands, 51, 295
New home economics (Chicago School), 37–38, 196, 204
New Jersey, 195–96
Newland, Kathleen, 7, 26
Newman, Barry, 183
New York City, 180
New York Times, 159, 202, 294
New Zealand, 84, 88, 286; animal market in, 193; censuses of, 115, 122n, 138–43; and child care time, 230; and contraceptive drugs, 243; Department of Statistics, 4, 115, 116, 138; External Aid Division of the Ministry of Foreign Affairs, 4; gang rape in, 245–46; labor force survey of, 138; legal compensation for genital organ damage in, 194–95; milk in, 208–9; and ozone layer hole, 294; Parliament, 1; recreation survey in, 160–61; sources of national accounts in, 115; suffrage in, 317; System of National Accounts, 1; Treasury, 4, 82–83; wildlife in, 265
New Zealand Herald, 324
Niger, 175
Nigeria, 241
Nipon Steel, 183
Nobel Prizes, 222; Friedman, 37; Kuznets, 36, 53; Leontief, 158; Samuelson, 220; Shockley, 221; Stone, 48, 159, 222
Noise pollution, 252, 253
Nomad women, 81–82, 176–77
Nondurable goods, in national accounts, 59
Nonmarket production. *See* Unpaid work
Nonmaterial sphere: in MPS, 327. *See also* Nonmonetary activities
Nonmonetary activities: in national accounts, 78–88, 103–6, 308; Pietilä's diagram for, 300. *See also* Unpaid work

Nonproducers: nonagricultural sectors as, 50; women as, 2, 12, 15–16, 28, 77, 90

Nonprofit organizations, 41, 68–69, 93, 105–6

Norhaus, William, 291

Norway, 51, 260, 296

Nuclear pollution, 32, 44, 155, 157, 252, 269–75, 316–18, 324

Nuclear power: Finnish women's reproductive policies re, 323; plants, 269, 272–74; research reactors, 269, 270–71. *See also* Nuclear weapons

Nuclear weapons, 9, 70–71, 140, 172, 186, 274–75, 284

Nuclear weapons-free policy, 140, 166

Nutrition, 235–38; global, 43; national accounts and, 54; and subsistence agriculture, 19. *See also* Malnutrition

Nye, Joseph, 9n

O'Brien, Mary, 10, 29, 187, 199

Occupational Safety and Health Agency (OSHA), 183

Occupations: classification of, 281–82, 312. *See also* Labor

OECD. *See* Organization for Economic Cooperation and Development

Oikonomikos, 18

Oil, 146, 167–68, 171, 291

Okeyo, Achola, 228–29

Old people. *See* Elderly

Omni, 227

Omvedt, Gail, 262

Ontario, Canada, 133

"On the Problem of Studying Women in Cuba" (Bengelsdorf), 247

Open economy, 300–301

Operators, in agricultural census, 132

Opportunity cost approach, 280–81

Organization for Economic Cooperation and Development (OECD), 82, 93, 140, 146, 153, 154, 309

Origin of the Family (Engels & Marx), 29

Oxford English Dictionary, 21, 28

Ozone layer, 44, 294

Packard, Vance, 190–91

Pakistan, 84

Palestinian refugees, 75, 220

Palmerole, 204

Papua New Guinea, 94, 98, 99, 100, 103–8, 149, 245–46

Paraguay, 258–59

Parker, Katherine, 161, 163

Parliament, New Zealand, 1

Parrots, 265

Parsees, 241

Patriarchy, 3–4, 10, 97, 262, 288, 314; Chicago School and, 37; ideology of, 44, 95, 96, 276; legal system and, 241; reasons for inaction of, 304–12; and reproduction, 188, 191, 203, 218–19; and suffrage, 316–17; UNSNA as applied, 224–49; and women's work, 78

Pay, 7, 69, 281; for government employees, 66; for household-confined work, 228; for housework, 7, 277–78, 280–81, 322–23; for lawyers, 190, 191; for medical personnel, 190, 191; for military personnel, 66; sex inequality in, 37, 184, 220, 280; sex preference theory and, 220; for surrogate mothers, 189–91; work assessed by more than, 301

Peace, "value" of, 3

Peason, Gail, 238

Penis damage, legal market and, 194

People's Daily, 211

Persian Gulf conflicts, 146, 170

Peru, 163n, 185, 214, 241, 305

Pesticides, 156, 181–82, 183, 269, 323–24

Petroleum. *See* Oil

Petty, William, 49–50

Pharmaceuticals. *See* Drugs

Philippines, 244

Physics, quantum, 225, 249

Pietilä, Hilkka, 300–304, 314, 316

Pigou, Arthur, C., 52, 59

Pill, contraceptive, 209

Plants, growing, 34

Poisoning: environmental, 155–57, 183, 254–56, 259, 269. *See also* Pollution

Poland, 163n, 260

Policy making, and GDP or GNP, 72

Policy. *See* Public policy

Politics: and food, 237–38; militarized, 171; of reproduction, 217–21, 222; of UNSNA, 47; women in, 247, 285, 316–19. *See also* Government regulation

Politics of Reproduction (O'Brien), 10, 29, 199

Pollack, Robert, 38–39

"Pollution Caused by Certain Dangerous Substances Discharged into the Aquatic Environment of the Community", 256

Pollution, environmental, 32, 44, 83, 149, 154–59, 252–61, 288, 313–14; air, 32, 158, 251, 252, 257–69 passim, 288, 289; chemical, 19, 156, 158, 181–82, 183, 254–55, 259, 269, 323–24; noise, 252, 253; nuclear, 32, 44, 155, 157, 252, 269–75, 316–18, 324; water, 158, 251–60 passim, 288, 289

Pool, Ian, 321

Population: of armed personnel, 168; census of, 117–30; Ethiopia, 175; New Zealand, 115; sex preference theory and, 221; sexuality market and, 205

Pornography, 210, 244

Porritt, Jonathan, 158

Poverty, 163–64, 178–81, 217, 310; aid and, 87–88; American, 31, 179–80; in female-headed households, 233–34; GNP and, 58; sexuality market and, 205, 206; war and, 172–76

Power, 292, 316

Power politics, of reproduction, 217–21

Pregnancy, protection of, 246

Prepubescent people, sexuality market and, 204. *See also* Children

Price indexes, 116; consumer, 115, 116, 136, 137, 170

Prices: breast milk, 208; bride, 108, 324; of children, 196–98; in national accounts, 147–49, 156; oil,

146; sugar, 240–41; timber, 261; of weapons, 170. *See also* Cost

Primary producers, 77–78

Primary responsibility censuses and, 119

Prisoners, female, 214

Private Property and the State (Engels & Marx), 29

Producers: defined, 75–77; primary, 77–78; women as, 4. *See also* Nonproducers; Production

Production, 3; "creative" and "destructive", 291; definitions of, 27–29, 50–51, 73, 75–77; industrial, 167, 182–83; in MPS, 51, 327–28; nonprofit organizations valued for, 41; for own consumption, 51–52, 78, 79, 107, 310–11 (*see also* Subsistence production); in Pietilä's diagram, 300–301; propaganda and, 222–23; reproduction of relations of, 188, 199–200, 216; UNSNA-excluded, *see* Production boundary; war and, 166–72. *See also* Household production; Unpaid work

Production boundary, 33–35, 91, 310–11; Barkay on, 113; and environmental pollution, 83, 254–56; and hidden economy, 308–9, 310; MPS vs. UNSNA, 327; and women's work, 33–34, 73, 74–88, 91, 102, 222–23, 310–11

Production unit (establishment), in New Zealand national accounts, 88

Productive capacity, of countries, vs. cash-generating capacity, 3. *See also* Production

Products, in agricultural censuses, 132

"Professional" women, 307

"Profile of Filipino Women" (USAID), 162

Profit organizations, serving households, 68n

Profits, in national accounts, 69

Prokopovitch, S. N., 51

Propaganda, 46, 249, 276; in censuses, 118; of international economic system, 44–45, 224; and legal system, 240–41; and

reproduction, 215–17, 222–23, 287; and women's production, 222–23
Property rights, 5; and air pollution, 32; of ownership, 59, 113, 121, 241, 242; of women, 201, 241, 242; to women, 188
Propietors' incomes, in national accounts, 69
Prostitution: breasts used in, 210; in China, 185; in Palmerole, 204; and protection, 244; starvation motivating, 238; in Thailand, 152–53, 244; tourists and, 244
Protected sector, in Pietilä's diagram, 300
Protection, 244, 246
Public Expenditure (Public Accounts and Budget) Select Committee, New Zealand Parliament, 1
Public Health Service, U.S., 214
Public policy, 49, 72, 145, 262, 302; and consumption, 59–61; and environment, 1–2, 262, 264–65, 303; on reproduction, 217–21, 287; and women's work, 284–86; and wrongful birth, 199. *See also* Politics
Putting People First (World Bank), 177–78

Quammen, David, 268
Quantum physics, 225, 249
Quebec, Automobile Insurance Act, 194
Quesnay, François, 50

Racism, 189, 203, 207
Radioactive pollution, 252, 269–75, 324. *See also* Nuclear pollution
Rape, 197n, 210, 212, 244, 245; gang, 245–46
Rarua, Kathy, 324
Reardon, Betty, 274–75
Recession, 136, 215
Recreation, 160–63, 293
Red Cross, 151
Reference persons, censuses and, 119, 123–30
Refugees, 219–20
Regenstein, Lewis, 155
Reid, Elizabeth, 316, 319
Reid, Margaret, 26

Religion, 21, 106n, 189, 241, 244, 246
Rent, 14–15, 51–52, 59, 69, 121, 149
Reporters, male, 325
Reproduction, 3–4, 12, 41; boundary of, 188–89, 204–6, 210; censuses and, 143; in China, 184, 197, 211; and definition of family, 89; definitions of, 27–29, 306; Fergie on, 94, 187, 287; Finnish antinuclear movement and, 323; in international economic system, 30, 34, 37; lesbians and, 205, 206; men paid for, 99; protection of, 246; reproduction of relations of, 99, 188, 199, 212; social, 41; value of, 3–4, 7, 10, 28, 41, 187–223, 286–87
Reproductive Freedom International, 190
Reproductive Revolution (Singer & Wells), 191–92
Research and development, military, 168
Resources. *See* Natural resources
Respect, 319
Revolt, sexuality market and, 205
Rhine river pollution, 255–56
Ricardo, David, 50
Rice, Gambian, 238
Riley, John G., 303
Roanbeck, Sissel, 260
Robbins, Lionel, 18, 19, 20, 73, 312
Robin, Chatham Islands, 265
Robinson, E. A. G., 54, 55
Robinson, Joan, 23–24, 36, 44, 118, 222, 287
Rogers, Barbara, 7
Roget's Thesaurus, 18
"Role of Household Surveys in Improving Statistics and Indicators on Women" (Ware), 305–6
Roosevelt, F. D., 56
Rosenfeld, Rachel, 133
Rowbotham, Sheila, 18
Royal Dutch Shell, 324
Rural areas: female-headed households in, 234; income in, 235–36; leisure time in, 162, 163n; work in, 76–87, 101, 131–36, 162, 228–30, 231, 232, 285, 307. *See also* Agriculture; Subsistence production

INDEX / *381*

Sachs, Carolyn, 133–34
Safety: on streets, 172; in Third World industry, 183; value of, 24–25
Sakupwanya, Melphy, 242–43
Salaries. *See* Pay
Sal trees, 262
Same-sex lovers, sexuality market and, 205, 206, 210
Samuelson, Paul, 18–19, 147, 220–21
Sandoz, 254–56
Sanitation, 11, 43–44, 212, 258
Sanitoriums, Soviet passes to, 161, 162
Saudi Arabia, 81, 235
Saving, household, 59–61
Saye, Burkino Faso, 322
Schettkat, Ronald, 282–83
School. *See* Education
Schreiner, Olive, 37
Schumacher, E. F., 290–91, 297–98
Scientific method, in economics, 39–43, 91, 97, 249
Scope and Method of Political Economy (J. N. Keynes), 73
Scott, Hilda, 233–34, 277
Sears, 169
Secretariat, UN, 93
Security, cost of, 293
Selamta, 174
Self-employed women, in informal sector, 8
Senate, U.S., 52–53
Senegal, 242
Sentimental worth, 197–98
Servants, domestic, 185, 225–26, 333
Services, national accounts and, 50–51, 52, 59
Seveso, Italy, 254
Sex abuse: of females, 212–13. *See also* Rape
Sexism. *See* Discrimination, sex
Sex issues. *See* Girls; Men; Sons; Women
Sex offenders, study of, 245
Sex preference, in offspring, 184, 188, 211, 220–21, 243–44
Sexual division of labor, 228–29, 234–35, 311–12
Sexual harassment, 245. *See also* Sex abuse

Sexuality: control over, 28, 188, 222, 242–46; Islam and, 244; market in, 204–6 (*see also* Prostitution); protection of, 244; slavery in, 152, 188, 205, 245
Shadow prices, "new home economics" and, 38
Shakespeare, William, 21
Shari'a, 241
Shelton, William C., 53, 55
Shockley, William Bradford, 221
Shopping, 42–43, 100
Sidel, Ruth, 201
Silence, 253
Singer, Peter, 191–93
Sisterhood Is Global Institute, 304, 320
Sisterhood Is Global (Morgan), 213
Sivard, Ruth Leger, 177, 215
Slavery, 248, 276; Engels on, 5, 6; patriarchal economics and, 44, 276; reproduction and, 188, 200, 205, 206, 222; sexual, 152, 188, 205, 245
Slaves of Slaves, 322
Small Is Beautiful (Schumacher), 290–91
Small scale development, 322
Smith, Adam, 22–23, 26, 47, 50
Smith, Judge, 196
Smith, Pat, 318
Smith, Phillipa Gemmel, 197–98
Smoke pollution, 260
"Social forestry", 261–62
Socialism, 42, 199, 242
Social relations: control of, 203–4; reproduction of, 99, 188, 199–202, 203–4, 210, 212–13, 216, 220
Social science, 10, 325
Social Security Administration, U.S., 278
Social services, 211–14; government spending for, 72, 180, 215, 216–17, 285; women seen as welfare cases for, 12, 37, 188. *See also* Health care
Sons, preference for, 184, 188, 211, 220, 243–44
South Africa, 171, 232–33, 324
Southeast Asia, 260. *See also individual countries*
South Korea, 244, 259

Soviet Union: aid to Ethiopa by, 173; arms trade of, 171; and compensation for loss of children, 197; invisibility of women's work in, 89–90; leisure time in, 163n; Material Product System in, 33, 34: and Mid-Decade Conference on Women, 4; military expenditures in, 168–69, 185; national accounts begun in, 51; women's overwork in, 161–62

Soviet Women, 34

Spain, 154

Spare Rib, 228

Spending: household, 59–61. *See also* Government spending; Military expenditures

Sporting recreation, 160–61

Sri Lanka, 241

Starvation, 173, 180, 211, 237–38

Star Wars, 19–20

Statistical Commission, UN, 92, 286, 294–95, 304, 309–12; and data collection difficulties, 113; and environment, 294–96; and nonmonetary activities (general), 79, 308; and voluntary work, 140; and women's work, 79, 82, 310–11

Statistical discrepancy, 70–71, 279

Statistical Office, UN, 48, 92–93

Statisticians, 53, 79, 92–114, 309, 314

Statistics. *See* Data collection; Measurement; Statisticians

Steele, Richard, 21

Steel industry, Third World, 183

Sterilization, female, 243

Stern, Ernest, 178, 307

Stone, Richard, 48, 79, 144, 249, 312; and environmental pollution costs, 158; and leisure time, 159–60; and reproduction, 222; and System of Social and Demographic Statistics, 155, 287–88; and war, 54–55, 66, 165, 313

Structure: of economy, 57, 302; of government, 317

Subsistence production, 5, 30, 79, 81–82, 101, 311; in Burma, 150, 151; commercial agriculture and, 237, 238, 239, 242; and consumption levels, 235; in Ethiopia, 174; and food trade, 238–40; and forests, 263, 264; migration and, 236; in Papua New Guinea, 103–5, 107–8; statistical measurement of, 34–35, 54, 107–8, 232. *See also* Gardening

Sudan, 81

Suffrage, 140, 316–17

Sugar prices, 240–41

Suicide rates, elderly Japanese women, 47, 58

Superannuation, 140, 145, 201

Supply, in national accounts, 69–73

Surrogate mothers, 189–93

Surveys: household labor force, 116–17, 136–38, 304–6, 320; New Zealand economic, 115–16; New Zealand recreation, 160. *See also* Censuses

Sweden, 154, 227, 269–72

Sweezy, P. M., 199, 203

Switzerland, 51, 255–56, 273–74

System of National Accounts: New Zealand, 1. *See also* United Nations System of National Accounts

System of National Accounts and Supporting Tables (UN Statistical Office), 48

System of Social and Demographic Statistics, UN, 155, 159, 287–88

Taiwan, 244

Tanzania, 242

Tao of Physics (Capra), 225

Taxation structure, women affected by, 12

Tax evasion, measurement of hidden economy by, 154

Tax forms, women's, 133

Taxpayers, aborted, 218

Teak, 262

Technology: household, 225, 226; in medical market, 189–93, 211, 220–21 (*see also* Drugs); in rural areas, 12

Techno-structure, 203

Teiler, Edward, 294–95

Terminology: economic, 17–29, 41, 46–47, 58–73; reproduction, 187–89

Thaba Bosiu, Lesotho, 233

Thailand, 152–53, 181, 244

Thesani law, 241
Third World. *See* Developing countries
Three Mile Island, 32, 155, 157, 269, 272, 273, 318–19
Thurow, Lester, 32, 158, 160
Time budget surveys, 282
Time: child care, 230; housework, 225–27, 228, 282–83; leisure, 149, 159–64, 217, 283; for politics, 247; value of, 189, 191, 193, 200, 208, 217
Tobin, James, 291
Togo, 241
Tongeren, Jan von, 309–10
Tourism, 244, 261
Trade: arms, 170, 171; drug (illegal), 152; drug (legitimate), 182; food, 236, 238–40; and Japanese defense expenditures, 185; pesticide, 182. *See also* Exports; Imports
Transaction cost approach, 38–39
Transportation: in Burma, 151; in Ethiopia, 175–76; in Nepal, 111
Treatise on the Family (Becker), 37–38
Trees. *See* Forests
Troppi v. Scarf, 198
Tuareg herders, 176–77
Tuchaninova, Svetlana, 89–90
Turu people, 33, 193

UN. *See* United Nations
Underground economy. *See* Hidden economy
UNECA (United Nations Economic Commission on Africa), 228, 234
Unemployment, in China, 247–48
UNICEF (United Nations International Children's Emergency Fund), 257, 321
Union Carbide, 158, 181
United Kingdom. *See* Britain
United Nations (UN), 93, 306; and breast milk price, 208; and Burmese economy, 151, 152; census topics recommended by, 117–18; Commission on the Status of Women, 152; Conference for Women, 319; Development Program, 151; Economic and Social Council, 93, 211–12, 215; and education for women, 216; Environmental Program, 293n; 294–95; Food and Agriculture Organization, 43, 93, 130, 131, 239, 307; General Assembly, 93, 166, 217; ILO, 14, 30, 82, 88, 89–90, 93, 231, 234; INSTRAW, 82, 305, 308; International Decade for Women (1975–85), 41–42; Mid-Decade Conference on Women, 4, 286–87; Secretariat, 93; Statistical Commission, *see* Statistical Commission, UN; Statistical Office, 48, 92–93; System of Social and Demographic Statistics, 155, 159, 287–88; World Economic Survey, 151, 181, 185; World Health Organization, 93, 212, 257, 268. *See also* United Nations System of National Accounts
United Nations Economic Commission on Africa (UNECA), 228, 234
United Nations Educational, Scientific, and Cultural Organization (UNESCO), 93, 216
United Nations Family Planning Agencies (UNFPA), 93
United Nations International Children's Emergency Fund (UNICEF), 257, 321
United Nations Multi-lingual Demographic Dictionary, 88–89
United Nations System of National Accounts (UNSNA), 1–4, 7, 44, 47, 111, 163, 276, 304–12 passim, 316; "building block" approach in, 296, 299; and censuses, 74–75, 88, 143; economists' views of, 144–64, 309; and environment, 1–2, 83, 91, 155, 156, 295–96; and fettered economy, 301; and GDP shift, 72; history of, 49–58; and investment category, 63, 65; and military, 49, 54–58, 166, 286; as patriarchy, 4, 44, 224–49; power of, 47–49; and production boundary, 33–35, 74–88, 91, 327; and reproduction, 44, 89, 222; rules of, 74–91; statistical discrepancy in, 70–71, 279; statisticians of, 79, 92–93, 103, 309; women's invisibility in, 2, 49, 53, 78, 81–91, 249; and women's production, 33–34, 44, 74–91, 94–95, 97–98, 222, 230, 310–11

United States: and abortion, 218; arms trade of, 171; breast-feeding in, 207; censuses of, 121n–22n, 134; Department of Agriculture (USDA), 134, 136, 236; Department of Commerce, 55, 72, 134; Department of Energy, 9, 272, 273–74; Department of Labor, 281–82, 307; displaced homemakers in, 233–34; divorce and unpaid work in, 201; and drugs, 182, 243; Environmental Protection Agency, 156, 259; and Ethiopia, 176; GNP, 71, 72, 146, 237; health care in, 169, 180, 214; hidden economy in, 152, 153, 154; and Honduran prostitutes, 204; housework decreased by appliances in, 225; housework in economy of, 31, 277–78; and International Fund for Agricultural Development, 176; leisure time in, 163n; military expenditures in, 9, 16, 55–56, 72, 168–70, 172, 180, 185, 274; national accounts begun in, 51–53, 55–56; national income account of 1981 for, 60; nuclear power in, 269, 272, 273, 274; penis damages awarded in, 194; in Persian Gulf, 146, 170; pesticides exported from, 182; pollution in, 155, 156–57, 259, 260; poverty in, 31, 179–80; rape in, 245; rural women in, 133–35; Social Security Administration, 278; starvation in, 180; statistical discrepancy in national accounts of, 71; surrogate motherhood in, 189–90; Third World industry of, 183; value of children in, 195–96; value of housewives in, 277–78; volunteer work's value in, 69; wife battery in, 245; wildlife in, 266–67; and World War II, 55

United States Agency for International Development (USAID), 162, 176–77, 262, 263, 283

Universities, UN statistics used by, 93

Unpaid work, 14, 97–98, 309–12, 323; agricultural, 74–81, 132–36

(see also Gardening; Subsistence production); censuses and, 122, 132–36, 138–43, 231–32, 306, 319–20, 321; divorce and, 200–201; hidden economy compared with, 153; imputation of value for, 7, 11–12, 68–69, 78, 82, 102, 105, 106–8, 223, 276–87, 310; and legal compensation for genital organ damage, 194; and leisure time, 159; Measure of Economic Welfare and, 291–92; of men, 99–102, 105; and social relations of production, 200. See also Housework; Reproduction; Subsistence production; Volunteer work

Unpaid Work in the Household (Goldschmidt-Clermont), 279

UNSNA. See United Nations System of National Accounts

Uranium, 303

Urban areas: costs associated with, 293; gardening in, 260; housework in, 225–28; income in, 235–36

USAID (U.S. Agency for International Development), 162, 176–77, 262, 263, 283

Users, of UN statistics, 93

"Use value", 29, 179

USSR. See Soviet Union

Utilization doctrine, with wildlife, 266

Validity, in censuses, 118

Value, 1–4, 14–19 passim, 33, 41, 102, 298, 302; bride price, 324; of children, 3, 38, 195–99, 202, 204, 243; of death, 8–10, 165–86; definitions of, 21–25; of housewives, 41, 200–202, 277–87, 311; imputation of, see Imputation; of life/reproduction, 3–4, 7, 8–10, 24–25, 28, 41, 166, 184, 186, 187–223, 286–87; market vs. moral, 22, 23; of time, 189, 191, 193, 200, 208, 217; of volunteer work, 69; of wildlife, 265–67; of women, 3, 7, 28, 41, 184, 200–202, 222, 277–87, 311, 324. See also Prices

Value added, 72, 156, 216, 309

"Value of Safety", 24
Vanek, Joann, 225, 282–83
Vanuatu, 324
Vatican, 4
Venezuela, 207, 213
Villainy, 147, 186, 306, 307–8
Viner, J., 58
Volume, work assessed by, 301
Volunteer work, 8, 27, 34, 323;
censuses and, 138, 139–41;
imputation of value for, 68–69,
106–7; money value of, 69;
religious, 246
Vuorela, Ulla, 218

Wages. See Pay
Walker, Kathryn E., 100
Wall Street Journal, 183
Ware, Helen, 305–6
"War Expenditures in National
Production" (Gilbert), 56
Wars, 165, 170–71; defined, 172;
economic value of, 165–72, 186;
how to pay for, 3, 54–58, 65, 313;
nuclear pollution and, 274–75;
Pietilä's diagram and, 302; value
of fighters in, 16, 99
Waste, hazardous, business in, 157
Water, 151, 256–60; carrying of, 79,
81–82, 91, 101, 113, 283; drinking,
11, 43–44, 209, 212, 250, 255, 256,
258, 259; polluted, 158, 251–60
passim, 288, 289; shortage of, 321–
22
Watkins, Justice, 198–99
Wealth of Nations (Smith), 50
Weather, 290
Weck-Hanneman, Hannelore, 153–54
Weeding, 79
Welfare services. See Social services
Welfare/Well-being, 147, 291–96, 314,
325; consumption and, 237;
environmental quality and, 251,
257, 303; household surveys and,
137; market vs., 299; national
accounts and, 8, 47, 54, 55, 57,
71–72, 145, 284, 285–86, 308, 313;
war vs., 299; women's
contribution to, 96; women's
health and, 211–12
Wells, Dean, 191–93
Wesson, Gwen, 35

West: aid to Ethiopa by, 173; drugs
in, 182; and International Fund for
Agricultural Development, 176. See
also individual countries
West Germany: aerospace industry
in, 169n; agricultural labor in, 232;
arms trade of, 171; drug
production of, 182; forests in, 260,
261; Green party in, 251, 255;
hidden economy in, 154; leisure
time in, 163n; nuclear
development in, 272; polluted
milk in, 234; Rhine pollution in,
255–56
Wet nurses, 207–8
Wheat, in national accounts, 72
Wildlife, 265–69
Wildlife Fish User Days (WFUD),
267
Wives: beating of, 245; property
rights of, 201, 241; rape of, 213,
244, 245; value of, 41, 200–202,
277–87, 311. See also Housewives;
Marriage
Women, 4, 251, 310–12, 316;
agricultural labor by, 24, 30, 74–
79, 131–35, 175, 176–78, 228–42
passim, 264, 307 (see also
Subsistence production); censuses
and, 8, 74, 89–91, 118, 122–23,
130, 131–32, 138–43, 231–32, 319–
20; Chicago School and, 38; in
China, 184–85, 247–48; and
consumption in national accounts,
61; and control over fertility, 28,
188, 205, 222, 242–46;
discrimination against, see
Discrimination, sex; education of,
203, 215–17, 234 (see also Girls); in
Ethiopia, 175; and forests, 261–62,
263, 264; head of household, 100,
211, 232–34, 237; health of, 211–
14, 215–16; household surveys
and, 116–17, 137–38, 304–6, 320;
and household work, see
Household production; invisibility
of, see Invisibility; in Iran, 81, 219;
and leisure time, 159, 160–64, 217;
malnutrition of, 164, 211, 237–38;
Mossi, 321–22; in national
legislatures, 1, 44; Nepalese, 111–
12, 241; in paid labor force, 37,

42–43, 184, 227, 246, 247–48; in politics, 1, 44, 247, 285, 316–19; postmenopausal, 204; in poverty, 164, 179, 233–34; production boundary and, 33–34, 73, 74–88, 91, 102, 222–23, 310–11; prostitute, *see* Prostitution, scientific method and, 40, 97; and slavery, *see* Slavery; in Soviet Union, 89–90, 161–62; statisticians and, 53, 79, 93–108 passim, 113–14; suffrage for, 316–17; surveying, 116–17, 137–38, 160, 304–5; in Thailand, 152–53; and transaction cost approach, 39; Turu, 33–34; value of, 3, 7, 28, 41, 184, 200–202, 222, 277–87, 311, 324. *See also* Mothers; Wives
Women and Food Conference (1982), 4, 94
Women and Life on Earth Conference (1980), 317–18
Women at Work (ILO), 231
Women of Tomorrow (Keeton & Baskin), 227
"Women's Employment in the USSR" (Tuchaninova), 89–90
Women's Role in Economic Development (Boserup), 41–42
Women's Worth (Leghorn & Parker), 161
Wood collection, 79, 81–82, 101, 107–8, 110, 263

Woods, Margaret E., 100
Work: definition of, 25–27; vs. leisure time, 160. *See also* Labor; Unpaid work
Working class, wet nurses from, 207
World Bank, 2, 93, 307, 309; and forests, 262, 263; Living Standards Measurement Series, 82, 95–96, 111–12; Office of Environmental Affairs, 288; and reproduction, 215; and women's agricultural work, 177–78, 238
World Economic Survey, UN, 151, 181, 185
World Fertility Survey Individual Core Questionnaire, 305
World Health Organization (WHO), 93, 212, 257, 268
World War II, 54–58
Wycko v. Gnodtke, 196

Xenophon, 18

Yugloslavia, 163n

Zambia, 90–91
Zeebord v. Gay, 197
Zelizer, Viviana, 197
Zero-Sum Society (Thurow), 158
Zhao Ziyang, 211
Zimbabwe, 242–43
Zurich Insurance Company, 255

ACKNOWLEDGMENTS / 387

This constitutes a continuation of the copyright page.

Hilkka Pietilä, for the diagram "The Complete Picture of the National Economy" appearing in "Tomorrow begins Today."

International Association for Research on Income & Wealth, for extracts from *National Accounting with Limited Data: Lessons from Nepal,* published in 1982.

Senator Janine Haines, for quoting from personal correspondence.

Ron Fergie, for extracts from his unpublished paper on the establishment of national accounts in Papua New Guinea.

Howard J. Sherman and Gary R. Evans, for the figure "Expenditure and Income approach to GNP" in *Macroeconomics.* Published in 1984 by Harper & Row, Publishers, Inc.

Rowman and Littlefield Publishers, Inc., for the table "Farm Women's Involvement in Farm and Home Tasks" in *The Invisible Farmers: Women in Agricultural Production* by Carolyn E. Sachs. Published in 1983.

The Population Council, for the table "Substitution of Labour for Performing Market Women's Household and Related Tasks," reproduced with permission of the Population Council, from Achola Pala Okeyo, "Women in the household economy; Managing multiple roles," *Studies in Family Planning 10,* no. 11/12 (November/December, 1979); 341, Table 1.